From Antiquity to the COVID-19 Pandemic: The Intellectual Property of Medicines and Access to Health

From Antiquity to the COVID-19 Pandemic: The Intellectual Property of Medicines and Access to Health

A Sourcebook

Nuno Pires De Carvalho

Wolters Kluwer

Published by:
Kluwer Law International B.V.
PO Box 316
2400 AH Alphen aan den Rijn
The Netherlands
E-mail: international-sales@wolterskluwer.com
Website: lrus.wolterskluwer.com

Sold and distributed by:
Wolters Kluwer Legal & Regulatory U.S.
7201 McKinney Circle
Frederick, MD 21704
United States of America
Email: customer.service@wolterskluwer.com

ISBN 978-94-035-2850-2

e-Book: ISBN 978-94-035-2851-9
web-PDF: ISBN 978-94-035-2852-6

For Ana (for ever)
For André, Hugo and Carolina

For Charles R. McManis, Thomas and Karole Green Professor of Law Emeritus, Law School of Washington University in St. Louis, MO, U.S.A., with my admiration and gratitude.

Table of Contents

Table of Illustrations

Preamble

When applied to medicines and access to health, intellectual property, in all its modalities, such as patents, trademarks, and trade secrets, is a matter of great controversy. In general, not only the public at large, but also governments, international organizations, and academics, tend to see intellectual property as a source of distortion of prices and competition in the field of health, with its attendant risks of monopolization, excessive prices, and scarcity. Of course, in times of the COVID-19 pandemic, those concerns increase.

This book shows that things have not always been much different throughout history. Actually, there has always been some tension between, on the one hand, the public interest and the public policies that stand behind access to medicines, and, on the other, the legitimate, private interests of individuals and companies that put their time, resources and creativity at the service of finding new medicines and methods of curing diseases.

Intellectual property, in its many specialties, has emerged quasi spontaneously as a legal tool that supports merchants and manufacturers in their struggle to lure and keep customers. Intellectual property is inherently associated with commercial rivalry because it helps competitors to protect the differentiating elements of their activities from rivals. It is those elements that businesses use to lure clients, by persuading them to choose their products and services, instead of those of their rivals.

So, behind any element of intellectual property, there is a notion of difference. Patents protect inventions that are *different* from the other techniques that are publicly known. Trade secrets concern information that is *different* from what other persons know. Trademarks cover signs that are *different* from those that designate similar goods and services. Products whose special, *different* characteristics result from their particular geographical origin are designated by geographical indications. And so forth.

It follows that intellectual property has been designed for supporting industrial and commercial activities that are carried out against a background of economic freedom.

Since early times, the inventors and the merchants of medicines, like all entrepreneurs, have used all methods possible to secure the preference of customers.

But, unlike other entrepreneurs, they have stumbled with difficulties that stem from the very nature of the products they create and sell. Those difficulties arise from the fact that the production and the commerce of medicines have been subject to the intervention of authorities since early times. As this book shows, since the Middle Ages, pharmacists would not be allowed to sell their products without prior control as to their quality and safety. In some cases, that control would be exercised by physicians. In other cases, the supervision was carried by the jurors of the apothecaries' guilds. In this way, medicines have been more scarce than foodstuffs, whose availability is no less essential for the sake of public health. They are, therefore, naturally more expensive. On the other hand, the fact that medicines are acquired by customers with the purpose of defeating ailments tends to generate a certain amount of anxiety as to their prices and availability.

The combination of these factors has led to the intervention of governments in the way medicines are made, distributed, advertised and sold. In short, the trade of medicines has been the subject of regulation since early times—and regulation has profoundly affected the way in which inventors and distributors of medicines have resorted to the mechanisms of intellectual property to protect the different features they introduce in their businesses.

An example taken from physics serves as an illustration. When a ray of the sun passes through a piece of transparent glass, the same white ray of light comes out on the other side. But when that sunray passes through an optical prism, what comes out is a rainbow. The reason is that the prism causes the refraction of the light and breaks it down into different colors. The same is true of intellectual property. When used in a free market, intellectual property reveals itself as a bunch of exclusive rights, which, to a large extent, permits right holders to lure customers by means of securing exclusivity in the differentiating features of the products they offer. Therefore, it also permits them to ask for prices as high as consumers are willing to pay. The very existence of competitors, who also have introduced differentiating features in their products, and who also seek to lure customers by offering those features, provide for a natural, self-regulated mechanism of prevention of abuses. When that does not work, legal mechanisms will have to be enforced. But if the operation of businesses is impacted by regulation aimed at implementing public policies (such as those that concern public health), such regulation operates as if it were a prism refracting the light—the exercise of intellectual property in medicines is distorted by measures that change the way the respective rights are acquired and enforced, such as exclusions from protection, special requirements on acquisition, compulsory licenses, special terms of protection compensating for certain administrative delays, etc.

In other words, the intellectual property of medicines and pharmacists is not the same as, say, the intellectual property of furniture and their makers. Actually, the title of this book implies that notion: there is an intellectual property that is specific to the products that pharmacists make and sell, this meaning that the rules of intellectual property that apply to those products are not always the same as those that prevail in other areas of entrepreneurship. In other words, intellectual property is not technology-neutral. The more important from a public policy perspective its subject matter is, the more governments will interfere in its operation.

It is not difficult to find evidence of this assertion. A brief look at the 1994 Agreement of Trade-Related Aspects of Intellectual Property Rights (the TRIPS Agreement) of the World Trade Organization reveals that its 73 articles contain no less than six provisions dealing *explicitly* with health and pharmaceutical products (Articles 8.1, 27.2, 27.3, 31bis; 39.3, 70.8 and 70.9), and six provisions dealing *implicitly* with health and pharmaceutical products (Articles 20, 27.1, 31(b), 65.4, 70.6, 70.7). To these provisions, one might still add the Doha Declaration on TRIPS and Access to Health, which has led to the adoption of a number of decisions by the TRIPS Council extending the transition periods for LDCs as regards pharmaceutical products. For a legal text that has been initially proposed and designed as a tool to prevent the discriminatory treatment of certain technologies and products—in particular, in the pharmaceutical field—and which led to the language of Article 27.1 ("patents shall be available for any inventions, . . . in all fields of technology") and of Article 15.4 ("The nature of the goods or services to which a trademark is to be applied shall in no case form an obstacle to registration of the trademark."), those provisions confirm that the intellectual property that applies to medicines and their inventors is not the same that applies to other products and their creators.

So, where the title of this book reads "From Antiquity to the COVID-19 Pandemic—The Intellectual Property of Medicines and Access to Health," it does not refer just to a special category of entrepreneurs or to the sort of products they make and sell—it refers to a different type of intellectual property altogether, which, in many points, differs from the rights that are normally granted to the entrepreneurs in other areas of business.

As it happens with intellectual property in general, the intellectual property of medicines is an old tool and has emerged spontaneously. But two main lines of tension can be devised in the historical evolution of intellectual property for pharmacists and medicines that cannot be seen elsewhere.

The first line of tension is between trademarks and common names. Trademarks are signs that designate products (and services) and distinguish them from similar products (or services). Per definition, they are supposed not to be descriptive of the goods they designate. This has given rise to the many debates on the genericism of certain trademarks—those that, at their birth, were distinctive but later became synonymous with the product they designated. As a result, certain popular trademarks, in spite of their owners' genuine efforts, have been lost in favor of dictionaries.

In other cases, the interference of public policies goes as far as prohibiting the use of trademarks to designate certain medicines. The reason is that trademarks serve not only to distinguish products (and services) from those of competitors but also to capture reputation. Therefore, medicines designated by their common names or their active ingredients' scientific names tend to be cheaper than those same medicines if designated by trademarks. This argument has been decisive in persuading governments to impose restrictions on the use of trademarks in schemes associated with supplying national systems of health.

With a few exceptions, there was no movement towards the differentiation of pharmaceutical products before the sixteenth century. Then pharmacists were required to strictly follow the Pharmacopeias, which meant that they should prepare medicines in the same manner and with the same ingredients as every other apothecary. Thus, medicines were designated with their common names. This explains the absence of distinctive signs in the pharmaceutical jars and containers that are depicted in old illustrations of drugstores. Medicines were manually prepared in those stores, frequently under the direct instructions of physicians, and their public sale was made through undifferentiated vases and packages. The differentiation function of trademarks, therefore, would not target the products but was rather confined to the businesses. The trade dress of the shops and the indirect advertisement of pharmacists' names through the sale of technical books were mechanisms that circumvented the absence of trademarks.

The recourse to trademarks and advertising so as to ensure differentiation and capture reputation would hesitantly start in the sixteenth century and generalize in the seventeenth century onwards. This was caused by a significant increase in the emergence of new medicines, which was due to two factors. One was the sudden increase in the availability of ingredients used in making compounded medicines, namely spices and sugar. The Portuguese discoveries opened the way for direct trade of those spices from the East, with the consequent reduction of prices. Before Portuguese navigators reached India, spices were carried by caravans from India to Northern Africa, where Venetian and Turkish merchants would buy them. It happened that when the supply of a specific herbal ingredient was exhausted in Europe, it could take up to three years for apothecaries to have access to new supplies. The second factor was the advance in the chemical science in the sixteenth century, which permitted apothecaries to move from galenic preparations to chemical formulations.

This book brings several stories of how this evolution in the inventing and trading of medicines took place. One particular case deserves special attention. It is the dispute (with plenty of episodes) involving the ownership and the distribution of an antidote, which became one of the most popular medicines throughout Europe in the seventeenth and eighteenth centuries, known as *Orvietan*. Among other documents concerning that dispute, which had many participants, the book includes one court report that describes the principles of Roman law and the precedents on which the final decision was made. From a historical point of view, that judgment is of great significance, not only because of the breadth of its arguments and analysis but also because it touches upon several areas of intellectual property, namely copyright, patents, trade names and trademarks. As far as trademark law is concerned, the judgment reiterates the principle (already established by the precedents) that still prevails today (and is mentioned in the TRIPS Agreement) of first in time, first in right. But also interesting is that, although some distributors would claim (and obtain) exclusivity as to the use of the name *Orvietan*, a term derived from the name of the Italian city Orvieto, where its inventor was born, it has become a generic name for antidotes. We have here, therefore, the same sort of genericide that much later would lead to the loss of distinctiveness of some well-known medicine trademarks.

Another aspect of the tension between medicine trademarks and common names is that, where the use of trademarks is admitted, often the sanitary authorities reserve the right to have a saying on their particularities, thus constituting a sort of a parallel trademark office (in the same way that now and then sanitary authorities feel tempted to create a parallel patent office for pharmaceutical inventions). And because medicines are often dispensed with the intervention of physicians and pharmacists, the reduction in the distinctiveness of the respective trademarks may be admitted. But, by contrast, sometimes, medicine trademarks are under the requirement of strengthened distinctiveness, exactly in order to avoid the risk of confusion (this is the so-called duty of greater care).

The second line of tension, which emerged several centuries ago, cuts through some of the most controversial and sensitive areas of intellectual property, which are associated with the private appropriation of knowledge. Indeed, the question of whether inventions that are crucially important to save lives should be left in private hands to be exploited with a view on profitability has been raised many times. Since the Middle Ages, when the profession and the trade of pharmacists started being regulated, that question has been answered in different manners. In a few cases, inventors of new medicines have been able to capture the private and social value of their inventions through patents. But not always. Until the twentieth century, in many countries inventors were not authorized to appropriate their inventions in the field of medicine through patents. Consequently, from the sixteenth century onwards, the use of secrecy to secure private interests in pharmaceutical inventions was the most generalized practice. Actually, from a historical perspective, western societies are more familiar with the use of trade secrets to protect pharmaceutical inventions than with patents. These have replaced trade secrets as a general mechanism in the twentieth century only. Even in those countries where restrictions to the patentability of medicines did not exist, such as the United Kingdom and the United States, pharmaceutical inventors would still frequently use secrecy to protect their creations.

Secrecy, therefore, has been for several centuries the main mechanism used by inventors of new medicines to avoid the copying by competitors. Secrecy was so common that in France, medicines were designated by the term *secrets* (even though in many cases they were not even secret). But secrecy has also given rise to controversies of its own. Secrecy in a formula or composition would keep the medicine indefinitely in the hands of its holder, which would keep it largely unavailable or scarce. This has caused various public appeals against the secrecy of pharmaceuticals. Another measure aimed at reducing the negative impact of secrecy was the acquisition by the sovereign and the subsequent public disclosure of those formulae corresponding to the most successful drugs. That scheme appears to have been invented in France and followed in other countries. But in France, it was even subject to a special regulation.

Upon the spreading of the printing press, pharmacists would also resort to a manner of indirectly appropriating their inventions: they would describe them in books and would obtain exclusivity, through printing privileges, in the making and distribution of those books. Thus, they would not only gain a reputation as pharmacists (and, eventually, as inventors) but could also extract revenue from the books.

This second line of tension in the evolution of the intellectual property of medicines and pharmacists arises from, on the one hand, the strong reaction of society at large against the manoeuvers of pharmaceutical inventors in securing their private interests in inventions, and, on the other hand, the measures taken by governments through regulation (which is frequently dictated by the political need to accommodate that strong reaction).

But why does society respond so negatively to the private appropriation of knowledge in the pharmaceutical sector? In a humorous text I wrote several years ago,[1] I linked that negative response to a paradox over the happiness machine patent—an imaginary machine that, by pressing a button, would make anyone very happy forever. The machine has been invented by someone who fancied to become the richest person on earth. He would, of course, charge a fee from anyone who wished to press the button. And, also as a matter of course, crowds would queue in front of his door—indeed, who does not want to be happy forever?

Analyzing the three possibilities available to the inventor for his capturing the (enormous) social value of such an invention—a patent, a trade secret, or the acquisition of the invention by the government—I concluded that the operation of the social forces against such capture would make that inventor very unhappy at the end of the day. Those social forces would operate on the basis that the private appropriation of such valuable invention would be immoral—after all, everybody is entitled to be happy, the rich and the poor alike. My conclusion was that no inventor, aware of how those social forces operate, would dare to invent a happiness machine.

The article (actually, a sort of a fable) gives three concrete examples of that paradox: Dr. Steinbock's patented invention of a device and a method to increase the amount of vitamin D in foodstuffs (the patent would be later invalidated by a United States federal court on a frivolous ground); James Watt's patent on the steam engine (the inventor and his capitalist partner had to spend huge sums of money to defend the patent against widespread infringement as well as against various challenges to its validity); and Monsanto's patent on the RoundUp Ready technology, which expired in 2014 (Monsanto, often cited on the Internet as a "company of evil," has also been frequently engaged in litigation to the defense of that patent, as well as of its contractual practices that permitted it to capture royalties from farmers and breeders).

On a more serious tone, one may see three main reasons for the general criticism against the efforts of research-based pharmaceutical companies to secure their control over their inventions. The first reason is the essential nature of medicines. These are an indispensable item for keeping persons healthy. Therefore, society tends to see with discontent the claim of proprietary—i.e., exclusive—rights in medicines and the attendants' risks of short supplies and high prices. However, one could say the same about the essentiality of foodstuffs, and yet, there is not the same negative social feeling against patents and trade secrets for culinary recipes.

It is here that the second reason intervenes: regulation. Because of the risk to public health that ineffective and/or unsafe medicines may cause, in the first part of the twentieth century, governments reintroduced a practice that had been used in the Middle Ages, under the corporatist regime, which consisted of the requirement that any new drug be tested and approved before its commercialization. Today, testing drugs and obtaining the marketing approval from governments require reasonably long

---

1. *The Theorem of the Social Value of Inventions and The Happiness Machine Patent Syndrome*, September 27, 2010, available at <works.bepress.com/nuno_carvalho/1/>.

periods (as well as significant amounts of money). This means that the first drug for a specific therapeutic purpose that reaches the market gains an important leading time by comparison with subsequent competing drugs. It is during that period that pharmaceutical companies make efforts to recoup the costs of inventing and testing the drugs. During that leading time, prices tend to be relatively high as compared to those that are fixed subsequent to the entry of competing drugs in the market.

Indeed, it is not patent protection that makes some drugs to be expensive because, at a certain point, there may be on the market, for the same therapeutic purpose, four or five competing drugs likewise covered by patents, and all of them pushing the prices of their rivals downwards. What makes the prices of some drugs to be high is the relatively short leading time that their inventors have that permit them to recoup the costs of inventing and testing.

In the absence of this regulatory factor, the economic behavior of pharmaceutical companies would be necessarily different because they would always be under rivals' pressure—as soon a drug claiming a specific therapeutic effect was released, immediately competing products (untested, of course) would be made available, with all the dangers to the public that would naturally ensue. This logic has never been tested, except for a very short period (one month, actually) after the French Revolution, when the libertarian ideals led to lifting all guild controls from apothecaries, including those on the quality of the drugs they made and sold—controls which were reinstated very soon after.

But there is a third factor, which has to do with social perception, rather than with reality. Even though the weight that regulation has on the high prices of particularly innovative drugs is well known, that does not reduce social discontent. The reason is that the public tends not to realize the economic value of the invention. Invention is intangible, so it is not perceptible except for those companies that invest vast sums in pursuing it. Therefore, the public tends not to accept to pay high prices for something that is essential for them but that they do not see.

All these factors intertwine in ways that make the intellectual property of medicines and access to health to be different from the intellectual property that applies to other products. They also add hardship to the struggle of creative entrepreneurs in the pharmaceutical field to obtain a living from their trade. This book is about that struggle and all the contradictions to which it gives rise.

But instead of describing that struggle, and the many approaches that both pharmacists, on the one hand, and governments, on the other, have adopted to deal with it, this book takes an impartial perspective and uses images and texts in order to provide for a comprehensive sourcebook. The book is structured in two main chapters, which correspond by and large to those two lines of tension that were described above.

Before I give the voice to those who have made (and continue to make) the intellectual property of pharmacists and access to health, five preliminary editorial notes are in order.

First, on terminology: the term "pharmacists" is used in this book in a very broad sense, meaning those professionals who invent or formulate or sell medicines. The term "pharmacist" is relatively recent in the history of medicine, and his/her role very often has overlapped with that of barbers, surgeons, herbalists, grocers, and physicians, who many times would engage in making and selling medicines. The term "medicines" is also used in a broad sense of substances that are employed to treat human ailments. "Access to health" is even a broader term and comprises any human creation that deals with the prevention, treatment, and cure of human diseases.

Second, most texts are preceded by notes that explain their respective contexts. I have tried to keep those notes as succinct as possible, so as to give preeminence to the sources. Hopefully, the sources selected will be able to speak for themselves.

Third, the sources are particularly focused in France, the United Kingdom (indifferently designated in the book as Britain, or Great Britain, even if that is not correct) and the United States. The reason is the same as indicated in the Preamble to FROM BABYLON TO THE SILICON VALLEY:[2] the first two countries were the greatest European powers for many centuries, and thus molded and influenced the way intellectual property developed. The United States took the same role after the nineteenth century when, moved by its people's innate entrepreneurial spirit and respect for private property, it redesigned intellectual property—and especially patent law—and fitted it to serve its industrial development. Another country will be cited several times in this book: Brazil. Brazil does not have the economic and political dimension that could make it a *maker* of intellectual property policies—instead, it is and has been a *taker* of intellectual property policies. In that sense, the country in 1996 had to adapt its industrial property law to the standards it imported from policymaking countries, through the implementation of the TRIPS Agreement. However, in the field of pharmaceuticals, Brazil has taken several measures with the aim of promoting the establishment of a national industry of generics that are worth mentioning

Fourth, many of the sources in this book have been translated. When the translations are not mine, translators' names are provided in the Credits section. But because a majority of those are indeed mine (with, in some cases, the assistance of Google Translation—a superb tool), a word of caution is appropriate: given that translation is (re)creation, eventual inaccuracies in those translations are entirely my fault. I only hope they are not too many.

Finally, the selection of sources is exactly that: a selection. The criteria for choosing one special document and not another were exclusively dictated by my belief that the former could be more illustrative of the way intellectual property has developed in association with medicines and public health than the latter. Moreover, as a selection, the collection of sources is not, nor is it intended to be, exhaustive. My choice focused on those sources that appeared to me as being of more relevance, as stones in a road's pavement. I did not include all the stones, but just those that, as I view them, are sufficient to permit one's walking the road without having to jump over deep gaps. This book has been structured in accordance with the same design as FROM BABYLON TO THE SILICON VALLEY, another sourcebook that Wolters published in this year. Actually, it may be seen as a spin-off of that book, in that it follows the same logical arrangement of sources, in accordance with the types of intellectual property involved and, as much as it is possible, in chronological order. In the last years of my

2. FROM BABYLON TO THE SILICON VALLEY: THE ORIGINS AND EVOLUTION OF INTELLECTUAL PROPERTY—A SOURCEBOOK (Wolters Kluwer, 2020).

professional life, the belief that many of the current debates on intellectual property are mere repetitions of discussions maintained by the generations that preceded ours has grown in me, along with the idea that it might be useful to learn how arguments and counterarguments have been absorbed or discarded by the laws. This puts things in perspective, which is always useful—and in particular, at a time of the COVID-19 pandemic when fear and a feeling of urgency are speaking against a reasonable and efficient use of intellectual property.

This time I have included a few pictures and drawings that illustrate some aspects of the peculiarities of intellectual property as applied to medicines and access to health. The reason for that is well known: a picture is worth one thousand words, as the saying goes. Well, frequently, it is worth more than one thousand words.

I cannot close the presentation of this book without thanking my wife, Ana, for her care and her almost infinite patience while I, confined with her in pandemic times, went through a lot of reading, searching, browsing, and looking for expressions of intellectual property in association with medicines and access to health. To me—and, I hope, to the reader too—these texts are not just literary expressions of frequently conflicting interests in trade and health, but also, and mainly, expressions of human beings trying to make a living from their work. It is true that not all those human beings have pursued their interests in an honest manner, but that is life—and imposing honesty in trade is, after all, the ultimate goal of intellectual property.

Through this journey, Ana has been by my side, always interested in listening to the fascinating stories I found in some of the selected sources. Ana has greatly contributed to this book. More than her patience, care, and suggestions, this book has greatly benefited from her companionship and love.

Jarandilla de la Vera, Caceres, Spain, July 17, 2020

CHAPTER 1

The Business Identifiers of Medicines and Access to Health

This chapter shows how governments and entrepreneurs have used medicinal business identifiers (trademarks, shop signs, geographical indications, etc.) to pursue public policies, on the one hand, and to ensure distinctiveness for the sake of obtaining profits, on the other.

The use of business identifiers by pharmacists started early—in Antiquity, druggists would use them as they saw fit, as the first two sections show. Afterward, however, in the course of the Middle Ages, things changed. In that period, pharmacists had to struggle with governmental requirements on the use of common designations for identifying the products of their trade. The main reason for those requirements was to avoid confusion by the pharmacists themselves as to the ingredients they used. This was the consequence of the reduced number of medicines available and the general imposition that pharmacopeias should be observed, thus leading to a general uniformity of the drugs. Pharmacists did not have a significant need for the use of trademarks.

A few centuries later, this changed, when the necessity of identifying the pharmacists for certification purposes arose from the increase in the number of available pharmaceutical ingredients and, consequently, of professionals. Subsequently, a golden period of almost uncontrolled freedom of action by pharmacists ensued—roughly between the sixteenth and the nineteenth centuries. The nineteenth century brought a new public awareness about the importance of imposing controls on the marketing of pharmaceuticals. This has given rise to a new debate on the requirement of distinctiveness that pharmaceutical trademarks should present.

Distinctiveness, the fundamental condition for the registration and protection of trademarks, has been understood in a different manner when we compare pharmaceutical brands and those that are used in other fields of trade. One major line of tension that has developed in the last century concerns the opposition between distinctive trademarks and common pharmaceutical designations (hence, nonproprietary). That is not a new tension because the same concerns on the mandatory use of common designations in medicines and their ingredients have existed for several centuries. However, the debate has shifted to avoiding the private appropriation of those designations by their use as trademarks. In parallel, and with the same purpose of ensuring distinctiveness, debates have also arisen about the genericism of certain trademarks, as well as about their use by rival pharmacists as informative elements of their own products.

Another more recent line of tension emerged, which is also linked to public health and has to do with the price that certain holders have to pay as a consequence of the acquired distinctiveness of their trademarks. Certain business identifiers have the power to become symbols of happiness or well-being, or simply of coolness, and, therefore, awake an inclination towards the consumption of certain regulated goods, such as tobacco, fast food, and breast-milk substitutes. A picture of a camel, or of a clown, or of a smiling, healthy baby, are examples of those symbols. Their use to promote the socially undesired consumption of the goods they designate and to which they lend symbolic meaning has been restricted, if not prohibited altogether, by health authorities.

The first chapter shows, in this way, that the intellectual property of medicines and access to health has singularities that are not found in other fields of industry and trade.

§ 1.01. TERRA SIGILLATA—THE GREEK ISLAND OF LEMNOS EXPORTS ITS BRANDED MEDICINAL EARTH, WITH REPUTED THERAPEUTIC EFFECTS—SECOND CENTURY BC

Merchants and artisans started employing business identifiers in very early times. As noted in From Babylon to the Silicon Valley,[3] *those identifiers emerged as spontaneous tools of identification and distinction of goods and businesses as soon as the first written records of free trade appeared. Business identifiers, in the form of seals, were found in abundance in Anatolia and Mesopotamia, the first civilizations where artisans and merchants engaged in business as private entrepreneurs.*
It is possible that some of those seals were used to designate medicines, or their makers, or their distributors. However, this cannot be asserted with certainty because of the particular nature of the figures that appear on those seals, mostly of a religious nature—i.e., without a specific link to the nature of the goods to which they related. The first business identifiers that we can be certain of having been used to designate medicines appeared on a Greek Island, Lemnos, in the Northern Aegean Sea. Those identifiers designated a particular type of earth that had medicinal properties.
The earth of Lemnos, as was called a mineral extract from a particular cave on that island, acquired a great reputation as an antidote in Antiquity. The earth was exported after being molded into tablets, on which a sign was printed, as a seal of origin and certification of authenticity. Indeed, because of its success, the Lemnian earth, known by the Romans as "terra sigillata" (or "sealed earth," because of the seal that was imprinted on it) was subject to competition, either by counterfeiting or by the trade of earths from other places. The Lemnian seal, with the figure of a goat, invoked one of the (allegedly)

3. See *supra* note 2.

medicine's ingredients: the blood of a goat, which was mixed with the earth, so as to form a paste.

One of the earliest references to the sealed earth of Lemnos was made by Pedanius Dioscorides, a Greek physician who lived in the first century AD, and who wrote a five-volume treatise on herbal medicines. One century later, the famous physician and pharmacist Claudius Galenus, or Galen, visited the Island of Lemnos and described how the medicinal earth was extracted and prepared. In Galen's time, the producers of the earth stamped the tablets with Diana's seal.

The tradition of stamping business identifiers on hardened pieces of medicinal earth continued for many centuries, until the end of the Middle Ages. As a historian of pharmacy has written:

> *"Almost every country in Europe strove to find within its boundaries a source of supply of so valuable and profitable a commodity. Some of these rival medicaments acquired a considerable reputation, one of the most celebrated being Terra Sigillata Strigoniensis or Strigian earth, which was found in Silesia and for which remarkable properties were claimed."* [*C.J.S. Thompson,* THE MYSTERY AND ART OF THE APOTHECARY, *at 47 (John Lane the Bodley Head Ltd., 1929). Source:* < archive.org >].

The same author refers to various other types of terra sigillata, *each with its own claimed medicinal properties, and each likewise distinguished by special seals or trademarks:*

> *"Among other earths, mention should be made of Terra Samia from the island of Samos, Terra Sicula from Sicily, Terra Portugallica found in Portugal, which bore the impress of a rose, Terra Chia and Terra Cymolia, which were both white earths and considered of great value, and Terra Lignicensis, which was impressed with an eagle. The latter was also called Axungia Lunas, as it was excavated in the neighborhood of a silver mine and was supposed to contain a small proportion of that metal. Earths for which similar properties were claimed were also found in Bohemia, in Griffenstein, Velden, Blois and Laubach, an account of the latter having been left by Geilfus.*
>
> *An earth excavated in the vicinity of Jerusalem called Terra Sigillata Hierosolymitanas was also in great demand. It was white and bore the impress of a crucifix, the symbol of the Jesuit Fathers." (Id., at 49-50).*

In Galen's time, the seals from Lemnos had become so well-known that the physician employs this term as being synonymous with the product: "For that reason I have not been negligent in experimenting with this drug: from which I have taken twenty thousand sphragids, that is to say, seals or signs."

Several centuries later, a French pharmacist, Jean de Renou, in his celebrated treatise published in Lyon under the title LES OEUVRES PHARMACEUTIQUES DU SIEUR JEAN DE RENOU, *described the Lemnian earth and emphasized the importance of the distinctive sign that identified the genuineness of the product. He also mentioned the counterfeiting of Lemnian earth by the Turks, who would print on it their own marks.*

The following texts are excerpts from the reports by those three authors. All three have put emphasis on the seals that were imprinted on the tablets, certifying their geographical origin.

§ 1.01.1. Dioscorides' observations on Lemnian earth and the seals used to brand it (*c.* 40 AD-*c.* 90 AD)

On the Lemnian earth. Chap. LXXII.

The earth called Lemnia comes from Lemno, an island with many lagoons, where it is generated in a certain very cavernous cave: from which the residents of those parts take it: and after cleaning and mixing it with goat blood, they make it into tablets and they mark them with a seal that has a goat sculpted on it, calling it from there onward, σφραγίδα αιγός, which is the same as goat seal. Drunk with wine, it is very valuable and powerful against deadly poisons: and if it is drunk before, it makes them go out by vomiting. It also serves against the punctures and bites of the beasts that expel venom from themselves. It is mixed in the antidotes: and some use it in sacrifices. Moreover, it is useful against dysenteria.

Figure 1 Picture of a goat on one the faces of a bronze coin minted at Hephaistos, north of Lemnos, c. fourth century BC. The same motif was employed for stamping medicinal earth from Lemnos.

§ 1.01.2. Galen (Claudius Galenus) (*c.* 129 AD-*c.* 200 AD) describes his visit to Lemnos and what he learned about the preparation of Lemnian earth

There are other different earths, by blending bodies of various kinds: like stony, and sandy earths. Which segregate, or separate the substance, and blend the said bodies: by pouring on a lot of water, so that everything becomes wet. Because in doing so, all the stony, and sandy material goes to the bottom, and subsides: but the real earth swims on top. Such thing appears in the land known as Lemnia, which some name *miltos Lemnia, id est, rubrica Lemnia.* Others call it *sphragis Lemnia, hoc est sigillum Lemnum*: because of Diane's seal printed on that earth. For the priestess of Diana, taking this land with honor and reverence (according to the costume of the country) not by sacrificing beasts, but by giving ferment and barley to the land, for atonement, and sacrifice, brings it into town. And after she has greatly disturbed and agitated the said earth soaked in water, and drawn up in mud, and after she has let it rest a little, she removes the water, which lingers on top. And immediately she takes the mud, which is under the water: and leaves only the rest, which stays in the bottom: that is to say, what is stony, and sandy, as useless, and superfluous. This mud is oily, and dried, as much as it has the consistency of a soft wax. And the priestess, taking small pieces of this mud, prints the seal, or sign of Diana, on them. And then she puts it to dry in the shade, until it loses all its humidity, and it becomes this medicine known to all doctors, named *Lemnia sphragis, id est, sigillum.* Because that is how some designate it, because of the seal printed on it, which the Greeks call σφραγις (*sphragis*, seal). Likewise, some call it *miltos Lemnia, id est, rubrica,* because of its color. However, there is a difference, especially because *Lemnis suphragis, id est, terra sigillata,* does not contaminate the hands, as *rubrica Lemnia* does. *Item* terra sigillata is only found just in one mountain, in Lemnos Island, which mountain is completely yellow. In which neither tree, stone, nor plant grows. There are three varieties of this earth. The first is the one we named above, namely, the sacred earth of Diana, which no one in the world is allowed to touch, except the priestess. The second is called *miltos, id est, rubrica*: which is mainly used by the fairies. The third is neutral: used by those who wash the linen sheets and the dresses. After I had read in Dioscorides, and other authors, that there was goat blood mixed with lemnian earth, and that from the mud made from such blend the priestess formed and sealed the seals, called *sphragids lemnia*, I had a great desire to see the symmetry, and the measurement of the blend. . . .

So when I came to the island called Ephestias,[4] the priestess of Diane had gone to the said mountain. Who, after having put in the ground a certain number of ferment and barley, and also after having performed some rituals, according to the custom and religion of the country, she completely filled a trolley cart with the earth. And after she had brought it into the city, she prepared the seals and the signs called *lemnia sphragids*, so celebrated by the fame of men; in the way that I said. So I asked her if she

4. Today, Ephestias designates an archeological site in the northern shore of Lemnos.

knew whether there was goat blood mixed with the said earth. And when I had said that, they all laughed loudly, not only the common [people], but also several learned men in many other things, and mainly in the history of the country. Furthermore, I took a book once written by one of the inhabitants: which demonstrated all the use and usefulness of this earth. For this reason I have not been negligent in experimenting with this drug: of which I have taken twenty thousand *spragides*, that is to say, seals or signs.

§ 1.01.3. Jean de Renou (1568-c. 1620) explains the difference between the genuine earth of Lemnos and its most common counterfeits

The land of Lemnos is similarly prepared with common clay dried, pulverized, and mixed with plantain water, then formed and shaped in pellets, which are marked with the seal of the great Turk similarly falsified, because Bellon writes that the seal is marked in a hundred different ways. But the forgery is easily discovered by dissolving both [earths] in water, because the one that is natural and legitimate leaks its water almost as oil and [it becomes] smooth after it has deposited, and the other leaks [a substance] that is it much more subtle and clear. . . .

On the Lemnian Earth

Chapter I

> The most excellent of all the earths that are used in Medicine it seems to me it is this one, which our Apothecaries sometimes call earth of Lemnos, or Lemnian earth, because of the island of Lemnos, from where it is brought to us, and sometimes also sealed earth, because of certain character that is imprinted on it. And in fact this one, which had formerly the shape of a small cake, which bore for mark the effigy of Diane represented in the shape of a goat, and which was prepared by one of its Priests, was the most recommendable of all. The real sealed earth or Lemnian must be yellow, or reddish, according to the saying of Galen and Dioscorides, eventually the same color of the hill that is in the island of Lemnos, from where it is brought to us, on which hardly any plant grows, not even any stone [can be found], and nothing else on it can be seen other than sealed earth. As for the one brought from Constantinople, it is ash-colored, and marked with the seal of the Emperor of the Turks, which does not consist of any figure of any animal whatsoever, like that of Lemnos, but rather in certain and various characters; and nevertheless it is purchased as true and legitimate in spite of its color not being similar to that of the other, which makes me believe that those are greatly mistaken who write that the inhabitants of the island of Lemnos or those who trade in that country, put goat blood in that earth, and make pellets from it to sell it. . . .

§ 1.02. ROMAN OPHTHALMOLOGISTS' TRADEMARKS AND SLOGANS—FIRST CENTURY BC-THIRD CENTURY AD

One of the most developed branches of medicine throughout Roman civilization was ophthalmology. Dozens, if not hundreds, of professionals dedicated themselves to the study of eye diseases and to the preparation of medicines to treat them. Famous physicians, such as Galenus and Cornelius Celsus, have dedicated these drugs—generally referred to as collyria—accurate attention.

But it should be noted that not all Roman medicinal preparations designated as collyria had an application in ophthalmology. Some of those preparations were also used for treating other ailments, such as wounds. For this reason, not all signs concerning collyria should be understood as ophthalmologists' trademarks.

In general, the collyria were prepared using cremation or another technique that reduced them to a paste. That paste was allowed to dry. Once dried, it was given a different configuration, depending on the container to be used. The collyria could be made into powder and put in a small glass or metal bottles. In this case, the medicines would then be dissolved in milk or egg white. Or they could be left in the form of a solid paste (not unlike certain cosmetics that are used today). The words designating the makers, the substances and their therapeutic uses, eventually in combination with figures, were printed on stamps, which generally had the form of a small parallelepiped, prism or cone. The sidewalls of the stamps were generally reserved for technical indications: the name of the collyria and their therapeutic purposes. The upper and lower faces were engraved with the name(s) of the inventor(s) of the formulae and, eventually, with drawings. Graffiti appeared on many ophthalmologist stamps. Often ophthalmologists not only made collyria and sold them but also administered them to patients themselves. Those stamps were used to print on the paste that formed the collyria, the trademarks, the names, and the slogans of the ophthalmologists who invented them.

The purpose of these notes is not to describe the practice of ophthalmology in Rome, but to show how business identifiers were already used in its context. And, in fact, the trademarks of collyria, which were used mainly in the first three centuries of our era, with a particular concentration in the Roman provinces of Gaul and Germania (but which are found everywhere in the Roman Empire), reveal surprisingly modern aspects of commercial rivalry.

At least three of these aspects deserve to be highlighted: the frequent use of figurative marks; the frequent use of evocative trademarks, that is, trademarks that are directly related to the ingredients used; and the use of slogans.

One of the figurative elements mostly used by Roman artisans as a component of their trademarks was the gladiator. (see Figure 2) Gladiators are found as figurative marks on various industrial objects, such as lamps and amphorae. But they are also found on collyria. A stamp found in Sens (Burgundy, France) displays on the upper and lower sides two figures of gladiators (one probably of Samnite origin, the other of Thracian origin). On the sides of the stamp are the inscriptions annotated and translated next. The presence of four names on the four sides of the stamp indicates that it was used by four different ophthalmologists (Paternianus, Severianus, Malafans, and Divixeus) for designating their products. The final distinction would be made by the physicians through annotations they would add afterward upon the dry and molded stamp. This is an interesting case of an association between competitors, who may have set a small drug manufacturing company. The four ophthalmologists may have adopted the gladiator as a fanciful, figurative, common trademark. In the case of medicines, the

figure of the gladiator could have a suggestive effect of implying good health and physical shape.
Roman ophthalmologists would frequently write graffiti on the stamps, given that the names of the collyria were often difficult to read by the physicians themselves since they were engraved on the stamp in reverse (so that once printed on the paste, the names would appear in the correct form).
One of the collyria used by ophthalmologists at that time was the thalasseros collyrium made with ingredients obtained from the sea. A stamp found in Vieux, in the French region of Calvados, containing the name of this collyrium, shows the drawing of a seahorse as a figurative element. It is, therefore, a suggestive mark, associating the seahorse with the type of collyrium, the thalasseros collyrium (which, in Greek, means "of the sea, marine"). Another example of a suggestive figurative trademark: the figure of a dove printed on a collyrium stamp, found in Lillebonne, France, which evokes the idea that this collyrium employed, as an ingredient, dove blood or bile—both materials then used to treat albuginea ailments and scars.
Another marketing technique Roman ophthalmologists used was slogans. One of the sides of a stamp found at Martres d'Artrières (Puy-de-Dôme, France) bears the following inscription: C. T. BALBINI. A/MIMETUM. AD. S [G(aii) T(itii) Balbini amimetum ad s(uppurationes)]. This means "Gaius Tittius Balbinus' inimitable collyrium against suppurations." Gaius Titius Balbinus was the inventor of the composition. Worth noticing in this stamp is the use of the word "amimetum" for designating the collyrium. That word is the Latin transcription of the same Greek term, which means "inimitable, unique." In using this particular term, the inventor wished to make it clear that his product was unique, exclusive, inimitable by his rivals.
However, not all ophthalmologists enjoyed a great reputation in Rome. In two of his famous epigrams, Martial (Marcus Valerius Marcialis, first century AD) did not spare those professional—mostly, freed Greek slaves—from his scathing criticism:

> *Lately was Diaulus a doctor, now he is an undertaker.*
> *What the undertaker now does the doctor too did before. (Book I, XLVII)*
> *You are now a gladiator: you were an eye-specialist*
> *before. You did as doctor what you do now as gladiator. (Book VIII, LXXIV)*[5]

5. Walter C.A. Ker (transl.), MARTIAL EPIGRAMS, WITH AN ENGLISH TRANSLATION, in 2 volumes (G.P. Putnam's Sons, 1920). *Source*: <archive.org>.

§ 1.02.1. Graffiti and inscriptions on an ophthalmologist's stamp

First Century BC-Third Century AD

Graffiti on the top and lower sides of the stamp, across the figure (gladiator):

PATTIRNIA / NVS / DIAMISO [Paternianus diamiso[s]] and DLCMTRV / S [D(e)l(a)c(ry)m(a)t(o)r(i)us]

On the four sides of the stamp:

1. PATERNIANVS / COL / S / LIRI / DIAMISOADA [Paternianus colliri(um) diamisos ad a a(spritudines)]

Translation: Collyrium Paternianus diamisos against the granulations of the eyelids.

2. SEVERIANUS / DLCMTRVS [Severianus d(e)l(a)c(ri)m(a)t(o)r(i)us]

Translation: Collyrium Severianus for eye drops.

3. MELANFANS / DIALEPINVS [Melafans dialepinus]

Translation: Collyrium Melafans dialepinus.

4. DIVIXEV [Divixeu(s)]

Translation: Collyre Divixeus

Figure 2 Roman collyrium stamp used by four Roman ophthalmologists found in Sens, Burgundy (France), showing two gladiators on the top and bottom faces, in addition to the physicians' and ingredients' names. A. Héron de Villefosse and H. Thédenat, Notes sur quelques cachets d'oculistes romains, in Bulletin Monumental ou Recueil de Documents et Mémoires relatifs aux différents branches de l'Archéologie, *5th series, vol. 11, at 309 et seq. (1883).*

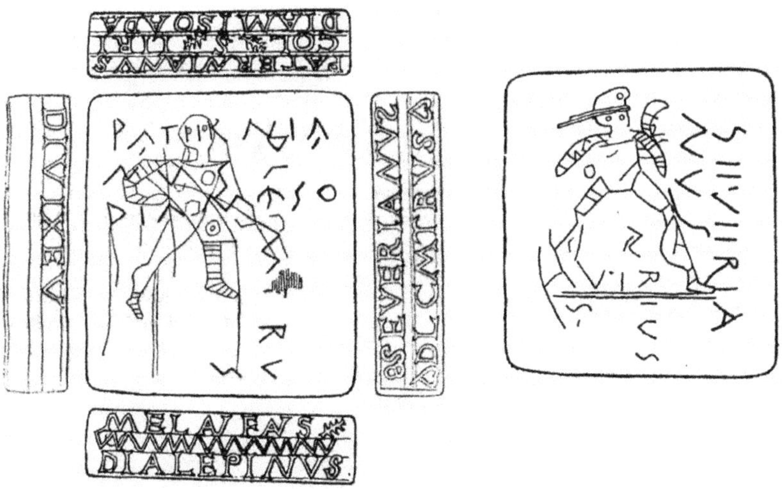

§ 1.02.2. Graffiti and inscriptions on another ophthalmologist's stamp

First Century BC-Third Century AD

On the top:

C.TIT.BALBI [*Gaius Tittius Balbinus*]

On the four sides:

1. C.T. BALBINI.A / MIMETUM.AD.S [*G(aii) T(itii) Balbini amimetum ad s(uppurationes)*]

Translation: Gaius Tittius Balbinus' inimitable collyrium against suppurations.

2. C.TITTI.BALBINI.CHLO / RON.AD.EXPVR.ET.REPLET [*G(aii) Titti(i) Balbini chloron ad expurg(ationem) et replet(ionem)*]

Translation: Gaius Tittius Balbinus' chloron collyrium, for modifying and filling the wounds.

3. BALBINI.CHAR / MA.AD.CYLON [*Balbini c(ollyrium) harma ad cylon*]

Translation: Balbinus' harma collyrium against cylon.

4. C.T.BALBINI.CHARMA / AD CYLON ET CHALAZOS

G(aii) T(itti) Balbini c(ollyrium) harma ad cylon et chalazos(in)

Translation: Collyre harma of Gaius Tittius Balbinus against cylon and chalazosis

§ 1.03. IN VENICE, PHARMACISTS WERE REQUIRED TO DESIGNATE MEDICINES WITH COMMON NAMES

1258

The following text, extracted from the charter of pharmacists of Venice of 1258, illustrates the absence of incentives for an early introduction of brands in medicines. In 1258, the Giustizarii—the magistrates in charge of supervising the arts and crafts of Venice—approved the "capitulare," or charter, of the pharmacists (designated as "speziali"). The charter placed the pharmacists under the technical supervision of the physicians (whose by-laws were approved at the same time) and required that most medicines elaborated by the former should be examined and approved by the latter prior to their commercialization. Moreover, pharmacists were required to designate all medicines they sold with their common names—a practice that would last for several centuries.

The "capitulare" were phrased in the form of a pledge that pharmacists were required to read as one of the conditions for being admitted to the profession. That is why the text is articulated in the first person.

Cesare Foucard, Lo STatuto dei Medici et dei Speziali in Venezia scritto nell' anno 1258 (excerpt)

2. Moreover, I will not make, nor will I order the making of preparations concerning medicine that exceed the value of ten *soldi*, if I do not first show them to the examiners or to the examiner that will be established for the moment by the *Giustizarii*, except, however, if any of the physicians wished to compose some special medicine for one of his patients. I have the right, however, to add electuaries to other preparations, but I will not compose either these or those, nor will I order the composition, if I have not previously shown them to the examiners or examiner who will then be appointed by the *Giustizarii*. The examiner or examiners must be present until the preparation is perfectly completed. The medicines in which the balm enters are excluded; and if I do not mix them, I will not sell them, nor will I sell them for balms. Neither will I sell anything, or will I have it sold without its proper (common) name. For this I will not make conspiracy or society with any physician so as to deceive buyers as regards the medicines, that is, as regards the electuaries, the powders, and the syrups.

§ 1.04. LAWS REGULATING THE PROFESSION OF APOTHECARIES IN PARIS—FOURTEENTH CENTURY

In the fourteenth century, France imposed the technical inspection of medicines prepared by pharmacists. In the same token of the capitulare of Venice, and by contrast with the regulations and by-laws concerning other professions, master apothecaries were not required to inscribe their names or individual marks on the products they prepared or on the containers thereof, for the purposes of quality certification. The reason for this exception is that medicines were subject to previous certification—they were, therefore, pre-certified. The illegality of selling medicines of poor quality resided then not in the low standards of the drugs themselves, but in failing to obtain the prior approval from the inspectors.

On the other hand, there was no market pressure for apothecaries to adopt business identifiers other than their own trade names because the preparation of drugs followed the prescriptions of a pharmacopeia. The second text mentions the pharmacopeia that, in the fourteenth century, was generally adopted: the antidotary of Nicholas, which was elaborated in the twelfth century by an unknown pharmacist of Salerno, Italy.

Medicine trademarks would appear much later, when apothecaries, although, in some cases, still subject to the technical supervision of physicians or of master apothecaries, engaged in a commercial rivalry with other makers and distributors of medicines, drugs, and medicinal herbs. The only information that the 1353 regulation required apothecaries to inscribe on the medicinal jars concerned the year and the month of the making of the product.

§ 1.04.1. Directive determining the inspection of Paris apothecaries' remedies by the physicians of the [medical] school

Paris, May 22, 1336.

Philippe [VI] by the grace of God king of France: to the provost of Paris, or his deputy, greeting.

The dean and the masters of the medical school have led us to understand, that formerly, for the common good, certain directives were passed and sealed with the seal of our Châtelet of Paris, between the said masters of medicine on the one hand, and, on the other, the apothecaries, concerning the profession of the apothecaries and grocers; and that especially, and expressly, it is provided in those directives that all and every apothecary who want to engage in that business, must swear before the [person] who by us will be appointed, to loyally hold and keep them.

Therefore, as the said masters of medicines know better the true understanding of those directives than those who do not hold the science of medicine would know, we command you to compel the apothecaries and their servants and the herbalists, to hold and keep them, before the faculty; or before the dean, or two, or three of masters thereof. And that you compel them to show the said masters the laxative medicines, and the opiates, which are kept for a long time, so that they see them, before they are prepared, and to know that they are good and fresh and not corrupted and desiccated, according to what it will appear to you, by the said directives, that they will be required to show them to their masters, or one of the jurors.

And do this diligently so that no infringement be reported to us.

Given in Paris on May 22, the year of grace one thousand three hundred and thirty-six.

§ 1.04.2. Directive on the exercise of the profession of apothecary and herbalist, subjecting them to the inspection

Paris, August 1353

Jean [II], by the grace of God, king of France; we make known to all present and to come.

As we have heard the report of several persons worthy of faith that in our city of Paris, by pure greed and ignorance of some, some medicines are administered that, at the same time, have no virtue or do not produce effects, other times because they are too old and otherwise, from which several scandals and great inconveniences ensue and could ensue, if by us remedy was not provided on this as appropriate. And therefore, we, wishing the prosperity and health of our subjects, willing to obviate the scandals and perils above mentioned, by the consent of the sages, and having in such matter full will, have provided by our command the following.

First. We have commanded and command that from now on, every year, twice—that is, about the Easter feast, and about the All Saints feast—shall be made diligent inspection, by the master of the apothecary's profession, who for the time will be mainly the apothecaries of the city of Paris, and suburbs, which inspection will not be left to be made at any occasion whatsoever. And said master of the apothecary's profession shall inspect, with the advice of two masters of medicine, whom the dean of the medical school will appoint, loyal to and experts in it, according to his conscience, and also of two apothecaries, whom our provost of Paris, or his deputy, will sufficiently elect according to his conscience, to the above said things. . . . They will reveal the truth of the things that will be in front of them, both old and new, or in whatever quality they are, and will not adjust, either in fact or verbally, by themselves or by others, any lie, or fraud, but they will reveal the plain and pure truth, and with this the apothecaries will swear that they will loyally carry out the profession of apothecary, and that they will have their book, which is called antidotary Nicholas, corrected by the masters of the profession, on the advice of physicians and [their] assistants, on the matter of the above mentioned inspection, and that they shall not include in their prescriptions any corrupt medicine, or from which the virtue is removed so that it cannot produce an effective result, and that they will not remove the new medicines, to put the old ones [in their place], and that they shall have their weights all true and loyally advertised, and will be seen by the above mentioned inspectors and counsellors. . . . And also they shall swear . . . that they will not accept any fraud, if any physician wished to sell medicine for a higher price with the intent of profit, and that they shall not sell it for a higher price because of some hatred that they may have towards the patient. And that if any of the masters prescribes in the apothecary's shop some recipes of syrups, or of his own medicines, for any patient, he shall not prepare it again at the request of the [patient] for whom it has been made, or given, without the advice of the one who prescribed it, or of another known physician, as it is said, and that they take good care of working according to their conscience. And also that [as regards] the electuary or opiate medicines, or any long lasting medicine, made and put in jars, or other vessels suitable to contain them, they shall put on the jar the year and the month of their making, and that they shall sell at loyal, fair and moderate prices, and loyal and fair with regard to currency fluctuation. . . .

We command the current and the future provost of Paris, or his deputy, that for the common good, they keep and make hold and keep entirely, without infringing, all the above mentioned things and each of them, by all concerned, [including] the royal ordinances of our predecessors [as far as] all the other things that have remained the same [are concerned]. And so that it be firm and stable forever, we have put our seal to these present letters, except all things that are our right and the right of others.

Given in Paris, the year of grace one thousand three hundred and fifty-three, in the month of August.

§ 1.05. FRENCH AUTHORITIES START ACKNOWLEDGING APOTHECARIES' INDIVIDUAL AND COLLECTIVE TRADEMARKS—EARLY SIXTEENTH CENTURY

As seen above, the first rules concerning the profession of apothecaries and the commerce of medicines would not include provisions on distinctive signs, in sharp contrast with other professions. Things started to change, very gradually, in the sixteenth century.

The two texts that follow show the hesitation of authorities in acknowledging such signs. In 1508, the by-laws of the city of Rouen ignored the use of trademarks by the apothecaries. Instead, they should identify the ingredients and the medicines with their common names, weights, and dates of preparation. But just six years later, the by-laws of Paris extended to the master pharmacists and grocers the same requirement that for decades, even centuries, had been already in place for other professions: they should communicate their trademarks to their masters or jurors, for the purpose of certification of the quality of the products they sold (and branded).
It is worth noticing that these rules were written by the master apothecaries and grocers themselves, which suggests that the use of individual trademarks might have already become a practice in their trades.

§ 1.05.1. By-laws of the Apothecaries-Wax Makers-Grocers, written at the Hotel-de-Ville of Rouen, by three medical doctors and by three Apothecaries-Wax Makers-Grocers

1508

It is ordered that all those of the said profession and business who are currently in the city, outskirts and suburbs of Rouen, may enjoy, use, and exercise them from now on, as they have done before, observing the orders and taking an oath to keep and observe them well and loyally to the best of their power, which will all be enrolled and registered with the common registrar of the fraternity of the said profession. . . .

Art. XV. — That they shall write on the jars or containers, in which they put and preserve the waters, syrups, opiates, or others, the day, the month and year of the composition, or distillation of those things contained therein.

Art. XVI. — That they shall not change or have changed the sign or the date of that container, on pain of being punished as infringers.

§ 1.05.2. Letters for the separation of the profession of an apothecary from that of a grocer, and on the mode of election of the trustees, and the reception of the apprentices

Vincennes, June 14, 1514

Louis [XII], etc., we make known to all present and those to come that we have received the humble request from of our dear and beloved sworn masters, guards of the community and goods of the master grocers and apothecaries of our good town and city of Paris, saying that our predecessor kings, considering that for the good of the public thing and conservation of human bodies, several trades were sworn in our said town and city, such as the profession and the trade of pharmacy, which consists in great art, science, experience and knowledge of drugs, composition of the receipts that enter the human body (which profession had the more reason to be so considered among the others), had in their regard good and great deliberations, made, ordered and established certain statutes and fine ordinances on said profession and trade, and to the members of that profession had given several privileges, franchises and freedoms which they enjoyed and used, as they do today, and likewise to the simple grocers, which belong to a profession and trade that are distinct and separate from the profession of apothecary grocers, because who is a grocer is not an apothecary and who is an apothecary is a grocer; and given that several questions and debates have since arisen between the members of one profession and of the other and continue arising every day at the election of their guards and inspectors, which otherwise, with the purpose of obviating those debates, questions and disputes, the mentioned applicants have put and redacted certain articles in writing, which they very humbly made us present in the form and manner that follows. . . .

(5) *Item*. That all those who wish to succeed in becoming master of the said professions of grocers and apothecaries or of one of them, once the respective reception [passing the exam] is done, shall be required to communicate their marks printed on lead or otherwise to the masters of the fraternities who will keep them in that fraternity's safe, so that all the works which henceforth they will make be known, and if there is a fault, the offenders may be identified so as to punish them and provide as appropriate.

. . .

We command this, etc., etc.

Given at the bois de Vincennes in the month of June, the year of grace of 1514, and the xviith of our reign.

§ 1.06. THE INTENSIVE USE OF JARS BY APOTHECARIES IN THE SIXTEENTH CENTURY GIVES RISE TO A NEW LINE OF POTTERY PRODUCTS: THE APOTHECARIES' JARS. AN EXAMPLE FROM ROUEN: MASSEOT ABAQUESNE.

The interior of drugstores between the sixteenth and the eighteenth centuries showed one predominant element in the arrangement of their layout: the shelves along the interior walls loaded with containers of many sorts.

These containers, beyond their technical purposes, as Jean de Renou explains in his recommendations on how an ideal drugstore should be organized, were, in most cases, the main esthetic element added by the apothecaries to their shops, so as to make them attractive to customers.

With the increase of the availability of some of the main raw materials of drugs across Europe (sugar and spices), after the Portuguese reached the East by sea, the industry and trade of medicines grew significantly. The number of pharmacists grew accordingly, in direct competition with the drugstores of monasteries and noble houses. The ingredients for medicines, as well as the elaborated end products, would carefully be conserved in jars, whose shapes and features evolved so as to make them more appropriate to serve their purposes. Certain shapes corresponded to certain types of ingredients and medicines. The jars would reserve a rectangle empty so that the apothecary could write the name of the ingredient in it—the idea of designating medicines with fanciful brands was still unknown. Eventually, the apothecaries would command jars from potters already with the names of the ingredients or medicines printed on them.

In this manner, potters developed a line of business in making and selling to apothecaries the jars they needed. Because potters were already users of intellectual property to ascertain their identities in the face of commercial rivals, many of apothecaries' jars displayed their makers' trademarks.

One example of one potter who has dedicated a part of his production to the making and selling of apothecaries' jars follows. It was Masseot Abaquesne, a potter who established the first industry of earthenware in Rouen, France, in the sixteenth century. Masseot acquired a great reputation and supplied remarkable works of faïence to French noble houses. Some of his works still can be seen in palaces and public buildings.

The intellectual property element that appears here did not belong to the pharmacist, but to the jar maker. The contract (in somewhat confusing language) that follows contains an interesting element: Abaquesne promised not to manufacture jars for other apothecaries while making those commanded by Dubosc; moreover, after delivering the last pot, he would have to wait six weeks before he could deliver any pot or jar to another client. This clause of exclusivity is a fine demonstration of the importance that ensuring the supply of the appropriate containers had for apothecaries.

Contract between Pierre Dubosc, apothecary, and Masseot Abaquesne, potter, concerning the supply of medicinal jars

Registered with the notaries of Rouen, May 24, 1545

Was present Masseot Abaquesne, potter, living in the parish of St-Vincent de Rouen, which declares having sold by these presents to Pierre Dubosc, bourgeois apothecary residing in the parish of St-Martin-du-Pont de Rouen, present, and who declared having bought from Abaquesne the number of pieces of glazed earthenware, as follows: 40 dozen enameled jars containing one jar each; 50 dozen vases also containing a painted piece; *item* 60 dozen of jars holding one *choppine*;[6] *item* 80 dozen pots holding a *demyon*; *item* similar number of 80 dozen pots holding a *demyart*, all holding for each [piece] at least the measure above stated and all in the manner of earthenware and reasonable and competent height and width and, as it has become the custom in the practice of pharmacy, good, loyal and marketable and well enameled as it is appropriate. *Item* 36 dozen pots in the manner of *chevrettes*, i.e., 24 dozen containing three *choppines* with five *demyons* each pot, and 12 dozen holding a *pinte*, also of reasonable and competent height and width and, as it has become the custom in the practice of pharmacy, loyal and marketable, all of which pottery as above said, Abaquesne promised and accepted to transfer and sell to Dubosc as soon as possible and continue working in making the mentioned jars ordinarily and which delivery will be made by Abaquesne and received by Dubosc; and while the task will be carried, Abaquesne may not work for anyone other than Dubosc until he has completely made all the number of pots for Dubosc and nor shall he deliver [any pot] to anyone whatsoever until six weeks after the complete delivery . . . this sale is made for the sum of 36 *solz* for each dozen pots holding a pot; for each dozen pots holding a *pinte* for the sum of 27 sols; for each dozen choppines, the sum of 18 sols; for each dozen *demyon* for the sum

6. *Choppine*, *pinte*, *demyart* and *demyon* were liquid measures used in medieval France.

of 12 sols; for each dozen of *demyart* for the sum of 9 solz, and for each dozen of chevrettes for the sum of 45 sols for each kind of *chevrette*, one carrying the other, etc.

Figure 3 Medicinal jars made in the workshop of Masseot Abaquesne, c. 1550. On the left, a jar with the space left in blank for the later inclusion of the content's name. On the right, the back of another Abaquesne's jar, with the artisan's trademark. Collection of the Museum of Victoria & Albert, London.

§ 1.07. JEAN DE RENOU, A FRENCH PHYSICIAN (C. 1568-C. 1620), DESCRIBES A TYPICAL DRUGSTORE AND MENTIONS ITS MOST DISTINCTIVE ELEMENT—THE ESTHETICAL FEATURES OF PHARMACEUTICAL JARS AND CONTAINERS

In the seventeenth century, the trade of pharmacists imposed the use of business identifiers. However, there was some sort of struggle between the notion of pharmacists as merchants, on the one hand, and pharmacists as workers for the public good, on the other. The following description of an ideal drugstore in the seventeenth century reflects such conflict in suggesting that in a pharmacist's store, the only distinctive features should be the ornamental figures and shapes of jars and containers where drugs and ingredients would be kept. In other words, it is implied that trademarks and other signs of ownership should be avoided.
This is reported by Jean de Renou in the second part of his famous treatise DISPENSATORIUM GALENICO-CHIMICUM, *published in Paris in 1608 and translated into French by another physician, Louis de Serres. De Renou was a French physician (c. 1568-c. 1620),*

and a counselor and physician to the King. As seen in the previous section, since the sixteenth century, the intensive use of jars had given rise to a new line of pottery (earthenware and porcelain) products, with their particular styles.
De Renou's recommendation that pharmacists wrote down the names of the medicines and ingredients on the vases and sachets that contained them had the purpose of avoiding that they made some quid pro quo—i.e., *that they made mistakes as to the nature and quality of the drugs.*

On the House and Store of the Pharmacist.

CHAPTER I.

. . . And so that all medicines are well and duly stored in his shop, it is expedient that it be organized in several and various shelves, for the most part equally distant from each other, tied and nailed to large pieces of wood similarly attached to the walls, and thus having all kinds of them, thereby with room to house properly and spaced out all his Pharmaceutical containers, both large and small, both those made of wood, and those which are made of earth, glass, or tin, and so that they will not be forgotten by the same means to locate them in a way that those that are most often necessary to handle and stir are in a close and convenient place, and the others the least used on some more distant shelf.

Finally, concerning the aspect of the vases, as well as of the sachets that he deems convenient to hang from the joists of his shop, he will use this caution: i.e., that he will write the name of each of the medicines in front of the vases and sachets, so that he finds them more quickly when necessary, and also for fear that he will do some *quid pro quo* of an Apothecary. . . .

On the boxes, bottles, and other vases needed in the Pharmacist's shop.

CHAPTER XII

All the vases that are in the Pharmacist's shop are intended for the preparation of medicines, as we said above, or to contain them after they are prepared, as we will say hereafter. Now, these vases are seven or eight in number: that is, bottles, or oil jars, or earthenware jars, or baskets, or chests, or small boxes, or normal boxes. . . .

Besides, there is only this place of normal and small boxes that are visible to those who enter the shop, which are decorated, and embellished with all kinds of decorative paintings, such as kites, feathered snakes, centaurs with peeled asses, bridled gooses, flying ducks, and the like, in the middle of which it is usual to leave a small empty square to write in it, in golden or azure letters, the name of the drug that is contained in each of them; as for the other boxes they are usually without any paint. . . .

Figure 4 A drugstore in the seventeenth century: a very functional layout, with the jars' ornaments as its only distinctive element. Extracted from Jean de Renou, Les Oeuvres Pharmaceutiques.

§ 1.08. THE IMPORTANCE OF CERTIFICATION MARKS IN THE PHARMACEUTICAL INDUSTRY GROWS IN THE EARLY SEVENTEENTH CENTURY

The text that follows is an illustration of the growing importance of marks of certification in the pharmaceutical industry. As said above, this is a direct consequence of the increase in the number of pharmacists and available medicines. This sort of ruling had already been applied to other industries for at least two centuries.

The Parliament of Rouen sets a specific trademark to certify the quality of the drugs and medicines exported from the city

1609

> It is said: That the Court has dismissed the Appeals; [that] it will settle the matter under appeal and give it is full and entire effect. . . . And concluding on the arguments of the Parties, it has Ordered and Orders that the Drugs and Groceries that will be transported and unloaded from the Vessels of this City of Rouen, to be sold et transported in other places, will be garbled, screened and cleaned by the Garbler[7] in the presence of the Masters and Guards of the profession of Apothecary-Wax Makers and Grocers who would make the Visitation, so that the Goods that will be found to be good, fair and marketable, [shall be] put in various Bags, according to the different kinds of the Groceries and Drugstores, and the Bags marked with the Mark of the City, namely a Lamb and, on top, the Fleur-de-Lys, to signify that the said Goods have been garbled and visited, and that what is inside is the best kind of Groceries and Drugs, and the other Drugstores and Groceries of the same kind, but not of such a good quality nor of the same price shall be put in other Bags, which will also be marked with the same Mark of the Lamb, but with a Circle above only, without the Fleur de Lys, so as to distinguish and differentiate the best from those of inferior quality. . . .

§ 1.09. A COURT SETTLES THE DISPUTE BETWEEN TWO APOTHECARIES WHO USED THE SAME SHOP SIGN—A RED CROSS—TO IDENTIFY AND DIFFERENTIATE THEIR BUSINESSES

After several centuries, the profession of apothecaries was consolidated both as a trade and technical art, in particular, upon the enormous contribution it received from the advances in alchemy and chemistry. Pharmacists carried their trade in specialized shops, where they would hold their laboratories for the preparation of drugs and for attending to the customers. In the shops, pharmacists would have their products inspected by the guards or jurors of the profession, where there was no corporation, or by the masters, where there was one, or by the college of physicians. Moreover, they would be visited by physicians, who would pass their prescriptions to them, with instructions

7. The garbler was a person specialized in preparing medicinal herbs to be used as ingredients. In garbling the herbs, the garblers would select, clean and cut them.

(the physicians, in many cases, also performed the role of inventors of new formulae). Gradually, those shops would be identified and distinguished by shop signs, which would help customers to locate the places where they could buy the medicines from those apothecaries they trusted.

The text that follows is a report of a judgment of 1612 by the Grand Chamber of the Parliament of Paris settling a dispute between two neighboring apothecaries who disputed the exclusivity in the use of the red cross as a shop sign. It seems that this was not the first judgment on a dispute involving shop signs because the reporter himself acknowledges a precedent of 1609. But it seems to have been the first case of a dispute over apothecaries' business identifiers. These disputes, in the course of the seventeenth century, with the increase of the business of pharmacy, would become more common. Interestingly, a dispute involving the use of the same shop sign of the red cross would arise again in France at the beginning of the twentieth century (see § 1.28).

Judgment by the Grand Chamber of the Parliament of Paris

March 2, 1612

The Grand Chamber, on the 2nd of March, 1612, examined whether in Paris, on the same street, an Apothecary, whose shop was separated from the shop of another Apothecary only by a party wall, and that had a red cross as a shop sign hanging above its door, could prevent that neighbor from using the same cross as his sign, with the intent of commercial rivalry (as it always happens with the artisans and the merchants, when they imitate with fraudulent intent, as Nonius explains), whereas the oldest cross had been known in the neighborhood for many years, which *lex 3. de oper. publ. ff.* prohibits.

The neighbor against whom the cause was launched had an explanation for what was seen: that there was a difference between the crosses, one being larger, the other being smaller; it seemed to him that a number of other towns accepted the same sort of signs, ones being bigger, the others smaller.

However, the Senate has confirmed the judgment of the Mayor of Paris, by which he condemned the newer shop to cease using the sign of the cross of the older shop, because the facts showed that jealousy, anger, and envy, were the reason for the use of the sign by the new shop, as Germanus and Charrerius said.

§ 1.10. IN THE SIXTEENTH AND SEVENTEENTH CENTURIES, WITH THE GROWTH IN THE NUMBER OF DRUGSTORES, PHARMACISTS INTENSIFIED THE USE OF SHOP SIGNS

The following text is formed by a few excerpts from a history of signboards, authored by Larwood and Hotten. In the seventeenth century, the business of pharmacy, pushed by the advancement of chemical science, opened the room for a significant increase in the number of drugstores in the main European cities. With that increase, the urge for luring customers to their shops grew dramatically, which led to an added tension among pharmacists as regards their business identifiers. Shop signs were one of their most valuable assets, given that most of the business was carried within the shop.

The two historians give an interesting account of the choice of some specific signs by apothecaries.

Dragons, when apothecaries' signs, were not derived from heraldry, but were used to typify certain chemical actions. In an old German work on Alchemy [note omitted] one of the plates represents a dragon eating his own tail; underneath are the words,

> "This is a great wonder, and very strange:
> the dragon contains the greatest medicament."

In mediaeval alchemy, the dragon seems to have been the emblem of Mercury, which appears from these words on the same print: "Mercury rightly precipitated or sublimated in its own water dissolved and again coagulated." To which are added the following rhymes:

> "There is a dragon that lives in the forest
> Who has no want of poison:
> When he sees the sun or fire he spits venom,
> Which flies about fearfully.
> No living animal can be cured of it;
> Even the basilisk does not equal him.
> He who can properly kill this serpent has overcome all his danger.
> His colours increase in death;
> Physic is produced from his poison,
> Which he entirely consumes,
> And eats his own venomous tail.
> This must be accomplished by him
> In order to produce the noblest balm.
> Such great virtue as will point out herein
> That all the learned shall rejoice."

Hence the dragon became one of the "properties" of the chemist and apothecary, was painted on his drug-pots, hung up as his sign, and some dusty, stuffed crocodile hanging from the ceiling in the laboratory had to do service for the monster, and inspire the vulgar with a profound awe for the mighty man who had conquered the vicious reptile.

The Salamander was another animal of the same class, and also represented certain chemical actions, owing to its fabled powers of resisting the fire. The notions of early naturalists concerning this creature were very extraordinary. A Bestiarium in the Royal Library of Brussels, No. 10074, says that it lives on pure fire, and produces a substance which is neither silk nor linen, nor yet wool, of which garments are made that can only be cleaned by fire; and that if the animal itself falls into a burning fire, it would at once extinguish the flames. Bossewell, besides incombustibility, attributes to the salamander some other qualities fully as extravagant.

"Among all venomenous beastes he is the mightiest of poyson and venyme. For if he creepe upon a tree, he infecteth all the apples or other fruit that groweth thereon with his poyson, and killeth them which eate thereof. Which apples, also, if they happen to falle into any pitte of water, the strength of the poyson killeth them that drinke thereof." [note omitted]

This incombustibility made it a very proper sign for alchemists and apothecaries, and with the last it still continues as such, at least on the Continent. Why the early Venetian printers adopted it as a sign is less evident. In France it was certainly a favourite sign with this class of workmen; but this was from the fact of its having been the badge of Francis I, a liberal patron of the arts and sciences.

One of the signs originally used exclusively by apothecaries was the Mortar and Pestle, their well-known implements for pounding drugs. Among the celebrities who sold medicines under this emblem was the noted John Moore, "author of the celebrated Worm Powder," . . .

His shop was in St Lawrence Poultney Lane. Every week the newspapers contained advertisements proving, by the most wonderful cures, the efficacy of his powders. In the sixteenth century a publican in Paris adopted the sign of the Pestle, on account of his living in the Rue de la Mortellerie (Mortar Street). . . .

Figure 5 Shop sign of an apothecary of the sixteenth century in Nantes, France, showing a young apothecary (an apprentice?) pulverizing some ingredient in a mortar. The apothecary wears clothes in use at the time of Louis XII. Extracted from Elie Seignette, TRAITÉ DU FAUX POLYCHRESTE.

§ 1.11. IN 1638, THE BY-LAWS OF THE GUILD OF THE APOTHECARIES AND WAX MAKERS OF PARIS REQUIRED THE LATTER TO HAVE INDIVIDUAL TRADEMARKS

Several centuries ago, the wax was an ingredient frequently used in the preparation of medicines. For that reason, for many years, the business of wax making was associated with that of pharmacy and led to the reunion of the two professions in the same guild. The following text is another example that, gradually, apothecaries incorporated the use of business identifiers to their trade. The text concerns the by-laws of the guild of apothecaries-grocers of Paris of 1638, but the same rule requiring the printing of wax makers' trademarks was found in other cities, such as the by-laws of the corporation of apothecaries of Montauban of 1601 [Édouard Forestier, APOTHICAIRES, MÉDECINS ET CHIRURGIENS MONTALBANAIS DU XIVÈME SIÈCLE, at 7 (Édouard Forestier, 1887)] and the by-laws of the corporation of the merchant apothecaries-wax makers-druggists of the City of Rouen and Suburbs, amended in the reign of Louis XIII (1610-1643) [*STATUTS, ORDONNANCES, ARRESTS ET REGLEMENS DES MARCHANDS APOTICAIRES-EPICIERS & DES MARCHANDS EPICIERS-CIRIERS-DROGUISTES ET CONFISEURS DE LA VILLE, FAUXBOURGS & BANLIEUE DE ROUEN, at 79 (Jacques-Joseph Le Boullenger, 1742). Source*: <gallica.BnF.fr>.]

By-laws and Ordinances for the Apothecaries-Grocers and the Merchants Grocers-Wholesalers-Druggists of the City, Suburbs and Outskirts of Paris

November 28, 1638

XXVI

The said Merchants-Grocers, or Apothecaries-Grocers, may not use in the preparation of their Medicines, Drugs, Jams, Preserves, Oils and Syrups, any sophisticated, discarded or corrupted Drugs, nor mix or use old wax with new wax in their works of wax, or old syrups in sugar-made works, and those works will be alike on top and below, under the penalty of confiscation of said drugs, goods and works, and even of their being burnt in front of the home of those who find themselves seized, as well as of fifty pounds, and exemplary punishment, if applicable.

XXVII

Item, all straws, powders, screenings or flakes, both of said Drugs and Groceries, are condemned and forbidden on the same terms as above: And the Grocers, or Apothecaries-Grocers may not sell or have in their shops any oily, damaged, mixed or sophisticated wax, under the same penalties as above.

XVIII

And to obviate the frauds and abuses committed henceforth as regards the works and manufactures of wax, We order that all those works shall be of pure wax, not mixed or sophisticated with oily or resinous wax; that on those works shall be placed and affixed the mark, both of their weight and the particular mark of the one who made and manufactured them; . . . all this under the same penalties of confiscation, of a fine of fifty pounds, and exemplary punishment, if appropriate. . . .

For such is our pleasure. Given at Saint-Germain en Laye, on the twenty-eighth day of November, the year of grace one thousand six hundred and thirty-eight, and of our Reign the twenty-ninth. Signed, Louis.

§ 1.12. A FRENCH APOTHECARY, ELIE DE SEIGNETTE (1632-1698), USED SEVERAL INTELLECTUAL PROPERTY TOOLS TO ASSERT HIS PROPRIETARY INTERESTS IN THE MEDICINE HE INVENTED WITH HIS BROTHER, THE SALT OF POLYCHRESTE: TRADE SECRECY, TRADE NAME, TRADEMARK, A PATENT LETTER

Elie de Seignette, a pharmacist from La Rochelle, France, along with his brother Jean, in around 1660, invented a medicine that became very popular in France, England, and the British American colonies: the Sel de Polychreste. *The name "Polychreste" was chosen*

because of its Greek meaning—something with several utilities. And the salt, indeed, was prescribed as a purgative with positive effects in a large number of illnesses.
Seignette kept his invention in secret with great care and extracted good money from it, in spite of the frequent counterfeiting—including by the pharmacist he had designated to distribute the drug in Paris. In order to fight counterfeit, Seignette adopted nominative and figurative trademarks that indicated the genuineness of his drug. The favor the product gained with authorities led to the issuance of a patent letter permitting Seignette to make and sell the Salt of Polychreste throughout France in spite of the fact that he never presented himself to be examined by the jurors and masters of the apothecaries in La Rochelle. This was indeed a major exception to the corporatist rules then in force.
In spite of several attempts of reverse-engineering the composition, its secrecy remained after the inventor's death, in 1698, and the drug continued being made with exclusivity by his son and daughter until 1731 when two chemists/pharmacists found the formula and revealed it to the Academy of Sciences of France.
The episode of the Salt of Polychreste shows that in the middle of the seventeenth century, trademarks were already a common feature in the trade of medicines. Most medicinal brands would consist of the names of their inventors, but it was not rare that they would include fanciful terms and figurative elements, such as elaborated monograms and drawings.
The following three texts illustrate the fascinating story of inventiveness, commercial acumen, and greed around the Salt of Polychreste. The first text was extracted from a booklet authored by Elie Seignette, in which he told the story of how the drug was invented by him and his brother, as well as of all the problems he faced as a result of commercial rivalries with other apothecaries. The second text is the notice by the Academy of Sciences of the revelation of the secret by two chemists. The third text is a piece of advertisement published considerably later (in 1754) when the formula of the Polychreste was already widely known, but Seignette's reputation was still a powerful invitation to consumers' preference.

§ 1.12.1. Elie Seignette explains how he and his brother invented the salt of polychrest and the troubles they faced to keep it exclusive

1675

In order to make use of all these lights, and so that the Public could take advantage of them, we chose three kinds of Salts out of those of which we had the most knowledge and certainty, which we prepared, and mixed, and made a Remedy slightly composed, yet very useful, very innocent, and very easy to take, because by an infinity of experiments we have been persuaded and convinced of the good and praiseworthy effects both of this Remedy and of the Salts of which it is composed, and we have also noticed that it had various virtues, according to the different applications that one could give it, as it will be said later: And it is for this reason that my Brother gave him the name of πσλύ ξηςσς, which is a Greek word that means several utilities.

Then, my Brother sent it to various places in France, to several Doctors and to several Apothecaries, his Friends, to use it for the various uses to which we had noticed that it was appropriate: who, in a short time recognized its usefulness and its innocence, which they often testified to us by letters, and even one of them, very advanced in age, took the trouble to come from more than sixty leagues to this city, in order to confer with us, and to strive by money or otherwise, to have knowledge of this Remedy; but unwilling to reveal it to him, we gave him some of it, so that he could use it only, as he had done before: and he and all those to whom we sent it, were very satisfied, as well as the patients who took it, which made the reputation of this remedy spread throughout France, and even in the other Kingdoms, and the esteem that we had conceived of it has increased more and more.

As soon as the Polychreste began to settle, jealousy arose, and various interested persons opposed its reputation and its establishment by all kinds of means; they tried to pass it off as a very bad remedy, composed of Arsenic, Réalgar [sulfur of arsenic], of Sublime and Antimony; they said that he ulcerated the stomach, the chest and all the places through which it passed, that he was so pernicious that he accelerated death, and that those who would take it would not live a year afterwards; briefly, they looked for all kinds of ways to harm us: but notwithstanding all they could do, the truth has always been recognized; and the public has always been convinced of the usefulness and innocence of this remedy: by an infinity of experiments which have been done on various illnesses, it has been recognized that it was only jealousy and envy that led these people to criticize it; that is why we had no trouble in obtaining a Judgment at the Municipality of this City, on May 13, 1660, by which each package of Polychreste was set at thirty sols, which price has always been kept. . . .

Being obliged to return to this city in 1666, I chose a person whom I thought quite trustworthy to distribute it, I entrusted him with a number of packages, which were all sealed with my stamp, along with a small Treatise that taught the public the utilities and how to use it (this person was Mr. Rousseau, Surgeon, Vieux Augustins street . . .), he distributed many, and the reputation of this remedy increased day by day. Having arrived in this City, after having well established the reputation of this Remedy in various other places in France, I very often received letters, by which I learned that everyone praised it for its goodness, and that it made surprising cures. . . .

But when I thought that I only had to work to improve a few other Remedies, which I have been using for a long time, and to collect the fruits of so much pain, I saw that in all the places of France the means to imitate the Polychreste were being looked for, particularly in Paris, where I was informed that the one whom I had appointed to distribute it, made false [remedies] in his own way instead of mine, under my name and with my stamps, which he did without giving me notice, notwithstanding the damage that this could do to the reputation of my remedy, and regardless of that being against conscience, and to the prejudice of the sick. . . .

The good effects of my Polychreste, the truthfulness of the Certificates, and of the approvals of which I have just spoken, are more than sufficiently justified by the opinion that Intendant Colbert du Terron sent to the King on December 5th, 1675, responding to his Ordinance of the twenty ninth October of the same year, by which, after having informed His Majesty of the whole fact, he says in these terms, word for word, speaking of me: "It turns out that having acquired a lot of capacity and experience in his art, through long practice, and having provided various good remedies to the Public, and in particular a Polychreste powder, which is particular to him, and of which he alone has the secret, which has been found very useful for the cure of various ailments, as it appears by the approval given by the First

Physician to His Majesty, and other famous Doctors in Medicine, and the Certificates of several people of consideration, who received relief from the use of said Polychreste powder; For all these reasons, my opinion is that it is in accordance with the justice of His Majesty and the public good, to allow the said Seignette to continue the public exercise of his Profession of Apothecary in the City of La Rochelle, and to keep there a shop, as well as to compose and administer throughout the entire Kingdom the remedies of which he is the Inventor. . . ." In consideration of which the King gave me a Patent of the sixteenth of January 1673, by which he awarded me my request, which is contained in the notice that was sent to him, in the following terms. "His Majesty wishing by reasons to gratify and favorably treat the said Seignette, he has permitted and permits him, in accordance with the opinion of Mr. du Terron, to continue henceforth if he sees fit the public exercise of Apothecary, in the City of La Rochelle, etc. . . ." . . .

And finally, since the name of Polychreste Salt has been given to various preparations of Saltpeter, in imitation of the name that we had given to a remedy that we had made with three Salts, I believe that it will not be deemed wrong that in the future I give it the name of *true Polychreste,* and that I distribute it under the name of *true Polychreste of the Seignette de la Rochelle,* instead of the name of powder Polychreste, which we had given it; not only because it is the first remedy composed of Salts to which this name has been given; but also because it produces many more different effects than the false Polychreste; and that we are its first Inventors; and again because our true Polychreste has long been recognized as good and true, that the other is only a false imitation or rather a dangerous counterfeit; and so nobody should give the name of *real Polychreste of the Seignette* to any other remedy that can be invented, since that is the name of our family, which I will always distribute it in the same way, because I do not believe that anything better could ever been made.

Those who, like Mr. Rousseau, have viciously and maliciously distributed the false Polychreste, although they were aware, like himself, that they were very different remedies, and which should not be administered for the same uses, will undoubtedly no longer dare to distribute the false one, as they have done; because they will no longer be able to hide their deceit in the future, any more than Mr. Rousseau; especially because I have given in this Treatise and in that of the true Polychreste, several marks and various infallible means to easily recognize its differences, and to distinguish my Polychreste from all those that one might counterfeit; thus, so if they still sell it, they will be forced to say that it is Polychreste Salt in their own way, and not in mine.

[A description of the very many uses of the True Polychrest follows—it essentially operated as a purgative with claimed efficacy against an enormous quantity of illnesses. The treatise ends with the following text:]

And so that my Polychreste powder can be distinguished from the others, so that it be taken with more confidence from those who distribute it for me, and so that the Doctors can order it with more safety, each sachet containing the powder will be stamped with my Stamp, and will have the mark printed below.

END.

[A statement by an "uninterested physician," praising the virtues of the real Polychrest, closes Elie Seignette's booklet.]

Figure 6 Seignette's signs and trademarks. The swan was part of Seignette's coat of arms. The motto that surrounds the swan reads: Com sole et sale omnia fiunt (Everything can be done with sun and salt). The swan was printed on the front side of the sachets that contained the salts. On the back, the monogram was printed along with the words: "Le vray Polycrest de Messrs *Seigneurs de la Rochelle." Extracted from Elie Seignette,* TRAITÉ DU FAUX POLYCHRESTE.

§ 1.12.2. Notice by the Royal Academy of Sciences on the composition of the Salt of Seignette

1731

On the Salt of Seignette and on that of Epsom

We put these two salts together, not because they have any similarity by their nature, but because they have a lot of common in their history, which is the only point to which we will touch, and even briefly. Both are new, both of great use in Medicine, and authorized by frequent successes, both of an origin, or of an unknown composition, which has escaped until now to everyone, and both have been discovered in the same year.

Mr. Seignette, Doctor of La Rochelle, inventor of the salt which bears his name, had the pleasure during his life that all the Chemists had made only useless efforts to discover his secret, and which he left intact, so to speak, to his children, who have enjoyed it. But learned Chemists are themselves instigated by missing a famous secret. We will see in the memory of Mr. Boulduc the pains he gave himself, reaching despair sometimes, then regaining courage, and finally he found that the salt of Seignette was cream of tartar made soluble by alkali of soda. In this compound the cream of tartar was quite recognizable, but it was this soda which hid most stubbornly, and which we did not dare to suspect.

The same day that Mr. Boulduc brought his discovery to the Academy, Mr. Geoffroy declared that he had made it too, and verified it by the facts that he showed the same day. The two Chemists, although friends, had not shared their views. The word of the enigma was all the more surely found that it was by them two, and it was a pleasant effect of the fate, that it was [found] precisely at the same time.

§ 1.12.3. Advertisement of the True Salt of Polychrest, in the Mercure de France [a French gazette and literary magazine]

1751

The said Vacossain [Merchant Grocer Druggist, Street and across from S. André des Arts] warns that he also has [at] his office the real Polychreste salt, composed by M. de Seignette, from La Rochelle, which salt is initialed inside each sachet, and sealed by Mr. de Seignette's hand, so as to avoid any surprise and ordinary counterfeit.

§ 1.13. THREE RENOWNED ITALIAN CHARLATANS, DESIDERIO DESCOMBES, LEVANTIN AND CONTUGI, AND THEIR DISPUTES AND CONTROVERSIES ON THE EXCLUSIVE MAKING AND DISTRIBUTION OF A FAMOUS ANTIDOTE—THE ORVIETAN

The Orvietan was a very successful medicine, a true blockbuster, in Europe, through the seventeenth and eighteenth centuries. In its essence, it was an antidote with a very old composition, created by the Greeks (under the name of Theriac). In the seventeenth century, one Italian charlatan, Ieronimo Ferranti, added a few ingredients (of a dubious or null effect) to that composition, such as sarsaparilla, and claimed the miraculous properties of his product as the solution to almost all sorts of illnesses. Being born in Orvieto, Italy, he was known as "the Orvietan." Later his alias would become the common designation of his invention.

Two main reasons explain the commercial success of Orvietan: its intensive advertisement and its general availability across France and other European countries.

Soon charlatans would offer an enormous amount of different formulations under the same name of Orvietan, both in the cities and in the country, where naïve populations, without easy access to apothecaries and physicians, were eager to buy them.

In the cities, the first charlatans were received with tolerance, if not disguised interest, by the registered apothecaries (i.e., those that belonged in guilds or were otherwise controlled by the medical schools) because they brought new ingredients and formulations to urban markets, and thus were not in direct competition with them.

One of the common techniques of advertisement by charlatans was through performances in theaters and on improvised stages in rural villages. These practices would generate a great commercial success for a few charlatans. We will see several licenses to be granted to charlatans for mounting on stages and selling their drugs. It is said that the career of Molière, one of the greatest French playwrights, included a few stints on the stages of mountebanks.

Some of those charlatans obtained permission to settle in cities. That was when registered apothecaries and physicians started complaining against them.

The texts that follow illustrate the struggles of three famous charlatans to secure permission and exclusivity in the distribution of Orvietan, including their rights in business identifiers, such as trademarks, shop signs, and even in the generic name of the drug.

The lawsuit between the Contugi family and the societies of physicians and apothecaries that took several years, and was filled with numerous procedural incidents (which would today be described as unashamed abuses of the due process), was just one example of that struggle. An excerpt from the judgment that put an end to that lawsuit is included below. With hindsight, the file concerning this case is worthy of study and analysis by a modern antitrust law because there we can easily detect practices that, being aimed at acquiring market power, today are known as sham litigation, forum shopping, unfair competition, and plainly abusive procedures.

Naturally, exclusivity in selling Orvietan was a coveted goal. In the absence of an industrial privilege covering the formula, its distributors would claim exclusivity in the name (being worth repeating that the designation of Orvietan would not necessarily correspond to one single formulation.)

The first text that follows makes reference to other disputes involving the same allegation of a pretense entitlement to the exclusive sale of the drug, as well as the conflicting use of the same figurative trademarks, such as that of the sun, by different "operators" (a term that then designated the distributors of medicines). Several privileges granting exclusivity in the distribution of medicines under the name "Orvietan" were granted by the King of France, thus adding to the conflicts among the operators. The use of the sun as a trademark figurative element was also a coveted tool for luring customers, as a symbol of light, hope, and well-being.

The same judgment concerning the dispute between Beaulieu and Levantin that is included below was reported by another French jurist, Hyacinte Boniface, also in great detail. There is no interest in reproducing it here because it contains the same discussions as in the first one. However, Boniface has added an additional report concerning another dispute on the use of the same name, with a very interesting episode of experimenting the product in animals as a precautionary (sanitary) measure determined by the authorities.

§ 1.13.1. One of the many recipes of Orvietan, as it was described in a treatise on drugs

1735

. . . when the Orvietan of Rome started being known in France, we brought it from Rome and a few other places in Italy, such as Orviette, where its name came from, but since Mr. Contugi has come to Paris, and that under the pretext of having received a permission from his Majesty, he pretended to make of himself its owner, druggists had abandoned this trade, either because of great terror, or because the business was not significant; but then they recognized that when His Majesty gave Mr. Contugi the privilege of selling and distributing the Orvietan in Paris, he did not intend to exclude the Merchant Grocers from bringing it, or even the Apothecaries of Paris from making it, as it has been decided by a Judgment, [see next Text] so as not to deprive France of a remedy so authentic and so necessary to the public: being certain moreover that notwithstanding all the precautions that Mr. Contugi has taken in dispensing this antidote, he has never been able to do it like in Italy, in that the ingredients which are in great number do not have the same properties in France as in Italy, either because it is a hot country, or where the simples have much more virtue.

Orvietan.

Take roots from Scorsonnère, Carline, Imperatoire, Angelique de Boëme, Bistorte, light D'Aristoloche, Contra-Yerva, white Dictame, Galangal, Gentiane, small Arabian Costus, true Acore, seed of Macedonian Parsley, Sage Leaves, Rosemary, Galenga, blessed Thistle, Dictame de Candie, Bay leaves, Geneva, each: one ounce.

Cinnamon, Clove, each: half an ounce.

Dry vipers garnished with their heart and their liver, old Theriac, each: 4 ounces.

Skimmed white honey, eight pounds, Medicine peas, which is twelve ounces each pound, that is to say, six pounds on the weight of marc, or of Merchant, so as not to do the same as some Apothecaries, who by negligence, or ignorance, or, if I dare to say, perhaps out of greed, use only the Merchant pound, or marc, and in this way increase by twenty-five percent, all the compositions that they make.

§ 1.13.2. One of the several patent letters authorizing Desiderio Descombes to make and sell Orvietan in various parts of France, on the condition that he did not engage in the practice of medicine and surgery

1626

Louis by the grace of God King of France and Navarre, to our beloved lord Counselors, the people holding our Great Council, greeting; Our dear and beloved Desiderio des Combes, a native of our Province of Angoulmois, Operator and Ordinary Distiller, has shown Us that with a long and painful work, with great expense and danger of his life, had acquired the particular secret of the composition of the antidote called the Orvietan, unique and secured remedy to cure all kinds of poisons and bites of poisonous animals, suitable for preserving from and guaranteeing against the contagious disease, the experience of which is so recognized by the experimentation and proof that he made of it, both before the Queen our very honored Lady and Mother, and several Princes and Lords of our court, in the good and main cities of our Kingdom, so as that our Parliaments of Rennes, Rouen, the Provost of Paris, or his Deputy, the Municipality of Lyon, Judge of Laval and Saumur, the Municipalities of Angers, Blois, Orléans, Troies and Auxerre, have authorized him to sell and distribute it publicly by Decisions and Judgments contradictorily issued; Accordingly, on the fifteenth of March of one thousand six hundred twenty-three, we granted him passport, and by our other letters of the subsequent twenty-third of May, authorization to sell and distribute this Antidote in such cities, Towns, places and localities of our Kingdom as he sees fit, and given that he has declared, and is declaring again now, that he has neither intended nor intends to engage in Medicine, Surgery, or Pharmacy, he fears that you make it difficult for him to enjoy the content of those authorizations, unless he obtains our letters for that purpose, addressed to you, which he has begged us to grant. For these reasons, taking into consideration the appeals that were made in his favor, both by our Lady and Mother, and several Princes and Lords of our court, for treating him favorably, and for not depriving the public of the help they receive from his remedies, otherwise he would withdraw to a foreign country, as we have been told that he is willing to do, after having had our Council seeing the mentioned Decisions, Judgments, and Sentences, together with the attached copy of the Patent of gift that our Lady and Mother has had issued in his benefit, [in the amount of one hundred and fifty pounds] in consideration of the experiment he has made in her presence; In addition to the permission from our Provost of Paris, or his Deputy, with the consent of our Prosecutor at the Châtelet, this with the mentioned letters attached under the counter-seal of our Chancellery, these confirming, we have agreed that it was necessary to authorize and grant it again, we authorize and grant by these present [letters] signed by our hand, that he may and it be allowed to him to sell and distribute in public and in private, or have distributed and sold by his own, that Antidote in all cities and places of our Kingdom as he sees fit, and that he be not or may not be disturbed or prevented in any way and manner whatsoever: We wish: we command you, and very expressly enjoin you that you make des Combes and his [partners or family] enjoy fully and peacefully of the content of these present and previous letters, without tolerating or allowing that he suffers any trouble and impediment to the contrary, [and that you shall provide] any aid, favor and assistance, which by him will be required, you having for this purpose committed and attributed any Court, Jurisdiction and knowledge, and the latter prohibited to all our Courts and Judge, Because such is our pleasure, notwithstanding oppositions or appeals whatever, letters, or anything else to the contrary, by which and without prejudice to those we do not wish to be contradicted. Given in Paris on the nineteenth day of December, the Year of Grace one thousand six hundred and twenty-five, And of our reign the sixteenth; Signed Louis, and below, by the King, Le Beauclerc. And next to it is written: Given the provisions of the King and Queen Mother, and the certificates of the experiments, I am happy that he be permitted. Done at Saint German en Laye, the twentieth of November of one thousand six hundred and twenty-five, Signed Herouard. And it is also written, Recorded in the Registers of the Great Council of the King, according to the Decision given here, in Paris, on the twentieth-seventh of April of one thousand six hundred and twenty-six, Signed Collier, And sealed with the great seal of yellow wax.

§ 1.13.3. Desiderio Descombes advertises his Orvietan on the Pont-Neuf, Paris, by staging theatrical representations, and magical tricks

1620-1630

Il signor Desiderio had everything it takes to act powerfully on the minds of the crowd. In him the scholar and the charlatan, the speaker and the swashbuckler lived together. To see him proudly camped on his theater, arched back, head held high, austere and dark physiognomy, you would have taken him for one of the enchanters of modern epic, or for one of those ardent champions whom the wind of reform had caused to blossom at all corners of Christian Europe. Add to this that he fascinated by the magnetism of his gaze, that he captivated minds by the display of an erudition that was alternately superficial and true, and that he struck the imagination with in an inexhaustible, singular fluency, full of scientific words and enhanced by the bursts of a foreign accent. Contemporary and compatriot of the Stupini, the Styfoni, the Ricci and the Andrea Bajani, those tireless characters of the macaronic style [note omitted], Desiderio surpassed them all by the boldness of his inventions in this genre, and sewed to all his speeches shreds of this strange language, in which his haughty sentence was draped insolently like a beggar in his Spanish cape.

For a long time now, he had acquired a great reputation for his ability to cure diseases reputed to be incurable. He had remedies for all pains, balms for all wounds, filters for all moral infirmities. But what made his pride and his glory above all was that he had recently invented a remedy, the *panacea panacearum*, [the Orvietan] a unique, universal remedy, which he summed up by concentrating in it the virtue of all the other specifics, and had the particular property to extend life up to a hundred and fifty years, to say the least.

To make announcements to the public, distribute his drugs, play the interludes, in short to help him in the execution of his operative functions, he had taken in his service a jester of the *Burgundy hotel*, named Galinet la Galine, and whom he called *Galina Galerita*, hen with crest, by allusion to the enormous red feather that rose vertically on the pointed hat of the funny man.

The latter was a master, expert in the art of entertaining the audience, either by haranguing them for his own account, or by serving as an accomplice to signor Desiderio, giving him the reply, and complementing the oratorical action of the master by a variety of grimaces and gestures each more grotesque than the others. . .

In addition, it was on the faithful Galinet that, to demonstrate the effectiveness of his drugs and the superiority of his surgical methods, the illustrious Desiderio made his most decisive experiments. Thus, he purged him, he gave him emetic drugs, he phlebotomized it, he made him swallow molten lead, he pierced him through with his sword, and a few moments later, he presented him cured in the eyes of the amazed spectators. . . .

In the circumstance that we mentioned above, signor Desiderio had retired behind the backdrop, and after the explosion of four rockets, after the execution of the infernal symphony, Galinet occupied the theater alone, calling the audience by gesture and voice, urging them to take their place, to listen with attention, and above all to distrust thieves and pickpockets. . . .

Then, he added confidentially and by lowering his voice so as to be heard only by the audience, that signor Desiderio, his master, was not a joker. . ., but just a scientist, a philosopher, a great man, and the most skillful doctor who would have ever existed. Why was he not rolling on gold? why did he not live in a palace, surrounded by a large number of servants? Because he was as modest as he was learned, and that he loved others too much to think about himself. If he set up his trestles on the Pont-Neuf, it was for being closer to those he loved, and who, otherwise, perhaps, would not have dared to go up to him. . . .

- Gentlemen, [said Desiderio's assistant], here is the wonderful remedy that (with God's permission) prevents death; here is this famous *panacea panacearum*, which the rulers of the earth would buy at the price of all their treasures. Well, Gentlemen, it is for you, for you alone that it is intended. Signor Desiderio had so far sold his packages at the rate of eight sous for three pounds, but in your consideration and by a special favor, he ordered me to fold the three pounds, which makes a little *écu* for the benefit of each of you.

Apparently this reasoning was irresistible, because in the blink of an eye, all the small packages were sold, and that to the great contentment of Galinet, who delighted the spectators with his most beautiful tricks of skills and aerobatics. . . .

After this singular exordium, Desiderio began to talk about the superiority of his doctrine, the excellence of his drugs and the marvelous efficacy of the *panacea panacearum* [the Orvietan], medicine endowed with strength and intelligence to such an extent that no sooner had he entered the body, no matter how, it went straight to the cause of the disease and chose the moods that had to be expelled. Then, speaking of himself, he told how his incomparable knowledge was less a result of study than a gift from nature. Still in the cradle, he had operated marvelous cures and healed his nurse of breast cancer, just by touching it with his lips. This innate virtue had only grown over time, and now it had reached such a point of development and power, that he only needed a word, a gesture, a look, to drive out the infirmities that were most resistant to ordinary curative means. Had it not been enough for him to approach a blind beggar to restore his sight (which healing was unfortunate for the beggar, since it deprived him of his livelihood)? And thus the blind men who bordered one entire side of the Pont-Neuf had asked him to always walk on the other side, lest it happened to them what had happened to their unfortunate comrade. . . .

Figure 7 The countryside merchant of Orvietan, etching, by Louis-Marin Bonnet (1743-1793) and Jacques-Philippe Caresme (1734-1796).

§ 1.13.4. Judgment by Parliament of Aix-en-Provence granting Antoine Levantin exclusivity in the use of the term "Orvietan" to designate his antidote

May 20, 1678

Antoine Levantin, known as the Orvietan, Roman physician, claimed to have descended from Horace Levantin of the City of Rome, inventor of the Orvietan. For distributing this medicine alone, he obtained a bull from Pope Urban VIII, in the year of 1629, giving [him] permission to sell and distribute the Orvietan in the whole territory of the Lands of the Holy See, with prohibitions to all other persons of selling it, under the penalty of one thousand ducats of gold, and of excommunication.

He comes to France; he has also obtained various judgments, both from the Parliament of Grenoble and from the Parliament of Provence, which authorize him to sell this medicine, and prohibit all others from distributing it under the name of Orvietan, and under the mark of the Sun, under the penalty of a fine of three thousand pounds, and of confiscation.

After several years the named Charles Beaulieu, Operator, presents himself, who had a Patent from the King granting the authorization for carrying his manual operations throughout France, together with the distribution of his medicines in theaters, and carry there his comical performances; he has this Patent registered at the Court; the Decision of registration forbids any other person from composing and distributing an Antidote, named Orvietan of France, under the mark of the Name of Jesus, on the penalty of a fine of five hundred pounds.

These conflicting privileges formed the dispute between Levantin and Beaulieu, two famous Operators. Levantin has opposed the execution of the Decision of registration of the Patent that the King had accorded to Beaulieu, and the case was brought to the Hearing of the Great Chamber.

Decoris, Antoine Levantin's lawyer, said he had four grounds of opposition. The first [was] based on the registration being groundless. The second, that at its bottom, Beaulieu's claim was contrary to common Law. The third, that it was contrary to the policy principles for the culture of the Arts. The fourth and last, that his party had for him the possession of particular titles of family, and Decisions in a contrary sense.

With regard to the groundlessness of the registration, it is entirely obvious. The King's Patent gives only permission to Beaulieu to carry out his manual operations, and his comic performances throughout the kingdom, as regards which the plaintiff does not envy him whatever.

Thus the decision of registration that authorizes an antidote under the name of Orvietan of France is not in conformity with the Patent, which does not mention it; and this Order could not be issued to the detriment of the precedents, which had forbidden all persons, except Levantin, from distributing the Orvietan, under the penalty of a fine of three thousand pounds, and the confiscation of the medicines.

Even if we disagreed, that the King's patent had allowed the plaintiff to sell his antidote under the name of Orvietan of France, it is always understood that, in the absence of another's right, is the ordinary clause of the Royal Letters of Grant. Now, as there can be no doubt that this Privilege supersedes that of the plaintiff, it will always be necessary to return to the main question of knowing whether any other Operator, other than one of the descendants of the Inventors of Orvietan, and who by the way is grounded on [Court] Decisions, can publicly sell this medicine under the name of Orvietan.

Not only did Beaulieu surprise the Court, by alleging [the existence] in the King's patent of a Privilege that this Patent does not mention at all, but also because its claim is based on common Law.

No one doubts that all the authors of works have the right to impose upon them whatever name they please, without any other being permitted to take it. Law 2. *ff de operibus publicis* [of the Code of Theodosius] is formal in that regard, where the jurisconsult decides that if someone has ordered the erection of a public work, he has the right to have his name engraved on it, and that if another person wishes to erase it so as to put his own, the President of the Province must interpose his authority to restore the name of the Inventor or of the benefactor.

It is true that by law 7, of the same title *de operibus publicis*, it is said that if another adds something to the work, and if that is done with the consent of the People, he will also be permitted to engrave his name on it, and without erasing the first one, *manentibus priorum titulis*.

But Beaulieu has not added anything to Levantin's medicines, he does not know the drugs, he does not know their secret, he does not know their virtue; and so he can add nothing to the name that Levantin's Ancestors have given to this medicine.

Indeed, the name designates the Master, it is not allowed to impose names or marks on the things of others; there is in the Code one precise title in the following terms: *Nemini liceat judicis autoritate signa rebus imponere alienis*. This is what has made St. Augustine say about Psalm 21, that when a person has put his name on something, that is an ordinary mark that belongs to him: *titulos meos posui, mea res est, ubi nomen meum invenio, meo est.*

It does not follow that it is not regularly allowed to take the name of others. *L. 1. Cod. de mutations nominis*, but it must be *sine fraud & captione*; these are the terms of Mr. Cujas, interpreting law 13. *ff. ad L. Cornelian of falsis*. In this case, everyone can take the so-called Orvietan of France for the real Orvietan of Italy. One may believe Beaulieu to be the Inventor or descendant from the Inventors of this excellent medicine. He will deceive the Public, he will even make Levantin's secret useless and fruitless. There is fraud; there is public deceit, and that kind of crime of falsehood that one wants to commit.

Moreover, and this is the third ground of opposition, the public requires that the Arts be not confused, that a craftsman does not counterfeit the works of another Artisan, *ne promiscuis artibus rerum turbentur officia. L. consulta. Cod. de testamentis*. That is why as soon as a craftsman has found in his art a new secret, and of which no one had yet been aware, he is easily given the privilege of profiting from it alone, and of not being counterfeited, *munera alunt artes*, if it were otherwise used, it would take away the honor and the reward from those who excel in the Arts.

It is contested that there are here two Operators who plead against each other; that one wants to obtain by the path of the Judiciary what the other does not want to owe other than to the reputation of his medicine; and that, on the contrary, as both appear on the theater's stage, there would be no need for other Judges than those who hear them, and from whom they seek approval, not only by their speeches, but particularly by the trials of their medicines.

It is answered that the functions of these two Operators are very different, they have their particular secrets, and their medicines that are peculiar to them. All they have in common is that they both appear on the stage: but while Levantin does so to exalt and explain in public the virtue of his medicine, Beaulieu does the same thing, but it pretends to give pleasure to the people, mingling among the Actors of the farce, of which he is the main character. As far as the Levantin who appears on Theater's stage is concerned, he does not derogate whatsoever from the honor due to the Doctors and practitioners, he does not make the fool and the joker, he practices Medicine, as it has formerly been done. . . .

With regard to the quality of the medicines that these two Operators distribute, Beaulieu wished to distinguish his own with the Arms of France, giving it the name and the sign of Orvietan de France; but that is a ruse to ruin the commerce of Levantin, to the extent that the people will not be able to distinguish which Orvietan is best—that of Rome, or that of France; it will be enough for them that it be the Orvietan, they pay attention to the name only, which is nothing else than the shell, without looking in depth to its quality, which is its kernel, and they do not take the trouble, and are not even able to apprehend it. Yet it is upon this that Beaulieu calls upon the Judges, he does not want any others, because he knows how to distract them by his tricks of street acrobat, and his jokes of comedian; which can only proceed from an unjust jealousy that Beaulieu has developed against the reputation of Levantin, and which has always been condemned by the Judgments of the sovereign Courts among those of the same profession.

Mornac on the law 14. *ff. de periculo and commodo reivendita*, speaks of two neighboring apothecaries, both of whom had a well-stocked shop, and which were only separated by a party wall. The oldest had the red cross as his shop sign. The other had put the same sign, with the single difference that the cross of this last sign was smaller than that of the other, and bore the following title: *at the small red cross*. The ancient apothecary had complained about it, and the claim, having been brought to the Hearing of the Grand Chamber of the Parliament of Paris, led to an Order, which enjoined [the new apothecary] to take this new shop sign down, with the prohibition to take that of the ancient apothecary. This is reported by the Author of the *Journal des audiences du Parlement de Paris*. [Antoine Mornac, In Senatu Parisiensi Patroni Observaciones, vol. 1, at 1073 (Franc Montalant, 1721). *Source*: <gallica.BnF.fr>]. [See § 1.09].

The same author mentions another Judgment, delivered between two sword makers of the town of Moulins, one of whom had a very strong reputation for his trade, and had the Heart as the sign for his shop. The other, less skillful, took the Wounded Heart as a sign. The newcomer was forbidden to take this sign of the Wounded Heart, by the judgment of the twenty-fifth of February, 1619, *atque id ex conjectura emulationis, ac invidia, que novo illi operi causam dedisse visa est.*

We can add a third example. Two merchant hosiers from Paris, neighbors of one another, had the Pavilion as a shop sign. He who had taken this sign first having caused the other to take away his own, the latter, decided to have painted in his sign, instead of a Pavilion, a large butterfly, with wings wide spread, so that he represented, or at least imitated, the figure of a Pavilion. By a second judgment this hosier was ordered to change the sign.

All these examples persuade us that if [on the one hand] there is a good emulation between the persons of the same state to improve in their profession, there is [on the other] a bad envy, full of fraud, and which proposes to harm, which has always been repressed in Justice.

Lastly, it has been said that Levantin was founded in titles, that he succeeded Horace Levantin, author of the Orvietan, and to which he has given that name because of the City of Orviette [Orvieto], in Italy, where he comes from. That Pope Urban the eighth has allowed this Horace Levantin's successor, by a special Bull, to sell the Orvietan in all the lands of his obedience, with prohibitions to all others of distributing it, under the penalty of a fine of one thousand ducats of gold.

He also has Letters Patent of the King who give him the same permission as regards France, and although he has not proved that he is from the family of the Levantins, Beaulieu is definitely not able to challenge his condition. He has always been recognized as such by the family, both in Italy, where he has distributed his medicine for a long time, and in France, where he has since established himself under the name of Levantin. . . .

Ultimately, this matter has been decided by a contradictory judgment of the Court, and by another of the Parliament of Grenoble against Operators similar to Beaulieu, which have forbidden them to sell their antidotes under the name of Orvietan.

These were Levantin's reasons.

Differing, Gaillar, on Beaulieu's behalf, said that he admitted that the inventors of medicines deserve special praise. There is no need for another example than that of Asclepiades, of whom Pliny the Naturalist speaks, book 26. chapter 3., who, having promised health by abstinence from meat, by massages, by walks, was looked at favorably by everyone as a man sent from heaven for the salvation of mankind.

But this medicine that is called Orvietan is not a new invention, it is a sort of Theriac [an antidote invented by the Greeks] and of Mitridate [a medical concoction containing a number of ingredients, including opium, likewise invented by the Greeks]. Theriac is its main ingredient, to which sarsaparilla is added.

It is, therefore, a great temerity for Levantin to call himself the author of this medicine. Mr. Charras, Artist of the King, in his Jardin des Plantes, in his Royal Pharmacopeia, fol. 325, made it public. He explains there the composition of the

Orvietan, and reveals its authors. There he decides the cause of Levantin and similar products, and shows clearly their imposture.

Meissonnier, Doctor of Montpellier, in the Treatise on Poisonous Diseases, fol. 6, also shows us the impostures that these Quacks do on the theater stage, to give authority to their Orvietan, and said that some have called it Athavan, and others, Orvietan. He describes its composition, and adds that it was Cardinal de Mantoile who has given it to Brother Jean Germain Minime. That is how it has become fashionable among us. He says that the Turks use it in Asia and Africa, where Levantin certainly has not brought it, and that it is not more than a medicine subsidiary to Theriac and Mitridate.

It is not out of place to note also that a lady of quality of this Province, excited by a principle of charity, makes the Orvietan herself, and has added to her composition some ingredients that render this medicine still more assured, and that therefore she has made it public and common to everyone.

Here is a medicine that has no true author, which is called sometimes Athavan, sometimes Orvietan, to which everyone adds what art and experience teach him/her. And after that how can one say that Levantin has the sole right to distribute it?—unless one wishes to say he has descended from Cardinal Mantoile, or from Brother Germain Minime, or, finally, that he should prohibit the use of this medicine to the Turks and Barbarians—which must be regarded as a misguidance of spirit, and as one of his jokes that he can dispense on the stage, but not at this August Hearing of the Court.

Moreover, it has been proved by the posters of those who have sold the Orvietan, that the named Jean Pierre Mazari Venetian had sold it under the sign of the Sun; that the named Lis, who claimed to be the son of the Orvietan, a native of Rome, has sold and distributed it under the same mark of the Sun; and according to Christophle Contugi Romain, who lives in Paris, is not it sold on the Quai des Augustins, at the corner of Rue Dauphine, under the name of the real Orvietan of Rome, and with the sign of the Sun?

None of these Operators is called Levantin, like this one. They do not claim to descend from the God Aesculapius, any more than from the Italian Ptolomei, Master of this Levantin; they have learned the composition of the Orvietan, they have made it, they have distributed it, and no one has found any fault in that. . . .

There really would be something to say if Beaulieu pretended to distribute the Orvietan of Rome. But he loves his Nation too much to take this medicine from the Italians, he distributes it as Orvietan of France, that is to say, with the corrections and the ingredients that France has added. And if the Turks distribute it under the name Atavan, why should not the defendant distribute it under the name of Orvietan of France, for it is composed in a manner different than that of Rome, and that all sorts of manufactures by foreigners are distributed in France with more approval than the original ones from which they have been taken?

In a word, privileges and works of art are common to everyone, and their exercise cannot be forbidden to people who use them well. . . .

If Beaulieu usurped the sign of Levantin, he would have some reason to complain about it, and to use the examples that Mornac brings about the law 14. *ff. of periculo & commodo rei vendita*, between two apothecaries jealous of each other.

But in this particular case, there is neither jealousy nor imitation between Beaulieu and Levantin; one sells the Orvietan of Rome, the other that of France; one takes the sign of the Sun, Beaulieu has one more illustrious and more salutary, for it is the name of Jesus, by which the Apostles have cured all the sick.

As to the judgments that Levantin has invoked, they do not deserve consideration. That of the Parliament of Grenoble, of the fifth of July 1668, is not against Beaulieu, but against the daughter of François Fosse and others, calling themselves Operators, who have been prohibited to give their medicine the name of Orvietan, and to take the sign of the Sun. But this has no impact on Beaulieu, who thirty years before sold the Orvietan of France under the sign of the Name of Jesus, and not of the Sun.

The same can be said of the other Judgments, which have been rendered against other parties who wanted to sell their antidote under the trademark of the Sun.

Finally, Levantin lacks the permission of the king, *opus novum sine Principis authoritate fieri non licet*, says the law 3 *ff. of operibus publicis*. By contrast, Beaulieu has a Patent from the King of the last March 1662, which allows him to distribute his medicines all over France. It is registered by Judgment of this Court of the sixth of October, 1676. He has a Contract with the City of Narbonne of the thirteenth October, 1651, and a certificate of his Consuls. He served with success in this city of Aix, in Toulouse, in Marseille, where he resides, in Montpellier, Ufez, Beziers, Montauban, and other Cities of the Kingdom, where he has made his Orvietan of France to be esteemed, and obtained miraculous cures.

Thus a Tramp who deals with astrology and all those trifles, of which the Nation boasts, must not prevail over a subject of the King, Operator of his Naval Armies, who has the approval of the Naval Medical Officer, and all the Kingdom; This is what must not be done, if one reflects on what the Roman Orator says in his Oration *pro Cluentio*, of a Quack of his time named Lucius, whom he calls *Pharmacopolam circunsoraneum*: i.e., an Operator of this quality, *qui casu tum Lorinum Venum*, and had as many certificates as Levantin, and was of the same Nation. Opianicus promised him a sum of money to get rid of Dinea; he sold her his medicine, and as soon as this woman took it, she died of it, *simul atque introductus est, eam confecit prima potione mulierem*. This means that one should not trust these Italian Operators, who are either unfaithful or ignorant, and all quacks by profession.

The Attorney General of Saint Martin, after having gathered all the reasons of the parties, has shown that the Question had been settled in proper terms by the judgment of the Parliament of Grenoble, rendered with a great deal of knowledge in favor of Levantin, and that on the same restraints, said that the same judgment should be followed; and that consequently, he concluded that, as regards Levantin's request, without considering the registration of the fifth of November, 1676, obtained by Beaulieu, prohibitions and inhibitions should be made against him, and to all others to whom it concerned, to sell and distribute antidotes under the name of Orvietan, under the penalty of a fine of one thousand pounds, costs, damages and interests; and in the event of infringement, [it should be] ordered that it be informed by the first Royal Judge, or Bailiff of the Court; and nevertheless that Beaulieu were allowed to give his antidote such other name as he would see fit: which conclusions were followed by the Judgment of May 20, 1678.

§ 1.13.5. Settlement of a dispute between Contugy and the Corporation of Apothecaries-Grocers of Paris concerning the making and selling of Orviétan, its various business identifiers, and the right of inspection at Contugy's shop

1737

Contradictory [*inter partes*] judgment of the Privy Council, and related Letters Patent, of December 31, 1736 and February 18, 1737, registered in Parliament.

By which, among other things, it has been allowed that the Masters and Guards of the Community of Apothecaries continue carrying jointly with three Doctors of the Faculty of Medicine, at Contugy's shop, the ordinary and accustomed Visits of all the Drugs that may be found in his Shop used for the composition of his Orvietan, including testing the mentioned Drugs. . . . Orders Contugy to submit to those visits and tests, and to give both the Doctors and the Masters and Guardians of the Apothecaries the honor and respect that are due to them. . . . And in the event of a challenge, refer the Parties to the Lieutenant General of Police, and by appeal to the Parliament of Paris, and not elsewhere.

Extract from the Registers of the King's Private State Council.

Letters Patent.

Louis by the grace of God, King of France and Navarre: To our loved ones and lord Councilors, the People holding our Court of Parliament in Paris; Greeting. Our beloved Masters and Guards of the Masters and Merchants Apothecaries-Grocers of our good City of Paris, have very humbly exposed to us that Florent-Jean-Louis Contugy, grounded on the Letters Patent of April 10, 1727, bearing confirmation of the Privilege of composing, selling and distributing an Antidote designated Orvietan, has challenged the Masters Apothecaries' right and possession of composing, selling and distributing the Opiate called Orvietan, whose composition is written in the Books of their Art, available to the Applicants in their capacity as Masters and Guards of that Body, which right they have had since their establishment of visiting, jointly with three Doctors of our Faculty of Medicine, the drugs used for the composition of his Antidote; [a brief report of a discussion on a conflict of jurisdiction follows; the Council has concluded for their own competence] . . . We have through these Present Letters, signed by our hand, maintained and maintain Florent-Jean-Louis Contugy in the enjoyment of the privilege granted to him by our Letters Patent of April 10, 1727, and consequently in the right and possession of composing, selling, and distributing the Antidote called Orvietan, to the exclusion of all Operators and other unqualified persons, both in the City and Suburbs of Paris, and in the other Cities of our Kingdom; prohibiting the Community of Master and Merchant Apothecaries of the City and Suburbs of Paris from disturbing him in the composition, sale and distribution of the Orvietan, as set in his Privilege, without prejudice to the right of the Master and Merchant Apothecaries of the City of Paris, of composing, selling and distributing the Opiate called Orvietan, whose composition is taught to them by the Books of their Art; consequently We order that the Community of Apothecaries, together with Contugy, will be required to use Display windows, Distribution tickets, Boxes, Trademarks, Shop Signs and Posters distinct and separate, prohibiting Contugy from using the Trademark attributed to the Apothecaries, and likewise the Apothecaries shall not use those [signs] that will be attributed to Contugy; and for the purpose of reaching an agreement on the Display windows, Distribution tickets, Boxes, Trademarks, Shop Signs or Posters, both the Apothecaries and

Florent-Jean-Louis Contugy shall appear within one month before the Lieutenant General of Police, so that the mentioned Display windows, Distribution tickets, Boxes, Trademarks, Shop Signs or Posters be decided and determined by him, as appropriate. We authorize the Plaintiffs to continue carrying, jointly with three Doctors of the Faculty of Medicine at the shop of Florent-Jean-Louis Contugy, the ordinary and accustomed visits of all the drugs that may be found in his Shop, which are used for the composition of his Orvietan, including testing those drugs, but only after the Plaintiffs have obtained the permission by an Ordinance of the Lieutenant General of Police; We order Contugy to submit to the visits and tests, and to give both the Doctors and the Applicants the honor and respect due to them; and notwithstanding the Decisions of the Great Council of August 11, September 23 and of October 3, 1729, as well as the Sentence of the Lieutenant General of Police of August 26 of the same year, we have completely lifted and lift the seizures made at the request of the Contugy at the shops of Geoffroy, Chilaud, Dubois, Jeudon and Laban, which seizures We have declared and declare null and void; We order that in the event of a challenge over the execution of said Judgment, jointly with all those disputes that may arise during the visits and tests that will be made at the shop of Contugy, the Parties are required to proceed before the Lieutenant General of Police, and, in the event of an appeal, before our Court of Parliament, and not elsewhere; for which purpose Contugy will be required to register therein the Letters of Privilege granted to him, if that has not yet been done; and We have dismissed the remainder of the claims, and ordered Contugy to pay the costs, including those reserved by the Judgment of our Council of February 27, 1736, for all damages and interest, and allowed the Plaintiffs to have read, published and displayed the Judgment of December 31 of the same year where it will be necessary: We also order you that you have read, published and recorded the Present Letters, and ensure that the Applicants will enjoy and use their content fully and peacefully, ceasing and putting an end to all troubles and impediments to the contrary, notwithstanding all the Privileges, Decisions and Regulations that We have derogated and derogate by these Presents: because such is our pleasure. Given at Versailles on the 18th day of February, the year of grace 1737.

§ 1.13.6. Judgment by the private Council in favor of Christophle Contugi, known as the true Orviétan, against Poloni, pseudo-Orviétan

February 1, 1658

Upon the request presented to the King in his Council by Christophle Contugi, native of Rome, truthful Orviétan, husband of Clarice Vitrarie, sole and single heiress of Jean Vitrairie, living doctor, who had married Clarice, [who was] previously widow of Hierosme Fioranty, first to be designated the Orviétan, inventor of this antidote, and by him instituted heiress of his patrimony and his secret, stating that the named Polony, pseudo-Orviétan, having undertaken to sell bad drugs under the name of Orviétan at the sign of the Sun, which is the trademark of the supplicant, under the pretext of a few judgments by him unlawfully obtained in the parliament of Toulouse, to the detriment of letters patent issued in favor of the plaintiff, by which his Majesty forbids all persons to sell their remedies under the name of Orviétan without his consent, the plaintiff would have brought his complaint to the Council where he presented his request for the purposes that, in accordance with said letters patent, defenses were made to Polony and all others to sell or distribute their drug under the name of Orvietan, on which he obtained judgment on May 3, 1656, etc.

For these reasons the plaintiff requested that it pleased His Majesty, regardless of the judgment of the parliament of Toulouse of xxviii June, to order the execution of the decisions of the Council of iii of May, xvii of June 1656 and xxv May 1657, and in accordance to those and to the letters patent of ix April 1647, to prohibit Polony and all others from selling their drug under the name of Orviétan and the brand of the Sun, on pain of corporal punishment, having regard to the request signed by Baudouin, attorney in the Council, the letters patent obtained by the supplicant dated ix April 1647, and other documents attached to the request, heard on this report Mr. le Boullanger, commissioner designated for that purpose and all considered,

The King in his council has commanded and commands that for the purposes of the said request, the parties will be summarily heard before the commissioner who will be for this designated, and joined to the proceedings pending in the said Council between the parties and during this time they will stay all demands elsewhere than in the Council, including the execution of the judgment of the Parliament of Toulouse of June 28, 1657 rendered since and to the detriment of the Council's mentioned decisions until His Majesty orders otherwise.

§ 1.13.7. Report of another judgment [on the conflicting use of the name Orvietan] (by an unspecified court)

1686

The same question [between Levantin and Beaulieu, concerning the exclusive use of the name Orvietan] having been presented to the Court. . . in the year 1686, between . . . du Val, husband of Demoiselle Isabeau de Montoux de Castelane, widow of . . . Poloni, and the named Toscan, known as Cappel d'or, both Operators selling Orvietan on the Theater, each under their different trademarks:

By judgment of that same day, on the report of Maître du Chaffau, sitting as the first President Mr. Marin, the Court ordered that the test and the experience of the two Orvietans would be made on two pigs[8] in the presence of the Commissioner, who would take two Doctors, four Surgeons and Apothecaries who would prepare the poison, on the basis of two judgments which were produced, one of the Parliament of Toulouse of the year 1656, rendered between Poloni, husband of the said de Montoux, and the named Contugi. And the other of the Parliament of Grenoble, between the same Levantin and the same Toscan, which ordered the same trial and experiment on two pigs, and the same presence; by which experience ordered by the last Judgment one of the two pigs died.

8. In the sixteenth and seventeenth centuries, the tests of secret drugs on animals became a mandatory practice in several French cities, as a measure to impose some control over the operations of charlatans.

§ 1.14. ANOTHER EVIDENCE THAT IN THE SEVENTEENTH CENTURY THE USE OF TRADEMARKS BY DRUGGISTS HAD ALREADY BECOME A COMMON PRACTICE: THE BY-LAWS OF THEIR GUILD IN THE FRENCH CITY OF SAINT-QUENTIN

The following text is an excerpt from the by-laws of the guild of apothecaries and related professions of the city of Saint-Quentin, France. The by-laws were redacted by the Masters of the various professions concerned. As the provisions say, they repeat the text of the by-laws of the same guild of Amiens. The request having been received favorably by the king's attorney, the Royal Provost of Saint-Quentin, on September 27, 1685, ordered the registration of these by-laws.

By-laws and Regulations in Favor of Merchant Haberdashers, Wax Makers, Grocers, and Druggists of the City of Saint-Quentin

1685

To Messrs. the Mayor and Magistrates of the City of Saint-Quentin.

The Merchant Haberdashers, Wax Makers, Grocers, and Druggists of the mentioned City humbly beg and state that, their Art having never been well regulated, they would like to comply with the By-laws of the City of Amiens,[9] Capital of our Province, of which they would have attached and annexed one copy to the present Request:

Which you please, Gentlemen, to endorse, and order that those By-laws be observed and executed in the future by them, according to their form and content, as well as to the charges, conditions and penalties set forth, to which the said Applicants acquiesce and adhere, and for greater assurance, have them recorded in the Register of that City, and that it be allowed to take them and have them Recorded and Homologated in the Court and anywhere else as appropriate: By doing so, you will oblige the Applicants to pray to God for your prosperity and health. . . .

XLIII

Item, That no merchant of the mentioned Profession shall make or contract association with anyone, if [the latter] is not merchant and master approved [examined] to that Profession, or lend their names or marks for the effect of the goods dependent on that Profession and Trade, under the penalty of the loss of the Mastery and a fine of sixty *sols*, and use foreign names and marks, except if that [use] is for passing the strait [the English Channel] and the danger of the enemy, if they are constrained to do so, in which case they will be required to advert the Masters in charge, prior to arrival of said goods, under the penalty of [the goods] being declared foreign.

9. An identical provision was included in the by-laws of the haberdashers, candle makers, grocers and spice sellers of Amiens, of 1661. *See* FROM BABYLON TO THE SILICON VALLEY, *supra* note 2, at 113-114.

§ 1.15. PRIVILEGE FOR THE EXCLUSIVE DISTRIBUTION OF MINERAL WATERS, WHICH WERE TO BE DESIGNATED BY A CERTIFICATION MARK, ALONG WITH THEIR TRADEMARKS—1739

Mineral waters have been since early times considered as medicines, and thus their extraction and trade have been regulated. The following text refers to the mandatory use of a certification mark (the coat of arms of François Chicoyneau, counselor to Louis XV and his first physician), so as to ensure customers of their quality and genuineness.

Exclusive privilege for selling and distributing mineral waters granted to Dr. Nicolas Bise, at Versailles, on April 1, 1739, registered at the Seneschalty of Marseille on April 24, 1739.

> François Chicoyneau, counselor to the King in his state and private councils, His Majesty's first physician, Chancellor of the University of Medicine of Montpellier, general superintendent of Waters, baths and mineral and medicinal fountains of France, to all those who this letter will see, greeting. By virtue of the powers granted to our predecessors by letters patent of His Majesty dated September 7, one thousand seven hundred and eighteen, and those given in our favor on September 28, 1783, registered at the Great Council on September 12, 1719, and on December 7, 1783, well and duly sealed, which allow us to designate persons of probity and sufficient capacity, by patent signed by us and countersigned by our ordinary secretary, for carrying out the transport, sale and distribution of all mineral waters in all the cities of the Kingdom.

As we have been recently informed that in the city of Marseille several individuals without our permission have engaged in distributing various mineral Waters [in a manner] that results in abuses and disadvantages detrimental to the public, which would not happen if those mineral Waters were distributed and commercialized in the correct order and the required trust; therefore, we, by virtue of the mentioned powers, following King's orders, and wishing to enable that the Bourgeois and the inhabitants of the city of Marseille and its suburbs receive from the use of those Waters the help they can expect for, and for remedying the abuses that have occurred and which could be committed in the distribution of those Waters in the city of Marseille, and considering that Mr. Nicolas Bize, besides being well and duly embedded with good life, morals, Catholic, apostolic and Roman religion. For these reasons and others that have persuaded us to proceed in this manner, we have appointed and appoint, have provided and provide hereby Mr. Nicolas Bize, [with the authorization] to extract, load and transport the mineral and medicinal waters of Ballaruc, Vais and in general all other mineral Waters of France and foreign Waters as well, and sell and distribute them in the city and suburbs of Marseille and in its outskirts, to the exclusion of any other not provided with similar letters, allowing him to seize, in his name, by reason of these presents and the letters patent of His Majesty, Mineral waters that either by land or by sea enter the city of Marseille or which will be given without being provided with an express and written permission signed by us and countersigned by our secretary and to impose on the offenders the fine of fifteen hundred pounds and costs, damages, and interest, in accordance with the letters patent of His Majesty, on the condition that Bize delivers to our hands the oath of loyalty of well and faithfully trading and distributing mineral Waters in the way it is below mentioned and has these letters registered along with the oaths at the Seneschalty of the city of Marseille in the event of a contravention and by appeal to the Great Council; we command the privileged to have published and displayed the whole together in the city of Marseille and its suburbs as well as in the various sources of the Kingdom these presents and the Regulation by us given and not to distribute mineral Waters other than in glass bottles and, for greater security with regard to the people who make use of the said Waters; we command the aforementioned privileged and his agents to have affixed the stamp of our arms that we have sent him, by the supervisors and keepers of the various sources from which the Waters will be extracted on the seal of the bottle caps.

We forbid the privileged from distributing any waters that have not been sealed with the appropriate seal for the said waters, the name of which is marked around the coat of arms. We decide that the privileged brings us the receipt of the said seals of the fountain keepers from each source to whom he will have sent them, however the affixing of our arms shall not prevent the owners of those mineral waters, if there is any, from affixing their own, this precaution aiming only at establishing public security and the privileged shall not be obliged to provide the public with bottles of mineral water sealed with our arms before three months after the publication of these presents.

. . .

Today, fourth of April of the present year of 1789, we have received the oath of fidelity from Mr. Nicolas Bize concening the exclusive privilege that we have granted him for the transport, sale, distribution, and commercialization of all mineral and medicinal Waters of France and foreign. Done at Versailles on the day and place aforementioned. Chicoyneau, signed in the original.

Received the letters and Patent registered attached hereto in Marseille on April 25, 1789.

§ 1.16. A FRENCH DRUGGIST OBTAINS PATENT LETTERS PERMITTING HIM TO SELL AND ADVERTISE A SECRET MEDICINE WITHOUT ANY ENCUMBRANCE FROM PHYSICIANS AND APOTHECARIES

As a result of the increase in the number of periodicals and the evolution of printing and marketing techniques, since the sixteenth century, druggists and pharmacists have resorted to intensive advertisement to promote sales. The following texts are good illustrations of the importance that advertisement had in the particular context of medicines: a druggist obtained patent letters that not only gave him the right to sell and advertise his medicines but also forbade all "other persons from tearing off or covering by other Posters, those which the Applicant will cause to be placed concerning his Privilege." This was a legal provision that protected the druggist against unfair competition.

§ 1.16.1. Judgment of the Great Council that orders the enforcement of the Letters in the form of a Provision of the Profession and Distributor of the King, belonging to the Court, and of its Councils, granted to Mr. Pierre-Raimond Vaconssain, Merchant Grocer-Druggist in Paris, on the first of September 1750, in the Prévôté of the Hotel, and Great Prévôté of France

December 9, 1750

> Louis [XV], by the grace of God, King of France and Navarre: To all those who will see these Present Letters: Greeting. We make known, by decision delivered today in our Great Council, upon the Request presented to our Council by our beloved Raimond Vaconssain, Merchant-Grocer-Druggist in Paris, and King's Distributor, Privileged, belonging to the Court and of our Councils, that it please our Council, to command that our Letters in the form of Provision of Profession and Privilege of Distributor of the King and of our Councils, granted to the Applicant on the first of September, 1750. Sentence for the registration of those in our Prévôté of the Hotel and Great Prévôté of France of the 22nd of the mentioned month, together with the Sentence of the Lieutenant General of our Prévôté of the 30th of the same month, bearing permission to have printed and displayed both in Paris, Court and Suite, and in other Localities and Cities of the Kingdom, his Letters of Privileges, the Memoir concerning the Purgative Powder, and other Remedies that he uses, containing his Profession of Distributor, with the instructive Memoir, shall be executed by the authority of our Council, in accordance with their form and content; in doing so, given the Attestation and Certificate of Mr. Chicoyneau, our first Physician, of last October 25, and registered in our Prévôté of the Hotel on November 25 also last, allowing the Applicant to display and distribute the Explanatory Memoirs of his purgative Powder and other Remedies concerning his Profession of Distributor, and to sell them in the whole extent of the Kingdom, to forbid all Surgeons and Apothecaries, Distributors and others from disturbing the Applicant, or those who will act for him in the distribution of his Purgative Powder and other Remedies, in the full exercise and the functions of his Profession and Privilege of Distributor; likewise to forbid the Displayers and other people from tearing off or covering by other Posters those that the Applicant will have placed concerning his Privilege, under the appropriate penalties, and prohibit for the reason above from initiating prosecution and Procedures elsewhere than in our Prévôté of the Hotel, and by Appeal to our Council, on penalty of nullity, dismissal of Proceedings, 1500 pounds of fine, costs, damages, and interest: . . .

Sentence of the Prévôté of our Hotel, which orders the recordal of our Letters of September 22, 1750, . . . which allows Vaconssain to print, display in Paris, Court and Suite, as well as in other Localities and Cities of the Kingdom, his Letters of Privilege and Informative Memoir on these of September 30, 1750, and other Exhibits attached to the said Request, Conclusions of our Attorney General:

> Our Great Council, having regard to the said Request, has ordered and orders that the Letters in the form of Provision of the Profession and Privilege of our Distributor belonging to the Court, of our Councils, of September 1, 1750. Sentence on their Registration in the Prévôté of our Hotel and Great Prévôté of France, of the 22nd of that month; together with the Sentence of our Lieutenant General of the

Prévôté of our Hotel of the 30th of the same month, it shall be executed by the authority of our Council according to their form and content; and in so doing it allows the Applicant to display and distribute the Explanatory Memoirs of his Purgative Powder, and the other Remedies concerning his Profession of Distributor, and to have it sold throughout the whole extent of our Kingdom; to forbid all Surgeons, Apothecaries, Distributors and others, from disturbing the Applicant or those who will act for him in the distribution of his Purgative Powder and other Remedies, and in the full exercise and functions of his Profession and Privilege of Distributor; similarly forbids Displayers and other persons from tearing off or covering by other Posters, those which the Applicant will cause to be placed concerning his Privilege, under such penalties as shall be appropriate, and prohibits the Parties for the above reason, circumstances and dependencies, to prosecute and procedures elsewhere than in the Prévôté of our Hotel, and by Appeal to our Council, on the penalty of nullity, dismissal of procedures, and a fine of 1500 pounds, costs, damages, and interest.

This we instruct the first of the Bailiffs of our Council in what it is enforceable in our Court and Suite, and outside of it, to the first Bailiff or other Bailiff or Sergeant whom on this is concerned, that at the request of Mr. Raimond Vaconssain, he executes this Decision in its entirety, according to its form and content, notwithstanding any oppositions or appellations, for which and without prejudice to them it shall not be modified, and moreover to carry whatever requested and necessary Measures and Acts of Justice for the execution of the Presents, and for this I give you power, without asking for *Placet, Visa or Paretis*. Given in our Council in Paris on the ninth day of December the year of grace one thousand seven hundred and fifty, and of our Reign the thirty-sixth. Sealed on December 23, 1750.

§ 1.16.2. Piece of advertisement published by Vacossain promoting his medicine, whose genuineness was confirmed by his seal and signature

Other Notices.

Mr. Vacossain, Merchant Grocer-Druggist, residing in Paris, street and opposite to S. André-des-Arts, at the Golden Mortar, the only authorized by the King, by Judgment of Our Lords of his Great Council, with permission of Mr. Berryer, Lieutenant General of Police, continues to sell his purgative powder, approved by Mr. Chicoyneau, First Physician to His Majesty, who only gave his Certificate after a scrupulous examination of all the simples that compose it, and the experiences he made of it himself.

This remedy has nothing to displease the taste, purges copiously without pain, without altering strength or weakening the temperament. On the contrary, it makes one more agile and more vigorous, it may be taken always without danger. This powder purifies the bulk of the blood, removes obstructions, prevents and diverts apoplexy, and other diseases. It is suitable for jaundice, dropsy, hemorrhoids, and even all kinds of fever.

The gentleman would have thought he was failing in the duties of a good Citizen, if he had not communicated that to the Public; devoted to his King and to his Country, can he exercise his talent better than by interesting it in the preservation of the health of His Majesty's Subjects? It is with this in mind that he gives his Purgative free of charge to the poor, and that, guided more out of honor than out of interest, he sells to the Public for twenty *sols* each portion of his powder in a sachet sealed and signed by him. He will send it to those who order it from the Province, against payment of the transport, and he will give an instructive Memoir for its use.

Although this powder is already known, particularly in this City of Paris, in Versailles, and other cities of the Kingdom, Mr. Vaconssain must add to the Public that it has been tasted, examined with attention, and approved by Mr. Baron, Dean of the Faculty of Medicine, Messrs. Boyer and Payen, Doctors of the Faculty & Professors of Pharmacy; Messrs. Nouquet and Vaudenesse, Doctors of Medicine, accompanied by Messrs. Paschalis, Santerre and Salvant, Guards in Charge, Apothecaries, and by Mr. Piai, the young, Former Guard Apothecary, in the visit they made to Mr. Vaconssain expressly for this purpose, that they declared it good, not having found anything caustic therein which could affect health. This visit was made on September 2, 1751, so Mr. Vacossain flatters himself that his powder, known to and approved by all such respectable witnesses, being announced, will become more and more useful to the public.

§ 1.16.3. Another piece of advertisement of Vaconssain's purgative powder, this time under the disguise of a press editorial

Mr. Vaconssain, Grocer Druggist, street and opposite Saint André-des-Arcs, having seen the purgative Powder being attacked as very bitter and very burning, believed that it was in his interest to show that he had been authorized to distribute his powder. He presented us with a Decision of the Great Council that allows him, according to the attestation and the certificate of the first Physician, to cause the display and distribution of the explanatory Memoirs of his purgative powder, and his other remedies, concerning his profession of Distributor, and to sell it throughout the Kingdom. This Decision is issued upon letters, in the form of a provision of privileged Distributor, belonging to the Court, granted to Mr. Pierre-Raimond Vaconssain by the Provost of the King's Hotel. A physician from Nogent sur Seine has written to us that he had successfully used this powder.

§ 1.17. AN APOTHECARY DISPUTES WITH GROCERS THE QUALIFIED PRIVILEGE OF EXERCISING THE PROFESSION OF PHARMACY, WITH IMPLICATIONS ON THE USE OF SHOP SIGNS—1773

For centuries, the profession of pharmacy struggled to be acknowledged as a separate activity. In the Middle Ages, apothecaries and physicians (along with the barbers) would in many cities share the same guild. Later, because the main ingredients in the composition of medicines were the spices imported from the East, apothecaries would belong to the same professional corporations as grocers. What would distinguish the individual professions within each guild was the apothecaries' need to submit to technical examinations and to have their medicines inspected by physicians and master apothecaries.

As it happened with other professions, pharmacists would frequently enforce their professional exclusivity and resulting privileges against unfair competitors—who, without having met the same difficult requirements, would attempt to divert their clientele. The text that follows is a mix of a court report and an analysis of one of those disputes between pharmacists and grocers, in which the former asked the court to prohibit the latter from encroaching in their profession. Interestingly, this case invoked the use of shop signs by pharmacists, which were specific to their profession, namely, cannon jars and alambiques. Those signs correspond to today's green (or red) crosses that pharmacists put on display over the entrance of their boutiques, in addition to their trade names or marks.

Thus, strictly speaking, those signs are not trademarks; in a sense, they do not distinguish any goods or services individually, but they are nevertheless business identifiers, exactly in the same way as certification marks, given that they identify a class of certified merchants. The text that follows refers to the role those signs play in leading potential customers to believe in the technical capacity of the professionals who work inside the shops.

Nicolas Toussaint des Essarts, Causes célèbres, curieuses et intéressantes de toutes les cours souveraines du royaume, avec les jugemens qui les ont décidées, vol. 11 (excerpt)

Cause LXIII

Do Apothecaries Have the Right to Prevent Grocers from Selling Medicines to the Public?

The Grocers and a small town apothecary disputed the right to sell drugs to the public. The former claimed their possession [as a customary practice], and wished to enjoy the privilege of competition; the latter praised their lights, and presented a frightening picture of the danger of entrusting the preparation of medicines to ignorant hands. The first judge had received the request of the Apothecary; the Grocers had appealed the Judgment. This was the scenario of this cause, the facts of which we will recall.

Mr. Polette, after two years of apprenticeship in Pharmacy, and after having lived for several years with different Apothecary masters in Reims, Versailles, Paris, Soissons, had decided to settle in the latter city. On the refusal that had been made to admit him to mastership, he presented himself at the College of Medicine of Paris, which, after the necessary examinations in the presence of the Guards of the community of Apothecaries, and of the ordinary masterpiece, had delivered letters of capacity to him on October 22, 1760, with the permission to establish himself in Soissons or in any other city where there was no *Jurande*.[10]

Equipped with this patent, Mr. Polette had no longer considered it appropriate to settle in Soissons, he had preferred the small town of Chauny. Police officers, after receiving his oath, ordered that it be registered and allowed him to open a shop.

10. Organized body for the control of professions not organized in guilds.

He had noticed the abuses that had crept into this small town, in relation to his profession: all the Grocers without right or capacity exercised concurrently with him the Pharmacy, composed all kinds of potions, medicines, and ointments; they secretly groaned for the effects of such a dangerous license; but before exposing those who usurped the functions of his art, it was interesting that he made himself known.

As soon as he believed his reputation to be strong enough not to have reason to fear the consequences of his complaint, he presented his request to the Judge of Police, and explained to him the inconveniences that could arise from the Grocers' businesses, and the dangers in which his fellow citizens incurred every day because of their want of skills. These reasons impressed the first Judge, and he delivered a judgment that, in execution of the Judgments and Regulations of the Court, forbade the Grocers from keeping or distributing any compound medicines, of whatever nature, . . .; similarly he forbade them from making medicines, other than simple medicines, in competition with the Apothecaries, . . . as well as giving their shops the external marks of those of the Apothecaries; consequently it was ordered that the Grocers would be obliged to get rid, within a week, of the cannon pots, and to have the alambiques, and other attributes of the Pharmacy erased from their display windows; . . .

As soon as the Grocers learned of this sentence they filed appeal. . .

We must examine the different arguments, and assess their appropriateness.

The First Judge ordered them to remove from the top of their shops the signs of Pharmacy, such as cannon pots, alambiques, etc.

It would doubtless be indifferent if the Grocers had signs on their shops that were foreign to their trade, if the gullible public did not see in those signs proof of their knowledge and a title to deserve their trust. But unfortunately the ignorant people perceive on the shop of a Grocer the signs that announce his experience in an art that they need, they fly with haste towards the deceptive sign that offers itself to their eyes, and instead of finding healthy remedies there, they buy new seeds of death. Ignorance sells them for less, and the illusion of agreement with their interest conceals the misfortunes that gullibility and lack of trust represent.

Thus, although the Grocers of Chauny claimed the immemorial possession of [the right to] announce themselves to the public with these deceptive signs, the First Judge had made a very wise decision in ordering their removal, and to modestly confine themselves within the bounds of their profession, without undertaking on the privileges of an Art that is foreign to them. . . .

Thus, the Parliament of Paris had no difficulty in confirming the Judgment of the Judge of Chauny, by its Judgment rendered on the conclusions of the Advocate General de Vergès, on May 19, 1773.

§ 1.18. A BRITISH DRUGGIST CREATES HIS OWN LABEL TO ENSURE THE GENUINENESS OF THE PRODUCTS OF HIS TRADE

In the struggle to lure customers, manufacturers and retailers have always tried to acquire the loyalty of potential customers, particularly when they are engaged in fields where counterfeiting is a major concern. We have seen above Eli Seignette's claim on the genuineness of his salt of Polychrest, and the signs he printed on the sachets that contained his product, so as to distinguish it from counterfeits. (see § 1.12) But Seignette was a pharmacist, and therefore he had in his own hands the way to claim the

genuineness of the products he sold. In the case of William Bacon, a druggist who in the late eighteenth century had a shop in London, he created his own seal of genuineness for each product he sold. That seal showed a promise of the authenticity of the product in question, printed on a copper plate—which, it is assumed, would be delivered to the customers along with the products they acquired. In a prospectus he published in London in 1792, from which the following text has been extracted, he included a list of all the drugs he sold, a few of them under patents, such as the Spa Elixir. And for each listed drug, he would include words of appraisal, some in the form of letters of grateful patients or doctors addressed to the medicine inventors, others in the form of laudatory descriptions of their effects and uses. One example of this technique of advertisement, which became very common from the eighteenth century forward, is also given next.
The patentee of the Spa Elixir (Thomas Gale) was not the same chemist that appears as its manufacturer in Bacon's prospect. Eventually, the patentee may have been assigned or licensed his rights to William.
Today, the expression "Spa Elixir" still survives as a trademark registered for cosmetics and spa services in the USPTO database (TESS).

§ 1.18.1. Announcement of the method that William Bacon created to ensure the genuineness of the drugs he sold in his store, the Royal Patent Medicine Warehouse

1792

Important Caution.

The uniform Efficacy and Safety of the Medicines spoken of in the following Pages, have established their Character, and a great and increasing Demand throughout Great-Britain, Ireland, and other Parts of Europe; also from America, and the East and West Indies; but this Character and Sale have been sometimes found productive of very serious Consequence to the World, and the Proprietors, by giving Opportunity for base and avaricious unprincipled Men to prepare and vend poisonous Counterfeit Preparations, which they have done to an alarming degree, especially in Country Towns, and by Exportation; Mr. Bacon, considering it his Duty to the Public, and to the Patentees and Proprietors, for whom he acts, to render Assistance to the utmost of his Power, in checking this Evil, has devised the following Certificate, engraved in Copper-plate; and as henceforth every Medicine (in this Book), whereof he is the general Agent, will be certified under his Handy, and as the Forgery of such Certificate is a capital Crime, he is not without hopes, that the Sick will cease to experience deleterious Fraud, and the Discoverers of valuable Remedies be in future protected in the Fruits of their Labours in the Healing Art.

"Bacon's Royal Patent Medicine Warehouse.

"I William Bacon, the sole appointed General Agent for the Sale of this Medicine, do hereby certify it to be faithfully prepared and truly genuine.

"Witness my Hand, W. Bacon,

"No. 150, Oxford-Street, London.

"Twenty Guineas Reward will be paid on Conviction of a Forgery of this Certificate."

As each Certificate is trebly checked, by a new and infallible Method, reference to Mr. Bacon, where a Forgery is suspected, will explain every Doubt, and lead to Discovery.

§ 1.18.2. Advertisement of the Spa Elixir in Bacon's prospectus

1792

By the King's Patent.

The Spa Elixir,

A most efficacious Corroborant for either Sex.

This Elixir possesses unequalled tonic powers in the Cure of Debility, Weaknesses, and Relaxation in Men or Women, arising from whatever cause, and at any time of life. It is an elaborate Chemical Preparation of the component of the most salutary Springs in England and upon the Continent, and the dose is from 30 to 60 drops in a wine glass of water.

It is the peculiar property of this Elixir, gently to brace the fibers and vessels, and invigorate the Stomach, and the whole Nervous System.

Bilious Disorders, attended with Acidity and Want of Appetite, arising from a relaxed state of the LIVER, or excessive DRINKING, are immediately relieved and speedily cured by this Elixir. . . .

General Observations.

This Restorative Elixir acts, in all complaints for which it is directed, with uniform safety; it gradually affords Nature her lost Tone; imperceptibly rouses the system into action, and regulates the different Secretions; the patient experiences nothing heating or violent; Strength soon succeeds to Languor; Mental Anxiety and Torpor are followed by Cheerfulness and Serenity, giving fair and certain presage of returning Health.

The Spa Elixir is prepared, by the King's Patent, by T. Williams, Member of the Apothecaries Company; and, sold in bottles, price 2s. 9d. 5s. and 11S. 6d.

Each bottle is certified by Mr. Bacon, under his handy, as by page 8 of this book.

§ 1.18.3. Specification of the Patent on the Spa Elixir granted to Thomas Gale

1782 AD—No. 1334.

Gale's Specification.

To all to whom these presents shall come, I, Thomas Gale, late of New Bridge Street, London, but now of Greek Street, in the Parish of Saint Ann, Westminster, Chemist, send greeting.

Whereas His most Excellent Majesty King George the Third, by His Letters Patent under the Great Seal of Great Britain, bearing date the Thirty-first day of July, in the twenty-second year of His reign, did give and grant unto me, the said Thomas Gale, my executors and administrators, His Majesty's special licence, full power, sole privilege and authority, that I, the said Thomas Gale, my executors, administrators, and assigns, from time to time and at all times during the term of years therein expressed, should and lawfully might use, exercise, and vend, within that part of Great Britain called England, His said Majesty's Dominion of Wales, and Town of Berwick-upon-Tweed, my "New-invented Medicine or Drops, called or intended to be called Spa Elixir, or Gale's Elixir, or Gale's Spa Elixir;" in such manner as to me, my executors, administrators, and assigns, should seem meet, and that I, the said Thomas Gale, my executors, administrators, and assigns, should and lawfully might have and enjoy the whole profit, benefit, commodity, and advantage accruing and arising from the said Invention during the term aforesaid; and there is a proviso contained in the said Letters Patent obliging me, the said Thomas Gale, by an instrument in writing under my hand and seal, particularly to describe and ascertain the nature of my said Invention, and in what manner the same is to be formed, and to cause the same to be enrolled in His Majesty's High Court of Chancery within four calendar months next after the date of the said Letters Patent.

Now know ye, that the said medicine or drops are as follows, that is to say:—

"R. fer. q. 1.; cor. anima., sp. vin. esse., tinc. anima. super., aq. nat., sp. sal. q. s.; dissolve, digest,

correct, evaporate, and extract the elixir, S. A."

In witness whereof, I, the said Thomas Gale, have hereunto set my hand and seal, this Thirty-first day of October, in the year of our Lord One thousand seven hundred and eighty-two.

§ 1.19. THE MAKER AND SELLER OF ÁGUA DE INGLATERRA (WATER OF ENGLAND), A POPULAR SECRET MEDICINE IN PORTUGAL AND BRAZIL, OBTAINS (AND LOSES) EXCLUSIVE RIGHTS IN HIS TRADEMARKS, INCLUDING THE MEDICINE'S GENERIC NAME

Água de Inglaterra (Water of England) *was a medicine basically made of quinine and sweet wine, which, at the end of the eighteenth and through the nineteenth centuries,*

became very popular in Portugal and Brazil in the treatment of all sorts of fevers. It is worth reminding that at that time, both countries were infested by malaria.
The invention of the water has been attributed to Jacob de Castro Sarmento (1691-1762), a famous Portuguese physician, who exiled to London, where he obtained great professional success (he was made a member of the Royal College of Physicians and elected to the Royal Society). However, Sarmento himself admitted that he was merely an improver of the medicine. He kept the method of preparing the improved medicine under secrecy but not the active ingredients used in its composition. Eventually, it was this secret that André Lopes de Castro claimed to have received from Jacob Sarmento (his uncle, apparently).
André's son, José Joaquim de Castro, resorted to various mechanisms to ensure the commercial success of his Água de Inglaterra. *He advertised it intensively in Portuguese and Brazilian newspapers and gazettes, and, in order to obtain the condescendence of authorities, donated vast quantities of the Water to Public and Military Hospitals and to Charities. The availability of the antipyretic in Military Hospitals was of enormous significance at that particular time when the armies of Napoleon were running havoc in Europe.*
José Joaquim claimed exclusivity in the Água. *However, such exclusivity was granted to him by the regent of Portugal not in the making of the medicine because its composition and method of preparation were part of the Pharmacopeia, and were thus known to all apothecaries, but in its name, which had then become generic. The exclusivity in the name led, in that way, albeit indirectly, to a sort of exclusivity in the making and selling of the product. This may explain, in part, the extensive counterfeiting. It may also explain the various references made then to the exclusive privilege for its making and sale. For example, on November 10, 1806, the Municipality of Maragogipe sent to the Governor and General Captain of Bahia (Brazil) acknowledging receipt and compliance with the "Exclusive Privilege for the Introduction and sale of* Água da Inglaterra, *of André Lopes de Castro."* [*Source*: < bndigital.bn.gov.br/acervodigital >].
The texts that follow reveal an interesting escalation of the rights acquired by the Castro family: first, André de Castro obtained permission to sell the medicine (even if he was not a registered pharmacist); then, he and his son got permission to designate the manufacture as Royal Manufacture, *which implied a royal approval of the medicine's quality; then, they obtained enforcement measures to prevent counterfeiting; subsequently, Castro's son (and heir) was permitted to sell the medicine without the need for revealing its secret composition; lastly, and more importantly, Castro's son obtained the privilege for selling the medicine with exclusivity, including the right to the exclusive use of his father's trademark and stamp, as well as the generic designation* Água de Inglaterra.
It took more than one decade for these rights to be nullified.

§ 1.19.1. License for the making and selling of *Água de Inglaterra*

Lisbon. Royal Board of the Proto-Medicato.[11]

Letter of License, without time limitation, passed in favor of José Joaquim de Castro, so that he, in the company of his Parents, and after their death, may freely manufacture and sell throughout this Kingdom and its Domains, Water of England, of the true composition of Doctor Jacob de Castro Sarmento, whose secret was revealed to him.

The Deputies of the Royal Board of Proto-Medicato, Judges of all Pending Civil Causes, and the pronunciation of Crimes in all [causes] that belong to the Faculties of Medicine, and Arts of Surgery, and Pharmacy, in this Kingdom, and Domains of Portugal, all by His Most Faithful Majesty, God preserve him, etc. Having been shown to us the great utility, which has resulted to the Public from the use of the true Water of England, manufactured by André Lopes de Castro, according to Doctor Jacob de Castro Sarmento's true Recipe, who has been manufacturing and selling it in this Court, and throughout this Kingdom, and its Domains, and outside it, for over thirty years, with public and undeniable acceptance; and whereas it has been also presented to Us by an attestation, written by himself, that he had communicated that secret to his wife, Mrs. Antonia Maria Rosa de Castro, and to his son, José Joaquim de Castro, who, in the impediments of his Father, has manufactured it for years with all possible perfection, and who has an exact knowledge, and intelligence of the simple [ingredients] necessary for its composition, and all probity to perform this business well.

In view of the fact that the conservation and use of this Recipe in its purity must be perpetuated for the benefit of the Peoples' health, because this is the genuine recipe of the true Water of England by Doctor Jacob de Castro Sarmento, We make known, and We order, at the request of his son José Joaquim de Castro, that he, jointly with his Parents, and after their death, may freely manufacture and sell it, for an unlimited time, and for the price thus far established; and this in spite of the fact that the said manufacturer is not a Pharmacist by profession, since he has full knowledge, intelligence, and zeal to manufacture it well, as he has been practicing for years in the impediments of his Father. For this reason, we order the issuance of the present unlimited license to José Joaquim de Castro, so that at all times he may freely manufacture and sell it, not only during his parents' lives, but also after their death, as well as in all, and any part of this Kingdom, and its Domains, by means of his legitimate Correspondents, and for all the [matter] referred we give him the necessary authority. And we order that all our Officers, to whom the knowledge of this [letter] belongs, comply with and keep it, and have it executed and kept, as formally and inviolably as it provides for, which they shall do, etc. Given, and passed in this Court, and City of Lisbon, and made in it on the third day of November, one thousand seven hundred and ninety-eight. . . .

By Order of the Royal Board of Proto-Medicato, issued on October 31, 1798 . . . .

11. The Royal Board of Proto-Medicato was a body created in Portugal in the middle of the eighteenth century (and extinguished in the early nineteenth century) that had the attribution of supervising the medical professions, as well as the teaching of medicine and the operation of hospitals.

§ 1.19.2. In a booklet, André Lopes de Castro, introducer of *Água de Inglaterra* [Water of England] in Portugal, advertises that he has communicated the secret composition to his wife and son and warns against counterfeits

1799

Prologue

I do not print this leaflet to speak well of my Water of England again, because it would be a superfluous job writing to speak well of a remedy of which constant experience, and so many Professors, for so many years, have successively spoken well, as it is publicly known. The reason that compels me to this printing is to declare, for the benefit of the Peoples, that having communicated my real recipe to my wife Mrs. Maria Rosa de Castro, and to my son José Joaquim de Castro, and as the latter has manufactured it for years in my impediments; so that in no time there be doubts about the perfection with which he manufactures it, I also thought it convenient to prove by the attestations of so many and so respectable Professors that it is the same [medicine] that I have produced, for its identical and constant effects in these last years: which by many other attestations I could confirm, and which I will do in the future.

Admonition

I recommend, and I ask effectively all buyers of my Water of England, especially those in America, that they take special care, and make every possible inquiry, not only as regards the bottles and seals, but also as regards the probity and character of the people by whom they are dispatched, because the counterfeiters of this remedy are numerous, and tireless, as it is publicly known, to the point they have ordered large portions of empty bottles, and with my trademark, and also using my seal, have deceived the Peoples, with very serious prejudice to the reputation of my Water, and irreparable damage to public health; which will soon be shown to the public with undeniable and authentic documents.

[This introductory text is preceded by a print of Castro's trademark (see Fig. 8), and followed by several statements affirming the therapeutic efficacy of Water of England.]

Figure 8 The seal and trademark of André Lopes de Castro. Extracted from Aviso ao Público.

§ 1.19.3. The maker of Agua de Inglaterra receives permission to designate its manufacture as Royal Manufacture

1803

Notice

For the Count of Villa Verde

Illustrious and Honorable Sir.

The Prince Regent Our Lord [later, João VI, of Portugal], in response to the request to Him submitted by José Joaquim de Castro, who continues to manufacture and sell Water of England, in accordance with the recipe of Doctor Jacob de Castro Sarmento, and for just reasons that He takes into consideration: He is pleased to give him Grace and Mercy so that his factory established for such manufacture and sale be designated as *Royal Factory of Water of England of José Joaquim de Castro.* Of this Your Excellency will inform the Royal Board of Commerce, Agriculture, Factories and Navigation of these Kingdoms, and their Domains, so that the Board has understood it, and has it executed as far as it concerns it. God keep your Excellency. Palace, on July 9, 1803. Viscount of Balsemão.

With the same content and date, another Notice was issued for the Royal Board of Proto-Medicato.

And nothing else is contained in the Register, of which the present has been passed, to appear where appropriate. Nossa Senhora da Ajuda, on July 14, 1803.

§ 1.19.4. The Prince Regent of Portugal approves Castro's request that enforcement measures be taken to stop the generalized counterfeiting of his medicine

1803

Notice.

The Prince Regent Our Lord, taking into consideration what José Joaquim de Castro has exposed to Him in the attached Petition, and the justified reasons that he alleges in order to avoid the frauds he mentions: He is served that Your Lordship grants him the Measures he asks for. God keep your Lordship. Palace, on June 6, 1803. . . .

And attached to the Royal with the Real Notice, a copy of the Petition has been sent, with following content:

Petition.

Sir, José Joaquim de Castro says that, the news having reached him that many people from different Cities, Villages, and Localities of this Kingdom have engaged in the absurdity of buying empty bottles in which the Supplicant usually sells his Water called of England, for later, filling them with another counterfeit water, selling them as the Supplicant's own water, given that they display the same trademark and seal that the Supplicant uses, which yields to the great detriment of the Supplicant's reputation, and of the Public: and this being not avoidable in another way unless Your Highness, through your Royal Notice to the General Intendant of the Police, orders him to issue Circular Orders to the Ministers of each of the mentioned lands of this Kingdom, so that they do not consent that in the Districts of their Jurisdictions any person, other than those who show to be Supplicant's Correspondents, by his appointment, which shall be registered with the Municipality, sells bottled Water of England in bottles with the trademark and seal of André Lopes de Castro, recently deceased, Father of the Supplicant, which is the same that the Supplicant uses under special Grace, which Your Royal Highness has just granted him by your Royal Notices, issued by the Secretary of State for Affairs of the Kingdom, on the 26th of May of this year of 1803, to the Real Boards of Commerce, and of Proto-Medicato; nor to buy the empty bottles, with the mentioned trademark, since for this purpose the mentioned Correspondents are equipped with the necessary authority. And whereas the Supplicant's purpose is to keep the medicine's reputation, defrauded by the mentioned persons, and many other counterfeiters, and he cannot achieve it without Y.R.H.'s deigning to order that the measures that the Supplicant describes be taken, which the same Ministers must publish by Edicts in the Districts of their Jurisdictions, and have registered in the respective Municipalities: therefore he asks for Your Royal Highness to be served by ordering the issuance of a Royal Notice addressed to the General Intendant of the Police, so that he does so, and ordering to lawfully proceed against the infringers of those Royal Orders. And he will receive mercy. José Joaquim de Castro.

[One year later this same order was extended to the territories that Portugal controlled overseas.]

§ 1.19.5. Castro's son and heir is authorized to sell Água da Inglaterra without the need to disclose the secret

The Royal Board of Proto-Medicato has adopted the following

Decree.

The Requests of José Joaquim de Castro having been submitted to me, in which he wants the freedom to be able to manufacture and sell his Water named of England, as it was practiced before, without being obliged to disclose the Secret of the preparation of the same Water; the various Representations of his father André Lopes de Castro, already deceased, . . . And Accepting such Information, and Bearing in mind that the frequent use and good success of the Water designated of England has qualified it in such a way that makes its examination unnecessary;

I am Served by granting the free use of the Water designated of England of José Joaquim de Castro, which for the experience of almost a century has been known as useful. So has the Royal Board of Proto-Medicato understood it, and have it executed, regardless of any Laws, Regulations, or Provisions to the contrary. Queluz Palace, on 24 September 1805.

With the Signature of the Prince Regent Our Lord. . . .

§ 1.19.6. Castro obtains the exclusive right in the use of the designation "Agoa de Inglaterra" and the confirmation of the designation of his factory as "Royal Manufacture"

Decree

Accepting the Information and Opinion of the Governors of the Kingdom of Portugal, and Algarves, on the Request of José Joaquim de Castro, in which he asks to be declared that the water that is manufactured in his factory be the only one to be designated as Water of England, and that such factory be the only that may be designated as *Royal Factory of Water of England*, so as to eliminate the issues that have been raised, in order to discredit it with irreparable damage of his Trade, and reputation, whereas its frequent use for many years has qualified it as useful: And also taking into account in my Royal Consideration the Donations of a large number of dozens of bottles of the same Water, which the said José Joaquim de Castro has made to Military Hospitals in the present war, to Emigrants, and to invaded and evacuated Localities, which service much recommends him: I am pleased and graced to give him the Mercy that only the water that is manufactured in his Factory be called *Water of England*; expressly forbidding any other Inventor, or Manufacturer, from being able to give the same name to the Febrifugal Waters of their invention, and manufacture; which remains free, without any restriction:

And I am pleased, moreover, for giving Mercy to the Supplicant's Factory, that only it has the title of *Royal Factory of Water of England*, whose denomination had already been granted to it by Notice of nine of July of one thousand eight hundred and three. That the Royal Board of Commerce, Agriculture, Factories, and Navigation so has understood it, and has it executed in the part that concerns it.

Rio de Janeiro Palace, on October 2nd, one thousand eight hundred and eleven.

With the signature of the Prince Regent Our Lord.

[One year later this Decree was confirmed.]

§ 1.19.7. An apothecary challenges José Joaquim de Castro's right to the exclusive making of *Água de Inglaterra* and use of its generic designation

1821

Antônio José de Sousa Pinto, Apothecary of this City [of Lisbon] represented to the Sovereign Congress that a Decree that José Joaquim de Castro had obtained, by which he had been granted the exclusive privilege of using the name of Water of England in a certain febrifugal medicine, which he manufactured, deserved to be revoked in times that did not condone with exclusive privileges, concerning things that belonging to many, or being known by all Apothecaries, did not allow exclusion, or singular prerogative. This was decided by the Wise Health Commission, and the Sovereign Congress approved it. . .

Castro claims to be the son of André Lopes de Castro, and this, the Nephew of Jacob de Castro Sarmento: he says that Jacob had invented Water of England, whose secret recipe had come to his nephew, and from him to his son Castro. This invention, and this succession—that is, in short, all his right. Therefore, showing that there was an febrifugal water, called Water of England, long before that of Jacob Castro, the building of Castro's intended justice will fall, and his already longstanding imposture will finally appear. Demonstrating it is easy.

Jacob de Castro Sarmento was born in 1691.. . ..

Manoel d'Azevedo, designated Proto-Doctor in 1638 wrote a Work entitled *Correcção d'Abusos contra o Verdadeiro Methodo da Medicina* [*Correction of Abuses against the True Method of Medicine*], in which, on page 292, the offer of the recipe for the true *Water of England*, made in London on April 14, 1681, can be found—that is, ten years before Jacob de Castro was born. . . . [other references to previous descriptions of the composition of Água de Inglaterra follow.]

From all this it follows that many years before Jacob de Castro existed, the so-called Water of England existed already. Therefore, Jacob de Castro was not the inventor: therefore, he had no right to an exclusive privilege himself. So, with what justice can his second nephew claim (if the recipe is the same, which has been proved by printed material that it is not), who is not even Apothecary?

On the other hand: the formula is printed in Pharmacopeias and Medical Books. All Apothecaries can manufacture it: many do it, actually. . . .

§ 1.20. THE BRITISH HIGH COURT OF CHANCERY GRANTS AN INJUNCTION SECURING EXCLUSIVITY IN MEDICINE EVEN IN THE ABSENCE OF A PATENT

Entrepreneurs have always resorted to all methods possible to secure their trade advantages. Patents and trade secrets may be the preferred tools because of the legal certainty (although relative in case of secrets) that surround their enforcement. But all other ways available to protect the reputation of a certain asset are eventually sought by merchants aware of their advantage.

In an unreported case, cited in Canham v. Jones *(a case involving a secret medicine, in which the Court denied the injunction because the defendant's medicine was not the same as the plaintiff's), the High Court of Chancery granted an injunction against the defendant who used various dishonest means to pass his medicine as the same as the plaintiff, namely the reproduction of pieces of his advertisements. There was no claim as to the copyright in the verses used in the advertisement. No patent, either, or, apparently, not even a trade secret was involved, but only the assertion by false means of an identity between two medicines.*

Canham v. Jones

High Court of Chancery

June 23, 1813

In *Sedon v. Senate*, about two years since [i.e., 1811], the Defendant, having sold a medicine to the Plaintiff, set up another, under a similar description; and, in his advertisement, adopted verses which had been attached to the original medicine.

The *Master of the Rolls*, sitting for the Lord Chancellor, . . ., granted an injunction, though the Plaintiff had no patent.

§ 1.21. THE FRENCH GOVERNMENT ADOPTS A REGULATION FOR THE TERRITORY OF THE LOW COUNTRIES (BELGIUM), PROVIDING FOR THE MANDATORY USE OF COMMON NAMES AND THE (CERTIFYING) SIGNATURE OF APOTHECARIES FOR DESIGNATING MEDICINES AND THEIR INGREDIENTS

The clear designation of medicines and their ingredients has always been a concern. We have seen one of its early expressions in the capitulare of Venice of 1258 (see § 1.03). In the nineteenth century, the French government adopted explicit measures in that same sense, to be applied to the Lower Countries, then under France's domain. There was no prohibition against apothecaries' personal trademarks, however. But these, in the form of signatures, were just complementary.

Later, another measure strikingly modern in its concept was introduced: the physicians, in their prescriptions, should use the medicines' designations as inserted in the Pharmacopeia. At that time, the purpose of this measure was just a matter of clarity. But today, the eventual prohibition of citing trademarks in medical prescriptions has to do with incentives for the purchase of generic medicines and the reduction of the luring power of reputed trademarks (see § 1.35).

§ 1.21.1. Instructions approved by Royal Decree of May 31, 1818, for the Doctors of Medicine, Surgeons of the Cities and of the Interior, Obstetricians, Apothecaries, Midwives, and Druggists of the Lower Countries

Instruction for the apothecaries

Art. 1. No one shall establish him/herself as an apothecary in this kingdom, unless he/she has satisfied both the general laws and the local regulations issued on this subject and currently in force. . . .

Art. 5. The medicines must be clearly and exactly designated on the jars, vases, boxes, etc., which contain them, with an indication of their old names and those given to them by the pharmacopeia approved by the government. . . .

Art. 11. Apothecaries shall clearly write on the label of the medicaments they prepare the name of the person who is to use them, the date and manner of taking them, and they shall additionally attach their signature. . . .

Instruction for the druggists[12]

Art. 1. No one shall establish himself as a druggist in this kingdom, unless he has satisfied both the general laws and the local regulations in force issued on the exercise of this profession. . . .

Art. 5. All articles supplied to druggists, used in medicine, whether they have been purchased in bulk or from other druggists, must be good and of the required quality; the pretext of having been misled or deceived by others in this respect shall not be accepted as a justification.

Art. 6. These articles must be indicated, with their own names, in an exact and clear manner, on the jars, vases, boxes, pots, etc., which contain them. . . .

§ 1.21.2. Additional provisions on the designation of medicines on medical prescriptions in Belgium

1821 and 1859

Royal Decree of April 28, 1821, art. 5.

C. Medicines must be clearly and exactly designated on the jars, vases, boxes, etc., that contain them, which will be covered with a label bearing both the old names of each medicine, as well as the new names, such as that they are expressed in the Belgian Pharmacopeia.

12. The difference between apothecaries and druggists was that the latter were not allowed to make and sell medicines—that being an exclusive prerogative of apothecaries—but only the ingredients that could be used in their preparation.

Royal Decree of Dec. 28, 1859, art. 5.

B. [Doctors] will use, in their prescriptions, the names of the official Pharmacopeia to designate the medicinal substances described in this collection; if they want the remedy to be prepared otherwise, they shall give its formula in the prescription, or they shall indicate the pharmacopeia where it is found.

§ 1.22. THOMAS HOLLOWAY AND HIS PILLS AND OINTMENT—A SUCCESSFUL COMBINATION OF SECRECY, TRADEMARKS (AND THEIR ENFORCEMENT), AND INTENSIVE ADVERTISEMENT

Thomas Holloway (1800-1883) is an example of an entrepreneur who combined several intellectual property tools to be successful in the pharmaceutical field. In the 1830s, he started selling pills and ointments under a secret formula. It has been alleged that the ointment's composition had been partially revealed through a patent application filed in France by a Swedish doctor, Dr. Sillen. The latter had claimed the invention of a pomade, i.e., a cosmetic, rather than an ointment, because under the 1844 French Patent Act, pharmaceutical compositions were excluded from patentability (see § 2.44). Holloway was accused of stealing the formula of the ointment from an Italian businessman, Felix Albinolo, but Holloway's formula was basically herbal, and thus it was very different from Albinolo's. Holloway has never filed for a patent in the United Kingdom, and thus he was not requested to submit the specifications of his pills and ointment.

He used his own name as a trademark ("Holloway's pills and ointment"), which he would enforce strictly (including against his own brother, as the first of the following texts shows). In addition, Holloway resorted to intensive advertising of many sorts, all over the world, and in many languages. A real business genius, Holloway supervised the ads of his products attentively and would pay them only after receiving a copy of the newspapers or magazines where they were published so as to control the quality of the printing. This combination of branding with intensive advertising corresponds, actually, to the same business model under which today's global conglomerates of consumer goods operate. Holloway would not be strange to another modern form of advertisement: product placement. It is told that he has sent a check to Charles Dickens so that the writer could make a nice reference to Holloway's pills in one of his novels. However, Dickens has never discounted the check (and never cited Holloway's pills).

Holloway was not, however, an innocent businessman. Part of his success can also be attributed to aggressive, if not illegal, practices, such as copyright infringement and breach of contracts with distributors. He was, indeed, a serious litigator, both as plaintiff and as a defendant. His successors continued acting aggressively against competitors.

Holloway was a philanthropist, and he used some of the considerable fortunes he made by selling his pills and ointment to found in England a sanatorium and a girls' college. His acumen has inspired his heirs, who were able to keep the business afloat for some time, with recourse to the same aggressive strategy that had been so successful—including the infringement of copyright in a famous German painting.

Holloway's business was pure quackery and was based on the credulity of customers, influenced (if not cheated) by massive advertisement. Nevertheless, it is interesting to look at how he has incorporated various modalities of intellectual property into his business model.

§ 1.22.1. Holloway sues his brother for trademark infringement

Holloway v. Holloway

November 9, 1850. Lord Langdale, M. R. 13 Beav. 209

The Plaintiff Thomas Holloway had for some few years made and sold pills and ointments at 244, Strand, under the name of "Holloway pills and ointment," and had, as he stated in his affidavit, expended nearly 150,000 *l.* in making them known and establishing a connection for the sale thereof. The wrappers and pamphlets contained extravagant representations as to the universal curative effects of those medicines. His brother, the Defendant Henry Holloway, had recently commenced selling pills and ointment at 210, Strand, under a similar description of "H. Holloway's pills and ointment." The pill-boxes and pots were similar in form to, and the labels and wrappers were copied from those used by the Plaintiff.

Under these circumstances, the Plaintiff filed his bill, praying an injunction to restrain the Defendant from selling any pills or ointment described as or purporting to be "Holloway's pills," or "H. Holloway's ointment," in boxes or pots having labels so contrived or expressed, as, by colourable imitation or otherwise, to represent the pills or ointment sold by the Defendant to be the same pills or ointment as were sold by the Plaintiff. . . .

The Master of the Rolls (without hearing a reply).

This case, upon the evidence before me is perfectly clear. The Defendant's name being *Holloway* has a right to constitute himself a vendor of *Holloway's* pills and ointment, and I do not intend to say anything tending to abridge such right. But he has no right to do so with such additions to his own name as to deceive the public and make them believe that he is selling the Plaintiff's pills and ointments. The evidence in this case clearly proves that pills and ointment have been sold by the Defendant, marked in such a manner that persons have purchased them of the Defendant believing that they were buying the goods of the Plaintiff; and for proof of the fraudulent conduct of the Defendant, I need only refer to the affidavits of *Coyneau* the printer and of *Hall*. Can anything be more clear than what they state? The first states that the Defendant brought the Plaintiff's pamphlets as models for preparing his own, and directed him to prepare his, the Defendant's, "as nearly similar to those of the Plaintiff, in language and arrangement and in every other respect, as possible, without being copies, in order that they might pass with the public as the identical pamphlets," etc. used by the Plaintiff. The Defendant also informed him that his object was to sell "his pills and ointment for the pills and ointment made by the Plaintiff, without the chance of detection."

I think this as clear and as plainly avowed a fraud as I ever knew. I do not mean to say that I have any sort of respect for this sort of medicines. I have none; but the law protects persons from fraudulent misrepresentations, and this is a species of property which the law does allow, and so long as the law recognises it, it must be protected, and persons in the situation of the defendant will not be allowed to practice a fraud like that here complained of.

§ 1.22.2. A sarcastic article on the ointment sold by Albinolo, who claimed that Holloway had stolen its composition from him

February 24, 1861

> *The Art of Acquiring Vipers and Making a Small Income from it*, by Edmond Martin
>
> There are people who have never invented anything—not even the gunpowder, and who console themselves by thinking that the Chinese had taken the lead over them.
>
> Mr. Albinolo, from Turin, who cannot shelter himself under the Chinese hat, saw fit to take his part in the great industrial concert with his ointment of its composition.
>
> This ointment is named after him.
>
> Now it remains to be seen whether it was Mr. Albinolo who made the ointment famous, or whether it was the ointment that threw some glaze on Mr. Albinolo's name. This is what we have never found out.
>
> Anyway, the *Albinolo ointment* is an ointment without any parallel, an ointment like we have never seen.
>
> And as proof I do not need more than its composition:
>
> Composition of the *Albinolo Ointment*:
>
> (Usurped by the man named Holloway)
>
> 1 butter; 2 yellow virgin wax; 3 fir resin; 4 rosin; 5 crushed white salt; 6 snake fat; 7 viper fat; 8 turpentine from Venice.
>
> To have the quantities of the articles, one pays 25 fr. and receives them by post, free delivery, to their destination. . . .

Like all things useful in this world, Father Albinolo's ointment applies to all diseases and to all wounds of humanity. I believe, God forgive me, that one could use it if necessary to paint the bedroom.

Let us give the word to the inventor:

> "This unrivaled balm quickly and radically heals the most serious ailments, such as: Skin diseases, pustular and vesicular darters, etc.; rheumatism, lumbagos; muscle and joint pain, etc.; diarrhea, malignant fevers, tumors, even cancerous, etc.; inflammations, cramps, ulcers, etc.; contagious diseases and epidemics; dysentery, cholera, etc."
>
> This balm, which is sovereign for colic and dysentery, is not only sold in Paris, but also in Turin, at Félix Albinolo and son, under the arcades of the fair, ...

§ 1.22.3. A report on the lawsuit initiated by the Swedish physician Sillen against Holloway, involving the permission to sell Holloway's ointment in France

1863

Law and Crime.

Sillen v. Holloway—Ointment or Pomade?

This was an action tried before the Lord Chief Justice in Middlesex, when a verdict was found nominally for the plaintiff, with leave to move to maintain his verdict for £500 or for £150. A report of the case was given in our December number. In the Court of Common Pleas, on the 12th ult., Mr. Eovill, Q.C., with whom was Mr. C. Pollock, moved, on behalf of the defendant, to set aside the verdict, or for a nonsuit. The action was brought by the plaintiff, a foreign physician, to recover £500 for his services in procuring permission to sell Holloway's ointment in France and her colonies. The contract on which the plaintiff sued was contained in a letter from the defendant to the plaintiff, in which he promised to pay the plaintiff £1,000 if he obtained permission to sell his ointment and pills in France and her colonies, with liberty to advertise the same, or £500 for the like permission as to the ointment. In January, 1861, the plaintiff obtained a *brevet* or patent authorizing the defendant to sell his ointment. But that was of no use or value. By the law of France, no secret remedy was to be sold or advertised without the sanction of the Minister of the Interior or a decree of the Emperor; and if a patent were obtained for a secret remedy, it was simply void. The plaintiff had described the ointment as a pomade, and had sent for a box of it to be analyzed in France, and there it had been found to consist of white wax, yellow wax, hog's lard, and turpentine—and liberty to sell this pomade had been obtained; but the defendant contended his ointment was a secret, and that he would not divulge its constituents on any consideration. The patent had not been renewed, and on that account it was also void. On these grounds he contended that the plaintiff was not entitled to his verdict, nor to the sum of £150 as remuneration for his services.—*Rule nisi* granted.

On the 27th ult., this curious case reached another stage.—Mr. Brandt, on behalf of the plaintiff, showed cause against the rule obtained by the defendant's counsel. He stated that the action was brought by Dr. Sillen, a Swedish physician, against Mr. Holloway, who called himself Professor Holloway, the proprietor of Holloway's ointment and Holloway's pills, to recover £500, on an agreement entered into by the plaintiff with the defendant, that if the plaintiff could obtain permission, through some influence he had, for the sale of Holloway's ointment in France and her colonies, he was to have £500. Dr. Sillen went to France, saw Dr. Laraball, the physician of the Empress, but found he could do nothing without some specimen of the ointment and pills; and in answer to his application the defendant sent the plaintiff over two pots of his ointment and one box of pills, recommending the plaintiff to concentrate all his efforts to procure permission to sell the ointment, which the defendant represented to be wonderfully efficacious for the cure of old wounds, on which it should be rubbed "like salt on meat." . . .

On the receipt of the ointment, the law of France prohibiting the sale of secret remedies, it was submitted to the authorized French chemists to be analyzed, and it was found to contain butter, lard, Bordeaux turpentine, white wax, yellow wax, and nothing else. On finding these to be the constituents of the ointment, the fear of the French against secret remedies fled at once, and Dr. Sillen obtained a *brevet* or patent for the sale of the ointment. But it was objected that the patent was for pomade and not for ointment, the brevet being granted for "*Pommade dit Holloway.*" If this was not Holloway's ointment, the learned counsel did not know what it was. But Mr. Holloway said the patent was not what he wanted—he wanted a decree of the Emperor for the sale of his ointment, which he would not be very likely to get, or he would not pay Dr. Sillen. It was objected that a patent for the sale of pomade was not a patent for the sale of the ointment—that "*pommade*" meant *pomatum*, and that the patent ought to be for the sale of "*ointment.*" . . .

There was permission obtained to sell the ointment; it was not a secret remedy, and against the French law, because it had been analyzed, and the analysis stamped with an official stamp was affixed to the *brevet*. If there were some subtle ingredients in it which could not be detected, it was the same thing as if they were not there, so far as the French law was concerned. The learned counsel contended, that having got the permission desired, the plaintiff was entitled to the agreed reward of £500, or at all events to a *quantum meruit* of £150. The patent existed for 15 years, and had not expired by reason of the non-payment of fees.

On the 29th ult., Mr. Bovill, Q.C., appeared to support the rule in this case, to set aside the verdict, and enter it for the defendant.

The learned counsel contended that the defendant made a contract by letter to pay the plaintiff £500 if he could obtain him permission to sell Holloway's ointment in France and her colonies. If he failed to obtain that permission he was not to have anything. By the French law, which prohibits the sale of secret remedies, that could only be done by permission of the Minister of the Interior. This was not the obtaining of a common brevet d'invention, which anybody could get. Holloway's ointment was a secret remedy, and was so treated. To obtain a patent for it, it had been treated as a cosmetic, and called "*pommade,*" and as the analysis showed that it contained only butter, lard, turpentine, and wax, the French had laughed at it, and said there was nothing noxious in that; it might be sold as a pomade. . . .

Mr. Bovill proceeded to contend that even the patent so obtained to sell "*Pommade dit Holloway*" was worthless, for when offered to the defendant by the plaintiff it was long after it had been granted, and when it had become void for the non-payment of certain fees.

The Chief Justice said that was a fatal defect, and on that ground the Court thought the rule ought to be made absolute, that when the plaintiff offered the patent to the defendant it was a void patent, and worth nothing.—Rule absolute. . . .

§ 1.22.4. Notice of another litigation episode involving Holloway's trademark, this time involving a distributor of his pills and ointment in South America

1879

Mr. Holloway has advertised in some South American papers advertisements stating that a Mr. Samper, of Bogotà, Colombia, was importing spurious imitations of his pills and ointment from America. Mr. Samper declares he has not done so, and brought an action against Mr. Holloway to compel him to stop, or at least to alter, the advertisements. This was agreed to. It was stated by Mr. Holloway's counsel that profits of 50,000*l*. a year are made by him, 40,000*l*. of which are spent in advertising.

§ 1.22.5. Examples of advertisements of Holloway's pills and ointments

Holloway's Pills and Ointment—Marie Dicks, a fish merchant, in Zalt-Bommel, for five years had her legs in an awful state and was transported twice to the hospital where she was always told that amputation was necessary. Holloway's treatment, with its medicines, has given back to the poor woman the use of her legs without resorting to the painful surgery.

[The same advertisement appeared in many other newspapers in English and French.]

Le Moniteur Officiel des Etablissements Français dans l'Inde, December 9, 1884, at 2398.

Figure 9a Another of Holloway's ads. The audience, in a position of veneration, seems to listen to some elderly, quasi-religious figure, a prophet perhaps, who certainly speaks to them about the virtues of Holloway's pills and ointment. The text reads: "HOLLOWAY'S PILLS AND OINTMENT. HOLLOWAY'S PILLS. The greatest remedy known to date in the world. All disturbances of the liver and stomach quickly give way to their powerful influence. They strengthen and restore debilitated constitutions to health, correct all impurities in the blood, arising from old age, or from youthful recklessness, from intemperance, or other causes, and can be taken as a general remedy for most diseases. They are wonderfully suited to women and children. HOLLOWAY'S OINTMENT Is a powerful curative which, rubbed on the system, reaches the hidden location of the disease and even penetrates the bone, like salt introduces itself into the meat, and, by its balsamic influence, it cures the disturbances of the kidneys, of stomach, liver, throat, etc. It is also infallible for the cure of sore legs and breasts, stiff and contracted joints, gout, rheumatism and all skin diseases. Detailed instructions and in all languages surround every box and jar. These remedies are sold in almost every Pharmacist in the world, and in London, at their owner's house, Professor Holloway, 244, Strand. Published in LE MÉMORIAL DIPLOMATIQUE, 3rd year, no. 21, Sunday, May 21, 1865, at 314.

§ 1.22.6. *Hansfstaengl Art Publishing Company and another v. Holloway*, a case of copyright infringement by Thomas Holloway's heirs—1893

Mr. Justice Charles, sitting in the Queen's Bench Division on Saturday, delivered judgment in the case of the Hansfstaengl Art Publishing Company and another *v.* Holloway. This was an action by a company of Munich, Bavaria, and their agent in London, against Sir George Martin Holloway and Mr. Henry Driver Holloway, of 78 New Oxford Street, sole proprietors of Holloway's pills and ointment.

The plaintiffs, as proprietors both in Germany and the United Kingdom of the copyright in a picture entitles "The Guardian Angel," painted by Bernard Plockhurst, asked for an injunction against Messrs. Holloway, restraining them importing into the United Kingdom, exhibiting, or distributing copies of the picture as advertisements for their pills and ointments. Plaintiffs also claimed damages for the infringement of their copyright, and the delivery up to them of the 400,000 copies of the picture now in the hands of Messrs. Holloway.

The defendants did not admit that the plaintiffs were the owners of the copyright either in England or in Germany. The defendants pleaded that the International Copyright Act of 1886 did not apply to this picture, or, if it did, the plaintiffs had not the necessary registration. The trial of the action took place in January. . . .

Mr. Justice Charles, in giving judgment, said the plaintiffs were the proprietors both in England and in Germany of the picture entitled "The Guardian Angel." The picture was exhibited in Berlin in 1886, but no copies were allowed to be taken. The copyright was assigned to the plaintiff company on March 27, 1887. Messrs. Holloway, for the purposes of their trade, caused their agents to make copies of the picture on cards, and on the back of those cards were advertisements of Holloway's pills and ointments. Some advertisements were in prose; others in poetry. It was not denied that all the copies of the picture were infringements. Therefore the questions which he had to decide were questions of law. But before dealing with the law he should state that the plaintiffs in 1891, having discovered the infringements, registered their copyright. . . .

His Lordship having recited the articles in the Berne Convention, and certain sections of the Copyright Act, said he came to the conclusion that the three questions of law must be decided in the plaintiffs' favour. His judgment would be for the plaintiff for 100*l.* damages, as agreed, and costs. He also granted the injunction in the terms asked for, and ordered the defendants to deliver up all the unlawful copies of the picture in their possession. . . .

[A detailed report of this case was published in Le Droit d'Auteur, the official journal of the Bureau of the International Union for the Protection of Literary and Artistic Works, July 15, 1893, at 86 *et seq.*]

§ 1.22.7. Another instance of trademark enforcement by Holloway's heirs

Holloway v. Clent

June 19, 1903.

In the High Court of Justice — Chancery Division.

Before Mr. Justice Swinfen Eady.

Passing-off. — Trade name. — Motion for interlocutory injunction. — Purchase by Defendant of a business not shown to include the class of goods in question. — Interlocutory injunction granted.

The Plaintiff, who sold pills which had a wide reputation as *Holloway's Pills*, commenced an action to restrain the Defendant from passing off his pills as the Plaintiff's and from using the name *Holloway* in connection with pills, and moved for an interlocutory injunction. The Defendant had some years previously bought a business from a man named *Holloway*, and alleged that he had the right to use the name; and it contended on his behalf that, in any case, he should not be restrained from using the name in connection with pills except so as to cause deception.

Held, that the Defendant had not shown that his predecessor had dealt in pills; that on the facts proved the Defendant had acted fraudulently, and that an interlocutory injunction should be granted in the form asked.

Figure 9b Portrait of Thomas Holloway and his two main charities. Extracted from an Almanac entitled "Holloway's Almanac—Celebrated Homes," published in 1892. Each month of the year, with notice of its celebrations and ephemerids, was illustrated with the drawing and the description of one of England's most famous mansions and palaces. At the bottom of each calendar page, the Almanac displayed mottos and slogans recommending Holloway's products, such as: "HOLLOWAY'S OINTMENT is Invaluable for Influenza, Bronchitis, Pleurisy, &c.;" "HOLLOWAY'S PILLS are Marvelously Efficacious for Stomach and Liver Complaints;" "HOLLOWAY'S PILLS and OINTMENT in cases of Gout and Lumbago ate Unrivalled."

§ 1.23. A FRENCH COURT HOLDS THAT A BUSINESS IDENTIFIER CANNOT BE USED FOR INDIRECTLY SECURING EXCLUSIVITY IN A SECRET MEDICINE COMPOSITION

The rob végétal dépuratif de Boyveau-Laffecteur *(literally,* depurative vegetable syrup of Boyveau-Laffecteur*) was a very popular medicine in the second half of the eighteenth and through the nineteenth centuries, with allegedly proven therapeutic effects against syphilis. The invention of the syrup was claimed by a certain Boyveau-Laffecteur, who designated himself in one of the many booklets he produced as "Physician, Chemist and Author of this Remedy that, since 50 years, he has provided to the Hospitals of the Navy, concerning which he has taken care, on behalf of the Government, of the cure of the Sickness acknowledged as incurable by Mercury and all other Remedies." The booklet in question is* OBSERVATIONS SUR L'HISTOIRE ET LES EFFETS DU ROB ANTI-SYPHILLITIQUE DE M. BOYVEAU-LAFFECTEUR *(self-publication, 1810). Following the marketing technique of the charlatans of that time, that booklet, under the pretense of being a scientific discussion of the disease, was, in reality, an unashamed piece of propaganda. It has four sections: the first section gives a historical account of syphilis and the different methods developed through times to treat it. The second section tells about the invention, its making, the experiments to test it, and how it gained the trust of governmental authorities, before and during the French Revolution. The third section is pure propaganda: it contains numerous testimonies of the miraculous cures obtained with the syrup. The final section provides for the various official documents pertaining to the commercialization of the syrup, such as the patent letter of 1778 that permitted it, and the various examinations carried out by the Royal Society of Medicine (which, in the end, decided that the syrup had some beneficial therapeutic effects). The booklet ends with an ode dedicated to Boyveau-Laffecteur's syrup, authored by Luce de Lancival, a teacher of literature. These are the words of Boyveau about the poet: "This flattering tribute to his Recognition praises his heart as much as his talents."*

It is worth noticing that the 1778 patent letters granted to Boyveau-Laffecteur did not give him exclusivity in the making and the sale of the syrup, but only in the use of the trademarks he adopted.

However, there has been a cloud of doubt over the sincerity of the claims by the alleged inventor of the Boyveau-Laffecteur syrup, that being the identity of its real inventor. In fact, although the syrup was branded with a double family name (and trademark) Boyveau-Leffacteur, those names corresponded to two distinct persons. Pierre Boyveau being the inventor, for some reason he employed Denis Leffacteur for obtaining the permission for its commercialization on the latter's own behalf. The right acquired by Leffacteur that resulted from the permission was subsequently assigned to Boyveau. As the first of the following texts show, through a contract (registered with a notary of Paris in 1787), Leffacteur assigned his name to Boyveau, and, for the services of obtaining the marketing approval of the drug and of promoting its sales, received a fixed yearly sum of 1,500 pounds. Ten years later, given that, for unknown reasons, Leffacteur did nothing to promote the sales, and thus he was not paid the agreed sum, he asked for a lump sum payment of 3,000 pounds for the assignment of his name, which Boyveau has paid.

So, when the drug reached the market, it was initially sold under the single name (and trademark) of Leffacteur. Only later, as Boyveau wrote in another of his publications, NOTICE D'UN GRAND INTÉRÊT, POUR TOUS LES ORDRES DE CITOYENS, SUR LES OUVRAGES DE BOYVEAU-LEFFACTEUR *(self-publication, 1799) [where he summarized many of his writings on the drug]: "Particular reasons had obliged me, in the beginning, to submit my remedy to the Society of Medicine, under the commercial denomination of Leffacteur, which I do not own, as a family name: whereas today the law does not permit any name changes, I repossess that of my parents, and henceforth I will sign BOYVEAU-LEFFACTEUR."*

Why would Boyveau need to use another's name for obtaining the permission of commercialization? This question has been left unanswered.

The syrup was affected by the enactment of regulations in the early 1800s (see § 2.38) prohibiting the advertisement and sale of secret remedies. Only those that were acquired by the government, or that were approved by the Society of Medicine could continue being traded and administered to patients. Leffacteur secured that permission by means of a decree, thus avoiding the disclosure of the secret formula and, at the same time, escaping the prohibition of the commercialization of the "secret remedies."

Later Leffacteur sold the formula to an actual physician, Giraudeau de Sainte-Claire, who continued commercializing it under his original brand, which in the meantime had become well-known through the European Continent.

Any great commercial success brings a major risk—that of counterfeiting. Leffacteur's syrup was no exception. Because of that, as we will see in the following texts, several references to the fact that the original product was sold only under certain business identifiers appeared in official documents.

Giraudeau attempted to secure the exclusivity of the drug through the ownership of the brand but failed. The court of appeals (Cour de Cassation), reversing the judgment of the Imperial Court of Paris, held that the brand "Boyveau-Leffacteur," through its long use (for over a century) had become the synonym of the medicine, and thus had become a matter of public domain. In modern terms, "genericide" had occurred. So, Giraudeau could no longer claim exclusivity in the use of that brand to designate his composition, particularly because the formula had already become publicly known. Nevertheless, given that Giraudeau continued manufacturing and selling the syrup, competitors were required to make it clear on the labels and advertisements of their own drugs that their provenance was not the same as Giraudeau's syrup.

§ 1.23.1. Contract as per which Laffecteur assigned his name to Boyveau, inventor and distributor of the Syrup Boyveau-Leffacteur

1778

We, the undersigned, Pierre Boyveau and Denis Laffecteur, former food inspector, have agreed as follows:

That I, Pierre Boyveau, by virtue of the approval and consent obtained from Mr. Denis Laffecteur, having submitted to the king a request in the name of the mentioned Mr. Laffecteur to obtain the privilege of the sale and distribution of an anti-venereal remedy, known and announced under the name of *Antisyphilitic Syrup*, Mr. Laffecteur finds it convenient that the decision of the council and the letters patent that will result from such request, be obtained in his name; moreover, all the deals or agreements that may be made in relation to the exploitation of the said remedy, of which, by the said request, Mr. Laffecteur appears to possess and own, although, in fact, he has only rendered to Mr. Boyveau the good service of lending him his name; of course, Boyveau shall not, in any way, contract commitments that particularly burden Mr. Laffecteur, not lending him his name for another purpose than in the context of the use of the mentioned remedy.

And I, Denis Laffecteur, hereby declare to Mr. Boyveau, that I have no property whatsoever over the aforesaid remedy, that I even waive it as much as necessary, as well as over the products that may result from its sale, in any manner whatsoever, either in the military hospitals of the kingdom and others, or otherwise, paying an annual and fixed gratuity, as a total amount, of fifteen hundred pounds each year, which will be paid to me by Mr. Boyveau, against simple receipts, and this during all the time that Mr. Boyveau enjoys the permission to sell and distribute the mentioned anti-venereal remedy under my name, which annual gratuity of fifteen hundred pounds, I, Boyveau, grant to Mr. Laffecteur, on the same terms and conditions stipulated above, which gratuity of fifteen hundred pounds will not begin to run until the day of publication of the decision of the Council, bearing the privilege requested by Mr. Boyveau, so that the gratuity be paid every three months against the receipts of Mr. Leffacteur. Made in duplicate in Paris, July 1, 1778; . . . Signed: Leffacteur — Approved the contract. . . . — Signed: Boyveau.

I, undersigned, Denis Laffecteur, declare and acknowledge that in addition to the causes set out in the deed under private signature of the other parts, for which Mr. Boyveau had granted me an annual gratuity of fifteen hundred pounds, I was to serve Mr. Sieur Boyveau as a clerk and help him with my services in that capacity, without any other remuneration; but that other occupations and circumstances did not allow me to fulfill such condition; that consequently, I asked Mr. Boyveau to pay me, as a lump sum, the amount of three thousand pounds, for the reason of the loan I made to him of my name, both for the past and for the future, not intending in any way to derogate in this regard from the clauses and commitments by me contracted and stated in the above deed of July 1, 1778, which sum of three thousand pounds M. Boyveau actually has paid me and under the conditions hereinabove expressed, in cash of gold and silver with legal tender, of which and all things above I give receipt. In Paris, February 18, 1787. — Signed: Laffecteur.

§ 1.23.2. Laffecteur obtains the permission to distribute his Anti-Syphilitic Syrup and exclusive rights in his trademarks

Decision of the King's State Council

Extracted from the Records of the State Council

of September 12, 1778

On the Request presented to the King, being in his Council, by Mr. Denis Laffecteur, former Inspector of Foods, stating that he is the owner of an Anti-Syphilitic Syrup, by which, without the help of Mercury, the cure of the most inveterate venereal diseases can be obtained; that the public having been too often deceived by remedies whose effects did not correspond to the promises of those who announced them, the Supplicant has asked, above all, that it should not only be subjected to tests that guarantee the fidelity of the declaration he made that no ingredient drawn from the mineral kingdom enters into its composition, but also that its effectiveness has been verified by experiments made under the eyes of the Magistrates; . . .

The King being in his Council, with regard to the aforementioned Request, has allowed and allows Denis Laffecteur, to sell and distribute the Anti-Syphilitic Syrup throughout the Kingdom, on the condition nevertheless of not delivering it for the treatment of venereal diseases unless under the prescription of those professionals of the art, and administering it under their inspection only, and in particular in the city and suburbs of Paris, only under the inspection and direction of Messrs. Andry and Paulet, doctors of the faculty and members of the Royal Society of Medicine, whom His Majesty has committed and commits to monitor the effects of said remedy, and report to the Society. Consequently, His Majesty has authorized and authorizes Laffecteur to mark the bottles that will contain the Anti-Syphilitic Syrup, with his name, his seal, or such other mark as he will decide; His Majesty makes very express inhibitions and prohibitions to all persons from counterfeiting the mentioned trademark, under the penalties [applied to] counterfeiting, and of a fine of one thousand pounds, half to be attributed for the benefit of His Majesty, and half for the benefit of the mentioned Laffecteur; His Majesty orders that the Lieutenant General of Police of Paris, and the Intendants and Commissioners present in the provinces, take care, each within their own attributions, of the execution of the present Decision, concerning which all necessary Letters will be sent. Done at the King's State Council, His Majesty being there, held at Versailles, September 12, 1778.

§ 1.23.3. A French Court acknowledges the rights of pharmacists to use the designation of a medicine made and sold by a competitor, even if that designation contains the latter's name, provided that designation has become a necessary designation and additional elements prevent the public from being misled

Court of Appeals

January 31, 1860

The secret remedy that has fallen into the public domain may be announced and distributed by all pharmacists under the name given to it by the inventor and which is instrumental to the use it designates.

Reversal, on the appeal of Mr. Charpentier and company, of a Judgment rendered by the Imperial Court of Paris, May 15, 1858, in favor of Mr. Giraudeau Saint-Gervais.

The Court, . . .

Under Articles 3 of the law of July 5, 1844, and 32 of the law of 21 germinal year xi [April 11, 1803];

Whereas the dispute between the parties did not have for object the exploitation of a remedy according to its formula, which was on the contrary recognized as pertaining to common domain in pharmaceutical matters, but only the name under which this remedy would be designated in the advertisements by pharmacists Charpentier and company;

Whereas, when it is not disputed that the manufacture and use of an industrial product have entered the public domain, like those of a medicine in the common domain of pharmacy, it must be recognized that they enter it with the option open in the latter case to all pharmacists to advertise and distribute it under the name that is instrumental to the use that it designates; that to reserve to the inventor or to the first maker the exclusive right to use this designation would be to maintain for his profit, as far as the advertisement and the distribution of this drug are concerned, a monopoly that the law denies him; that in particular, by obliging pharmacists to change the name under which a remedy is known to substitute to it a new and particular name, one would risk putting them in contradiction with the rules of their profession and exposing them to the reproach of advertising a secret medicine;

Whereas the application of these principles may extend to the designation that comprehends the inventor's name, if, in such use and by the inventor's own initiative, his name has become the necessary element of the designation of a product; that, undoubtedly, its competitors could not, without infringing the rights that continue belonging to him, to borrow his name in such a way as to mislead the public as to the individuality of the manufacturer and the origin of the products; but that on condition that they give sufficient information to prevent any misunderstanding in this regard, they may, in certain cases, be permitted to use, as a reminder of a formula fallen into the public domain, the designation that has become usual [in association] with the name that would have become a necessary part of it;

And whereas, in fact, Charpentier and company, whose right of manufacturing and distributing the remedy in question in these proceedings has not been challenged, have asked in their concluding remarks to be authorized to use the denomination of *depurative vegetable Syrup according to the Boyveau-Laffecteur formula,* on the condition that they always write their advertisements and labels in a way that clearly explains the origin of the product as being their laboratory, and not that of Boyveau-Laffecteur's successors.

Whereas, without examining whether the use of this name had become the usual and necessary element of the product's designation, the imperial court of Paris, basing itself, not on an assessment of facts and intentions, but on the principle of an absolute right of ownership that it recognized in Giraudeau in relation to that designation, drew the general consequence that any use by a competitor of that name, even if only as a reminder of a formula, is a means of avoiding the principle and an abuse, forbade Charpentier and company from using it in any form whatsoever, and only allowed them to exploit the formula of the remedy in question by attributing to it a name which is particular to them; in which the mentioned court violated the aforementioned articles;

Reverses, etc.

Holds, etc.

Hereby decided and pronounced, etc. — Civil Chamber.

Figure 10 Advertisement of the True Vegetable Syrup of Boyveau-Laffecteur, "currently made by Dr. Giraudeau de Saint-Gervais, only successor of Boyveau-Laffecteur." On top, one reads the warning (in Latin): cave dolum (beware of fraud). In the bottom, the ad reads: "As there are dangerous counterfeits, it is essential to pay attention to the parchment envelopes as well as to the ribbons bearing the signature of Doctor Giraudeau de Saint-Gervais. The name of Boyveau-Laffecteur is imprinted on the glass and on the capsules." The tropical motives surrounding the text evoke the use of the anti-venereal medicine by sailors returning to France from distant, exotic places. Extracted from Almanac Bottin du Commerce, *Paris, 1854.*

§ 1.24. A US DISTRICT COURT ACKNOWLEDGES THE EXCLUSIVE EFFECTS OF A GEOGRAPHICAL INDICATION FOR MEDICINAL SALTS—1898

Carlsbad Sprudel Salt *was the designation of a mild laxative and diuretic medicine whose main ingredient was imported from Carlsbad, Germany. The product gained significant reputation and commercial success in the United States in the nineteenth and early twentieth centuries. For that reason, as it happens, it was subject to frequent counterfeiting. The city of Carlsbad has been successful in claiming the necessary correspondence between the city's name and the genuineness of the mineral water and of the medicinal salts it exported to the United States. One of the points the city made was that its name had not become a generic designation, unlike Epsom, whose name was taken from the spring waters that are found in the English city of Surrey. The generalized use of Epsom salts for magnesium sulfate led to the loss of its geographical meaning as an element of differentiation.*

City of Carlsbad v. Kutnow, 68 F. 794 (1895), as cited in *Pillsbury-Washburn Flour Mills Co., Ltd., v. Eagle*, 86 F. 608 620 (1898) (Circuit Court of Appeals, Seventh Circuit, April 5, 1898).

In *City of Carlsbad v. Kutnow*, 68 Fed. 794 [1895], the city of Carlsbad, as the proprietor of the Carlsbad springs, had for years evaporated the waters into salts, which were sold as "Carlsbad Sprudel Salz." Defendants, who were New York druggists, made a similar salt, without the use of the genuine Carlsbad water, and sold it under the name "Improved Effervescent Carlsbad Powder." Judge Wheeler, in granting the injunction, said:

> "If any artificial salts have come to be known by the name of 'Carlsbad Salts' from similarity or otherwise, of course the defendants have the same right to sell such salts by that name that they have to sell anything by the name by which it is known. But there is no real evidence to that effect. And if the defendants procured genuine Carlsbad waters or salts, and put them up in different forms, or with other Ingredients, to improve their taste or vary their effects, these words would be truthful, and they would seem to have a clear right to use them in such preparations: but the plaintiffs' proof tends to show that the defendants' salts are not, in substance, genuine Carlsbad salts, in any form, and the leading defendant has been a witness, and has not assumed to state—and, although the proof must be within their reach, none has been produced to show—that their salts come direct, in any form, from the Carlsbad springs. The impression left by the evidence is that they do not, but are artificial. No proof has been brought showing that the plaintiffs have used the name of 'Carlsbad' upon any but genuine Carlsbad Sprudel Salts. As the case stands here, the defendants appear to be using the name 'Carlsbad' upon artificial salts having no connection with that name, and to be using it only because of its connection with the genuine Carlsbad Sprudel Salts. Carlsbad, with its springs, is far away. This use of the name in connection with a preparation so similar to this well-known product of them is some representation that it is a genuine product of them. Calling the powder 'Improved Carlsbad' is a direct representation that genuine Carlsbad powder has been taken to be improved upon: and calling it also 'effervescent' is a representation that the improvement is in the effervescence. This is putting the plaintiffs' mark, to some extent, upon the defendants' salts, and is calculated to lead customers to think they are the salts of the plaintiffs. Such deception would be actionable at law, and is preventable in equity. *McLean v. Fleming*, 96 U. S. 245; *Menendez v. Holt*, 128 U. S. 514, 9 Sup. Ct. 143; *Improved Fig Syrup Co. v. California Fig Syrup Co.*, 4 C. C. A. 264, 54 Fed. 175: *Von Mumm v. Frash*, 56 Fed. 830. Allusion has been made to this word being the name of the city, to which ordinarily an exclusive right cannot be acquired: but it is also the name of these peculiar springs, and gives the name to their products."

And on appeal (35 U. S. App. 750. 18 C. C. A. 24, and 71 Fed. 167), the court, in affirming the order, by Judge Lacombe said:

"The Carlsbad Sprudel Salts in either form, therefore, is a natural product, and well known as such; and there is no proof in the case that the complainants have used the name 'Carlsbad' upon anything but genuine Carlsbad Sprudel Salts. And we concur with the circuit judge in the finding that there is no evidence in the record that any artificial salts have, from similarity or otherwise, come to be known by the name of 'Carlsbad,' as is the case with the Epsom salts, a term now generally applied to sulphate of magnesia whether such sulphate of magnesia comes from Epsom or not. Under these circumstances the complainant, the city of Carlsbad, has the right to indicate the origin of these natural salts by its own name, and would be entitled to the aid of a court of equity to prevent anyone from using that name to induce the public to accept as genuine artificial) salts not the product of the Carlsbad springs."

Figure 11 In this ad, a medieval parade announces the benefits of Carlsbad Sprudel Salt, which "is obtained from the Sprudel Spring, By evaporation." Published in the North American Review*, January 1891.*

§ 1.25. THE CASE OF VASELINE, DESIGNATION OF PETROLEUM JELLY: THE VICISSITUDES OF SECURING TRADEMARK RIGHTS IN POPULAR MEDICINES

"Vaseline" is one example of a trademark that may have become too successful in luring customers. Created in 1872 by Robert A. Chesebrough, inventor of the medicinal substance it designates, it was introduced in the specification of the patent, issued in that same year, in the United States, as a simple and practical word. Actually, the inventor was just following the tradition initiated several years before in England, where inventors would include in the specifications the fanciful names they gave to the results of their ingenuity.

The years passed by, and with the help of intensive advertisement, soon Vaseline became a very popular product—as well as a brand—not only in the United States but also in Europe, and, later, in other Continents.

With great success usually comes great infringement. And through the years, the company Chesebrough founded to manufacture and sell Vaseline saw itself frequently engaged in litigation to secure proprietary rights in its brand. In that, the company had mixed success.

*In the United States, in 1874, the word "Vaseline" was acknowledged as a valid trademark by the Supreme Court of the State of New York and was registered as such in 1878. But not all were persuaded that the word presented the characteristics of a trademark. In 1909, Justice Timlin, of the Supreme Court of Wisconsin, in his dissenting vote in a case involving the word "Carbolineum," expressed his reservations as to the registrability as trademarks of words (like "Vaseline") that, in his view, had become generic designations of products as a result of their having been used by the inventor himself as if they were necessary. He acknowledged that this matter had been overcome in a precedent case (*In re Chesebrough Mfg. Co.'s Trade-mark, *19 Rep. Pat. Cas. (1902) 342), but even in that very opinion, a voice of dissent had been heard.*

In the United Kingdom, the result was different. In 1901, the Chancery Division of the High Court of Justice, based on case law, held that the use in patent specifications of the word "Vaseline" for indicating the product obtained by the claimed process had per se *made of it a generic designation.*

But Vaseline's saga did not stop there. In France, in 1891, based on the doctrine of laches, a court held that the inertia of the Chesebrough Manufacturing Co. in enforcing its trademark rights in the word "Vaseline" against a significant number of competitors who announced and sold Vaseline products had caused the loss of property.

In 1910, the magazine THE CHEMIST AND DRUGGIST *brought the news that in Germany, a court held that the word "Vaseline" had become a generic name, and thus it was unenforceable as a trademark.*

Today, "Vaseline" is a registered trademark in the United States, owned by Conopco Inc. (part of the conglomerate Unilever). The most recent entry in the USPTO's trademark registry appears as "The Healing Power of Vaseline," Reg. no. 5360219, of December 19, 2017. "Vaseline" is also registered, in the nominative and figurative forms, under the Madrid System, with the designation of about twenty countries.

§ 1.25.1. Excerpts from the specifications of Robert A Chesebrough's 1878 US Patent for new products from petroleum, where he employed the term "Vaseline" several times to designate his invention

United States Patent Office

Robert A. Chesebrough, of New York, N.Y.

Improvement in Products from Petroleum

Specification forming part of Letters Patent No. 127,568, dated June 4, 1872 (excerpts)

To all whom it may concern:

Be it known that I, Robert A. Chesebrough, of the city, county, and State of New York, have invented a new and useful Product from Petroleum, which I have named "Vaseline;" and I do hereby declare that the following is a full, clear, and exact description thereof, which will enable those skilled in the art to make and use the same.

The substance from which Vaseline is made is the residuum of petroleum left in the still after the greater part of the petroleum has been distilled off. . . .

My method of making Vaseline is by filtering the aforesaid petroleum residuums through bone-black, according to my process described in my Letters Patent dated August 22, 1865, ...

Vaseline is the product of the filtration of the said residuums through bone-black, and varies in color as it comes from the filter. . . .

Vaseline is a thick, oily, pasty substance; . . .

When paraffine-oil is filtered by my process the result is a better article of paraffine-oil, and not vaseline. It will, therefore, be seen that vaseline cannot be made from any of the distilled products of petroleum, but only from the residuums of the still which have not been vaporized; and hence it is a distinct substance by itself, is a new article of manufacture, and is useful for various purposes.

Vaseline is especially useful in currying, stuffing, and oiling all kinds of leather. It is also a good lubricator, and may be used to great advantage on all kinds of machinery. The finest grade of vaseline is also adapted to use as a pomade for the hair, and will be found excellent for that purpose, one of its chief recommendations being that it does not oxidize. . . .

Claim.

What I claim as my invention, and desire to secure by Letters Patent, is—

The new article of manufacture named by me "Vaseline," substantially as herein described.

§ 1.25.2. A British court denies trademark protection to the word "Vaseline" because, having being used by its inventor in the patent specifications as the product's indication, has become a necessary, generic designation

In the High Court of Justice—Chancery Division.

February 9 and 12, 1901.

Before Mr. Justice Buckley.

In the Matter of the Cheseborough [sic] Manufacturing Company's Trade Marks. In the Matter of Pearson's Application to Register a Trade Mark.

Trade Mark.—Application for registration of "Vasogen."—Refusal.—Appeal.—Motion to remove "Vaseline."—Old mark.—Distinctive word.—Name of article made according to patented process.—Order made to remove "Vaseline."—Registration of "Vasogen" refused.—Trade Marks Registration Act, 1875, section 10.

An application having been made for the registration of "Vasogen" as a Trade Mark in Class 8 for chemical substances prepared for use in medicine and pharmacy, the Comptroller required the Applicant to obtain the consent of the registered proprietors of the Trade Mark "Vaseline," which had been registered as an old mark in 1877 in Classes 3, 4, 47, and 48 for certain goods including "Vaseline," six years' user being claimed, and, such consent not being obtained, he refused the application. The Applicant appealed, and the appeal was referred to the Court. The Applicant moved to remove the Trade Mark "Vaseline" from the Register on the ground that the word at the date of registration denoted petroleum jelly filtered through animal charcoal, and not the goods of a particular firm. He relied particularly on the use of the words in certain Patents taken out by the predecessor of the registered proprietors and in the application for registration. The proprietors alleged that the word indicated goods of their manufacture.

Held, that at the date of registration the word "Vaseline" indicated petroleum jelly as manufactured by a particular process, which had been protected by Patents, and that it accordingly was not distinctive within the meaning of section 10 of the Trade Mark Regulation Act, 1875. The Register was ordered to be rectified by the removal of the Trade Mark "Vaseline." The appeal as to "Vasogen" was refused for similar reasons.

Linoleum Manufacturing Company v. Nairn (L.R. 7 Ch. D. 834) followed. .

. .

Buckley, J.—This is a motion by Mr. Edward Theodore Pearson to rectify the Register of Trade Marks by removing the Trade Mark "Vaseline." The mark in question was registered in the year 1877, and therefore under the Act of 1875. The language of section 10 of the Act was:—"For the purpose of this Act a Trade Mark consists of (*inter alia*) any special or distinctive word or words"; and there are numerous authorities to show that those words mean distinctive in the sense that the Trade Mark shall indicate the manufacturer or trader who used the mark and not indicate the goods which are sold under the mark. It must be distinctive of the person who uses the mark and not distinctive of the goods which are sold under it. The question, therefore, which I have to try is whether in 1877 the word "Vaseline" was distinctive in that sense. The great difficulty in the case to my mind is that, being purely a question of fact, the evidence which is before me is meagre and unsatisfactory to the last degree.

The facts are these: that in the year 1865 the predecessor in title of the Respondents, by Mr. Newton, to whom he communicated the invention, took out certain Letters Patent in this country for an improvement in refining petroleum and other hydrocarbon oils. In his Specification he describes the invention as relating to the refining of petroleum and other hydrocarbon oils by filtration through animal charcoal, sometimes termed bone black, wood charcoal, or other filtering medium. What he claimed was "the refining or purifying of petroleum or other hydrocarbon oils by filtration through animal or wood charcoal or other filtering material or materials in the manner substantially as herein described." In 1871, according to the affidavit of Colonel Cheseborough [*sic*], the Respondents, or rather their predecessor in title, coined the word "Vaseline." . . .

I arrive therefore at the conclusion of fact here that the word "Vaseline," as used in 1877, is, upon the language of the documents to which Colonel *Cheseborough* [*sic*] was a party, namely, the American Patent of 1872, the English Patent of 1874, the "Trade Marks Journal" of 1877, used as indicating, not the manufacture of a particular firm but the petroleum jelly as manufactured by a particular process, and I do not think that there is anything in the evidence which assists me in arriving at any other conclusion.

Now, if that is a right conclusion of fact, then I have to apply the doctrine of the *Linoleum Company v. Nairn*, and other cases of that kind. In the *Linoleum* case floorcloth, of course, was made and known at that date, just as petroleum jelly was known at this date; but linoleum floorcloth, that is to say, floorcloth manufactured according to a particular patented process by the use of oxidised oil, was a new thing, and could only be made under the Patent. When the Patent had expired anybody was at liberty to make linoleum floorcloth; and Mr. Justice Fry, in the *Linoleum* case, asked, what were they to call it unless they called it "Linoleum?" So here, the Patents under which the filtration of petroleum jelly through animal charcoal was protected have expired, and anybody may make petroleum jelly prepared by that process. I ask myself what could they call it? They could only call it "Vaseline," if I am right in thinking that "Vaseline" meant the thing made by that process and not the thing made by that person. It is no doubt a serious matter. This Trade Mark has been on the Register since 1877, and it is a strong measure, no doubt, to remove it, and I have hesitated very much about the case; but I cannot see that the persons who maintain the right to the mark have satisfied the words of the Act of 1875 that the word was distinctive in the sense in which that word was used. I must therefore make an Order to rectify the Register by taking off "Vaseline."

§ 1.25.3. No matter how generalized the use of a trademark has been, its owner is entitled to its protection—so has decided a United States Court

In *Burnett v. Phalon* (June 1867. N. Y. Super. Ct.)

Per Pierrepont, J. "Every man has a right to the reward of his skill, his energy, and his honest enterprise; and when he has appropriated, as his trade-mark, letters combined into a word before unknown, and has used that word, and has long published it to the world as his adopted trade-mark, he has acquired rights in it which the courts will protect."

[Comment by Rowland Cox:

> The decision in *Burnett v. Phalon* is also of pronounced interest and value, as emphasizing the principle that although an article may have no other name that that which is claimed as a trade-mark, the name may be monopolized. There are considerations of great weight that tend to negative the correctness of this conclusion, but those which make in favor of it have been generally accepted in the United States. The coined words, "BOVILINE," "SAPOLIO," "CARBOLINE," "VA-SELINE," etc., may be mentioned as illustrations.]

§ 1.25.4. Justice Timlin, of the Supreme Court of Wisconsin, in a dissenting vote, expressed his reservations as to the registrability as trademarks of words (like "vaseline") which, in his view, had become a generic designation

Avenarius v. Kornely

Supreme Court of Wisconsin

May 11, 1909

As I understand the case last cited, there is properly deducible therefrom the fourth proposition of the syllabus, viz.:

> "When the right to manufacture became public, the right to use the only word descriptive of the article manufactured became public also."

This rule is not limited to the case of patented articles upon which the patent has expired. Such cases are merely illustrative of the rule—a narrow application of the more general rule that the right to use the only word descriptive of the article manufactured is the right of the public. It cannot make any difference how this word became the only word descriptive of the article. . . . It is not because there were letters patent, which letters have expired, that the public may make and sell the article by its patented designation, but because the designation of the patented article has become descriptive and has become the name by which the article is known.

In *In re Chesebrough Mfg. Co.'s Trade-mark,* 19 Rep. Pat. Cas. (1902) 342, this question is suggested in the majority opinion at page 353, but it was not decided, because there was evidence that the word "*Vaseline*" was used originally to denote the goods manufactured by the Chesebrough Company. In the opinion of Justice Cozens-Hardy it is said:

> "I have reluctantly come to the conclusion that it appears from the appellant's own evidence that the word '*Vaseline*' was an invented word to describe an invented

> thing, and, if so, I think it follows that any one was at liberty to make the invented article, which was not protected by patent in England, and at liberty to call it by the name attributed to it by the inventor. In the case of *Linoleum Mfg. Co. v. Nairn*, L. R. 7 Ch. D. 834, Mr. Justice Fry applied this principle to the case of a patented article after the expiration of the patent, but I think it cannot be limited to that case."

No one can claim protection for the exclusive use of a trade-mark or trade-name which would practically give him a monopoly. . . .

It may be said that the inventor of a new compound who at the same time invents a new name for such compound does not thereby prevent others from devising other new and fanciful names for the same compound, and this is true. This privilege on the part of others would be of little practical use to them, but that is quite immaterial. The real objection is that such use of a newly coined word as a trade-mark enables the owner at once to describe the new compound by that name without reference to who makes it or where it is made, and at the same time appropriate that word as a sign to the public that the particular goods so marked are not of or belonging to the class or genera indicated by that name, but are distinguished therefrom as the superior product in that line of his own skill, industry, or honesty. These two uses of the invented word are to me inconsistent. If so, it follows that the exclusive use must yield. This is my first ground of dissent.

§ 1.25.5. Decision by a French Court: the trademark "Vaseline" has been abandoned due to laches

The Chesebrough Manufacturing Company v. Agnel.—Vaseline case.

Court of Appeals of Seine (9th ch.), June 4, 1891.

A foreigner who has registered in France his trademark consisting of a fanciful name must be considered as having renounced the benefit of legal protection when he has allowed a certain time to pass without protesting against the filing by third parties of trademarks identical or similar and against the use that has caused that fanciful name to become the common and new designation of the product of its manufacture.

The Court.

Whereas, according to the records of Danlos, bailiff in Paris, dated November 19, 1888, the Chesebrough Manufacturing Company, of New York, has seized, in the shop of Agnel, perfumer, avenue de l'Opéra, no. 16: 1st a cardboard box containing one soap and bearing the following label: "Vaseline soap;" 2nd a jar covered with a label bearing these words: "Vaseline Cream or Coldcream Vaseline;" 3rd a bottle also covered with a label on which the words: "Vaseline Oil" are written;

Whereas that company, claiming to be the owner of a trademark consisting of the names "Vaseline," sued Agnel before the Court as accused of counterfeiting and of offering for sale products bearing a counterfeit trademark;

Whereas Agnel recognizes the facts attributed to him, but concludes that they should be dismissed outright on the basis that the company, in his view, has no longer any private right over the mark that it claims, and counterclaims the payment of 4,000 francs as damages;

On the main issue:

Whereas the word "Vaseline" was coined by Chesebrough who first used it, in 1871, in America, to designate a fat extracted from the residues of petroleum distillation;

That this word was duly registered as a trademark on March 23, 1878 and June 14, 1881, in the United States Patent Office, by the Chesebrough Manufacturing Company, which was recognized as its owner by a judgment of the Supreme Court of the State of New York of August 3, 1874;

Whereas the record shows that the plaintiff or its owners, in 1876 and during the following years, sold in France through the intermediary of Messrs. Faugera, Lancelot and Du Chambon, their representatives, under the name of "Vaseline," mineral fat extracted from the residues of petroleum distillation;

That the company filed regularly, on May 26, 1880, at the secretariat of the Commercial Court of Seine, in accordance with article 6 of the law of June 23, 1857 and the Convention of August 16, 1869, its trademark consisting of the name "Vaseline;"

Whereas, under these conditions, the Chesebrough Manufacturing Company can indisputably claim in France, against any person and by all legal means, the ownership of the trademark "Vaseline," unless it is demonstrated that it has abandoned it;

Whereas it is not alleged that it has ever expressly waived its rights;

That it is only necessary to inquire whether, as Agnel claims, it has tacitly abandoned them to the public domain;

Whereas, according to its own declarations, the Plaintiff only protested towards the end of 1888 against the use that was made of its trademark by various manufacturers or merchants for designating products similar to its own and not originated in its manufacture;

That it was only on December 1, 1888, that it invited, by registered letter, Agnel and several other merchants to stop using the designation "Vaseline;"

Whereas, however, from July 12, 1878, Mrs. Cottance, manufacturer of perfumery in Pantin, had filed with the Secretariat of the Commercial Court of Seine a label bearing the following inscription: "Vaseline Perfumery," taking the care of indicating that the word "Vaseline" was intended to serve as its trademark;

Whereas if this filing could not make Mrs. Cottance acquire the exclusive property of the designation "Vaseline" because of the use that had been made previously by the representatives of the Chesebrough Manufacturing Company, it should be noted however that the latter had not launched any lawsuit against the mentioned woman nor did it protest at all against the intent, thus expressed by her by means of a public act, to claim a private right in the designation that is the matter of this litigation;

Whereas three other filings claiming the word "Vaseline" as a trademark, have been made: the first, on March 7, 1883, by a Mr. Salomon, commercial agent in Lyon; the second, on December 27, 1887, by a Mr. Favert, chemist in Lyon; the third by a Mr. Alexandre, a perfumer in Paris, 9, avenue de l'Opéra, without the Chesebrough Manufacturing Company having pursued the applicants or sent them any complaint;

Whereas Agnel still produces a certain number of circulars, notices on prices and invoices from which it follows that several merchants have offered to the public and delivered to himself, after the filing of May 26, 1880, and prior to the seizure of December 19, 1888, products similar to those of the plaintiff, under the name "Vaseline" and that, in particular, he received on various occasions, in 1883, deliveries of products sold under that designation by a Mr. Schmitz, then resident at rue de Dunkerque, 22, and to whom that company had not addressed any protest concerning the use that it thus made of the trademark that it claims today;

Whereas, finally, it has been established by the documents provided during the debates, and that it is moreover common knowledge that, shortly after the filing of this mark at the Commercial Court of Seine, French pharmacists began to sell, under the designation of "Vaseline," products that most of them have purchased from competitors of the Chesebrough Manufacturing Company;

Whereas the latter could not ignore the increasingly considerable distribution of these products;

That, however, it has never opposed the use made in pharmacy of the designation "Vaseline" to identify mineral fats not coming from its manufacture;

Whereas its inaction is all the more significant because vaseline, considered as a medicine, not being susceptible of being patented, the plaintiff could only secure its rights by claiming the fanciful designation given to this product by Chesebrough, its founder;

Whereas by neglecting to do so, by tolerating for several years the sale, under the name of "Vaseline," by a considerable number of pharmacists, of products not manufactured and not supplied by it, as well as by not taking any legal action against the manufacturers who had registered trademarks consisting in whole or in part in the name "Vaseline," nor against those who have made use of this designation in their trade, the plaintiff has tacitly waived the rights that could result from the filing of its mark at the registry of the Commercial Court of Seine;

Whereas, as a result of this prolonged inaction, the name "Vaseline" had become, since before 1888 and hence prior to the first legal procedures against Agnel, the common and new designation of the product sold under this name by a certain number of merchants and by all pharmacists;

Whereas Agnel, therefore, did not commit any of the crimes that are attributed to him;

That it is appropriate purely and simply to acquit him of the facts;

On the counterclaim:

Whereas the Chesebrough Manufacturing Company could not have ignored that the tacit abandonment by it of its trademark to the public domain has entailed the loss of all the rights resulting from the filing it had made on May 26, 1880;

That the notice it has filed constitutes an effective abuse of direct notice;

That in addition, the seizure of December 10, 1888, has caused damages to Agnel, for which he is owed compensation;

That the Court has the elements necessary to appreciate the importance of this damage and to determine the amount that will have to be paid to Agnel to compensate him;

For these reasons,

Acquits Agnel of the pleadings and declares the Chesebrough Manufacturing Company ill-founded in all of its conclusions;

Dismisses [the lawsuit];

Admits Agnel as a counterclaimant;

Orders the Chesebrough Manufacturing Company to pay him a sum of 1,000 fr. as damages;

And condemns it to pay all the costs.

§ 1.25.6. Vaseline deemed to be a generic designation in Germany

1910

"Vaseline" in Germany — A summons brought recently against Dr. Graf & Co., Berlin-Schoneberg, by the Chesebrough Manufacturing Co., New York, for alleged infringement of their registered name, has been dismissed by Berlin courts. The defendant firm designated their product as "American Vaseline," and the Court decided that the term "Vaseline" is a generic term indicating a salve-like product obtained from petroleum residues. An appeal by the plaintiffs has been rejected.

Figure 12 An ad of Vaseline by the legitimate trademark owner, The Chesebrough Manufacturing Co. (1899?).

§ 1.26. A SCOTTISH COURT DENIES TRADEMARK PROTECTION TO A COMPANY THAT, FOR ACHIEVING COMMERCIAL SUCCESS IN THE SALE OF A MEDICINE, SYSTEMATICALLY LIED TO CONSUMERS ALLEGING THE MEDICINES' FICTITIOUS ORIGINS IN AUSTRALIAN ABORIGINAL PEOPLE'S TRADITIONAL KNOWLEDGE

The book FROM BABYLON TO THE SILICON VALLEY *contains excerpts from an Opinion given by a Brazilian court, which dismissed a criminal case against three managers of YKK, a Japanese Company, on the ground that the plaintiff's claim was based on fraud: he had benefited from an administrative mistake by the Trademark Office and registered a well-known worldwide trademark—YKK for zippers or slide fasteners—that belonged to the Defendants.*[13] *The text that follows is not very different, except that it applies in the field of pharmaceuticals and involves a more sophisticated fraud. Here, the plaintiffs alleged that the Defendants infringed their trademark, designating a very effective pill for liver ailments. Their trademark had, like YKK, acquired notoriety as a result of intensive advertisement. But its reputation near consumers resulted from a false story—that the pills were the product of scientific improvement over a medicine developed by the aborigines of Australia, who had used it for centuries.*

The text that follows is an excerpt from the Opinion of Scotland's Inner House (a senior court, of second instance), which agreed with the judgment given by the Ordinary Lord (a judge of the Outer House, which is a court of first instance).

The essence of intellectual property, as it is said in From Babylon to the Silicon Valley, *is honesty in trade. Absence of honesty leads to the loss of protection. This is true across the whole spectrum of intellectual property, but, for obvious reasons, it is of more significance as far as medicines are concerned.*

Bile Bean Manufacturing Company v. Davidson

In the Court of Session of Scotland.

Inner House—Second Session.

October 17, 1905, and June 12 to 15, and 26, and July 20, 1906

Trade Name.—"Bile Beans."—"Passing off."—Application for Interdict against Respondent using same trade name.—Complainers' advertisements containing false statements.—Trade name used in fraudulent trade.—Secondary meaning.—"Bile Beans" found not to have acquired a secondary meaning.—Sufficient distinction between Respondent's goods and Complainers' goods.—Interdict refused.

In 1899 the B. B. Co. started to sell in the United Kingdom liver pills which they called "Charles Forde's Bile Beans for Biliousness." They spent large sums in advertising and at once acquired an extensive business. The word "Bean" had not been previously used in the United Kingdom for a bill except by one Smith who, in 1887, registered the words "Bile Beans" as his Trade Mark, and whose rights the B. B. Co. acquired. In America the word "Bean" is occasionally used for a pill. The advertisements of the B.B. Co. stated that the basis of their Bile Beans was an Australian Herb discovered by Charles Forde, and eminent scientist, after long research. These statements and others in the advertisements were false. They did not appear on the Complainers' pill-boxes. In 1904 D. began to sell liver pills under the name of "Davidson's Bile Beans." The B. B. Co. raised an action of Interdict against him.

Held, by Lord Ardwall L.O. [Lord Ordinary]—(1) that the Complainers' trade was a fraudulent trade, and that no action ought to be entertained by the Courts of Scotland to protect it or the name used in connection with it; (2) that the Complainers had not and never had any right to the exclusive use of the words

13. *Supra* note 2, at 146 *et seq.*

"Bile Beans," and that such words did not denote their manufacturers alone so as to exclude the use them by other traders; (3) that in any case D. had by the get-up of his boxes sufficiently distinguished his Bile Beans from those of the Complainers. Interdict was refused. The Complainers reclaimed.

The Second Division adhered to the Lord Ordinary's judgment, with expenses, upon the same grounds.

The Lord Justice Clerk.—The evidence in this case discloses the history of a gigantic and too successful fraud. The Complainers, who ask interdict against others, do so to protect a business which they have brought to enormous proportions by a cause of lying which has been persisted in for years. The scheme they formed was to delude the public into the belief that a valuable discovery had been made of a medical remedy, hitherto known only to certain savage tribes in a distant part of the world but known to them for ages, that the medicine had been perfected by aid of "the implements of modern scientific research," and that "the best laboratories and most modern plant had been requisitioned for compounding" this wonderful Australian vegetable substance. The place of the discovery, the mode of the discovery, the discovery itself, the instruments of research, the laboratories were all deliberate inventions without any foundation in fact. The story was that a certain *Charles Forde* who was declared to be a skilled scientist, had, while in Australia, noted the fact that the aborigines were markedly free from certain body ailments, and that by patient research and exhaustive investigation he had ascertained that this immunity was obtained by the use of a natural vegetable substance, whose properties for the cure of such ailments were extraordinary, and that as the result of his research this wonderful remedy was now given to the world. All this was, in every particular, undiluted falsehood. There was no such person as *Charles Forde*. No eminent scientist had been engaged in researches, and no one had gone to Australia and learned of a time-proved native cure. The truth was that the Complainers had formed a scheme to palm off upon the public a medicine obtained from drug manufacturers in America, as being the embodiment of the imaginary Australian discovery by the eminent scientist *Charles Forde*. Accordingly, having got their supplies from the American drug dealer, they proceeded to create a public demand by flooding this and other countries with advertisements in the press, and by placards, leaflets and pamphlets, in which the lying tale was repeated, often embellished with pictorial representations of the healthy savage and with pictures of the imaginary scientist (duly bearded and goggled) having the precious root pointed out to him by the Australian native. It was of importance in exploiting a fraud of this kind to get a catching name, and the only trace of discovery if the whole proceedings was that the Complainer *Fulford* thought out the alliterative name of "Bile Beans of Biliousness." Even this was not, in a true sense, original, the word "beans," having been in several cases applied to boluses in oval form, and the words "Bile Beans" having formed part of a trade mark taken out so early as 1887 by one *Smith*. This descriptive name has proved so valuable a possession that it is desired now to establish a monopoly of these words in combination, and to interdict anyone else from using them, on the footing that these words are not merely a descriptive name, but have come to designate the goods sold by the *Bile Bean Manufacturing Company* formed by the Complainers, and that any use of the name by others is a fraud upon that company. The claim is not for right in a trademark. The claim is made at common law for protection of a trade, by preventing a name appropriated to it being used by others. Now, this name, which the Complainers desire to have protection for, was the name chosen to designate the article about which all these lying statements were put forward, in order to make a trade by inducing the public to buy the article as being what the Complainers said it was, the article being one to which the description was given and the historical statements made in regard to it were wholly inapplicable. And it is to be observed that these statements were not of the mere puffing order, not of the "never failing," the "incomparable," and the "unique," "worth a guinea a box" order, but were statements of alleged facts carefully elaborated and intended to be accepted as facts from which persons might draw a sound inference that the article sold would effect to the buyers what it had done for ages to another race in another part of the world. The purpose was not to catch those who listened to mere assertion about a thing, but to convince them that they were buying a drug, which incontestable facts had demonstrated to be a valuable remedy.

I agree with the Lord Ordinary in holding that the Complainers being engaged in perpetrating fraud on the public, in describing and selling an article as being what it is not, cannot be listened to when they apply to a Court of Justice for protection. It is their own case, brought out in the evidence, that stamps the whole business with falsity. In bringing forward their case they were compelled to disclose, what otherwise might never have been known, and which was not to the Respondent, that the business they sought to protect was tainted with fraudulent representation. I should have no hesitation in so holding on general principles. No man is entitled to obtain the aid of the law to protect him in carrying on a fraudulent trade, but the cases quoted at the debate by the Lord Ordinary establish, as I think, very clearly that the Courts have in the past given effect to the principle which allows nothing to the man who comes before the seat of justice with a *turpis causa*. I do not enlarge upon the precedents as I have had an opportunity of seeing an Opinion, prepared by *Lord Stormonth Darling*, in which they are more fully gone into, and the Lord Ordinary has in his Opinion very fully quoted the cases. I therefore agree with the Lord Ordinary that the demand of the Complainers must fail. This view is sufficient for the disposal of the case. The Complainers cannot succeed in obtaining assistance from the law for a business based on unblushing falsehood for the purpose of defrauding the public into a totally false belief as to the origin and material of the goods they sell.

It is not necessary in these circumstances to refer to the other matters alluded to in the Lord Ordinary's Opinion, but I may say shortly that I entirely concur in the Lord Ordinary's view that the name used by the Complainers, "Bile Beans," was not a fancy name invented by them, but was a descriptive name, the word "bean," as applied to drugs made up in oval form, having been in frequent use for many years, and the words "Bile Beans" having formed part of a Trade Mark obtained as far back as 1887; and the Complainers went to the expense of buying out the Company holding it. There is I think no ground for holding that it was a fancy name invented by the Complainers, and they had not the original and never had the sole use of it. . . .

Lord Kyllachy.—I agree with your Lordship, and I also agree with the Lord Ordinary's judgment upon all its grounds. I do not think it necessary to say more.

Lord Stormonth Darling.—I am perfectly satisfied with the first and leading ground of the Lord Ordinary's judgment in this case. I would have contented myself with expressing my concurrence in the reasons he assigns so clearly for coming to that conclusion, were it not that some points in the argument have probably been developed more fully before us than they were in the Outer House. . . . And, if the principle applies [that misrepresentation may lead to disentitlement of the trade], I agree with the Lord Ordinary that the facts of the present case are amply sufficient to raise it. Mere puffing will not do. Exaggeration, however gross, of the merits and virtues of a remedy will not do. In the case of *Holloway*'s pills (13 Beavon 209) [see ....] it was held that the description of the inventor as "Professor," and the statement in advertisements that the pills were adapted to cure all diseases, did not amount to misrepresentation disentitling him to have an injunction against a piratical brother. But here what the Lord Ordinary well calls the "foundation fiction," of the discovery by an eminent scientist of a vegetable substance growing in Australia, which had long ago enabled the natives of that country to defy disease, and had at last been reproduced in the most convenient form as "Bile Beans"—this flagrant piece of invention was no casual lapse into hyperbolical language, but was circulated systematically from the very inception of the trade, and plainly formed the basis on which the whole superstructure rested. It is said that, to have effect of disentitling the trade to the protection of the law the misrepresentation must not be collateral, but must be contained in the Trade Mark (where it exists) or in the trade name itself. It affected the very essence of the article offered for sale, and was plainly implied in the name *Charles Forde*, that being the name of the so called "eminent scientist" who had made the "Valuable discovery." . . .

Lord Low.—I agree with the result at which your Lordships have arrived. I am of opinion that the false and fraudulent misrepresentations by which the Complainers have built their extensive business disentitles them to have that business protected by Court. I therefore think that the application should be refused.

On the question whether if there had been no fraud the Complainers would have been entitled to interdict against the Respondent, I desire to express no opinion. The question is not necessary for the disposal of the case, and seems to me to be attended with great difficulty.

§ 1.27. A US FEDERAL COURT OF APPEALS HELD THAT SELLERS OF MEDICINES ARE ENTITLED TO USE EXPRESSIONS OF BOASTING OR PUFFING ABOUT THE QUALITIES OF THE DRUGS

The text that follows is an interesting expression of authorities' indecision—in this case, a court—concerning the boundaries between veracity and fantasy (or false promises) in the business identifiers that apply to medicines.
It is also worth noticing that the court discussed some aspects of secrecy in medicaments, namely that secret medicines should be banned to the extent that the ignorance of their ingredients might put health at risk. In addition, from a procedural standpoint, the court also looked at the refusal by a witness to give the medicine's composition. The court admitted such possibility, particularly in view that the other party did not insist in its request of disclosure, but did not rule on that matter.

Dr. Peter H. Fahrney & Sons Co. v. Ruminer

(Circuit Court of Appeals, Seventh Circuit. April 16, 1907)

Appeal from the Circuit Court of the United States for the District of Indiana.

The appellant (complainant in the court below) sought by its bill to restrain the appellees from using as a trade word the words St. Bernard Alpenkrauter; averring that the use of such trade words by appellees, upon appellees' bottles, and in their advertising, is in the nature of unfair competition with appellant's medicines, sold for the same ailments, and known as Dr. Forni's Alpenkrauter.

The Master found that appellant was an organization existing under the laws of the State of Illinois; that appellees were citizens and residents of the State of Indiana; that appellant manufactured and sold a blood purifier; that in this business they succeeded their father, Peter Fahrney, who in turn had succeeded his father Jacob Fahrney, who in turn had succeeded his father Peter Fahrney—the latter of whom manufactured and sold in Maryland, Pennsylvania, and Virginia, a blood remedy made from herbs; that about 1888 the term Alpenkrauter was given to this remedy; that there is spent annually, for the advertising of this remedy about eighty thousand dollars; and that appellees' use of the words St. Bernard Alpenkrauter is unfair competition.

The Master stated his conclusions of law as follows:

1. The defendants' use of the words "St. Bernard Alpen Krauter" is unfair competition.
2. The complainant is entitled to the injunctive relief prayed in the Bill of Complaint unless it should be denied such relief for either one of the following reasons: (a) the complainant has not come into Court with clean hands . . .

But each of these reasons is, in my opinion, well founded, and because of each of these reasons complainant should be denied relief in this suit. As to reason (a); complainant's representations in its advertising matter practically guarantee that its medicine, Alpen Krauter, will cure—bring about the regaining of perfect health by the person using the remedy according to the printed directions on the carton—all the diseases named on complainant's carton. Such a remedy would be a miracle worker. These representations are coupled with the cautionary advice to intending patrons which, fairly interpreted, comes to this: Do not consult a physician and do not take counsel of a druggist, avoid a medical diagnosis of your ailment, ignore the recommendation of a trained pharmacist and use a 'secret remedy, the ingredients of which cannot be ascertained by chemical analysis and which ingredients the proprietor declines to reveal. In view of the public policy of this State on the subject of the practice of medicine and pharmacy as expressed in legislative enactment. 3 Burns' Ann. St. 1901,§ § 7318 to 7322 and 8136a to 8136g—notwithstanding sale of proprietary medicines is permitted in these statutes—and in view of the provisions of section 1995 of Burns' Ann. St. 1901, which makes it a criminal offense for one to prescribe a secret drug or medicine, the true nature of which he, if inquired of, does not truly make known and thereby endangers life, it must be said of complainant's methods that while they gain success commercially, ethically they are reprehensible; that while they may bring relief to credulous hypochondriacs they, notwithstanding, suggest, none the less, the ways of a thaumaturgist; that while they protect a recognized property right, they do not square with the doctrine of clean hands. . . .

And upon these findings, recommended that the bill be dismissed for want of equity, which in the Circuit Court, upon the hearing of the case, was done. Further facts are stated in the opinion.

Grosscup, Circuit Judge, after stating the facts, delivered the opinion:

We are of the opinion that the Master was not in error when he found that use of the words St. Bernard's Alpenkrauter was unfair competition; and we concur with him, that unless relief on account of unclean hands or laches is denied, the injunctive relief prayed for ought to have been granted. This reduces this case to the questions, Did appellant come into court with unclean hands? . . .

Upon the subject of unclean hands, it is our opinion that the conclusion of the Master is not supported by his finding of facts. It is true that the remedy was advertised by appellant as a cure for more diseases, perhaps, than any remedy could possibly cure. But this, in itself, is not unclean hands. Proprietary medicines, generally, promise more than they do; and for that matter licensed physicians often do the same. And with proprietary medicines, as with physicians, the object often is to give mere temporary help, under the belief of the patient that he is obtaining a cure. But whether this be an improper use of the public's confidence, or constitutes a practice against public policy, is a question to be decided by the state, through its legislature, and not by the courts under the equitable doctrine of unclean hands; for so far as this case discloses, proprietary medicines are lawful commerce, and are to be given the freedom of mere trade boasting that ordinary commerce is allowed to enjoy.

It is also true that the name Alpenkrauter connects the herb out of which it is made, in the imagination of the purchaser, with the Swiss Alps. But this is not holding out to the public that the particular root that went into the medicine was grown on the Alps. Indeed the representation in the advertising was that only a part of the herbs were imported, and a part were grown by Quakers in this country. There is therefore, in this particular, no such deception as constitutes unclean hands.

It is true also, that when appellee on cross-examination, seeking probably to find out whether any of the herbs were imported, asked of one of the appellants what were the ingredients of the medicine, that the witness was instructed not to answer; and that when the further questions were put of what particular herb houses or firms the herbs were purchased, the witness was again instructed not to answer; from which the Master draws the inference that the herbs were not, in fact, imported; otherwise the questions would have been answered.

But all the facts of this case borne in mind, the inference drawn by the Master is not tenable. True, the witness may have been instructed not to answer, because a truthful answer would have divulged that no part of the herbs were in fact imported, or would have given a clue to the names of witnesses from whom that testimony might have been obtained. But it is equally obvious that the motive of the refusal to answer might have been an apprehension that if the ingredients were disclosed, or there was disclosure of the names of the people from whom the ingredients were purchased, the whole value of the medicine as a secret preparation would be destroyed—a danger that the appellant was not willing to incur unless ordered by the court. And though a motion to compel an answer was filed, the hearing of that motion was continued to the final hearing, at which time it was not pressed. Now it is the right of a witness, apprehensive that some wrong will be done to his personal or property rights, to refuse to answer to a Master any question propounded, and to stand upon that refusal until the question raised has been determined by the court; and when such refusal is followed by the failure of the other party to press the question in court, the legal inference is not that the facts are as the proponent claims them, but rather, the proponent failing to press the motion, that he acquiesces in the right of the witness to refuse to answer—the record thereafter standing as if no such question had been put.

It is true, too, that in their advertising, appellant advised the public not to inquire for the Alpenkrauter at drug stores. But this does not justify, it seems to us, the inference drawn by the Master that it was meant as counsel not to consult a physician, and to ignore the recommendations of a trained pharmacist—the plain motive for the suggestion being, that the Alpenkrauter was not on sale at drug stores, and that to inquire for it would result in no purchase of appellant's medicine, but/might lead to the inquirer's being induced to purchase something else. Surely, so long as proprietary medicines are lawful commerce, precautions of this kind, obviously commercial, are not within the doctrine of unclean hands.

That the whole traffic in proprietary medicines may be injurious to the public; that remedies, the ingredients and formula of which are secret, should be forbidden; that the sick and ailing should be protected against every offer of help except those coming from licensed physicians and pharmacists, are each questions that the public can take up and decide for itself, through the legislative branches of its governments; but that not having been done as yet, by the public will thus expressed, it does not seem to us that the facts in the record before us furnish a reason why the courts should formulate a public policy, or withhold the aid of the law to protect this commerce, as yet lawful, against the unlawful piracy of another.

The decree appealed from will be reversed, with instructions to grant the injunction as prayed for in the bill.

§ 1.28. EUGENE POUILLET, A RENOWNED FRENCH JURIST, EXPLAINS HOW IN THE LATE NINETEENTH AND EARLY TWENTIETH CENTURIES, FRENCH COURTS SET THE CRITERIA FOR DISTINGUISHING PROTECTABLE PHARMACEUTICAL TRADEMARKS FROM GENERIC DESIGNATIONS

In the nineteenth and twentieth centuries, the possibility of acquiring exclusivity in medicinal trademarks was a point of contention in those countries that excluded pharmaceutical inventions from patentability. The main concern was that inventors could use the designations of new products in a way that, indirectly, accorded them the same exclusivity that patent laws were aimed at eliminating. The same contention also emerged in the context of pharmaceutical products whose patent protection had expired. We will see some of the debates posed by this dilemma in the United Kingdom and in the United States, where patents for pharmaceuticals have been available.

But the text that follows is specific to France, where until the middle of the twentieth century, exclusivity in the making of pharmaceutical products was acknowledged in connection with secret medicines, only, and under strict criteria, as it will be shown in tne second Chapter—but not with patents. Thus, inventors felt naturally tempted to use trademarks to achieve the same exclusivity that was denied to them by patent laws.

However, it should be noted that when Pouillet wrote this text, the doctrine of exhaustion, even if already accepted in some jurisdictions, was not yet entirely disseminated as it is today (to the point that it has been inserted in the TRIPS Agreement). In the nineteenth century, the exclusivity stemming from pharmaceutical trademarks was aggravated by the fact that the manufacturers of medicines could prohibit pharmacists from reselling their products in the absence of a licensing agreement.

The following text gives an account of several of these debates as they were settled by French courts along several decades in the turn of the nineteenth and twentieth centuries, in the words of one of the most illustrious French jurists, Eugène Pouillé. Significantly, the text provides a few examples that some of the debates are not confined to one place or one era. For example, the discussion on whether a name given by the inventor to the pharmaceutical product in the specification can be appropriated as a trademark has also taken place in the UK and the United States (see § 1.25). And the dispute over the use of the shop sign of the red cross was heard in 1612 and in 1910—in the latter case, not as an issue of appropriation, but of unfair competition because the red cross had already become a worldwide known designation for health care (the International Committee of the Red Cross having been founded in 1863, in Geneva).

Eugène Pouillet, Traité des Marques de Fabrique et de la Concurrence Déloyale en Tous Genres—1912 (excerpts)

> 119. *Quid* if the matter is pharmaceutical products? —What we say about the names of patented objects also applies to the names of pharmaceutical products. These products, as we know, cannot be patented: they never enter the private domain, and fall, as soon as they are invented, into the public domain, subject, of course, to existing statutes (statutes, be it said, ill-defined) on pharmacy and secret medicines. So when it comes to drugs listed in the Codex or inserted in the Bulletin of the Academy of Medicine—they are the only ones that case law does not consider secret medicines [note omitted]—it is up to all pharmacists to prepare, and, consequently, to sell them under the designation that science or usage has established [note omitted]. Anyone, however, who, engaging particularly in the manufacture of one of these products, wishes to distinguish it from similar products produced by his/her competitors, is entitled to designate it by a distinctive, special sign, and, consequently, even by a name of his/her own [note omitted]. It goes without saying, anyway, that nothing in the law prevents a doctor from transferring to a pharmacist the property of the name that he gives to certain medicinal products, even when they belong in the public domain [note omitted].
>
> 120. Case law.—Proprietary pharmaceutical names [note omitted].—It has been held, in this vein, and we will see that it is by application of the same principles: 1st that the right, belonging to any pharmacist, to manufacture and commercialize a drug falling within the common domain of pharmacy, generally carries with it the right to announce it and to sell it under the denominations that are used to designate it; this possibility ceases however in the event that the use of these names would constitute an act of unfair competition to the detriment of another manufacturer, by misleading the public as to the origin of the product; it is therefore with good reason that the courts forbid a pharmacist from using a designation such as *Tonic anti-mucus elixir* (*Elixir tonique anti-glaireux*), when this designation is entirely fanciful, and the drug is listed in the Codex under another name, and prohibit him to include the name of the first manufacturer, even by preceding it with the words: *following the formula of* (Rouen, March 27, 1862, Gage, and Civ. Rej., Mars 15 1864, Ann., 65.394); 2nd that, if it is permissible for any pharmacist to manufacture a drug that has fallen into the [public] domain of pharmacy, to advertise and distribute it under the names that have become customary for its designation, that is on the condition that such designation be not used in such a way as to mislead the public as to the origin of the product, and of not making of that an act of unfair competition against another manufacturer (Grenoble, August 31, 1876, Nègre, Ann., 76.225, *Elixir antiglaireux de Guillé*); 3rd that the pharmacist who has given a known remedy a particular name, such as *iron dragées*, has the right to oppose another pharmacist's selling similar products under the same name (Trib. Comm. Seine, March 16, 1878, Clin, Ann., 78.78); 4th that, if pharmacists cannot in any case claim the industrial property of compositions, even those discovered by them, nor make of those discoveries the object of a patent of invention, they at least have, like any manufacturer, a right to the property of the mark adopted by them to designate the products of their manufacture; this means that the law recognizes them as exclusive owners of their mark, aimed at making known to the public the true origin of the products it designates

(Aix, March 20, 1879, Fumouze, Ann., 81.179); 5th that although medicinal preparations can only be validly sold by pharmacists, the infringer of a trademark taken for a secret medicine cannot defend him/herself against an action for infringement, alleging that the owner of such mark is not a pharmacist. The ownership of a trademark is, in fact, absolute and independent of the use to which it can be applied. (Cr. Rej., May 27, 1898, Choffé, Ann., 98.289, *Vin Désiles*).

121. Case law.—Non-proprietary pharmaceutical names [note omitted].—It has been held: 1st that the composition, designated under the name of *Eau de mélisse des Carmes*, is so well known to the public that the way of making it is described in the works that deal with pharmacy; that in particular in the Codex, [of mandatory observation] for pharmacists, this product is described under the name of *Eau de mélisse des Carmes*, from which it follows that this name is really nothing else than a generic name designating a special drug whose name has perpetuated at the same time as the matter (Paris, November 10, 1843, Boyer (2), Ann., 76.15); 2nd that a name, such as the word *dosimetric*, applied to a pharmaceutical product, when it designates a therapeutic method rather than a special product, cannot be the subject of a private right, especially when the person who created it has left, for many years, its use free to all (Paris, June 30, 1892, Chanteaud, Ann., 94.92); 3rd that the name chosen to designate a pharmaceutical product, unlike any other product, must be a purely fanciful name, and not a necessary mark capable of revealing, by its mere enunciation, either the particular nature or the specific and therapeutic effect of the designated product; in particular, the term *antipyrine* cannot be used as a mark, because it is a simple derivation from the adjective *antipyretic* used for many years to designate a febrifugal substance, which, having replaced the purely scientific word *dimethyloxyquinezine*, has immediately entered the vocabulary of physicians, pharmacists and even the least educated patients (Paris, May 4, 1900, Piettre, Ann., 01.271); 4th that the judges of facts rightly refuse to admit a case of trademark infringement, when they realize that the filing of this mark (*pyramidon*) was only an expedient conceived to confiscate a new remedy that was about to be popularized under that name and thus secure a real monopoly in violation of the provisions of the law of 1844, which excluded pharmaceutical products from patentability. They rightly decide, under these conditions, that the name under which the inventor, by abbreviation of the scientific name (*dimethylamidopyrazolone*), has made the new product and its therapeutic properties known to the world could not be validly registered, when it was under this name, which has become usual, that the medicine entered medical practice (Lyon, February 23, 1907 and Crim. Rej., June 24, 1908, Soc. Farbwerke, Ann., 07.1.160 et 08.1.286); 5th that the name *Phenosalyl* constitutes a fanciful name, not indicating the nature of the product, given that, in addition to phenic acid and salicylic acid, it also contains lactic acid and menthol. It can therefore be the subject of a private trademark. However the creator of this mark cannot claim it, when, in fact, without opposition on his part, it being a scientific abbreviation of product's name, has naturally become its usual and necessary designation, no other simpler and more natural [term] occurring to mind. Acknowledging a private right in it would grant its creator, for the advertisement and the distribution of a drug, a privilege that the law refuses to him. (Paris, November 3, 1905, de Christmas, Ann., 06.39). . . .

742. Case law [note omitted]—It has been held: 1st that the law refuses any patent for the invention or the improvement of pharmaceutical compositions; it follows that the author of a new or improved remedy cannot reserve the ownership of the name under which he signaled it to the trade, because otherwise he would indirectly keep in connection with commercial distribution the same private right that the law denies him: however, common law protects him against maneuvers

employed by competitors to deceive the public as to the origin of the products offered for sale (Paris, May 12, 1857, Gage, Ann. [note omitted], 60.86); 2nd that the industrial product (in this case, the *Boyveau-Laffecteur syrup* [see § 1.23]), the manufacture and use of which have entered the public domain, can be advertised and sold by everyone under the name that is usually used to designate it, even though, in this denomination, appears the name of the inventor, if, in the use and as its consequence, his name has become the necessary element of the description of the product; it is necessary, however, by sufficient indications, to prevent any misunderstanding concerning the individuality of the manufacturer and the origin of the product (Cass., January 31, 1860, Giraudeau [note omitted], Ann., 60.108); 3rd that any pharmacist may, in accordance with statutory and case law, commercialize pharmaceutical products under the designation given to them by their first manufacturer, even if the latter's name falls is part of that designation; but the labels and leaflets must at least contain the information necessary to prevent any confusion on the origin of these products (Trib. civ. Lyon, December 4, 1867, Bresson [note omitted], Ann., 69.92).

743. Case law (continued)—It has been held, according to the same principles, but under a stricter application: 1st that the rights of the creator of a pharmaceutical product cannot extend to its exclusive commercialization, however it is with good legal standing that he claims the name under which he has made his product known, and forbids his competitors from using, in any way whatsoever, his own name: especially, when a medicinal product is known as *Regnauld's balsamic pectoral paste*, no one other than the inventor or his successors in title can use the same designation to designate a similar product (Paris, November 17, 1854, Frère [note omitted], *Teulet*, 4.131); 2nd that, if it is permitted for any pharmacist to prepare a drug according to the formula of its author and to sell it under the name (*epispastic paper*) that its author has given it, this right does not comprise an authorization to distribute their preparation under the name of the formula's author, given that such complement is not essential for the designation of the product (Paris, January 12, 1857, Albespeyres, Ann., 60.86); 3rd that, if it is permitted for all pharmacists to manufacture a medicine of which they believe they have the formula, it is on the condition that they use it under their own name, by giving it such a name that suits them and which would be particular to them; but they must be prohibited, by virtue of soundly applied principles of commercial property, from using in any way the name of others to recommend their products, if that name itself has not fallen into the public domain; the advertisement of this name, applied even only as a reminder of a formula, would only be a means of evading this principle: it also constitutes an unfair abuse which must be repressed as well as the direct use of the name of the first manufacturer (Paris, May 15, 1858, Giraudeau [note omitted], Ann., 60.100). . . .

796. Case law to the contrary [note omitted][14].—It has been held: 1st that if, in principle, any pharmacist has the right to use on the products that he prepares the name of the formula's original author, so as to indicate its nature more clearly, it is on the condition, however, that such name be preceded by the words: *prepared according to the formula*, written in clearly visible characters (Bordeaux, February 6, 1873, Torchon, Ann., 77.226); 2nd that, when the name of the manufacturer has become a necessary element in the description of the product, it is permissible for anyone to use it to designate this product, on the condition, however, of attaching a statement so as to prevent any confusion over the origin of the product:

14. Pouillet explains that there was one single decision that went in the other direction, holding that competitors could not even use the expression "according to the formula of . . . ."

especially, given that since the expiration of the patent obtained by Reynault, the pectoral paste, subject of the patent, has fallen into the public domain, it is lawful to indicate on the label that it is manufactured *according to the Reynault's formula* (Paris, March 14, 1876, Pauliac, Ann., 78.243); 3rd that, given that the vinegar formula invented by Bully is in the public domain, there can be no unfair competition in selling it under the name of: *Vinegar composed according to the recipe of Claude Bully prepared by ...,*" when moreover the bottles and labels used bear no resemblance to the bottles and labels of Bully's successors (Paris, March 28, 1878, Leroux (1), Ann., 78.239); . . .

1170. Unwanted use of its own prospectuses.—There is unfair competition:. . . 2nd in the fact, by a pharmacist, of distributing near the competitor's store a leaflet stating the following: "before entering your usual pharmacist, consult this current price in the interest of your purse and your health" (Trib comm. Melun, December 11, 1906, Baillet, Ann., 07.2.46). . . .

1425. Case law (continued).—Various designations [note omitted]; . . . 2nd that if the Red Cross sign cannot be the exclusive property of a pharmacist, it is certain that the affixing, on the storefront, of emblems similar to those inaugurated by the neighbor may be of a nature to divert the customer. The act of unfair competition is the act of a pharmacist taking the title and ensign of the Red Cross inaugurated by a colleague established in the same neighborhood, and distributing leaflets bearing this name with the clear intention of creating a confusion to attract all or part of his clientele is an unfair competition practice (Poiters, December 19, 1910, Blanc, Ann., 11.2.27).

§ 1.29. THE BRITISH PARLIAMENT REPORTS ON THE FREQUENTLY DECEPTIVE BRANDING OF SECRET (PATENT) MEDICINES

At the beginning of the twentieth century, a special committee of the House of Commons looked at the practices involving the commercialization of secret medicines. The report is interesting because it takes a snapshot of the situation at that time, prior to the adoption of a system of mandatory registration of drugs. After hearing thousands of witnesses, with a special focus on branding and advertising, the Parliament published a report very critical of pharmacists' marketing practices.

Report

August 4, 1914

The Select Committee appointed to consider and inquire into the question of the sale of Patent and Proprietary Medicines and Medical Preparations and Appliances, and Advertisements relating thereto; and to report what amendments, if any, in the Law are necessary or desirable:

Have agreed to the following Report:—

. . .

Invented Names of Drugs.

38. A new and ingenious method of defrauding the public by the sale of secret remedies has recently been devised. This consists of inserting a "reader"

advertisement—without the suffix "Advt." whenever the newspaper or magazine will consent to omit this—recommending for an ailment or a physical blemish a simple prescription containing one drug or preparation bearing a fancy name, "which any chemist will supply." This is an ordinary drug put up as a proprietary remedy under the fancy name, and sold, of course, at a fancy price. Sometimes these advertisements take the form of "Answers to Correspondents," or are given under the authority of a fictitious person, "Madame Lucie Robert," for instance. Examples of such fancy names are " pure colourless kalamax," "salith leaves," "stallax," "pheminol," "pergol," "pure bisurated magnesia," "boranium," " karox," "pilenta soap," "jetraline," "allacite of orange blossom," "tennaline," "carmarole," &c. These names are all invented words and should properly be printed with a capital initial letter, the proprietors having the exclusive right to their use as trade names. They are, however, printed in these disguised advertisements without capitals, to deceive the public into the belief that they are not proprietary articles, but are familiar drugs purchasable in small quantities at ordinary prices, whereas, in fact, they are only sold in a considerable quantity at a fancy price.

Changes in Name or Composition of Remedies.

39. It is not uncommon for the composition of a secret remedy to be altered without any change in the name. "Anti-kamnia," as we have said, was acetanilide in America, and is now phenacetin, and "Daisy'' powders were similarly changed. "Powell's Balsam of Aniseed" was repeatedly proved in courts of law to contain morphine. It now contains none. The same is true of "Mrs. Winslow's Soothing Syrup." The formula of "Pond's Arthriticus" was said to be altered by the addition of potassium bromide and salicylic acid. The powders in one packet of "Steedman's Powders" varied in weight from 1. to 4.5 grains. Sir Joseph Beecham informed us that "Beecham's Cough Pills" at one time contained morphia, as that was considered to be a necessary medicinal ingredient; that when the law compelled the word "Poison" to be put on the wrapper of preparations containing morphia, the morphia was taken out of the pills; then so small a quantity was put in again that it was "comparatively innocuous or perfectly innocuous," and therefore did not need to be labelled "Poison." That is, a potent drug was put in this remedy, taken out, and put in again, without regard to its medicinal effect, but solely because of the legal conditions under which it could or could not be sold.

§ 1.30. IN THE UNITED STATES, THE BRAND FOR ACETYLSALICYLIC ACID—ASPIRIN—GOES GENERIC (IN PART), AND IN THE UNITED KINGDOM, THE MEDICINE LOSES PATENT PROTECTION

Aspirin, *like* Vaseline, *has commanded a huge commercial success, to the point that consumers acquired the habit of using that word as synonymous with the medicine, regardless of its maker.*

Also, like the inventor and maker of Vaseline, *Chesebrough Manufacturing Co., the company that claimed to invent* aspirin, *Bayer Co., resorted to various intellectual property mechanisms to secure exclusivity in its trade. However, they have not obtained the same results.* Vaseline, *as seen above (see § 1.25), was held to constitute a trademark in the United States, even if the inventor used the word to designate the product in the patent specifications. By contrast, the term* aspirin, *which was not employed in the respective patent specifications, was understood as a generic name by District Judge Learned Hand interpreted consumers' acquisition habits as evidence that the word did not mean a particular manufacturer, and concluded it had lost the nature of a trademark. The judge also understood that Bayer's own techniques for designating the product—"aspirin of Bayer"—implied that the same product might be obtained from other sources.*

However, also by contrast with vaseline, aspirin *continued being protected as a trademark in almost the rest of the world—whereas* vaseline *has become generic outside the United States.*

Interestingly, the facts show that Bayer has not gained much from the patent protection obtained for acetylsalicylic acid. In the United States, as Judge Hand said, as well as in other countries, the infringement of the patent was so generalized that Bayer Co. had no means to fight it. Moreover, in the UK, Bayer lost the patent due to lack of novelty. So, the company, instead, preferred to focus on protecting its trademark.

Another interesting aspect is that Judge Hand concluded that aspirin *had been the subject of a sort of a two-tiered level of genericide. Indeed, he decided that the word* aspirin *could be used by all pharmaceutical companies in direct sales to consumers, but not in their sales to druggists. His idea was that, while consumers were ignorant that* aspirin *might be associated with one particular manufacturer, retailers had an obligation to be more knowledgeable of the true product's name. So, on the first level, manufacturers of acetylsalicylic acid could not designate the product as* aspirin *in their sales to druggists. For those,* aspirin *was a trademark. On the second level, druggists could use* aspirin *to designate the medicine in their retailing sales. For the latter, therefore,* aspirin *had become a generic designation.*

§ 1.30.1. A US District Court held "aspirin" as a generic trademark, in part

Bayer Co. v. United Drug Co.

272 F. 505 (S.D.N.Y. 1921)

United States District Court for the Southern District of New York April 14, 1921

Learned Hand, District Judge

In Equity. Suit by the Bayer Company, Incorporated, against the United Drug Company. Decree for plaintiff for part only of the relief sought.

This is a suit in equity between the plaintiff, a New York corporation, and the defendant, a Massachusetts corporation, to enjoin infringement of the plaintiff's common-law trade-mark "Aspirin." The bill was filed in May, 1917, and alleged that the plaintiff or its predecessors had since 1899 been selling throughout the United States a drug known as "acetylsalicylic acid," to which they had given the artificial trade-mark "Aspirin;" that they had expended large sums of money in popularizing the trade-mark so adopted, which had thus become a synonym for the acetylsalicylic acid manufactured by them; that on May 5, 1899, the plaintiff's predecessor had registered this trade-mark in the United States, and that the plaintiff held both the common-law and the registered mark by proper assignments; that the value of the amount in controversy was more than $5,000; and that the defendant had infringed the mark by using the word "Aspirin" in the sale of acetylsalicylic acid. The bill also charged the defendant with unfair trade in its advertisements of acetylsalicylic acid in the failure to discriminate sufficiently between its own manufacture and the plaintiff's. It prayed the usual injunction in such cases.

The answer denied the main facts and alleged that on August 1, 1898, the plaintiff's predecessor had applied for a patent for "acetylsalicylic acid' which issued on February, 1900, and expired on February twenty-seventh, 1917, and that thereafter the product fell into the public domain and with it the word, "Aspirin," which had become the name for the drug and therefore descriptive. It denied the charges of unfair trade in the bill.

The facts shown upon the trial were in substance as follows: The predecessor of the plaintiff was a German corporation engaged in the manufacture of chemical products, among them the drug in question, which was its own invention. On August 1, 1898, it applied for a patent in the United States, and therein described the drug as "acetylsalicylic acid." This patent issued on February 27, 1900, and therefore expired 17 years thereafter. It was eventually sustained by the courts, and in theory should have given the plaintiff or its predecessors a monopoly of production. This, however, was not the case, at least for a long time, and probably not altogether at any time. Large quantities of it were surreptitiously introduced into this country and sold, and while the amounts are necessarily somewhat uncertain, the plaintiff showed that considerably more than 220 tons had in fact been imported, of which it is fair to presume that all or nearly all reached the eventual consumer. This represented a very substantial proportion of the drug manufactured and sold by the plaintiff itself or its predecessors. It is impossible to ascertain how much, if any, of this infringing drug was marketed under the name "Aspirin," but it is probable that little or none of it reached the retail druggists under that name.

The plaintiff called a number of retail druggists, who swore with substantial unanimity that they had never sold the infringing drug to the consumer under the name "Aspirin," and in many cases that the customers themselves asked for it as "Acetylo" or as "acetylsalicylic acid." In Europe, where the plaintiff's predecessor appears not to have enjoyed the benefit of a patent, the drug was manufactured in open competition, but the name "Aspirin" was uniformly respected as a trade-mark, other manufacturers selling either under the name mentioned in the patent or under artificial trade-marks invented by the manufacturers themselves.

The importation into this country by the plaintiff's predecessor began sometime in the year 1899 and before the patent issued. At that time it was all sold in the form of powder, and for some years only to manufacturing chemists, retail druggists, or to physicians. The plaintiff's predecessor, however, did make it up into sample tablets, which it sent gratuitously to all or nearly all the physicians in the country in small quantities. It registered the name as a trade-mark on May 2, 1899. It advertised very largely in technical magazines, and in all its advertisements and on all its labels claimed the word "Aspirin" as its trade-mark. For example, this legend was commonly employed: "The word 'Aspirin' identifies it as the manufacture of" the plaintiff or its predecessors. None of these advertisements, however, were to the public at large, nor did any of the packages reach further than physicians, manufacturing chemists, or retail druggists. In its powder form it was only prescribed by physicians, except as now to be stated.

About 1904 the plaintiff's predecessor began to sell the powder in increasingly large quantities to wholesale manufacturing chemists, understanding that they would make it up into tablets to dispense to retail druggists in bottles containing 5,000, 1,000, 500, and 100 tablets. These chemists, who comprised nearly all the large houses in the country, sold the tablets to retailers under the name "Aspirin," and in no case did the name of the plaintiff or its predecessors appear upon the labels. Moreover, the manufacturing chemist in each case used his own name upon the bottle, e.g., "Aspirin, Squibb," or simply, "Aspirin," with his name or initials below. The tablets soon occupied by far the greater part of the field, the prescription by powder very largely decreasing in proportion, and remaining only in those cases in which a prescription required the drug as one ingredient. The tablet trade grew to very large proportions, amounting in the case of the defendant alone in two years to nearly 16,000,000 tablets, and in the case of Smith, Klein & French in nine years to about 6,000,000. The drug proving useful, the public in time thus acquired the habit of self-medication by means of it and bought it either by fives or dozens from the retail druggists, or in bottles of 50 or 100, and possibly in some instances even more. During this period the plaintiff or its predecessors continued its former policy of addressing only the drug trade or physicians, and the public continued to have no greater information than before of who was in fact manufacturing the drug under the name "Aspirin."

On the charge of unfair trade the plaintiff proved that the defendant advertised the drug of its own manufacture as "genuine Aspirin," and asserted that in other ways not necessary to describe it gave color to the supposition that its product had been made by plaintiff.

On November 30, 1918, an examiner of the Patent Office declared that the trade-mark was no longer valid and ordered its cancellation. From this decision no appeal was taken, and that feature of the case therefore falls out of consideration.

The issues in this case do not, I think, depend upon the decision in *Singer Mfg. Co. v. June Mfg. Co.*, . . . so much as the defendant supposes. That case decided no more than that the existence of a patent during the period when the goods became known to the public might be a controlling element in determining whether the name under which they were sold indicated a single source of origin. Since then courts have several times said that the name of goods protected by patent might in fact indicate not only the kind of goods they were, but as well that they emanated from a single source. . . .

So here it might be that the name "Aspirin" in fact had come at once to describe the drug in question and also its origin from a single source. If it did, that would be enough to justify some protection, since the identity of the source need not be known. . . . Indeed, the whole law of "secondary meaning" is built upon that presupposition.

The single question, as I view it, in all these cases, is merely one of fact: What do the buyers understand by the word for whose use the parties are contending? If they understand by it only the kind of goods sold, then, I take it, it makes no difference whatever what efforts the plaintiff has made to get them to understand more. He has failed, and he cannot say that, when the defendant uses the word, he is taking away customers who wanted to deal with him, however closely disguised he may be allowed to keep his identity. So here the question is whether the buyers merely understood that the word "Aspirin" meant this kind of drug, or whether it meant that and more than that; i.e., that it came from the same single, though, if one please anonymous, source from which they had got it before. Prima facie I should say, since the word is coined and means nothing by itself, that the defendant must show that it means only the kind of drug to which it applies. The fact that it was patented until 1917 is indeed a material circumstance, but it is not necessarily controlling.

In deciding that issue I cannot, however, approach the question formally, as the plaintiff wishes; as to say that there was a user before the patent, and therefore the patent could not forfeit this property right, or that there was never any intention to abandon the trade-mark and so it must have continued. No doubt it is convenient for many purposes to treat a trade-mark as property; yet we shall never, I think, keep clear in our ideas on this subject, unless we remember that relief always depends upon the idea that no man shall be allowed to mislead people into supposing that his goods are the plaintiff's, and that there can be no right or remedy until the plaintiff can show that at least presumptively this will result. . . .

In the case at bar the evidence shows that there is a class of buyers to whom the word "Aspirin" has always signified the plaintiff, more specifically indeed than was necessary for its protection. I refer to manufacturing chemists, to physicians, and probably to retail druggists. From 1899 it flooded the mails with assertions that "Aspirin" meant its own manufacture. This was done in pamphlets, advertisements in trade papers, on the packages and cartons, and by the gratuitous distribution of samples. True, after 1904 it abandoned the phrase "acetylsalicylic acid" for "monoaceticacidester of salicylicacid," but even that extraordinary collocation of letters was intelligible to these classes of buyers who, except possibly the more ignorant of the retail druggists, were measurably versed in the general jargon of pharmaceutical chemistry. Moreover, the drug continued to be generally known by the more tolerable phrase "acetylsalicylic acid," which also adequately described its chemical organization. As to these buyers the plaintiff has therefore, I think, made out a case at least to compel the addition of some distinguishing suffix, even though its monopoly had been more perfect than in fact it was.

The crux of this controversy, however, lies not in the use of the word to these buyers, but to the general consuming public, composed of all sorts of buyers from those somewhat acquainted with pharmaceutical terms to those who knew nothing of them. The only reasonable inference from the evidence is that these did not understand by the word anything more than a kind of drug to which for one reason or another they had become habituated. It is quite clear that while the drug was sold as powder this must have been so. It was dispensed substantially altogether on prescription during this period, and, although physicians appear to have used the terms, "Aspirin" or "acetylsalicylic acid" indifferently, it cannot be that such patients as read their prescriptions attributed to "Aspirin" any other meaning than as an ingredient in a general compound, to which faith and science might impart therapeutic virtue. Nor is there any evidence that such as may have seen both terms identified them as the same drug. I cannot speculate as to how many in fact did so. No packages could possibly have reached the consumer, nor was any advertising addressed to them; their only acquaintance with the word was as the name for a drug in whose curative properties they had got confidence.

In 1904, however, they began to get acquainted with it in a different way, for then all the larger manufacturing chemists began to make tablets, and the trade grew to extraordinary proportions. The consumer, as both sides agree, had long before the autumn of 1915 very largely abandoned consultation with physicians and assumed the right to drug himself as his own prudence and moderation might prescribe. In all cases—omitting for the moment the infringing product—the drug was sold in bottles labeled "Aspirin" with some indication of the name of the tablet maker, but none of the plaintiff. It is probable that by far the greater part of the tablets sold were in dozens or less, and that the bottles so labeled did not generally reach the hands of the consumer, but, even so, a not inconsiderable number of bottles of 100 were sold, and as to the rest they were sold only under the name

"Aspirin." The consumer did not know and could not possibly know the manufacturer of the drug which he got, or whether one or more chemists made it in the United States. He never heard the name "acetylsalicylic acid" as applied to it, and without some education could not possibly have kept it in his mind, if he had. So far as any means of information at all were open to him, they indicated that it was made by most large chemists indiscriminately.

This being the situation up to the autumn of 1915, the defendant seems to me to have effectually rebutted any presumption which the coined word might carry. However, the plaintiff argues along with this user large infringing sales of the drug were being made to consumers under the name "acetylsalicylic acid." It has indeed proved that it was unable absolutely to protect the monopoly of the patent, and it is clear that large quantities were piratically sold, though, so far as this record shows, with uniform respect for its trade-mark. Further, a good many retail druggists swore, with undoubted truth, that their customers got accustomed to the use of the phrase and could either ask for the drug or get it written out on a slip of paper and present that. I think I must accept the record as showing that this went on to a substantial, though obviously to a wholly indeterminate, extent. However, I need not accept, because I do not believe, that all the piratical drug was sold to the consumer under the name "acetyl alicylic acid." This is inherently improbable, and evidence to the contrary was not produced by, and naturally not available to, the plaintiff. . . .

After the autumn of 1915 the plaintiff totally changed its methods, and thereafter no tablets reached the consumer without its own name. But it is significant that even then it used the word "Aspirin" as though it was a general term, although it is true that there was ample notice upon the bottles and boxes that "Aspirin" meant its manufacture. The most striking part of the label read, "Bayer—Tablets of Aspirin." While this did not show any abandonment of the name, which there has never been, it did show how the plaintiff itself recognized the meaning which the word had acquired, because the phrase most properly means that these tablets were Bayer's make of the drug known as "Aspirin." It presupposes that the persons reached were using the word to denote a kind of product. Were it not so, why the addition of "Bayer," and especially why the significant word "of"?

Disregarding this, however, it was too late in the autumn of 1915 to reclaim the word which had already passed into the public domain. If the consuming public had once learned to know "Aspirin" as the accepted name for the drug, perhaps it is true that an extended course of education might have added to it some proprietary meaning, but it would be very difficult to prove that it had been done in 17 months, and in any case the plaintiff does not try to prove it. The issue in this aspect, indeed, becomes whether during that period the word had obtained a secondary meaning, and I do not understand that any such thing is claimed. If it is, I own I cannot find any basis for it in the record. Probably what really happened was that the plaintiff awoke to the fact that on the expiration of the patent its trade-mark would be questioned, and strove to do what it could to relieve it of any doubts. . . .

There are words, such as "Lactobacilline" (29 Rep.Pat.Cas. 497), "Vaseline" (19 Rep.Pat.Cas. 342), "Argyrol" ((C.C.) 164 Fed. 213), "Valvoline" ((C.C.) 38 Fed. 922), or "Celluloid" ((C.C.) 32 Fed. 94), which may at once mean both the kind of goods and their maker. These will be entitled to a qualified protection. The most striking illustration is perhaps *Singer Mfg. Co. v. June Mfg. Co.*, *supra*, itself, where the putative mark was a proper name. The validity of a trade-mark does not, indeed, rigidly depend upon its meaning only the differential between a genus, defined by the kind of goods, and a species, defined by that kind when emanating from the owner. . . . When it means the owner as well as the kind, it will be entitled to a qualified protection; when, as here among the trade, there is another current word, it may be entitled to an absolute protection, patent or not. For a patent gives the public no greater rights than it has without patent. We speak of a dedication of the disclosure, but that is rather for convenience. In fact, the public may always practice the invention, except as the monopoly interferes, and it gets that right independently of the patent. But when, as here among consumers, a mark does not give even an intimation of the owner, there is no room at all for any protection. . . . After all presumptions and other procedural advantages have been weighed, the owner must show that his mark means him, else he cannot prevent others from using it. There is no invention in the word, which he can protect.

The case, therefore, presents a situation in which, ignoring sporadic exceptions, the trade is divided into two classes, separated by vital differences. One, the manufacturing chemists, retail druggists, and physicians, has been educated to understand that "Aspirin" means the plaintiff's manufacture, and has recourse to another and an intelligible name for it, actually in use among them. The other, the consumers, the plaintiff has, consciously I must assume, allowed to acquaint themselves with the drug only by the name "Aspirin," and has not succeeded in advising that the word means the plaintiff at all. If the defendant is allowed to continue the use of the word of the first class, certainly without any condition, there is a chance that it may get customers away from the plaintiff by deception. On the other hand, if the plaintiff is allowed a monopoly of the word as against consumers, it will deprive the defendant, and the trade in general, of the right effectually to dispose of the drug by the only description which will be understood. It appears to me that the relief granted cannot in justice to either party disregard this division; each party has won, and each has lost. . . .

As to the first class the question arises whether the injunction should be absolute or conditional. A strong case may be made for the defendant's present labels. They all bear the letters "U.D. Co." in juxtaposition with "Aspirin" and of equal size. These letters are universally known by the trade to signify the plaintiff, because the custom is general for manufacturing chemists in this way to mark their goods. I think that the plaintiff would be adequately protected but for the 10 years' history of the tablet trade. However, the fact is that during that time such legends were used to indicate that the manufacturing chemist who signed, as it were, the label, was making the tablets from the plaintiff's powder. Probably at present that belief has largely disappeared, but, since we are dealing with customers who are presumably aware of that history, and who have been repeatedly told that "Aspirin" signifies the plaintiff, I can see no reason for subjecting it to the chance. The phrase "acetylsalicylic acid" to them is intelligible; it means the same drug as "Aspirin," and its use ought not unduly to hamper the trade in its business. Besides, the case in this aspect is one of trade-mark proper. Therefore I will grant an injunction against direct sales of the drug under the name "Aspirin" to manufacturing chemists, physicians, and retail druggists. This will, of course, include invoices and correspondence.

In sales to consumers there need, however, be no suffix or qualification whatever. In so far as customers came to identify the plaintiff with "Aspirin" between October, 1915, and March, 1917, this may do it some injustice, but it is impracticable to give any protection based on that possibility. Among consumers generally the name has gone into the public domain. The defendant, as I understand it, makes no direct sales, and all its transactions will therefore probably fall within the injunction, but the sale of its stockholding retailers will be free, and it may so instruct them. Moreover, I see no reason why the defendant should be compelled to sell in such large bottles or boxes that the retailers must

> bottle or box tablets for themselves. This is a trade advantage which conceivably may be of capital consequence in competition. True, it must sell to these retailers clearly under the name "acetylsalicylic acid," but the retailers may themselves use the word "Aspirin." So it seems to me that the defendant should be allowed to pack its tablets in bottles or boxes of 50 or less, bearing the name "Aspirin" without more. These must, however, be sold to the retailers as acetylsalicylic acid, and when shipped must be enclosed in a container marked only "acetylsalicylic acid," with the defendant's name on it. I have limited the quantity to 50 because it seems to me that in greater quantities the permission might be a means by which the retailers could sell the drug to physicians as "Aspirin." True, some physicians may buy as little as 50 at a time, just as some consumers in fact buy more. But some compromise must be made. If there are physicians who buy in such small quantities, the plaintiff must rely upon preventing the retailers from using these bottles; if there are consumers who wish more, the defendant must submit to the disadvantage that the retailers must sell 2 at a time, or must relabel a bottle of 100.
> . . .

I append a form for the mandatory part of the decree as to the trade-mark, which will serve unless the parties wish to have it modified:

> "Against using the word 'Aspirin' in correspondence, invoices, bills of lading, and the like, or upon cartons, labels, or other marking, in any sales of 'acetylsalicylic acid' to manufacturing chemists, wholesale or retail druggists, or physicians. The defendant will be free to sell 'acetylsalicylic acid' direct to consumers under the name 'Aspirin' without suffix or qualification. The defendant in sales to retail druggists will also be free to pack tablets in bottles and boxes of fifty or less, labeled, 'Aspirin,' provided these bottles or boxes be wrapped or boxed in containers marked 'acetylsalicylic acid manufactured by U.D. Co.,' without the word 'Aspirin,' and that in making such sales the correspondence, invoices, bills of lading, and the like refer to the drug so sold only as 'acetylsalicylic acid'."

§ 1.30.2. Excerpt from the specifications of the United States patent for acetylsalicylic acid ("aspirin")

Felix Hoffmann, of Elberfeld, Germany, Assignor to the FarbenFabriken of Elberfeld Company, of New York.

Acetylik Salicylic Acid.

Specification forming part of Letters Patent No. 644,077, dated February 27, 1900.

To all whom it may concern:

> Be it known that I, Felix Hoffmann, doctor of philosophy, chemist, (assignor to the Farbenfabriken of Elberfeld Company, of New York) residing at Elberfeld, Germany, have invented a new and useful Improvement in the Manufacture or Production of AcetylSalicylic Acid; and I hereby declare the following to be a clear and exact description of my invention. . . .
>
> Having now described my invention and in what manner the same is to be performed, what I claim as new, and desire to secure by Letters Patent, is—
>
> As a new article of manufacture the acetylsalicylic acid having the formula: . . . being when crystallized from dry chloroform in the shape of white glittering needles, easily soluble in benzene, alcohol and glacial acetic acid, difficultly

soluble in cold water, being split by hot water into acetic acid and salicylic acid, melting at about 135° centigrade, substantially as hereinbefore described.

In testimony whereof I have signed my name in the presence of two subscribing witnesses.

§ 1.30.3. The Chancery Division of the High Court of Justice (England) held that the patent on acetylsalicylic acid is invalid (1905)

Farbenfabriken Vormals Friedrich Bayer & Co. v. Chemische Fabrik von Heyden

In the High Court of Justice.—Chancery Division

May 2 to 11, and July 8, 1905

Before Mr. Justice Joyce.

Patent.—Action for infringement.—Construction of Specification.—Claim for product.—Prior publication.—Patent held invalid.—Costs on higher scale allowed.

A Patent was granted to N. in 1898 for "the manufacture or production of acetylsalicylic acid." The Claims in the Specification were for two processes of manufacture of the acid for the alleged new body, and for its use for therapeutic purposes. The Plaintiffs alleged that, by the method of recrystallization from dry chloroform adopted by them, the acid (which was sold under the name of "aspirin" and used in medicines had been for the first time prepared in a state of purity. The Defendants alleged that K. in 1869 had published a description of the preparation of the acid by one of the said processes, that as so prepared the acid contained a small proportion of impurity, but that this impurity did not produce any difference or therapeutic effect, and that it could be removed by recrystallization from boiling water as described by K.

Held, that the Patent was for acetylsalicylic acid as a new body and not for the process of purification, and that the Patent had been anticipated and was invalid. The action was dismissed, with costs on the higher scale. . . .

On the 22nd of December 1898, Letters Patent (No. 27,088 of 1898) were granted to *Henry Edward Newton* for "The Manufacture or production of 'acetylsalicylic acid,' communicated to him from abroad by the *Faberfabriken vormals Friedrich Bayer & Co.* of Elberfeld, Germany. . . .

On the 19th of May 1904, the *Faberfabriken vormals Friedrich Bayer & Co* and *Henry Edward Newton* commenced an Action for infringement of the Patent (and of a Patent No. 9,123 of 1899, granted to *Henry Edward Newton*) against the *Chemische Fabrik von Heyden* and *Burgoyne, Burbidges and Company*, claiming the usual relief. . . .

Joyce J.—This is an action for infringement of a Patent, under which the Plaintiffs make a medical preparation popularly known as "aspirin," and sold under that designation. Its scientific or chemical name is acetylsalicylic acid. It is derived from salicylic acid by a process which alters its nature, but leaves the broad characteristics of salicylic acid in the compound obtained. In fact, the Patent is claimed for a body or product the name of which was known, the characteristics and properties of which had been described with more or less accuracy, and a method of getting it had been published. There was no novel idea in the Patent. The Patentee did not discover acetylsalicylic acid. The real and only question in the case is the validity of the Patent, and, speaking generally, the question turns upon a prior publication in 1869 by a distinguished German chemist named *Kraut*, who there discussed, among other things, the subject of acetylosalicylic acid, which is the same as acetylsalicylic acid. The Specification of the Patent is intituled "The manufacture or production of acetylsalicylic acid," and it claims (1) "The process for producing acetylsalicylic acid by causing acetic anhydride to act on salicylic acid or its salts substantially as hereinbefore described. (2) For the production of acetylsalicylic acid, the use of the process which consists in allowing acetyl chloride to act on salicylic acid or its salts substantially as hereinbefore described;" and, (3) (this is the principal claim) "As a new article of manufacture, the new body hereinbefore described. (4) The use of the new body hereinbefore described for therapeutic purposes"—as to which last it was, I think, admitted upon both sides that it must stand or fall with Claim No. 3. The Patent, therefore, is one for a new product, and for the use of certain processes of producing it. It is not a Patent for an improved or more economical method of manufacturing the product, or an improved or particular method of purifying the crude or raw product obtained by the process of causing acetic anhydride to act on salicylic acid or of allowing acetic chloride to act on salicylic acid.

The Defendants have not infringed the Patent by the use of any particular process, but only, if at all, by the manufacture of acetylsalicylic acid, as to their method of doing which nothing has been proved, and for the purpose of this case it may be taken to be unknown. . . .

The Specification is a somewhat remarkable document. Indeed, none of the experienced counsel engaged in this case had ever seen another Specification like it. It is not a plain statement of an invention with the method of performing it, but a controversial document framed with a view to showing that neither *Kraut*, nor any other chemist, had previously made or described the manufacture of acetylsalicylic acid; in other words, that there had been no anticipation, by previous workers, of the invention, whatever it was, claimed by the Patentee. Further, this document, as it appears to me, is, by accident, error, or design, so framed as to obscure the subject as much as possible. . . .

If the Patentee had said, *Kraut* told you how to obtain crude acetylsalicylic acid, or acetylsalicylic acid mixed with a minute quantity of salicylic acid or something else—it matters not much what—remaining uncombined, and my invention is for a new process for the separation of the crude product by re-crystallization with dry chloroform, still, as at present advised, I should say that such a Patent would not have been valid, and I am disposed to agree . . . that the Specification in this case contains no element of invention or discovery beyond what was either common knowledge among chemists, or known by the publication of *Kraut*. But, however that may be, the invention claimed is for the production of acetylsalicylic acid as a new body, may be a better way of cleansing or purifying the crystalline mass, produced by the reaction, than that which *Kraut* suggested.

The result is that, in my opinion, the Specification in this case is misconceived, the Patent is invalid, and the action must be dismissed, with the usual consequences.

§ 1.30.4. A German Court holds that the use of the trademark "Aspirin" by a competitor of Bayer, while an informative element of its own product, is, under the circumstances, a legitimate trade practice

Bayer and Co. v. Asche and Co.

High Court of Hamburg, July 4, 1904; Empire's Court, March 8, 1906

Protected word trademark "Aspirin."—Expression "Aspirin Equivalent" used in the labels of a third person to better characterize the product [which is] anyway designated by its real name.—No confusion; Use permitted.

The limited company "Fabrique de couleurs, hereinafter Fr. Bayer et Cie.," at Eberfeld, owns the word trademark Aspirin, which designates a certain pharmaceutical product. Neither this product nor the process used to manufacture it is protected, and thus it can be manufactured and sold by other chemical factories, among which is C. F. Asche et Cie., at Hamburg. The latter puts this product into circulation in the form of tablets contained in dark blue glass tubes, with a white label with a broad red stripe. On this stripe one reads, as an indication of the content, the name "Acid. acetylo-salicylic," and below, placed between two lines, the following mention: "Ersatz fur Aspirin" (equivalent to Aspirin). The company Fr. Bayer, having considered that the use of these labels infringed the rights acquired by it subsequently to the registration of the word trademark Aspirin, filed a lawsuit against Asche. But the lawsuit was dismissed, on the advice of the experts, by a judgment of the Superior Court of Hamburg dated July 4, 1905, whose grounds are the following:

By registering its trademark, the plaintiff has not in any manner obtained the right to exclude third parties from any use of the word Aspirin in the trade of pharmaceutical products. The affixing of this

word on the labels used by the defendant for its products would be prohibited, under Articles 12, 14 and 20 of the Law on the Protection of Trademarks of Goods, only if the word Aspirin was used as the denomination of the goods, or if it were used in a form which would lead the public to believe that this word is the distinctive sign of the goods and to lead it to confuse the defendant's product with that of the plaintiff (see judgments of the Tribunal of the Empire in Criminal Matters, vol. 30, at 353). However, the defendant designates its merchandise not as "Aspirin," but as "Acid. acetylo-salicylic." By adding to this name the expression "*Aspirin* Equivalent," it unequivocally indicates that it is a product other than *Aspirin*. It only remains, therefore, to enquire whether it is to be concluded that the words "equivalent of" elude the public, and that by reading the word *Aspirin* on the label, it does not believe to be in the presence of the plaintiff's product bearing the protected trademark. The Tribunal is convinced that this danger does not exist. The labels used by the defendant bear the words *Acid. acetylo-salicylic*, in the place that, by the red background, the graphic ornamentation and the use of larger characters, is characterized as being the place intended for receiving the name of the product. Anyone who takes a quick look at the tube with this label will only notice these words, and will only see "Aspirin Equivalent" on closer inspection. The words "Equivalent of," although printed in a type slightly smaller than the word *Aspirin*, are however too conspicuous to be overlooked. There is therefore no risk that the public will mistake the defendant's product for that of the plaintiff.

The complainant's appeal was dismissed by order of the Empire Court of March 8, 1906.

(*Gewerblicher Rechtsschutz und Urheberrecht*, August 1906, at 263; communication of M. A. Joseph, at Hamburg).

§ 1.30.5. Advertisement and notices concerning the successful enforcement of the trademark "Aspirin" published in a Canadian newspaper, 1936 and 1937

Find Out From Your Doctor if the "Pain" Remedy You Take Is Safe

Don't Entrust Your Own or Your Family's Well-Being to Unknown Preparations

Before you take any preparation you don't know all about, for the relief of headaches; or the pains of rheumatism, neuritis or neuralgia, ask your *doctor* what he thinks about it—in comparison with "Aspirin."

We say this because, before the discovery of "Aspirin," most so-called "pain" remedies were advised against by physicians as being bad for the stomach; or, often, for the heart. And the discovery of "Aspirin" largely changed medical practice.

Countless thousands of people who have taken "Aspirin" year in and out without ill effect, have proved that the medical findings about its safety were correct.

Remember this: "Aspirin" is rated *among the fastest methods yet discovered* for the relief of headaches and all common pains . . . and *safe* for the average person to take regularly.

"Aspirin" Tablets are made in Canada. "Aspirin" is the registered trade-mark of the Bayer Company, Limited. Look for the name Bayer in the form of a cross on every tablet.

Demand and Get "ASPIRIN"

"Aspirin" Trade Mark Sustained

A warning is found in the judgment by the Exchequer Court of Canada at Ottawa, in an action brought by The Bayer Company, Limited, owner of the trade mark "Aspirin." The action asked a judgment of the court restraining the defendant from infringing the trade mark by selling tablets as "Aspirin" which were not the product of The Bayer Company. The judgment restrains the defendant permanently from putting out any of his own tablets as "Aspirin" or under any name so similar to "Aspirin" as to be confusing and awards The Bayer Company damages and costs.

"Aspirin" Trade Mark Protected

Bring Actions to Restrain Infringement And Secure Judgment

The Bayer Company Limited having brought actions to restrain infringement of its registered trademark "Aspirin" the Exchequer Court of Canada has given judgment against the five defendants. In each case the Exchequer Court perpetually restrains the defendants Ivan Lambert, Joseph Nozick, Standard Botlers and Packers Ltd., B. Neuman and Joe Beckman from using the trademark "Aspirin" on preparations put out by themselves and awards the Bayer Company costs and damages.

The descendants were marketing the infringing product under various names, including Pioneer Sales Co., Western Sales Co., Advance Specially Co., and Acme Specialty Company. The tablets labelled "Aspirin" were not of Bayer manufacture and were packed in small envelopes, each containing three or four tablets, and mounted on cards.

It is the intention of The Bayer Company, Limited, to take every legal method to uphold its trademark.

"Aspirin" is the trademark of The Bayer Company, Limited, Windsor, Ontario.

§ 1.31. A UNITED STATES FEDERAL COURT AFFIRMS THE REQUIREMENT OF GREATER CARE IN SETTING THE DISTINCTIVENESS OF MEDICINE TRADEMARKS

Distinctiveness is an essential requirement for trademarks. Their main role being to ensure consumers that they are able to distinguish between competing products and services, trademarks must be distinctive. Over the centuries, courts have set certain parameters for making that characteristic effective. However, the nature of the products that medicine trademarks designate has caused some changes in how that requirement is imposed in their regard.

Here, we can detect a certain tension between a diminished requirement of distinctiveness and the duty of greater care. On the one hand, health authorities in certain countries may be tempted to impose less strict standards of the distinctiveness of trademarks that apply to pharmaceuticals subject to medical prescription. The reason is that the targets of those trademarks are physicians and pharmacists, i.e., educated, scientifically educated people. They are, therefore, less prone to confusion if confronted with trademarks that, being distinctive, bear some similarities.

On the other hand, the orientation may go exactly in the opposite direction. The argument is that because confusion in the consumption of medicines may raise serious problems of health, greater care in the differentiation of those products as compared to other commercial goods is necessary. This is the so-called duty of greater care.

The need for greater care had been already in the radar of courts since some time, but it was for the first time unequivocally enunciated (and the doctrine coined) by the former United States Court of Customs and Patent Appeals (which, in 1982, was merged with the Court of Claims, and renamed as the U.S. Court of Appeals for the Federal Circuit, known as the CAFC): "Moreover, it seems to us that where ethical goods are sold and careless use is dangerous, greater care should be taken in the use and registration of trade-marks to assure that no harmful confusion results."

Campbell Products, Inc. v. John Wyeth & Bro.

Decided June 26, 1944

Court of Customs and Patent Appeals

143 F.2d 977 (C.C.P.A. 1944)

Opinion delivered by Bland, Associate Judge.

Appeal from the Commissioner of Patents, Opposition No. 21,376. Proceedings on the application of Campbell Products, Inc., for the registration of a trade-mark, opposed by John Wyeth Brothers, Inc. From a decision of the Commissioner of Patents reversing a decision of the Examiner of Interferences in favor of applicant and sustaining the opposition, applicant appeals.

Affirmed.

This is a United States Patent Office trade-mark opposition appeal. The appellant-applicant applied in the Patent Office for registration of the trade-mark "Alutropin." Appellee-opponent filed notice of opposition to the registration of said mark, basing its opposition upon the prior use and registration of its trade-mark "Alulotion." Priority of use by appellee is not disputed. Concerning appellant's mark, we quote the following from appellant's brief:

> Beginning in March, 1941, the Appellant-Applicant, Campbell Products, Inc., after extended investigation as to its merits by the Department of Therapeutics, New York University, College of Medicine and in the wards of Belleview Hospital, New York City . . . first marketed its trade-marked product "Alutropin," in accordance with its invariable custom, as an ethical preparation solely through the medical profession. . . .
>
> Such medicinal product is a mouth-administered, nonpoisonous, colloidal aluminum-hydroxide fortified with another of the Applicant's trade-marked products "Novatropine" (homatropine methylbromide) for the treatment of peptic ulcer and gastric hyperchlorhydria (hyperacidity), and it has been supplied in tall, 12-ounce, clear-glass, rectangular bottles bearing gray-and-blue labels describing the product and displaying in addition the following: "Warning: Use cautiously if dryness of the throat occurs: discontinue if rapid pulse or blurring of vision appears." "Caution: To be used only on the prescription of a physician." "Shake Well." . . . "Such long, narrow, substantially-rectangular labels . . . state no dosage or frequency of use because it is essential, for safety and for the preservation of the established good reputation of the Applicant's product, that these be determined by the physician, depending upon the condition of the patient, and specified in his required written prescription.

Opponent's registered mark is the word "Alulotion." It is pointed out by appellant that appellee's trade-marked product is a "poisonous, externally-applied lotion for the treatment of that repulsive, highly contagious, skin disease *Impetigo contagiosa* . . .," and appellant states (the record is silent on the point) that in order to comply with the requirements of the Federal Food, Drug, and Cosmetic Act, 21 U.S.C.A. § 301 *et seq.*, since the main ingredient of the product is poisonous mercury, appellee is required to state also, in connection with its mark, the following (which appears in the same size letters as the mark): "Ammoniated Mercury with Kaolin." Appellee's goods are sold upon physicians' prescriptions in a short, small, 3-ounce blue bottle, which does not disclose the exact color of its contents but makes the contents have the appearance of being milky and slightly darker than the product of appellant. The label on appellee's bottle is oval-shaped. Near the top the word "Wyeth's" appears in script. Below that is the word "Alulotion,", with the notation "Reg. U.S. Pat. Off." in very small type. The latter notation is followed by the words "Ammoniated Mercury with Kaolin" in the same size type as the trade-mark. The label then points out the ingredients—ammoniated mercury 5%, Kaolin 15%, and aluminum hydroxide 2.3%. Then appears the statement, "Poison—External Use." There are other instructions as to use, and the injunction to shake well and to be used only on the prescription of a physician. Appellant states that appellee's lotion is used on the skin after removal of the scabs resulting from the disease.

The Examiner of Trade-mark Interferences held that there was no reasonable likelihood of confusion, dismissed the notice of opposition, and further adjudged that the appellant was entitled to register its mark. He had the following to say:

> These goods of the parties, while they are believed to possess the same descriptive properties, are thus specifically different medicinal preparations, and, other than that they contain an aluminum compound as a common ingredient, the differences therebetween in composition correspond to the wide differences in the respective essential properties and uses.
>
> The marks "Alutropin" and "Alulotion" here involved contain obvious resemblances. The terminal portions "Tropin" and "Lotion" constituting the major portions thereof, however, are quite different in significance and serve also to emphasize the differences in the properties and uses of the goods. When these differences in marks are viewed together with those present in the goods to which they are affixed, the examiner is persuaded that the marks may be concurrently used in trade without reasonable likelihood of confusion. Particularly so, since it is to be expected that products of this type will be sold under conditions which will greatly minimize any possibility of confusion or mistake. . . ."

Upon appeal, the First Assistant Commissioner of Patents (acting for the commissioner) reversed the decision of the Examiner of Trade-mark Interferences, held that the goods of the parties were of the same descriptive properties and that the trade-marks were confusingly similar, and sustained the opposition. . . . From the decision of the commissioner, appellant has here appealed.

Appellant argues that, by reason of the differences between the packages, labels, and use of the merchandise, as well as for other considerations presently stated, there is no likelihood of confusion flowing from the concurrent use of the two marks on the respective goods, and that the decision of the commissioner should be reversed. Appellant further argues that since the goods of both parties are used only on physicians' prescriptions (thus assuring less likelihood of confusion than otherwise); that since appellee must put on its label in large letters the phrase "Ammoniated Mercury with Kaolin;" that since the medicines are used for wholly different purposes, one internal and the other external; that since the goods are packaged differently (as before stated); that since there is no competition between the two medicines; that since one could not be used for the treatment of the diseases for which the other is recommended; that since the meanings of the words "Alulotion" and "Alutropin" are wholly different; and that since appellee has no monopoly on the term "lotion" and was not the originator of the syllable "Alu" (which is supposed to signify alumina) in connection with a trademark, there is no probability of any confusion resulting.

We are in agreement with the holding of the commissioner. It is too obvious to require discussion here that the marks "Alulotion" and "Alutropin" are quite similar in sound and appearance, and that the goods are of the same descriptive properties within the meaning of the Trade-Mark Act, 15 U.S.C.A. § 81 *et seq.* The prefix "Alu" in both marks evidently refers to an ingredient common to both products. While they are both sold on physicians' prescriptions, and while appellee's product (according to appellant's statement) is required, under the Federal Food, Drug and Cosmetic Act, to be sold with certain printed matter on the label, it does not necessarily follow that these conditions may continue to prevail. . . . Moreover, it seems to us that where ethical goods are sold and careless use is dangerous, greater care should be taken in the use and registration of trade-marks to assure that no harmful confusion results. The shape of the bottles in which the preparations are sold and the color, shape, and other features of the labels, etc., are subject to change. Since they are both sold from the same shelves in the drug stores, it is our view that the commissioner was correct in concluding that the goods of the parties are of the same descriptive properties and that the trade-marks are confusingly similar.

Appellant relies largely upon a case decided by the Sixth Circuit Court of Appeals, *Solventol Chemical Products, Inc. v. Langfield*, 134 F.2d 899, 903, where "Solventol" was allowed registration over "Solvite," the court holding that both marks being highly suggestive, other persons likewise had the right to use suggestive marks for similar goods. It stated that the marks "look unlike, are spelled differently and are phonetically dissimilar." Attention was called to the fact that neither of the marks in question was arbitrary or fanciful. It was also pointed out that there was some difference in the descriptive properties of the goods. The merchandise of one party was a cleaning preparation which, when mixed with gasoline, was used for cleaning garments, draperies, etc., while the merchandise of the other party was used for cleaning floors and walls.

It is obvious that considerations which there influenced the court are not present here, and the case is not authority supporting the contentions of appellant here. Moreover, this court in *Langfield v. Brady*, 101 F.2d 530, 26 C.C.P.A., Patents, 908, which involved the marks "Solvoline" and "Solvite," held that the marks were confusingly similar and that the goods of the respective parties (a dry-cleaning fluid and a dry-cleaning soap) were of the same descriptive properties and denied registration of the mark "Solvoline." And in *Langfield v. Solvit-All Corporation*, 49 F.2d 480, 18 C.C.P.A., Patents, 1313, where the marks were "Solvit-All" and "Solvite" and the goods, respectively, were sanitary solvents for cleaning toilet bowls and similar articles, and a cleaning preparation for garments, draperies, etc., our holding was substantially the same as in *Langfield v. Brady, supra.*

For reasons which are obvious and need not be discussed here, the cases relied upon in the decision of the Examiner of Trademark Interferences are not controlling.

> We think the case to which appellee has called our attention—*Guggenheim v. Cantrell Cochrane, Ltd.*, 56 App.D.C. 100, 10 F.2d 895, 896—is quite pertinent. In that case Mr. Justice Robb, speaking for the court "In this court, it has been repeatedly declared that there is neither legal nor moral excuse for even an approximate simulation of a well-known mark applied to goods of the same descriptive properties, and that, when an attempt to effect such simulation becomes apparent, the two marks should not be examined with a microscope to

detect minute differences, but, on the contrary, should be viewed as a whole, as the general public would view them; in other words, that the points of similarity are of greater importance than the points of difference.

It seems to us that the following cases are in point, although it has many times been said that the decision in cases like that at bar is rarely controlled by decisions in other cases, since the facts almost invariably differ, and each case must rest on its own bottom: . . .

We think that the commissioner arrived at the right conclusion, and his decision is affirmed.

Affirmed.

§ 1.32. FOR THE SAKE OF PUBLIC HEALTH, THE UNICEF AND THE WHO ORDER THE REDUCTION OF THE DISTINCTIVENESS OF TRADEMARKS CONCERNING BREAST-MILK SUBSTITUTES

The general understanding is that the more distinctive trademarks are, the better because distinctiveness ensures the differentiation of products and services by consumers, and ensures fair competition. Merchants and manufacturers, grounded on robust trademark rights, are able to capture the reputation they have gained by serving consumers well, with care, creativity, and acumen.

But trademarks may become symbols, thus acquiring meanings that go beyond the products or services they designate. Trademarks, especially when accompanied by effective advertisement, may awake in consumers the feelings of happiness, personal success, and well-being. Such symbolic meanings are frequently sought voluntarily by merchants, with the intention of increasing sales or obtaining the loyalty of customers—or both. In general, there is nothing wrong with this practice. But as regards some specific products, those symbolic meanings may be undesirable in the eyes of public authorities, to the extent they may lead to certain patterns of consumption that should be avoided.

One type of product whose trademarks may give rise to that sort of public concern is that of breast-milk substitutes. The argument is that no product can replace breast-milk completely. The policy of organizations such as the United Nations' Children's Fund (UNICEF) and the World Health Organization (WHO) has been of encouraging mothers to breastfeed their babies so that they do not fall in the temptation of feeding them with artificial substitutes. In this same token, the two organizations have expressed a special concern with the symbolism of certain trademarks that, when associated with breast-milk substitutes, evoke feelings of good health, beauty and well-being for the babies who are fed with them. This concern is particularly strong in the context of poverty. Poor, uneducated mothers may fall more easily prey to the misguiding symbols of certain trademarks, especially those that are figurative, as far as the nutritive qualities of milk-substitutes are concerned.

In the late 1970s and early 1980s, the decision bodies of the UNICEF and the WHO adopted rules restricting the ways manufacturers of breast-milk substitutes can brand those products. The main purpose of those rules, codified as the International Code of Marketing of Breast-milk Substitutes, is to avoid that breast-milk substitutes are promoted as if they effectively replaced the natural product. As far as intellectual property is concerned, Articles 4.2 and 9.2 of the Code reduce the freedom of manufacturers in branding their products, to the extent that they prohibit the use of certain nominative and figurative elements that may be understood as promoting the consumption of breast-milk substitutes. Consequently, the photos or designs of infants should not compose the trademarks that are printed on the packages of infant food formulae. The same applies to any other sort of designs that "idealize" the consumption of breast-milk substitutes, namely those that associate the consumption of those products with feelings of happiness, joy and well-being. As said, the idea is that many pregnant women in poor countries are illiterate, and to them, a face of a healthy, smiley baby, as well as figures depicting idealistic scenarios, such as rainbows, unicorns, chirping birds, are persuasive elements as to the effectively nurturing power of the branded substitutes.

The UNICEF website informs that "since 1981, 84 countries have enacted legislation implementing all or many of the provisions of the Code and subsequent relevant World Health Assembly resolutions. In addition, 14 countries have draft laws awaiting adoption." (www.unicef.org/nutrition/index_24805.html).

The implementation of the Code gave rise in the 1990s to a dispute between the United States and the then US company Gerber Products Co., on the one hand, and the government of Guatemala, on the other. Guatemala's Ministry of Health refused to register Gerber's infant formula as a substitute of breast milk because of its trademark, which, in its original configuration, includes the picture of a smiley baby's face (based on a drawing of Ann Cook Turner's face, when she was four months old). In view of the 1986 Guatemalan law and its implementing regulations (see the following texts), such a trademark would need to be modified, with the elimination of the baby's picture. The company refused to comply and sued—alleging, among other matters, that the government of Guatemala had expropriated its trademark. The United States' diplomacy intervened in its favor, and, in the end, the Supreme Court of Guatemala decided that Gerber's trademark was acceptable because the 1986 statute and its regulations only applied to formulae nationally manufactured, not to imported products. In the meantime, Gerber Company was acquired by Novartis, and later, Novartis sold it to Nestlé. So, today, the Gerber's worldwide well-known trademark is part of the vast line of Nestlé's infant products.

The International Code of Marketing of Breast-milk Substitutes, in fact, inaugurated a movement towards the reduction of the differentiation of trademarks and other business identifiers for the sake of public health. In this particular case, the issue is the fear of promoting the consumption of breast-milk substitutes, and, consequently, inducing the reduction of breastfeeding.

This is not the place for debating the merits of this relatively new trend in health-related laws vis-à-vis trademark rights and the international treaties that protect them,[15] *but, as we will see again in the context of tobacco products and their plain packaging, the total*

15. For an extensive discussion of the consistency of this sort of limitations in the acquisition and protection of trademark rights, *see* Nuno Pires de Carvalho, The TRIPS Regime of Trademarks and Designs, at 365 *et seq.* (4th ed., Wolters Kluwer, 2019).

elimination of the distinctive features of trademarks seems exaggerated. Health authorities, instead of reducing the distinctive capacity of trademarks and their inducing power, should engage in campaigns of education of future mothers, which would be much more effective than simply attacking the brands, with the attendant effects of destroying product differentiation and reputation.

§ 1.32.1. International Code of Marketing of Breast-milk Substitutes (excerpts)

World Health Organization Geneva 1981

The Member States of the World Health Organization:

> Affirming the right of every child and every pregnant and lactating woman to be adequately nourished, as a means of attaining and maintaining health;
>
> Recognizing that infant malnutrition is part of the wider problems of lack of education, poverty, and social injustice; . . .
>
> Conscious that breast-feeding is an unequalled way of providing ideal food for the healthy growth and development of infants; that it forms a unique biological and emotional basis for the health of both mother and child; that the anti-infective properties of breast-milk help to protect infants against disease; and that there is an important relationship between breast-feeding and child-spacing; . . .
>
> Considering that, when mothers do not breast-feed, or only do so partially, there is a legitimate market for infant formula and for suitable ingredients from which to prepare it; that all these products should accordingly be made accessible to those who need them through commercial or non-commercial distribution systems; and that they should not be marketed or distributed in ways that may interfere with the protection and promotion of breast-feeding; . . .
>
> Recognizing further that inappropriate feeding practices lead to infant malnutrition, morbidity and mortality in all countries, and that improper practices in the marketing of breast-milk substitutes and related products can contribute to these major public health problems; . . .
>
> Considering that manufacturers and distributors of breast-milk substitutes have an important and constructive role to play in relation to infant feeding, and in the promotion of the aim of this Code and its proper implementation; . . .
>
> Believing that, in the light of the foregoing considerations, and in view of the vulnerability of infants in the early months of life and the risks involved in inappropriate feeding practices, including the unnecessary and improper use of breast-milk substitutes, the marketing of breast-milk substitutes requires special treatment, which makes usual marketing practices unsuitable for these products;
>
> Therefore:
>
> The Member States hereby agree the following articles which are recommended as a basis for action.
>
> Article 1. Aim of the Code
>
> The aim of this Code is to contribute to the provision of safe and adequate nutrition for infants, by the protection and promotion of breast-feeding, and by ensuring the proper use of breast-milk substitutes, when these are necessary, on the basis of adequate information and through appropriate marketing and distribution.

Article 2. Scope of the Code

The Code applies to the marketing, and practices related thereto, of the following products: breast-milk substitutes, including infant formula; other milk products, foods and beverages, including bottlefed complementary foods, when marketed or otherwise represented to be suitable, with or without modification, for use as a partial or total replacement of breast milk; feeding bottles and teats. It also applies to their quality and availability, and to information concerning their use.

Article 3. Definitions

For the purposes of this Code:

Breast-milk substitute means any food being marketed or otherwise presented as a partial or total replacement for breast milk, whether or not suitable for that purpose.
Complementary food means any food whether manufactured or locally prepared, suitable as a complement to breast milk or to infant formula, when either become[s] insufficient to satisfy the nutritional requirements of the infant. Such food is also commonly called *weaning food* or *breast-milk supplement*.
Container means any form of packaging of products for sale as a normal retail unit, including wrappers. . . .
Infant formula means a breast-milk substitute formulated industrially in accordance with applicable Codex Alimentarius standards, to satisfy the normal nutritional requirements of infants up to between four and six months of age, and adapted to their physiological characteristics. Infant formula may also be prepared at home, in which case it is described as *home-prepared*. . . .
Marketing means product promotion, distribution, selling, advertising, product public relations, and information services. . . .

Article 4. Information and education

. . . 4.2 Informational and educational materials, whether written, audio, or visual, dealing with the feeding of infants and intended to reach pregnant women and mothers of infants and young children, should include clear information on all the following points: . . . Such materials should not use any pictures or text which may idealize the use of breast-milk substitutes. . . .

Article 9. Labelling

9.1 Labels should be designed to provide the necessary information about the appropriate use of the product, and so as not to discourage breast-feeding.

9.2 Manufacturers and distributors of infant formula should ensure that each container [h]as a clear, conspicuous, and easily readable and understandable message printed on it, or on a label which cannot readily become separated from it, in an appropriate language, which includes all the following points: . . . Neither the container nor the label should have pictures of infants, nor should they have other pictures or text which may idealize the use of infant formula. They may, however, have graphics for easy identification of the product as a breastmilk substitute and for illustrating methods of preparation. . . . .

§ 1.32.2. Guatemala's law on the marketing of breast-milk substitutes (excerpt)

Decree-Law No. 66-83, of June 7, 1983

Article 1. Objectives and scope. The purpose of this law is to seek the establishment of the necessary measures to protect and promote breastfeeding, ensuring the proper use of breast-milk substitutes, based on appropriate information, when necessary, and the modalities of trade and distribution of the following products: breast milk substitutes, including infant formulae; other dairy products, foods and beverages, including complementary foods administered by baby-bottles, when marketed or when otherwise indicated that they can be used, with or without modification, to partially or totally replace breast milk. It will also apply to the quality and availability of the related products and to the information on their use.

. . .

§ 1.32.3. Guatemala's regulation on the marketing of breast-milk substitutes (excerpts)

Ministry of Public Health and Social Assistance

Governmental Agreement No. 841-87, September 30, 1987

Article 5. Informative, didactic, advertising material or any other intended to disseminate the feeding of infants, of children under two years of age, as well as [those addressed to] pregnant women or mothers of children under two years of age, shall include the following:. . .

b) It will not carry photos, figures, sounds or messages [relating to] children under two years of age or other images that idealize the product or cause confusion about its properties;

. . .

Article 12. The label announcing breast milk substitutes or industrialized baby foods shall not contain information that may stimulate the use of the baby bottle. Moreover, it shall not contain messages like the following:

a) Images of infant children or others that may idealize the use of the baby bottle;
b) Legends, drawings or illustrations that directly or indirectly tend to create the conviction that the substitute food is equivalent or superior to breast milk.

. . .

Figure 13 The worldwide well-known (and registered) Gerber trademark, which appears on the packages and labels of a large series of products destined to infants and toddlers.

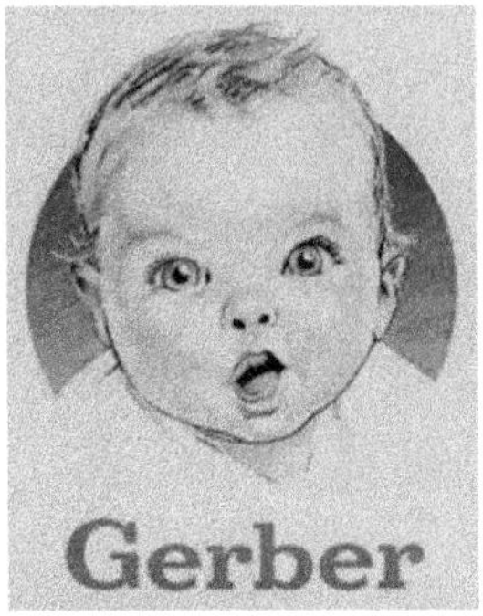

Figure 14 Examples of figures that are recurrent in baby milk formula. The teddy bear is perhaps the most recurrent motive, but other friendly animals also appear, as well as rainbows, colorful stars, and fanciful, dreamful figures, such as unicorns.

§ 1.33. THE IMPEDIMENT TO THE USE OF TRADEMARKS AS A MANNER TO PRESS GENERIC PHARMACEUTICAL PRICES DOWNWARDS—THE EXAMPLE THAT COMES FROM BRAZIL

Since the Middle Ages, pharmacists had to struggle with governmental requirements on the use of common designations for identifying the products of their trade. The main reason for those requirements has changed through times, however. At first, the purpose was simply to avoid confusion by the pharmacists themselves as to the ingredients they used (the so-called quid pro quo*). As noted above, the reduced number of medicines available and the general imposition that pharmacopeias were observed did not give rise to a significant need for the use of trademarks. A few centuries later, this changed when the necessity of identifying the pharmacists for certification purposes arose from the increase in the number of available pharmaceutical ingredients. Subsequently, a golden period of almost uncontrolled freedom of action by pharmacists ensued—roughly between the sixteenth and the nineteenth centuries. The nineteenth century brought a new public awareness about the importance of imposing controls on the marketing of pharmaceuticals (as well as on the ownership of new medicines' formulas, as we will see in the next Chapter). This has given rise to a new debate on the requirement of*

distinctiveness that pharmaceutical trademarks should present. We saw above several examples of this discussion, which continued into the twentieth century.
But in the twentieth century, a new social institution introduced new requirements on the use of pharmaceutical trademarks: public healthcare systems. Soon, after their introduction, these systems proved to impose a heavy burden on national budgets, which led some governments to adopt measures aimed at reducing the prices of medicines dispensed through those systems. One of those measures was put in place in Brazil, in 1999, in the context of a statute aiming at encouraging the local manufacture and trade of generic pharmaceuticals.
Essentially, generic pharmaceuticals are those that are not covered by patents. But this does not mean that they are completely non-proprietary. First, generic pharmaceuticals may have their formulae, totally or partly, hidden under secrecy. The processes for their making may also be kept secret. Second, generic medicines may be trademarked. When well reputed, those trademarks lead to consumers' and doctors' brand loyalty, which give their owners a certain amount of market power.
Therefore, those trademarks may command higher prices, to the extent they capture reputation—and reputation captures clientele's preference.
In order to avoid this consequence in the context of its public healthcare system, Brazil has determined that the generic pharmaceutical medicines that are acquired by the centralized mechanism of purchase of the Ministry of Health shall not be identified by trademarks. This does not mean, however, that the use of trademarks is banned altogether in connection with generic pharmaceuticals. Such use is prohibited in the context of the public healthcare system only. But generic pharmaceuticals that are sold directly to customers who do not apply for their reimbursement by the system can still bear trademarks.

Law 9,787, of 1999, amending Law 6,360, of 1976, which deals with sanitary vigilance, establishes the generic medicine, provides for the use of generic names in pharmaceutical products and contains other provisions

> Article 3
>
> XX—Similar Medicine—the medicine that contains the same concentration, pharmaceutical formula, route of administration, dosage and therapeutic indication, preventive or diagnostic, as the medicine of reference registered in the federal agency responsible for sanitary vigilance; it may differ only in characteristics related to the size and shape of the product, shelf-life, packaging, labeling, excipients and vehicles, and must always be identified by the trade name or trademark.
>
> XXI—Generic medicine—medicine similar to a product of reference or pioneer product, which is intended to be interchangeable with the latter, generally produced after the expiry or the abandonment of patent protection or of other exclusive rights, upon proof of its efficacy, safety and quality, and designated by the CBD [Common Brazilian Denominator] or, in its absence, by the ICD [International Common Denominator].

Figure 15 An example of the package of a generic medicine in Brazil. The active ingredient is designated (Ibuprofen), along with the dosage, the use, and the therapeutic effects. Originally, the package is red. This color is the choice of the manufacturer. But the stripe at the bottom should appear mandatorily in yellow. Its color and text announce a generic medicine. The manufacturer has inserted its logo in the top right corner of the package.

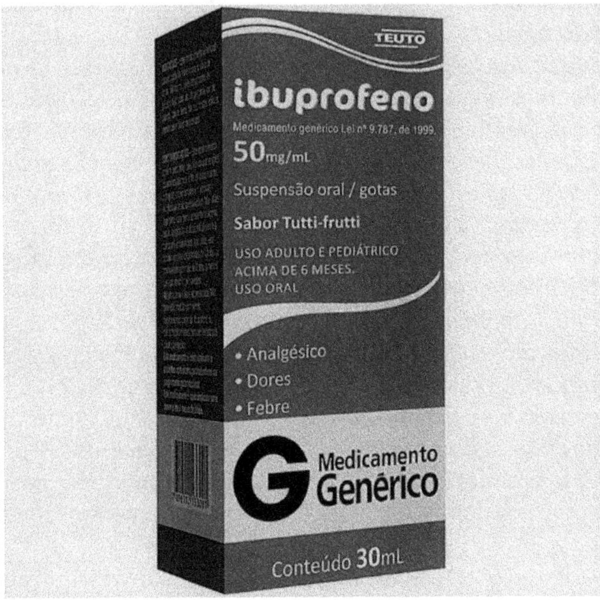

§ 1.34. PROPRIETARY NAMES OF PHARMACEUTICAL SUBSTANCES VERSUS NONPROPRIETARY NAMES

Another concern that governmental authorities have expressed regarding pharmaceutical trademarks is the risk of private appropriation of scientific or common designations through the adoption of business identifiers that derive from them. In this token, the WHO, with the help of the World Intellectual Property Organization (WIPO), has adopted and disclosed a comprehensive list of generic pharmaceutical designations, which, as a consequence of their inclusion in such list, become nonproprietary per se, i.e., *not registrable both as trademarks and trade names.*

The idea is to establish an agreed nomenclature for selecting a single name of worldwide acceptability for each substance that is to be marketed as a pharmaceutical product—and thereby originating a generic name for the active substance. Those names are published in a WHO periodical as a proposed INN (International Nonproprietary Name), and interested parties can oppose that selection. Two lists of proposed INNs and two lists of recommended INNs are published every year, in several languages, including Latin.

Marks and International Nonproprietary Names for Pharmaceutical Substances (INNs)

Document prepared by the Secretariat (WIPO)

SCT/16/3, of September 1, 2006.

4. INNs identify pharmaceutical substances or active pharmaceutical ingredients. Each INN is a unique name that is a globally recognized generic name for an active substance used in pharmaceutical preparations. The system of INNs as it exists today was initiated in 1950 under the auspices of WHO by World Health Assembly Resolution WHA3.11 and began operating in 1953, when the first list of INNs was published. The cumulative list of INNs stands now at some 8,000 published INNs. The aim of the INN system is to provide health professionals with a unique and universally available designated name to identify each pharmaceutical substance [note omitted].
5. With the growing number of INNs and trademarks, the possibility of conflicts between them has gradually increased. The main source of conflict is usually an attempt by a manufacturer to propose a new trademark containing "stems", which are word elements established in the INN system to demonstrate the relationship between pharmacologically related substances. By the use of common "stems" the medical practitioner can recognize that the substance belongs to a group of substances having similar pharmacological activity. To prevent conflicts between INNs and trademarks, the World Health Assembly Resolution WHA46.19 was issued in 1993, requesting the Member States of WHO to develop policy guidelines on the use and protection of INNs, and to discourage the use as trademarks of commercial names derived from INNs and, particularly, names including established INN "stems" [note omitted].
6. WHO collaborates closely with INN experts and national nomenclature committees to select a single name of worldwide acceptability for each active substance that is to be marketed as a pharmaceutical. The INN Expert Group convened by WHO rejects any proposal that could result in a conflict with known trademarks. Selected names are published in a WHO periodical ("WHO Drug Information") [note omitted] as proposed INNs and interested parties are given a period of four months to raise an objection to a proposed INN. An objection may be based, for example, on similarity between the proposed INN and a trademark in which the interested party has proprietary rights. When an objection has been raised, WHO will actively pursue an arrangement to obtain the withdrawal of such an objection or will reconsider the proposed INN. As long as the objection exists, WHO will not publish it as a recommended INN [note omitted].

§ 1.35. SPAIN PROHIBITS THE DESIGNATION OF MEDICINES BY TRADEMARKS ON MEDICAL PRESCRIPTIONS

In 2011, Spain introduced a provision into a statute of 2006 prohibiting medical doctors from designating medicines on their prescriptions by making reference to their trademarks. Instead, medicines must be indicated through their active principle. The measure applies to the medicines to be delivered through the public healthcare system.

The purpose of this measure is purely fiscal. The idea is that, when showing the prescription at the drugstores, patients will obtain the cheapest medicines containing the prescribed active ingredient. This, multiplied millions of times every year, naturally reduces the weight of medicines' costs in the public healthcare system's budget. The Preamble of the statute is unequivocal on this point: "This Royal Decree-Law specifies a series of austerity measures on the supply of pharmaceuticals that seek to alleviate the financial strain on health services, ..." The heading of the statute itself makes it clear that it aims at "contributing to the fiscal consolidation."

This measure may be seen by some as an unwarranted restriction on the physicians' freedom of choice. But, when they see a particular (i.e., exceptional) reason for prescribing a special brand of the medicine, physicians can do so (but they have to justify the choice). And yet, to a large extent, Spain has reduced the differentiation of medicines and inhibited the appropriation of reputation.

Spain is not the first country to take such a measure. Before Spain, a few countries in Latin America have done so. In 1997, in the context of its Trade Policy Review, in the WTO (World Trade Organization), Mexico was questioned by Switzerland about the compatibility of a similar provision with the provisions of Article 20 of the TRIPS Agreement. Mexico refused to enter the substance of the matter and simply replied that the country was still within the transitional period for adapting its norms.

Measures like that of Spain and Mexico may cause some concern, as they eliminate all sorts of trademark differentiation in a significant portion of the market for medicines. Both governments might have alternative ways of reaching the same fiscal result without such a drastic imposition of completely eliminating differentiation in medicines—for example, by setting maximum prices for those drugs dispensed through the public healthcare system. As said in regard to the mandatory plain packaging of breast-milk substitutes, the ban on trademarks appears as an exaggeration, as well as an unjustified restriction to trade, which the TRIPS Agreement might not admit.[16]

The 2016 amendment has been challenged in a Spanish Court by Farmaindustria, the national association of research-based pharmaceutical companies. The Court has sustained the compatibility of the provision in question with Spanish and European Union laws. It has not, however, discussed the possible (actually, probable) infringement of the TRIPS Agreement (see Sentence 338,2016, by the Supreme Court, Chamber of Administrative Litigation, 4th Section).

16. See *supra* note 15, and accompanying text.

Royal Decree-Law 9/2011, of August 19, on measures to improve the quality and cohesion of the national health system, to contribute to fiscal consolidation, and to increase the maximum amount of State guarantees for 2011

Preamble (excerpt)

For its part, the modification of Article 85 of Law 29/2006, of July 26, proposes to generalize the prescription by active principle as a means of, without reducing the quality of the pharmaceutical service, introducing criteria of responsibility in the adequate financial management of resources available to the health system. For this purpose, it is established that the prescription of medicines and health products will be carried out by their active principle or their generic name respectively, except when there are causes of therapeutic needs that justify the prescription by brand, or in the case of medicines that belong to groups consisting exclusively of a drug and its licenses at the same price.

However, when, exceptionally, the prescription has been made by the commercial name of the medicine or health product, the prescribed product will be dispensed if it is the one with the lowest price of the corresponding group; otherwise, the one with the lowest price will be dispensed. This measure entails the dispensing of the lower priced medicine or health product, which represents a significant saving for the National Health System, ...

Article 85 is modified, which will have the following wording:

1. The prescription, indication or authorization of dispensing of drugs will be made by active principle, in the official medical prescription or order of dispensing, of the National Health System.

   Likewise, in health products for non-hospitalized patients that require an official medical prescription or dispensing order from the National Health System for dispensing at the pharmacy office, the prescription, indication or authorization of dispensing will be made by generic name by type of product, and by the characteristics that define it, specifying its size and content.

   In both cases, the pharmacist will dispense the presentation of the medicine or health product with the lowest price, ... However, when, as an exception to the general rule, the prescription, indication or authorization of dispensing had been carried out identifying the medicine or the medical device respectively, by its commercial name, except in the case of the assumptions provided in point 2 of this article, the pharmacist will dispense said medicine or product provided it is the one with the lowest price of the corresponding group, and if it is not, it will dispense the one with the lowest price of the group.
2. However, when the therapeutic needs justify it, as well as when the drugs belong to groups made up exclusively of a drug and its licenses, at the same price as the reference drug, the prescription, indication or dispensing authorization may be carried out by identifying the medicine or, where appropriate, the medical device by its commercial name.

§ 1.36. TOBACCO PLAIN PACKAGING—ANOTHER ASSAULT ON TRADEMARKS' DISTINCTIVENESS FOR THE SAKE OF PUBLIC HEALTH

Like patent rights, which have been under attack because of its allegedly negative effects on access to pharmaceuticals; like copyrights, which have been criticized because of the barrier they might generate for the poor who wish to access culture and education; and like industrial designs, which have been censored because of their monopolist effects on spare parts necessary for repairing complex products—trademarks also have been under siege. Today the attack focuses on trademarks for tobacco products, but the same public health concerns also have inspired the assault on trademarks for other regulated products, such as foodstuffs, infant formulae, etc. [see § 1.32]. The debate has developed around trademarks' potential capacity to lure consumers to the consumption of unhealthy products. In taking measures against that capacity, governments have introduced mandatory "plain packaging," a scheme that varies from country to country, but which essentially restraints the colors, sizes and figurative presentation of trademarks, thus reducing—when not eliminating completely—their distinctive function.

Several bodies of the United Nations have encouraged the Member States to actively engage in the fight against the alleged effect that those trademarks have in inducing the consumption of tobacco. In that sense, the World Health Organization (WHO) approved, in February 2005, the Framework Convention on Tobacco Control (FCTC). Following the example of the International Code of Marketing of Breast-milk Substitutes [see § 1.32.1], the FCTC also recommends the Member States to impose restrictions on, or even to eliminate, the use of certain trademarks that differentiate tobacco products.[17]

A few WTO Members have challenged in the organization's dispute settlement mechanism the adoption by Australia, in 2011, of a statute transposing to national law some of the constraints recommended by the FCTC. In 2018, the arbitration panels, reunited in one single panel, issued a Report that concluded in favor of Australia. An appeal is pending at the time of this writing. The text that follows has been extracted from that Report.

§ 1.36.1. Australia—Certain Measures Concerning Trademarks, Geographical Indications and Other Plain Packaging Requirements Applicable to Tobacco Products and Packaging

Reports of the Panels [excerpt]

WT/DS435/R, WT/DS441/R WT/DS458/R, WT/DS467/R

June 28, 2018

> 7.2604. Overall, we are not persuaded that the complainants have demonstrated that Australia has acted beyond the bounds of the latitude available to it under Article 20 to choose an appropriate policy intervention to address its public health concerns in relation to tobacco products, in imposing certain special requirements under the TPP [Tobacco Plain Packaging] measures that encumber the use of trademarks in the course of trade. While recognizing that trademarks have

17. The same comment made above as regards trademarks for breast-milk substitutes also applies here: some of these restrictions are exaggerated, ill-conceived, and against international law. *See supra* note 15, and accompanying text.

substantial economic value and that the special requirements are far-reaching in terms of the trademark owners' possibilities to extract economic value from the use of figurative or stylized features of trademarks, we note that the TPP measures, including their trademark restrictions, are an integral part of Australia's comprehensive tobacco control policies, and designed to complement the pre-existing measures. As noted above, the fact that the special requirements, as part of the overall TPP measures and in combination with other tobacco-control measures maintained by Australia, are capable of contributing, and do in fact contribute, to Australia's objective of improving public health by reducing the use of, and exposure to, tobacco products, suggests that the reasons for which these special requirements are applied provide sufficient support for the application of the resulting encumbrances on the use of trademarks. We further note that Australia, while having been the first country to implement tobacco plain packaging, has pursued its relevant domestic public health objective in line with the emerging multilateral public health policies in the area of tobacco control as reflected in the FCTC [United Nations Framework Convention on Tobacco Control] and the work under its auspices, including the Article 11 and Article 13 FCTC Guidelines.

§ 1.36.2. Australia's Tobacco Plain Packaging Act 2011 (Excerpts)

Section 20. Prohibition on trademarks and marks generally appearing on retail packaging

No trade marks

(1) No trade mark may appear anywhere on the retail packaging of tobacco products, other than as permitted by subsection (3).

No marks

(2) No mark may appear anywhere on the retail packaging of tobacco products, other than as permitted by subsection (3).

Permitted trade marks and marks

(3) The following may appear on the retail packaging of tobacco products:
   (a) the brand, business or company name for the tobacco products, and any variant name for the tobacco products;
   (b) the relevant legislative requirements;
   (c) any other trade mark or mark permitted by the regulations. . . .

Section 21. Requirements for brand, business, company or variant names, and relevant legislative requirements

Requirements for brand, business, company or variant name—general

(1) Any brand, business or company name, or any variant name, for tobacco products that appears on the retail packaging of those products must comply with any requirements prescribed by the regulations.

Requirements for brand, business, company or variant name—cigarette packs and cigarette cartons

(2) Any brand, business or company name, or any variant name, for cigarettes that appears on a cigarette pack or cigarette carton:
   (a) must not obscure any relevant legislative requirement; and

(b) must not appear more than once on any of the following outer surfaces of the pack or carton:
   (i) for a cigarette pack—the front, top and bottom outer surfaces of the pack;
   (ii) for a cigarette carton—the front outer surface of the carton, and the 2 smallest outer surfaces of the carton; and
(c) may appear only on the surfaces mentioned in paragraph (b); and
(d) must appear across one line only; and
(e) must comply with the requirements in the table in subsection (3).

(3) The following table has effect: [a table follows with specific requirements on the way brands, business and company names are to be displayed on tobacco packages]

Requirements for relevant legislative requirements (other than health warnings)

(4) Any relevant legislative requirement (other than the health warnings) must comply with any requirements prescribed by the regulations. . . .

Figure 16 A banned trademark under all plain packaging schemes in force: the Camel and its exotic eastern middle eastern background may induce the youth to start consuming tobacco. Camel is a trademark owned by Japan Tobacco Inc.

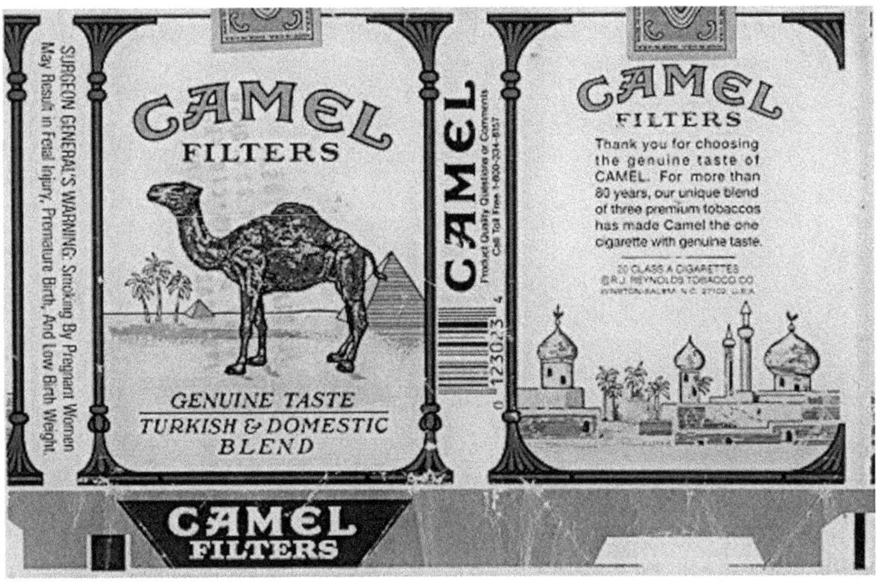

Figure 17 Australian government's guide to tobacco plain packaging and a sample of a law compliant pack of cigarettes: the brand appears once, in a word form. No drawings, no pictures, other than those illustrating the evils of tobacco consumption.

CHAPTER 2

The Private Appropriation of Pharmaceutical Knowledge (Patents, Trade Secrets, Printing Privileges)

The second chapter illustrates the second line of tension that, throughout history, has presided over the intellectual property of medicines and access to health: on the one hand, the efforts of inventors to appropriate their creations and thereby to capture private revenue; on the other, the reluctance from various corners of society to permit the private appropriation of those inventions.

The first trend has been based on patents and trade secrets, the latter being more frequently used by inventors as regards medicines until the beginning of the twentieth century—when governments gradually started imposing the disclosure and registration of medicinal formulae as requirements for their commercialization. During the seventeenth century, some European sovereigns purchased the secret compositions of a number of drugs and ordered their publication. As seen in the first chapter, inventors would also resort to indirect means of appropriation through the building of reputation, by means of intensive advertising and branding. The foundations of this line of conduct lie on the natural right of inventors to appropriate the fruits of their intellectual labor. Additionally, the economic rationale also assists inventors, whereas patents and trade secrets serve the self-interest of private inventors who, using their own resources, find new drugs and medical devices only because they are lured by the perspective of gains. An additional economic explanation is that private property in drugs reduces the (high) transaction costs that naturally, in its absence, result from licensing rights in medical technology.

The second trend has been asserted through the imposition of restrictions on the patentability and on the commercialization of secret medicines. Four reasons have been proposed to justify those restrictions: (i) first and foremost, the private appropriation of medicinal compositions is immoral—inventions of such importance to human life should not rest in the private hands of invariably selfish individuals; (ii) the grant of patents implies a right to use, and thus it should not lie in the hands of patent examiners, but rather of sanitary agencies; (iii) obtaining patents is the same as acquiring monopolistic tools, with attendant high prices, either on direct sales or as a consequence of royalties, and the impossibility of poor people having access to them; and (iv) in situations like the COVID-19 pandemic, there is the urgent need for achieving a huge level of production of a vaccine, which an individual patent owner would never be able to secure. In addition, there have been attacks against the private appropriation of certain aspects of medical knowledge that not only result from research and development, and, eventually, good luck, but also from the personal skills of physicians. This concerns therapeutic, surgical, and diagnostic methods, whose patentability is seen by many as an unethical confrontation with the values of the medical profession.

These two trends are illustrated in the texts that follow. The sources show that there is no winning trend, with the various stakeholders flagging their arguments in various fora and under different circumstances. The sources also show that proposed alternate means aimed at conciliating the conflicting positions, such as granting prizes to inventors instead of patents, have already been tested.

Like the first chapter, this second chapter also shows that the intellectual property of medicines and access to health has many aspects of its own, which cannot be found in other areas of business. The reason is perhaps that the notion of access to health as a business is repugnant to many people. And yet, in the absence of that dimension, and of the lure of gains obtained from product differentiation obtained through the development of new medicines and methods of treatment and cure, public health would be in a much worse state than it is now.

§ 2.01. THE SECRET MEDICINE OF ANTONIUS PACCHIUS—FIRST CENTURY AD

Secrecy was the first way to which inventive pharmacists resorted for appropriating the results of their ingenuity. In the absence of formal mechanisms, secrecy has always been the easiest, fastest and cheapest way of securing private gains in knowledge.
This assertion is confirmed by the story of Antonius Pacchius and his improvement of an old formula for an analgesic that gained great popularity in the first century of our era. Antochius Pacchius was a renowned physician and pharmacist who lived during the time of the first two Roman Emperors, Augustus and Tiberius. As an inventor, he produced new medicines and improved old ones, from which he obtained great financial success. He created, for example, the formulae of several lotions employed as collyria. His name appears in several stamps (see § 1.02) associated with the names of a number of doctors, such as Maritimus, who would sell (and stamp) a collyrium ad aspritudines *("for trachoma"). [Ernest Desjardins, Notice sur les Monuments Epigraphiques de Bavai et du Musée de Douai, at 111-112 (L. Crépin, 1873). Source: <gallica.BnF.fr>.]*
Pacchius' most famous medicine was a "hyera" (which, in Greek, means "sacred medicine"), with analgesic and anti-inflammatory effects, used against back pain and gout. "Hyera" was a term employed generically to designate a type of compositions that usually contained aloes as their main ingredient, to which aromatics would be added. Pacchius kept his composition as a secret during his entire lifetime. Upon his death, a description of the composition was found in a letter that Pacchius had addressed to Tiberius, and that was kept in the public library.

In his lifetime, Pacchius took strict measures not to disclose the secret composition: he not only refused to deliver the formula in exchange for money but also kept it away from his own servants, who assisted him in the preparation of his medicines. When the time came for making the hyera, Pacchius would not only lock himself and the servants in a room but would also have them adding more substances than necessary, so that they would not be able to learn the true recipe.

The text that follows is a report of Pacchiu's secret by Sribonius Largus, physician to Tiberius, who left a description of about 250 medicines in De Compositione Medicamentorum. *The same story can be found in Marcellus Empiricus'* De Medicamentis. *Marcellus, a medical writer, born in Gaul (fourth-fifth century AD), incorporated in his book excerpts from classical writers' works, including those of Scribonius.*

Scribonii Largi, Medici Vetustissimi, de compositione medicamentorum liber—First Century AD

XCVII. The hyera antidote of Pacchius Antiochus against all pains, especially back pain, and gout

For the back pain, with or without fever, the effects of the marvelous composition were not ignored by the ancient, but its principles were taught by Pacchius Antiochus and its use shown to auditor Philenidis Catinensis. And he [Pacchius] made immense profit out of the repeated success [of his drug] against most difficult illnesses. But during his lifetime he would not impart the composition to any, not even for money. After his death, the composition was found in a letter he wrote to Tiberius Caesar, and found in the public library. In that way it came to our hands, what beforehand in no way otherwise we could have extracted, even though we had tried everything we could. But [Pacchius] would lock himself up to prepare [the medicine]; he would not trust even his own [servants] that he employed to add the several perfumes [ingredients], because he would have many more things to be added than [the recipe] contained, purposely to deceive his people. Afterwards we could, safely and freely make the medicine, which [Pacchius] had not invented, but whose uses he had proved against certain illnesses, and the respective mode, and in this way we could profit from that information. Because it might be not unknown to the ancient, and yet [they did not know] what to add, or to subtract. And the value of [Pacchius'] recipe was in its composition, whereas the one known to the ancient was unsuitable. In spite of the numerous old compositions, they had not the same effect [as Pacchius' composition], whose wonderful temperament produces marvelous results.

§ 2.02. PLINY THE ELDER COMMENDS THE INVENTIVE LABOR OF THOSE WHO FIND NEW MEDICINES IN NATURE BUT CRITICIZES THEIR GREED AND THEIR "SECRET SPIRIT"—FIRST CENTURY AD

Gaius Plinius Secundus, known as Pliny the Elder, in his NATURAL HISTORY, *wrote extensively about medicine and the drugs used in Rome. The two following excerpts reflect Pliny's views on the intellectual property of those medicines. In the first text, he explained that the work of inventing and preparing medicines justifies that their prices are not as low as that of their respective ingredients. In the second, he refers in a critical tone to the appropriation of the knowledge in drugs through secrecy. Some inventors would also be recognized through the attribution of their names to plants. However, Pliny admits that if it were not for the wish of those inventors to somehow capture the prestige and the financial rewards from their inventive work, they would not have searched for roots and vegetation that were hidden in deserts and behind mountains for the preparation of useful medicines.*
The last two sentences in the first excerpt refer to the fact that most physicians and drug makers in Rome were of Greek nationality.

NATURAL HISTORY, by Pliny the Elder

First Century AD

Book XXIV. Ch. I.

Hence sprang the art of medicine. Such things alone had Nature decreed should be our remedies, provided everywhere, easy to discover and costing nothing—the things in fact that support our life. Later on the deceit of men and cunning profiteering led to the invention of the quack laboratories, in which each customer is promised a new lease of his own life at a price. At once compound prescriptions and mysterious mixtures are glibly repeated, Arabia and India are judged to be storehouses of remedies, and a small sore is charged with the cost of a medicine from the Red Sea, although the genuine remedies form the daily dinner of even the very poorest. But if remedies were to be sought in the kitchen-garden, or a plant or a shrub were to be procured thence, none of the arts would become cheaper than medicine. It is perfectly true that owing to their greatness the Roman people have lost their usages, and through conquering we have been conquered. We are the subjects of foreigners, and in one of the arts they have mastered even their masters.

Book XXV. Ch. I.

This peculiar glory of plants which I am now going to speak of, Mother Earth producing them sometimes for medicinal purposes only, rouses in one's mind admiration for the care and industry of the men of old; there was nothing left untried or unattempted by them, and furthermore nothing kept secret, nothing which they wished to be of no benefit to posterity. But we moderns desire to hide and suppress the discoveries worked out by these investigators, and to cheat human life even of the good things that have been won by others. Yes indeed, those who have gained a little knowledge keep it in a grudging spirit secret to themselves, and to teach nobody else increases the prestige of their learning. So far has custom departed from fresh research and assistance to life; the supreme task of our great minds has long been to keep within individual memory the successes of the ancients, so allowing them to be forgotten. But, heaven knows, there are some whom a single discovery has added to the number of the gods, whose life on earth at any rate has been made more glorious by their names being given to plants, so kind the thanks of a mindful posterity. This careful research of theirs is less wonderful when rewarded by plants of fascinating growth or attractive as food; but they have scoured also trackless mountain heights, unexplored deserts and all the bowels of the earth, finding out the power of every root and the uses to which can be put mere slim threads of vegetation, and turning to healthful purposes that which the very beasts refuse to touch as food.

§ 2.03. OATH OF SECRECY BY THE NEW MASTER APOTHECARIES IN PARIS—FOURTEENTH CENTURY

For many centuries, secrecy has been the mechanism of election for the private appropriation of knowledge by the inventors of new medicines. G. Mandich, who found and described the Venetian statute on industrial privileges of 1474, mentions a regulation approved in 1297 in that same city that provided that, when physicians created a new medicine and kept it under secrecy, the other members of the guild should not interfere with it. See G. Mandich, Primi riconoscimenti veneziani di un diritto di privativa agli inventori, *Rivista di Diritto Industriale 7 (1958), 101-155.*
*The same respect for secrecy was imposed in the fourteenth century to the masters of the guild of apothecaries of Paris. Probably, not many medicines would be kept secret because apothecaries were required to strictly follow the recipes described in the prevailing Pharmacopeias. Thus, secrecy in medicines in the thirteenth and fourteenth centuries in Europe might not be an obligation specific to the nature of the trade, but rather to the very nature of the guilds. Indeed, old guilds were initially created around religious beliefs and duties of fraternal assistance, and that is why they were also designated as "mysteries." Secrecy was in the social fabric behind those organizations. Therefore, even if in professional terms, secrecy might not constitute a relevant way of appropriating knowledge—*i.e.*, as a competitive advantage over commercial rivals—apothecaries' guild members were bound by it.*
The following text, taken from an oath that, in the fourteenth century, the apothecaries of Paris had to swear before they could start practicing, states the purpose that then was attributed to apothecaries' secrecy: to avoid that significant information fell in the hands of "idiots and ungrateful persons." In reference to idiots, we may see a concern with public health (so that idiots would not adulterate medicinal formulae). The reference to ungrateful persons possibly revealed a concern with the payment of the services provided by apothecaries—if their secrets were revealed, patients could attempt to reproduce the drugs, thus avoiding the payment of fees.

C.J.S. Thompson, The Mystery and Art of the Apothecary (Excerpt)

Oath that the apothecaries of Paris had to swear before they were allowed to practice

> I swear and promise before God, Author and Creator of all things, one in essence and distinguished in three persons, everlastingly blessed; that I will observe on every point all the following articles. And first, promise to live and die in the Christian Faith; to love and honour my parents to the best of my ability; to honour, respect and serve, as far as in me lies, not only the doctors of medicine who have instructed me in the knowledge and precepts of the art, but also the teachers and the master-apothecaries under whom I have learnt my business; not to speak ill of my former doctors, master-apothecaries, or any one else.

To do all I can for the honor, glory and adornment of medicine, not to teach its secrets and curiosities to idiots and ungrateful persons, to do nothing rashly without the advice of Physicians and only in the hope of gain. To give no medicament or purge to those laboring under any disease, without first taking counsel of some learned doctor; not in any way to touch the shameful and forbidden parts of women, unless in case of urgent necessity, that is to say when some remedy has to be applied to them. To disclose to no one any secret entrusted to me, never to give anyone any kind of poison to drink, nor to advise anyone to give such a potion even to his greatest enemies; never to give any abortive potion; never in any way to attempt to induce the expulsion of the foetus from the belly of the mother, unless acting on the advice of the doctor, do dispense exactly, without adding or leaving out anything in the prescriptions of the doctors, as far as they are in accordance with the rules of the art. To use no succedaneum or substitute without taking counsel of someone of greater knowledge than myself; to repudiate and avoid like the plague, the scandalous and utterly pernicious methods of practice now employed by empirical charlatans and alchemists, to the great shame of the magistrates who tolerate them; to give help and succor alike to all who shall employ me, and lastly to keep no bad or old drug in my shop.

May the Lord bless me always, as I shall observe these things.

§ 2.04. JACOPO DI DONDI RECEIVES AN INDUSTRIAL PRIVILEGE FOR A PROCESS OF EXTRACTING MEDICINAL SALT FROM THE THERMAL WATERS OF ABANO, ITALY—1355

In 1355, the Prince of Ferrara granted Jacopo di Dondi a privilege for the extraction of salt from the hot mineral springs of Abano that are found near Padua. The good medicinal effects of that salt were vigorously contested by some people, which obliged Jacopo to write in defense of his invention. The text that follows is an excerpt from a notice on that privilege written by Francesco Scipione and on the treatise that Jacopo wrote in defense of his invention.

Jacopo was a renowned inventor, his name being generally associated with the invention and making of the astronomical clock of the Torre dei Signori of the Palazzo del Capitanio in Padua. His fame made him to be remembered as Jacopo dell'Orologio.

Francesco Scipione, *Notizie sopra Jacopo e Giovanni Dondi dall'Orologio*

Our Jacopo, in that occasion, reveals his invention on producing salt to the Prince [of Ferrara], who in his good disposition decides to grant him the permission to make it, through an honorific Decree that accorded him the exclusive right [of making it] and transport it to wherever he saw fit, with exemption of any duties and taxes.

In the following year, in order to contest his enemies and describe how to make that Salt, he wrote a brief treatise on this topic. Here is the title: *Consideratio Jacobi de Dondis de causa salsedinis aquarum, & de modo conficiendi sal ex eis* [Treatise by Jacobi de Dondis on the cause of the saltiness of the water, and mode of making salt from it]. . . . In order, says Jacopo [in the Preamble of his treatise] to repress the calumnies of my enemies & envious detractors of the work that is more the product of divine grace than of human ingenuity, I am obliged to write a treatise on a method that I recently invented of extracting salt from the hot springs near Padua, [divided into four chapters]. . . .

§ 2.05. THE ORDINANCES OF THE GROCERS' COMPANY AND THE OBLIGATION OF APPRENTICES TO KEEP TRADE SECRETS—1525

As already noted, in the Middle Ages, apothecaries did not feel the pressure for the invention of new medicines. Most drugs were described in old Greek and Roman pharmacopeias, which served as technical guides for the guilds. Moreover, the ingredients of most of them—sugar and spices from the East—were very rare and expensive. It was not a coincidence that the Guild of Apothecaries and Grocers of London, formerly called the Pepperers, had in their coat of arms, granted in 1429 by Henry the Sixth, the picture of a loaded camel. Indeed, it was on the back of camels that Arabs brought the spices from India and other Eastern countries, to sell them to the Turks and the Venetians. British grocers would obtain the matters of their trade—spices—from those intermeddlers, who would charge very high price mark-ups.

It was in the fifteenth century, with the navigation successes of the Portuguese around the African coast, that the trade of spices changed, and their availability increased significantly. This led not only to a reduction of the prices of medicines but also to significant growth in the availability of new ones—and significant growth in the number of apothecaries as well.

In the sixteenth century, there was another push to the creativity of apothecaries: the emergence of chemistry, built in part on alchemic research.

These two factors led to a significant increase in the invention of new medicines, with the attendant eruption of competition among inventors and the unfortunate, but always inevitable, emergence of charlatans and quacks.

It was then that the appropriation of new medicinal compositions and formulae became a matter of relevance and subject to more or less established public policies. Secrecy was the way inventors preferred to reserve the use of new drugs, and, as we will see in the next sections, kings would not refuse to accord exclusive protection in their regard. But this would come later.

Anyway, in the sixteenth century, the notion of secrecy was already part of the normal trade of apothecaries and their apprentices. Although European countries were then already familiar with the notion of industrial privileges, which frequently (but not always) would include a requirement for the disclosure of inventions, very rarely would they be granted for inventions with medicinal use. Indeed, the privilege granted to Jacopo di Dondi (see § 2.04) was quite unique. Not a single of those inventions appears in the available lists of privileges granted in Venice, under the statute of 1474, or in Germany, or in Spain.[18] *And none appears in the calendar of patent rolls. Clearly, the first industrial privileges covered mechanical inventions and processes only. This would change much later, with the enactment of the Statute of Monopolies (see § 2.21).*

The following text confirms the care that in the sixteenth century London apothecaries and their apprentices were required to have in preserving the secrets of their trade.

J. Aubrey Rees, THE WORSHIPFUL COMPANY OF GROCERS—A HISTORICAL RETROSPECT (excerpt)

Regulation 42, Ordinances of the Grocers' Company, 1525

The Oath of the Apprentices—"Ye shall swear to be good and true to our sovereign lord the King, and to his heirs, kings, and well and truly ye shall serve your master for the terms of your apprenticeship, and in all lawful and honest causes ye shall be obedient to the Wardens and to all them that be of the clothing, and to have the same in due reverence. The lawful secrets of the said fellowship ye shall keep, and give none information nor instruction thereof to no person but of the said fellowship. In all these things ye shall well and truly behave and surely keep this said oath to your power, So help you God and His saints, and by that Book. And if it fortune that you depart from your master, ye shall not serve any person out of the said fellow ship without licence of the said Wardens for the time being, upon pain to forfeit to the use of the said fellowship such penalty as shall be assessed upon you by the said Wardens and associates of the said fellowship."

§ 2.06. A SECRET SURGICAL METHOD—1550

With the rise of the medical profession in the sixteenth century, based on the growing wealth of knowledge that was then being developed systematically, as the Scientific Revolution moved on, not only new pharmaceuticals appeared in profusion, but also new techniques of diagnosing and treating ailments were created. Often engaged in bitter commercial rivalry, physicians would not disdain to seek intellectual property protection for their creations as an effective way of ensuring competitive advantage.

18. *See* the Appendixes to Giulio Mandich, *Venetian Patents (1450-1550)*, 166, 207 J. OF THE PAT. OFF. SOC'Y (1948), and to Hansjoerg Pohlmann, *The Inventor's Right in Early German Law—Materials of the Time from 15831 to 1700*, 121, 135 J. OF THE PAT. OFF. SOC'Y (1961). See Nicolás García Tapia, TÉCNICA Y PODER EN CASTILLA DURANTE LOS SIGLOS XVI Y XVII (Junta de Castilla y León, 2003).

It seems that at that time, there was no social or political reluctance in granting exclusivity in surgical methods. In the text that follows, French historian Alfred Franklin briefly describes the facts involving a secret method of extracting stones from the gall bladder, which would have been invented in France. Apparently, the inventor had the king's support because he not only was designated as personal surgeon to the king but was also appointed to work in a public hospital.

Alfred Franklin, Dictionnaire Historique des Arts, Métiers et Professions exercés dans Paris depuis le Treizième Siècle (excerpt)

In Paris, [the lithotomy] remained for a long time the specialty of a family whose members kept the secrets and passed on to one another certain chirurgical procedures. Laurent Collot or Colot, surgeon of Henry II and lithotomist at the Hôtel-Dieu, taught his method to his son, who applied it successfully. He had a son, a third Laurent Colot, whose skills equaled that of his ancestors. This one gave birth to Philippe Colot, *peritissimus artifex*, . . . he himself afflicted by the stone, was operated by his son, and his nephew, who was associated in his labors. Severin Pineau, his son-in-law, put in possession of the famous secret, thought his duty to divulge it; but the Colots did not for that reason ceased to practice their art, and two of them, Jerome and Francis, left a famous name.

§ 2.07. ALTERNATIVE MEANS OF THE APPROPRIATION OF PHARMACEUTICAL KNOWLEDGE: PRINTING PRIVILEGES, SECRETS, REPUTATION

In the sixteenth and seventeenth centuries, pharmacists resorted to various means alternative to patents to secure the appropriation of their knowledge. The first and preferred alternative was, as shown, trade secrets. They do not depend on any formality. Taking some protective measures to avoid their disclosure to competitors is enough. Eventually, authorities have acknowledged their value, by ensuring their exclusive use, or by paying the inventors for their communication. These various mechanisms are illustrated in this book. But those in possession of useful pharmaceutical knowledge had recourse to other ways of appropriation. Some pharmacists did publish the secret of recipes of medicines. But in this case, they applied for and obtained privileges on the respective publications. For almost three centuries, printing privileges were the sole mechanism guaranteeing exclusivity in the distribution and sale of printed books—in other words, it was copyright before copyright. In that way, pharmacists and their publishers were able to extract revenue from pharmaceutical inventions. Moreover, published books would show the publishers' trademarks and shop signs, thus integrating a panoply of legal tools, ensuring exclusivity and enforceability in intangible assets.

The texts and figures that follow give two examples of those alternative means of appropriating pharmaceutical knowledge.

The first example concerns Alessio Piemontese, who, at the age of 82, wrote a famous treatise on medicinal and botanical "secrets"—De Secreti del Rev. Donno Alessio Piemontese—first published in Venice, in 1555. The book had enormous success and, besides being reedited several times in several Italian cities, was soon translated and published in other European countries. In the preface to the first edition of his book, Alessio provided for a few biographic details, as well as, importantly, his motivations in publishing his secrets. Alessio was not a typical pharmacist because, as he explains, he was well-off, and, therefore, kept his many recipes secret because of vanity, not because he wished to gain money with their use. Nevertheless, he acted as regards his secrets exactly in the same way as other pharmacists did. Alessio's "conversion" against the secrecy of medicines was based on moral and religious values. Also importantly, Alessio emphasized the experimental nature of his scientific knowledge of medicines—something that corresponded to the principles of the Scientific Revolution, which was at that time spreading in Europe.

The second example is more typical of the practices of some pharmacists in obtaining revenues from secret knowledge: Godefroy Roussel, a master apothecary from Paris, published a book on some of his alchemic secrets, obtained a printing privilege from the king, and sold the books himself, rather than assigning that task to a printer/bookseller. Curiously, according to the notice in the cover, Roussel's books were available at the store of a candle maker (eventually a colleague of Roussel because at that time, candle makers and apothecaries were reunited under the same guild). This seems to be a violation of the laws concerning the printing business because only registered booksellers were, in principle, allowed to sell books. However, the contrary was true: many booksellers would sell medicines and their ingredients.

§ 2.07.1. Alessio Piemontese, Prologue to his book De Secreti

1555

Don Alexis Piemontois to the reader.

Those who have known me in the past, or, to put it better, those who have been familiarly related to me during my entire life, may know, perhaps, how our Lord God, by his great kindness, made me rise from noble house and blood, according to the costume, against the vain opinion of those who base the nobility more on the merits of others than on their own, and that besides I have always been at ease, and have acquired many goods of fortune, eventually much exceeding the smallness of my merit. I will say even more, not to boast, but in order to inform the gracious Reader, and to thank God for it, because there are several persons who are aware that since my earliest youth I have dedicated myself to the studies, I [thereby] have acquired not only the knowledge of the Latin, Greek, Chaldaic, Arabic languages, and of several other diverse nations: But above all that, by natural inclination, having taken a singular pleasure in philosophy, and in the Secrets of Nature, I travelled the world for fifty and seven years, in order to have the knowledge of all kind of learned people. By which diligence and curiosity I learned beautiful Secrets: not only from people of great knowledge, and great Lords, but also from poor women, craftsmen, peasants, and all kinds of people. And three times I have been in the Levant and reached almost all the other parts of the world, being able to say for sure, that I have never stayed in a country for more than five months. This study of mine, or this desire of mine to know, both the universal sciences and the particular secrets, besides being natural in me, as in most of the men, which everyone by instinct of nature wishes to know, has always been in me the basis of a true ambition, and vain glory, to know what others did not know, and I have always been very avaricious to wish to communicate any of my secrets, even to the dearest friends I have had. And I always have said that if the secrets were known by everybody, they would no longer be called *secrets*, but *publics*. And then when, after several months, I found myself in Milan, and being already eighty-two years and seven months old, a poor craftsman was suffering from [kidney] stones, and he had been two days without urinating, and a physician who took care of him, knowing that I had many secrets, and especially for the stone, came to request me to teach him, or give him the medicine to heal the patient. I, seeing that he wanted to avail himself of the things of others for his benefit and honor, did not want to give it to him, but I said that he should lead me to the patient, that I would have made the medicine without wanting any payment. The doctor, either because of being ashamed of having recourse to the help of others when perhaps he had boasted of having the secret, or because he wanted to earn money, was upset, and now with one excuse, and then with another, or with some pretext, delayed the thing for two days, and then finally took me there. When I got there, I found the patient already at the end [of life], and, raising slightly his eyes, and compassionately looking at me, he passed away, without needing that [medicine] any more, nor any other remedy for his health. Thus I remained with so much compassion, or with so much pain, that I hated myself, and I wished I could die too, seeing that the ambition, and my vain glory had been the reason for that Christian having not been helped with that secret and grace that the most merciful God, and universal father, and our Lord, had given me. And so much the remorse affected my conscience that, wishing to seclude myself from the world, and not finding myself in disposition, nor in the spirit of living in monasteries among religious people, who are stronger, and better-formed than I was, I restricted myself to moving to a place away from the city, where I have a small piece of land, and a few books, and a study, in order to flee idleness. Here I live a life which I call monastic and religious, with only one servant, who goes to the City, not to beg, but to buy the provisions, and other necessary things: to minimally sustain his life, and mine, as long as it will please our Lord to allow me to live it. Now, not being able to take away from the mind that I have been a true murderer, because I refused to the doctor the recipe to cure that poor man, I have decided to publish and communicate to the world all those recipes that I have, being assured that few [other persons] will be found who have as many as I. However, not wanting to bring to light but the most truthful and experimented [secret recipes], I have these past days, withdrawing partly from my writings, partly from my memory all those that I have learned, made a collection of those that I am certain to be true and tested, not caring that some of them are written, or printed in other Books, and not only in this one. Because from this collection of mine the Reader will draw at least this utility, that where beforehand he could doubt whether such remedies brought to light by others were true, or not, he will now be assured under my oath: for, as a matter of course, at this age, with disposition of body, and of spirit, I would not like to put myself to write lies, which would last forever. On one point I want to warn the Reader, it is that he should do things with due diligence, and that with regard to medicines concerning the human body, he should use the help of physicians: in spite of the fact, however, that it seems that several of them, moved by a certain rustic and ill-founded boredom, with a jealous passion, have become accustomed to blaming things that do not come from themselves. Therefore, as much in this as in any other point, if the one who wants to use it found, by fortuitous event, that the thing did not come into effect to his contentment, that he checks whether he has not been abused in something, and that he starts it, again, with greater diligence, making sure that, as I said, there is nothing in this Book that is not very true and well experimented. And, of all, always giving glory to God alone, be hopeful that, by means of his divine grace, I will consequently make you present of the rest, of all that I have acquired of good, by so many years, travel, costs, and diligence of study.

Figure 18 Cover of the Belgian edition of Alexis Piemontese's De Secreti (Christophle Plantin, 1559).

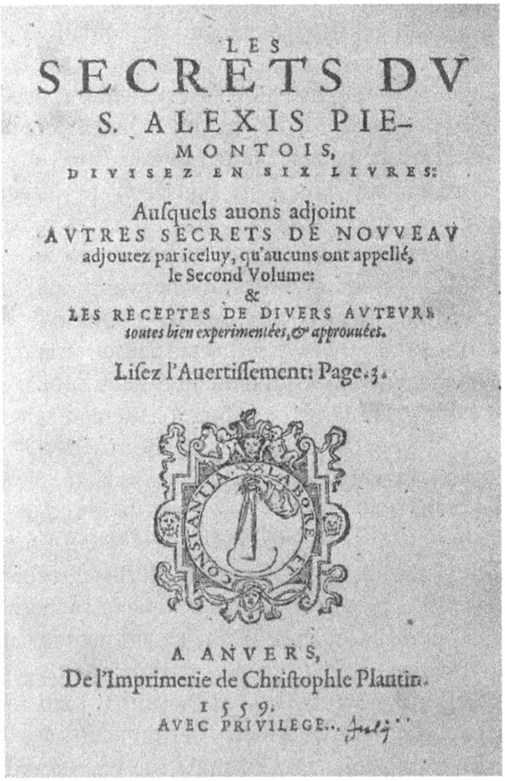

LES
SECRETS DV
S. ALEXIS PIE-
MONTOIS,
DIVISEZ EN SIX LIVRES:
Auſquels auons adjoint
AVTRES SECRETS DE NOVVEAV
adjoutez par iceluy, qu'aucuns ont appellé,
le Second Volume:
&
LES RECEPTES DE DIVERS AVTEVRS
toutes bien experimentées, & approuuées.
Liſez l'Auertiſſement: Page.3.

A ANVERS,
De l'Imprimerie de Chriſtophle Plantin.
1559.
AVEC PRIVILEGE...

§ 2.07.2. Excerpt from the Privilege to the Belgian edition of Piemontese's De Secreti

Extract from the Privilege

The Royal Majesty has given Privilege to Cristophle Plantin, Sworn Printer of the City of Antwerp, allowing him to print, or have printed, sold and distributed, both in Brabant, and throughout all the Low Countries,

Les recettes de plusieurs auteurs: &
Secrets de reverend Seigneur Alexis Piemontois, tous bien approuvés.

Forbidding all printers, booksellers, and other anyone, to do the same in all these aforementioned countries, or elsewhere print, sell, or distribute in any of these three languages, namely, French, Flemish, and Spanish, during four full years, under penalty of confiscation of the printed Books, and in addition to [the fine of] twenty Carolus for each time that someone would have contravened or infringed this, as it is more fully stated in the original Privileges given at Brussels on November 13, 1559. Signed Ph. From Lens. And at the Privy Council, of March 2, 1557. Signed de la Torre.

§ 2.07.3. Excerpts from the Preamble to the Revealed Secrets of the Arts, both of Pharmacy and of Distillation, commonly called Alchemy, or Spargyric: through which perfection will be reached, both in Theory and in practice, in making gold drinkable, succinctly described in the form of Dialogs, by Godefroy Roussel

1613

To the Reader,
The Art of distilling, commonly called Alchemy, to which I refer (Dear Reader) is a science approved by some, and by others disapproved. This diversity is the cause that many remain unsure of its truth. Which is very difficult to know (although there is nothing so true:) Even given that the Doctors who have written about it make it confusing with texts that seem to contradict each other, because their intention is covered with the veil of the enigma, or must it be understood by a mystical or allegorical sense, which has caused many to get carried away by the persuasion, or rather, by the biased opinion that, based on natural reasons, is so much forgotten by those who condemn it, without even wanting to take the trouble to seek the basis of it, and of its principles and causes, to know if they are necessary and profitable for the use of men. . . . if not that the truth takes the right way, and the lie the left one. This right path is the one where nature begins, and where it ends, which will level our judgment as far as it is necessary that it plant these limits, inside which we can make gold Drinkable, against the opinion of those who, ignoring the secrets of nature, affirm that gold cannot become Drinkable, saying that it is of immutable substance, which cannot

be changed against its nature. This Argument being based only on the opinion that is the lie's daughter, which has persuaded them, and not on experimentation, the truth's daughter, also makes that its consequence cannot be true, as the reason demonstrates it. Because being the Gold composed of the substance of the elements, whose shape is generated by the higher bodies, it cannot be that it is not subject to the vicissitude and revolution of them. . . . I want to believe that the cause that makes it immutable comes from its perfect coction and digestion, by which the composition of its elements are so strongly chained and linked together, that one cannot overcome the other, which makes it resist to fire, to air, to water, and to the earth, which cannot dissolve, corrupt, confuse, and rot it. Being therefore this digestion the base and foundation that make that its substance remains indomitable and unchangeable, if it was removed from it, and that its elements were untied. There is no doubt that it would be made drinkable. . . . I have written this Treatise, which is divided into two Dialogues, the first shows that nature has five main parts, namely matter, form, movement, time and place, of which the matter and the form are the principle, and as far as the causes are concerned, [they are] the efficient, the final, the exemplary, and the instrumental. . . . The second Treaty teaches how to prepare the drugs and mainly to make the gold Drinkable, after some decision on certain points, which seem to contradict each other, and in short the rules of the Art are as seriously as succinctly represented in accordance with that of the nature, which makes our way easier, which you are advised (Benign Reader) to follow if you wish to achieve the Art of distilling. . . .

Figure 19 Cover of Les Secrets Découverts des Arts, Tant de Pharmacie que de Distiller, *Invented by Godefroy Roussel, Master Apothecary in Paris (self-publication, 1613).*

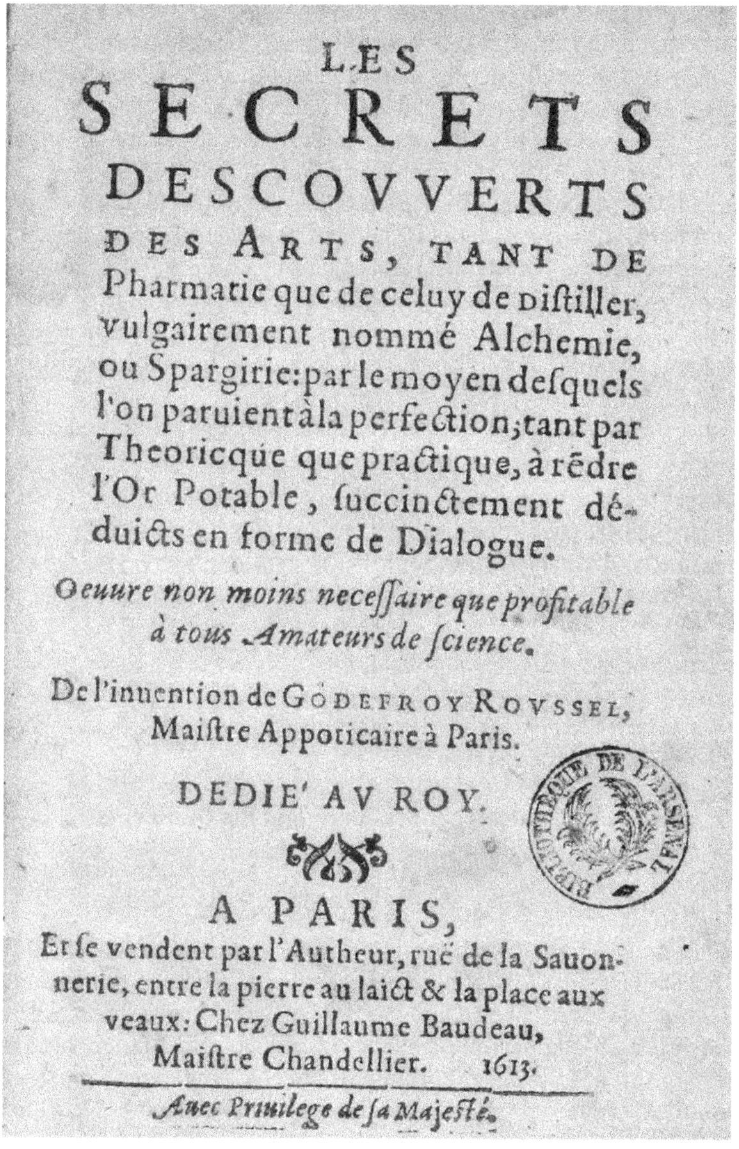

LES
SECRETS
DESCOVVERTS
DES ARTS, TANT DE
Pharmacie que de celuy de diſtiller,
vulgairement nommé Alchemie,
ou Spargirie: par le moyen deſquels
l'on paruient à la perfection; tant par
Theoricque que practique, à rẽdre
l'Or Potable, ſuccinctement dé-
duicts en forme de Dialogue.

Oeuure non moins neceſſaire que profitable à tous Amateurs de ſcience.

De l'inuention de GODEFROY ROVSSEL,
Maiſtre Appoticaire à Paris.

DEDIE' AV ROY.

A PARIS,
Et ſe vendent par l'Autheur, ruë de la Sauon-
nerie, entre la pierre au laict & la place aux
veaux: Chez Guillaume Baudeau,
Maiſtre Chandellier. 1613.

Auec Priuilege de ſa Majeſté.

§ 2.07.4. Extract from the exclusive privilege granted to Roussel for having his book on the Secrets of Arts printed, exhibited and sold—1612

Extract from the King's Privilege.

By the King's grace and privilege, Godefroi Roussel, Master Apothecary in Paris, is allowed to print, exhibit and put on sale throughout the whole Kingdom of France, a Book entitled *Les Secrets des Arts, tant de Pharmacie, que de celui de Distiller, vulgairement nommé Alchemie ou Spargirie, &c.* [*The Secrets of the Arts, both of Pharmacy, and that of Distilling, commonly called Alchemy or Spagyria, &c.*]. And inhibitions and defenses are made to all Booksellers or Printers to print or have printed, sell or distribute the mentioned Book, without Roussel's express consent, on the penalty of confiscation of the books, and a fine of one thousand pounds, and all expenses for damages, during the time and space of six years, starting on the day on which it will be finished printing, which is the fourteenth day of the month of January, one thousand six hundred and thirteen. As it is more fully demonstrated by the said Privilege.
Given at Paris, the fourteenth of November, one thousand six hundred and twelve.
Signed, Brigard.

§ 2.08. CHRISTIAN IV, OF DENMARK, ACQUIRES THE SECRET FORMULA OF THE OINTMENTS OF TERKEL ESKILDSEN, A DANISH PEASANT—1621

In the text that follows, a Danish physician and historian tells about the acquisition, under the instructions of Christian IV, king of Denmark and Norway, of the secret formulae of a number of medicinal ointments owned (and apparently created) by an empirical pharmacist, Terkel Eskildsen.

The peasant Terkel Eskildsen and his Ointments

by Dr. K. Caröe

During the last half of the sixteenth century a peasant named Terkel Eskildsen lived in Jested, a small village near Ribe, the former residence in Jutland of the Danish kings. It seems he knew how to rise well above the level of his colleagues, because he married in 1576 the priest's daughter and he had an enviable reputation because of his knowledge in the art of treating and healing wounds, a reputation that made his name known not only throughout Denmark, but also outside the kingdom. We know that in 1594, an individual from Königsberg, Prussia, resorted to his good offices, despite the length and difficulties of the journey.

Terkel Eskildsen died in Jested on April 1, 1624, then in his nineties. He seems to have been born in 1534, in the same village, where the names Terkel and Eskild alternated between father and son (Eskildsen = Eskild's son) for many generations, but his life is quite unknown, no date can be specified and neither can we know where he had learned medicine, to the point of practicing it, as a healer. We know, however, that his reputation was such that on September 7, 1620 King Christian IV asked the bailiff of the Ribe castle to talk to Terkel Eskildsen and buy from him the secret of the preparation of his ointments, offering him a price of 500 *rigsdaler* (1400 francs) and more. Terkel accepted this offer and sold the prescription for the preparation for 300 *sletdaler*, i.e., for 550 francs (one *sletdaler* = 2/3 *rigsdaler*). On April 30, 1621 Master Terkel issued the receipt for this purchase so advantageous for the king.

This sale has long been known, but what has remained unknown is the preparation of these ointments and other remedies. A favorable chance brought them to light, the recipes (in Danish) having been found in a manuscript, the first that was given to the Medical-Historical Museum of Copenhagen. Two ointments in particular have enjoyed great popularity, one to be applied to wounds, the other to be used in affections where the skin is intact. By reviewing all the books of good advice, written by hand, which are in the Royal Library and the Medical-Historical Museum, one sees that these two ointments are mentioned in seven manuscripts (dating from 1630 to 1800), while three other ordinances, the only ones known, are found only twice in two manuscripts. It is certain that these two ointments carried Terkel Eskildsen's name out of our country, and that is why I thought this note would be of interest to the readers of the Bulletin.

Forty years passed after the king's purchase, and the ointments were still in vogue in Denmark. It was then that the famous anatomist Thomas Bartholin included them in Latin in one of his many books, entitled HISTORIARUM ANATOMICARUM RARIORUM CENTURIAE VI, published in Copenhagen in 1661.

§ 2.09. THE FIRST BRITISH PATENT FOR A MEDICAL DEVICE—1629

As this text sows, by contrast with medicinal compositions, patents for medical devices started being granted soon after the enactment of the Statute of Monopolies.

Excerpts from the first patent granted under the Statute of 1624 for a medical device, invented by Thomas Grent

June 22, 1629. Patent No 47.

Charles, by the grace of God, &C. to all to whom these presents shall come greeting.

Whereas we have been informed by the humble petition of our trusty and welbeloved Thomas Grent, Doctor of Phisick, that he had by his long studies and great expenses, attained unto a mistery of framing "A new Kind of Baths, being of a Mixed Nature and consisting of Divers distinct Heats, Termed Circular Baths or Bathing Waterworks for divers Uses," which, as we are informed, are likely to prove very profitable to all our subjects as well in the times of health as sickness, which also are framed and contrived in such manner as had not heretofore been practiced and put in use within any our realms or dominions; and whereas we, taking into our princely consideration the great care, Industry, travaile, and expenses which the inventing and bringing to perfection of works of this nature do require, and finding it convenient and agreeable to justice that the first inventors of every laudable and profitable Invention should in some measure receive a reward answerable to their demerits.

Know therefore, that we, for the considerations aforesaid, and for divers other good causes and considerations, us hereunto specially moving, of our especial grace, certain knowledge and mere motion, have given and granted and by these presents for us, our heirs and successors, do give and grant unto the said Thomas Grent, his executors, administrators, and assignees, full and free liberty, licence, power, privilege, and authority, that he, the said Thomas Grent, his executors administrators, and assignees, or his or their deputies, servants, and workmen, and none other shall and may, for and during the term of years hereafter in these presents mentioned [for and during and unto the full end and term of fourteen year from thence next ensuing, and fully to be complete and ended], make, frame, use, exercise, and put in practice within our Realm of England and Dominion of Wales, or any of them, the circular baths or bathing waterworks above mentioned, which have been first by him invented as aforesaid, and which have not heretofore been used or put in practice by any other person or persons whatsoever within any our realms or dominions, and also to make, found, erect, and form, as many engines or instruments as he or they or any of them shall think meet or necessary for the making or using of the baths aforesaid.

And to the end the said Thomas Grent, his executors, administrators, and assignees, may have and enjoy the full benefit of this our present grant, we do by these presents, for us, our heirs and successors, straightly charge, prohibit, and command, that no person or persons whatsoever of what estate, degree, or condition soever other then the said Thomas Grent, his executors, administrators, and assignees, or his or their deputies, servants, agents, or workmen, shall presume, attempt, or go about at any time or times whatsoever during the term hereafter mentioned, to make, form, frame, or erect the baths hereinbefore mentioned, or any the instruments or engins so invented, as aforesaid, nor shall imitate or resemble the same, or any of them, or make any other like thereunto, or like unto any of them, nor shall use, exercise, or employ any such engines or instruments to the purposes aforesaid, without the special license, warrant, authority, or consent of the said Thomas Grent, his executors, administrators, or assignees, first had and obtained in writing, under his, their, or some of their hand and seal, or hands and seals, upon pain of forfeiture of all and every such engins and instruments so made, framed, and used, as aforesaid, contrary to the true intent and meaning of these presents, and upon such further pains, penalties, and imprisonments as by the laws and statutes of this our Realm of England, or by our prerogative royal can or may be inflicted upon the offenders for their contempt and disobedience of our royal pleasure and commandment in this behalf. . . .

And, lastly, we do by these presents, for us, our heirs and successors, graunt unto the said Thomas Grent, his executors, administrators, and assignees, and every of them, that these our Letters Patent shall be and shall be construed, adjudged, and deemed to be good and effectual in the law, according to the true intent and meaning of the same; notwithstanding the not reciting or describing the way, means, or materials by which the said circular baths or bathing waterworks be made or used; and notwithstanding any misprison, defect, or incertainty in these present contained, and any other matter or cause whatsoever to the contrary in anywise notwithstanding; although expressed mention, &c.

In witness whereof, &c. Witness our self at Westmynster the Two-and-twentieth day of June [1629].

§ 2.10. THE BY-LAWS AND REGULATIONS FOR THE SWORN APOTHECARIES OF METZ PROHIBIT THE "DÉBAUCHAGE"—MAY 22, 1631

*A clause prohibiting the practice of what in French is called "débauchage" was very common in the by-laws of European guilds or corporations. According to that clause, one master could not hire the services of another master's apprentice without the consent of the latter. One of the purposes of that clause was to avoid the disruption of the normal operation of the workshop where the apprentice worked. Another purpose was to avoid the communication by the apprentice of the secrets he had learned from his master to outsiders (*i.e.*, competitors).*

In From Babylon to the Silicon Valley, *we have seen that this clause is very old: it was part of the Code of Hammurabi, c. 1,750 BC. The same clause is now mentioned in note 10 of the TRIPS Agreement, of 1994, as a modality of an unfair trade practice.*[19]

The "débauchage" clause has two modalities, both of which are found in the following text, extracted from the by-laws of the guild of apothecaries of Metz, of 1631. One is the prohibition of hiring the apprentice of another master during the apprenticeship contract. The second is the requirement that, once the apprenticeship contract has expired, the former master gives his consent for another master to hire the apprentice.

Paul Dorveaux, Les Apothicaires de Metz, Leurs Satuts (Honoré Champion, 1909) (excerpt)

> V.—Prohibitions made to take any Apprentice breaching his Contract of Apprenticeship, without the knowledge and consent of his first Master, to whom he will be required to go as if he had not started his Apprenticeship; for this purpose he will be registered again by the aforesaid Masters and Jurors, and the day of his Reception noted, under the penalty of a fine of twelve pounds [assigned] to the Pension Fund against each of the offenders.
> VI.—That none of the said Masters will take any Servant leaving the Shop of another of the City, without the consent of his first Master.

19. See *supra* note 2, at 157.

§ 2.11. DURING THE 1636 EPIDEMICS OF THE BUBONIC PLAGUE IN LONDON, CHARLES I ORDERED THE PUBLICATION OF INSTRUCTIONS ON HOW TO PREPARE CHEAP MEDICINES

Claims of ownership of medicines with therapeutic effects against epidemic diseases have been extremely rare. The historical trend has been to make those medicines freely available.

In 1636, Charles I—the same king that, in 1624, approved the Statute of Monopolies and its special provision on the granting of patents for inventions—ordered the College of Physicians to publish recommendations on how to prevent and treat the illnesses resulting from the bubonic plague that, during the seventeenth century, erupted in London several times.

The advice on therapies against the plague (published under the royal seal) included a number of statutes dealing with emergency situations, such as on the help to be provided to the poor. A few medicines described in this publication were indicated for the "richer sort," implying they were out of reach of the poor.

An advice set down by the College of Physicians, by his Majesty's special Command, containing certain necessary Directions, as well for the cure of the Plague, as for preventing the Infection, with many easy Medicines and of small charge the use whereof may be very profitable to his Majesty's Subjects.

Doctors, Apothecaries, and Surgeons.

The Church orders for prayers being first observed as in former times, it is thought necessary that by the government of the City there be appointed three or four Doctors at least, who may apply themselves to the cure of the Infected: and that these Doctors be stipendiaries to the City for their lives: and that to each Doctor there be assigned two apothecaries and three Surgeons, who are also to be stipended by the City, that so due and true care may be taken in all things, that the people perish not without help, and that the Infection spread not, while none take particular care to resist it, as in Paris, Venice, and Padua, and many other Cities.

And if any Doctor, Apothecary or Surgeon stipended by the City shall happen to die in the service of the attendance of the Plague, then their widows surviving shall have their pensions during their lives.

[Practical recommendations concerning confinement and sanitization are provided under the following chapters: "Men or goods from foreign places. That all good orders be revived. To be cautelous upon any suspicion. The care to be taken when a house is visited. Caution concerning flying into the Country. Burial of the dead. Caution about apparel and household stuff."]

Preservatives.

Correction of the air.

For the correcting of the infectious air, it were good that often Bonfires were made in the streets, and that sometime the Tower Ordinance might be shot off, as also that there be good fires kept in about the visited house and their neighbours.

Take Rosemary dried, or Juniper, Baileaves or Frankincense: cast the same up on a Chafingdish, and receive the fume or smoke thereof.

Also to make fires rather in pans to remove about the chamber, then in chimneys, shall better correct the air of the houses, adding a piece of old iron to the fire.

[Subsequent suggestions are given under the following chapters: "By perfuming of apparel. By carrying out of perfumes. Or may use this Pomander. The richer sort may make use of this Pomander. By inward medicines."]

By Cordials.

Mithridates medicine of Figs.

Take of good figs and walnut kirnels of each twenty four; Rue picked two good handfulls, of Salt half an ounce or what better; first stamp four figs and walnuts well together in a stone mortar, then add your Rue, and last of all Salt, mire thein exceedingly well; take of this mixture every morning fasting the weight of sixteen pence, to children and weak bodies less.

Or this will be effectual also.

Take twenty Walnuts, pill them, figs, fifteen, Rue a good handful, Tormentill roots three drams, Juniper berries two drams, Bole Armoniack a dram and a half. First stamp four roots, then your figs and seeds, then add your walnuts, then put thereto five drams of London Treacle, and two or three spoonfuls of wine vinegar, mire them well in a stone mortar, and take of this every morning the quantity of a good nutmegg fasting they that have cause to go much abroad, may take as much more in the evening two hours belong supper. . . .

[The instructions on the preparation of medicines continues with the following chapters: "For women with child, children, and such as cannot take bitter things, use this. For the richer sort. By Medicines Purgative. Blood letting. Vomits. Medicines expulsive. In summer this is good. Medicines external. Tobreak the tumour. Or this. To draw. For the carbuncle. Or this. Another. Another."

[A number of statutes dealing with assistance to the poor and with maintaining the public order follow.]

§ 2.12. SUED BY THE APOTHECARIES OF BEAUNE, FRANCE, A DRESSMAKER, OWNER OF A SECRET MEDICINAL FORMULA, WAS AUTHORIZED TO CONTINUE DISTRIBUTING IT, PROVIDED SHE WOULD NOT CHARGE FOR IT—1661

In another incident showing that in the seventeenth century, authorities had no qualm with the secrecy of medicines, the owner of a secret remedy for gravel and kidney stones, who had no technical qualification (she was a seamstress), was allowed by the court to continue making and distributing them—provided she did not charge for their sale.

A. Baudot, Etudes Historiques sur la Pharmacie en Bourgogne avant 1803 (excerpt)

Around 1661, Jacquette Damoiseau, dressmaker in Beaune, had the secret, hereditary in her family for eighty or a hundred years, "of water for gravel and kidney stones," a remedy that she distributed to whoever wanted to use it. The apothecaries, based on their regulations and public utility, wanted to prevent her from doing so, and for that they sued her. But she brought so many certificates from doctors and important people, she demonstrated so well the proven utility of her remedy, even offering not to sell any, but to distribute it free of charge to her friends and acquaintances, and especially to give it charitably to the poor; she refuted so well the arguments of the apothecaries maintaining that she was "a charlatan and that her remedy was bad and composed of unprepared antimony;" finally, she was so persuasive that the king's attorney, taking her evidence into consideration, declared that, if the apothecaries "knew the remedy, they would be right to prevent Damoiseau from distributing it, but that, ignoring it, she did them no harm, and that they had nothing to complain about." Jacquette was nevertheless condemned in Beaune; but the Parliament annulled this judgment under the condition that "Lady Damoiseau would limit herself to distribute her remedy free of charge." (Judgment of July 24, 1661).

§ 2.13. SOME COMMERCIAL PRIVILEGES GRANTED TO MOUNTEBANKS DURING THE REIGN OF CHARLES II, INCLUDING THE LICENSE FOR ERECTING STAGES—1665 ONWARDS

In the seventeenth century, as in France, charlatans wandered through the territories of the United Kingdom to sell their medicines, mostly quacks. And also, as in France, one of their preferred marketing techniques was to climb on stages and, by means of spectacular performances and magic tricks, convince innocent spectators to buy their products. [see § 1.13] That is exactly where the word "mountebank" derives from: to mount on a bank, i.e., *a stage. The French idiom has a literal translation of the same word: "saltimbanque." A large proportion of the mountebanks awarded with commercial privileges in England, as in France, were of Italian origin.*

The following texts show some privileges granted to a number of those charlatans, with repeated reference to the erection of stages—which was then an integral part of their business. The privileges show two aspects: on the one hand, they were permissions for the mountebanks to carry their trade; on the other, some of them conveyed certain sorts of protection against competition.

§ 2.13.1. License to George Moretto, 1665

1665. April 11. Whitehall. License to George Moretto, in consideration of his skill in medicine and surgery, to practice in any part of the King's dominions, and to expose his medicines for sale publicly, by erecting a stage in the market place, or any other mode which he deems convenient, without molestation to himself or servant.

§ 2.13.2. License to Joanees Michapilo, 1667

1667. August 5. Whitehall. License for Joannes Michapilo, a mountebank, to dispose of his medicines, and practice the skill on medicine and surgery, in any city, town or borough of the kingdom, none disturbing him, nor erecting stages near any erected by him.

§ 2.13.3. License to John Ryssell, 1667

1667. August. Memoranda [from the Signet books] of warrants, grants, etc., passed during the month, the uncalendared portions of which are as follow:—

> License to John Ryssell, mountebank, practitioner in physic and surgery, to erect a stage in London or elsewhere, to vend his medicines, prohibiting all strangers not naturalized to practice near him, in such times and at such places he does.

§ 2.13.4. Certificate and license in favor of Toussain Le Jond, 1667

1667. September 2. London. Certificate by P. Massonet, physician in ordinary to the Duke of York, that he has known Mr. Toussain Le Jond, operator in physic and surgery, practice and exercise such professions with great skill and success, in this and other kingdoms, and that he has compounded and publicly sold an excellent Oriental balsam, and other remedies. Endorsed, "Toussain, the Empiric."
1667. October 5. Grant of license to Joussain le Jond, operator in physic and surgery, to erect a stage or theatre in any town of England or Wales, and to vend his balsams and remedies, remaining in any town as long as he desires.

§ 2.13.5. License to John Baptista Quaranteni, 1668

1668. Feb. 19. Warrant licensing John Baptista Quaranteni to sell medicines on a stage or otherwise, in the same form as that granted to James Micaphilo.

§ 2.13.6. Licence to Tamberlaine Harvey, 1673

1673. July 28. Whitehall. License to Tamberlaine Harvey, the king's sworn servant, who has attained great skill in preparing and administering medicines, and performing difficult operations in surgery, and is of the company of Barber-Surgeons, London, to sell his remedies and perform manual operations in public, in any place in England or Wales, he being already licensed thereunto by the Master of the Revels, and order that no stage be allowed to be erected by or near the place where he has erected one.

§ 2.14. CHARLES II, OF ENGLAND, CREATES A SPECIAL PUBLIC POST—OF CHEMICAL PHYSICIAN—FOR THOMAS WILLIAMS, A PHYSICIAN AND INVENTOR OF NEW MEDICINES—1669

Not all inventors sought to be paid for their labors and investment in the market by resorting to trademarks, trade secrets and patent protection (or, as seen, copyright protection in books revealing their skills and knowledge). Some inventors preferred to be rewarded by governments, thereby avoiding the risks associated with commercial endeavors. Of course, such an option does not eliminate uncertainty because it depends greatly on the humor and biases of governmental authorities.

Thomas Williams succeeded in obtaining government protection for him and his inventions: not only did he get a royal recommendation for receiving the title of M.D. from the University of Cambridge and the appointment for a well-remunerated civil post at the King's court, but was also ennobled with the title of Baronet.

1669. March 5. Whitehall. The King to the [Vice-Chancellor] of Cambridge. We recommend Thos. Williams, who has for some time past attended our Royal person, and shown singular knowledge in compounding medicines, to the degree of M.D., without fees or exercises, dispensing with our letter of 15 July last, or any other statute to the contrary.
1669. May 7. Warrant for erecting an office of chemical physician to the King, fee 20 marks a year, and appointing Dr. Thos. Williams thereto, his Majesty wishing to encourage so important an art, and hearing of the extraordinary learning and skill which he shows in compounding and inventing medicines, some of which have been prepared in the royal presence; with leave to make experiments in all his Majesty's chemical laboratories.

§ 2.15. IN 1670, UNDER THE CHARTER OF THE GUILD OF THE APOTHECARIES OF LONDON, APPRENTICES WERE REQUESTED TO TAKE AN OATH OF SECRECY

In 1617, the apothecaries of London finally became independent from the grocers and received from the king a Charter for their own guild. Following the traditional formula, the Charter included a clause that obliged apprentices to keep the secrets of the trade. It also included another customary clause prohibiting the "débauchage," i.e., *the hiring of an apprentice under a contract with a master by a competitor unless the former gave his consent.*

The following text has been extracted from a fascinating historical account of the profession of the apothecary by C.J.S. Thompson.

C.J.S. Thompson, The Mystery and Art of the Apothecary (excerpt)

The apprentice, who had to serve eight years to his master, was required to take the following oath on beginning his term, which was ordered "to be administered by the Master and Wardens of the Apothecaries unto every apprentice of the Company," in 1670:

> "You shall swear to be good and true to our Sovereign Lord the King's Majesty, His Heirs and Successors, and well and truly you shall serve your master for the term of your apprenticehood and in lawful and honest causes you shall be obedient unto him and unto the Masters, Wardens and Assistants of this Company and have them in reverence. The lawful secrets of the said Fellowship you shall keep, and give no information or instruction thereof to any person but the said Fellowship.
>
> "In all these things you shall well and truly behave you and surely keep your Oath to your Power.
>
> "So help you God.
>
> "And if it fortune you to depart from your Master his service, you shall not serve any person out of the said Fellowship without licence of the Master and

Wardens for the time being, upon pain to forfeit and pay to the use of the Company such penalty as shall be assessed upon you by the Master, Wardens and Assistants for the time being.

"God save the King."

§ 2.16. CHARLES II BUYS THE SECRET OF A MEDICINAL FORMULA CREATED BY JONATHAN GODDARD—C. 1670

Jonathan Goddard (1617-1675), a reputed scientist, member of the Royal Society, invented (or, as it is said, improved) a composition that produced good effects against an uncertain number of illnesses, including gout. The medicine, known as "Goddard's drops," or "English drops," was very popular. As it happens today with some very successful medicines, many complaints against the high prices charged by Goddard and his licensed chemist were heard. There were also complaints against Goddard's secrecy. In response to both criticisms, Goddard wrote in defense of his practices, namely on the advantages of the private appropriation of useful medicines.

Among other aspects, Goddard proposed the idea that new medicines should be invented by physicians, relegating thus the role of apothecaries to that of mere manufacturers and dispensers. Obviously, this proposal encountered serious resistance from the apothecaries.

Some detractors of Goddard's spread the rumor that his formula included some very exotic, if not horrible, ingredients, such as human skulls of men dead from a violent death, and dried vipers. It turns out that was not true, Goddard' drops being just a variation of a traditional medicine. The real composition of Goddard's medicine was given by an English physician, Martin Lister, who said it had been revealed to him directly by Charles II.

Charles II (1630-1685) was a chemistry enthusiast. He maintained a fully equipped laboratory near his apartment, at the Whitehall Palace, and would spend many hours there, engaged in "philosophical experimentation." Attracted by the enormous success of Goddard's drops, he acquired from the inventor his secret composition. But Charles II did not buy the secret with the purpose of making it publicly known, but exclusively for his own scientific entertainment. Charles II would produce some Goddard's drops in his laboratory, hence the medicine's other name of "King's drops."

However, it seems, according to Dr. Lister, that Charles II acquired and ordered the disclosure of another medicine, the "Jesuit's powder," which was another name for the "remède de l'anglais" (whose formula Louis XIV acquired as well). Incidentally, it is worth noticing that Charles II and Colbert, Louis XIV's minister and a strong proponent of the use of intellectual property in pursuance of public objectives, were in frequent correspondence.

Goddard's drops are considered the first "patent medicine," not in the sense of having been the matter of a patent for an invention, under the Statute of Monopolies, of 1624, but in the sense of Goddard having been accorded the permission (by means of a patent letter) of advertising and selling it, without the need for disclosing its specification. It is with this contradictory meaning that many secret medicines were designated as "patent medicines" in the United Kingdom and the United States, until the late nineteenth century, when their trade was prohibited. Their composition being secret, they were not subject to any control or inspection as to the ingredients used or to their therapeutic effects.

The texts that follow illustrate not only Goddard's strong defense of his keeping the composition secret but also some aspects of the controversy surrounding his medicine and the way it was commercialized.

§ 2.16.1. Jonathan Goddard defends the private appropriation of physicians' inventions concerning new medicines, either by patents or trade secrets

1669

Jonathan Goddard, A Discourse setting forth the unhappy Condition of the Practice of Physick in London, and offering some means to put it into a better; for the Interest of Patients, no less, or rather much more, than of Physicians. London, 1669. (excerpt)

This communication of Medicines by Physicians to Apothecaries (whereby they come to be so great Masters of Receipts) is in the plain reason and nature of the thing, a Trust, whereof they are free to make the advantage or profit that belongs to their Trade, by selling such Medicines at valuable rates, according to their costliness or elaborateness in their preparation: but the advantage of directing and prescribing their use in all cases, belongs to the Physician: and the hindering him herein, to the impairing him of his Practice, is a breach of Trust, and unworthy, as well as injurious dealing by him, as may farther appear by the following Consideration.

All Laws of Nature and Nations, all Justice, Equity, and Reason of Mankind, do allow to every person the benefit of his own Invention; which, if it be of that Nature, that the bringing of it into use and practice, doth necessarily import the discovery of it, according to our Laws, Patents for terms of years are granted: but if an Invention be of such a nature, that it may be concealed in the use and practice, no limitation for private advantage or profit thereby, is set by Law; it is only Honesty, Ingenuity or Interest, that can restrain from making unreasonable or unconscionable advantages in such case. Now any Medicines or Receipts for Cure of Diseases, invented by Physicians, or coming to their private knowledge only; or any new use or virtue of an old known Medicine, discovered by any Physician; in relation to those Physicians by whom they have been invented or discovered (as far as they are of any consideration or value) are of this Nature, that is, Inventions that may be kept secret by them; and whereof nothing hinders them from making the advantage; the Laws of the Land (as well as in other Countries) allowing and authorizing Physicians to practice their Art in all its parts and members, and so by consequence to make any Medicines, themselves. The case being thus, how unreasonable and unequal is it, that when a Physician hath by his Industry found out, or by some Felicity lighted upon a Discovery that hath proved remarkably successful in some particular disease or case; upon his communication of it to an Apothecary, he shall have only an inconsiderable matter (not worth the owning many times) in case the Patient come or send to him; or at most an ordinary Fee in case of Visiting the Patient; whereas the Apothecary being one that takes upon him to practise, shall not only repeat the same Medicine many times over, to the same Patient, but also give into any other Patients, whose case he judges to be the same, or of affinity to it; and drive a Trade with it all his life time; and so gain (as it is well known, and hath been upon occasion, by some confessed or boasted of) by one Receipt, an hundred times as much as the Physicians Reward or Fee for prescribing it: so that he only cures the Patient once for an ordinary Fee at most, and teaches the Apothecary, when the same case occurs, to do it ever after.

The consequence of this to Physicians, must be the impoverishment of many; who, in regard of the charges of their Education, and the use and consequence of their Profession, deserve to get as great Estates, as are gotten in any Profession or way of Trading, and yet shall scarce be able to subsist, though as Learned and able in their Profession, as their Predecessors, who thirty or forty years ago, got great Estates, when the Apothecaries kept within their own bounds, or inconsiderably encroached upon the Physicians. For now a Physician will be of use only amongst great persons, or persons of learning and parts to value him: whereas others that are of ability enough for Estates, and would be ready to entertain him, are so amused by Apothecaries, their ostentations and pretensions before mentioned, their canting upon the common notions and terms of Humours, Fumes, Obstructions, *&c.* (which an empty illiterate pretender, having confidence enough, may so manage, as to make a more graceful sound, than the most solid and able Physician) that they are generally entertained in the beginning of sicknesses, and made Judges whether or not, and when any, and what Physician shall be sent for: (being accounted a check upon the Physician by such a sort of People) who for the most part, is not called, till the other is willing to go no farther, because it is not his interest, that the person should die under his Cure; and then he says it is work for a Doctor; who shall have nothing to do amongst these people but in desperate cases: whereas (as hath been hinted already) in difficult cases, the best Physician may stand in need of all advantages, especially timely opportunities to apply proper and effectual Remedies for Cure.

And where the Apothecary hath the nomination of the Physician, it is easily judged, what one he is like to be, that is one between whom and him a design is driven of mutual furtherance, or one that he knows will comply with him, that is content to succeed him, and approve of what he hath done before; or one that is noted in general to prescribe most for the Apothecary's profit. Upon such accounts some Physicians are cryed up, and others decryed (if not traduced) of no less, or of much more and longer approved ability, worth, and honesty. To be sure no Physician taken notice of to have and give any Medicine of his own preparation, shall be called in, if the Apothecary can hinder it. Persons may if they please be undeceived upon this account, and understand how little reason they have, and how little it may be their interest to be ruled by Apothecaries in their choice of Physicians. . . .

But if there be any advantage in the power of Physicians themselves, which they may lawfully, honestly, and fairly make use of, to put themselves into a better condition for the exercise of their profession, it may be of good consequence to consider thereof. Since all Law, Equity, and Reason allows them as well as others (as was touched before) to make advantage of their own Inventions, and since they are of such nature, as they may keep them secret to themselves, in the use and practice of them, they being not bound to discover them to Apothecaries or any others, but free to prepare them themselves, as hath been made appear: whether may not this Course set upon, though attended with some trouble and inconvenience, be an effectual means, at least in reasonable time, very considerably to advantage and better the condition of Physicians in their Practice?

§ 2.16.2. A [wrong] account of the composition of Dr. Goddard's drops

BIOGRAPHIA BRITANNICA OR THE LIVES OF THE MOST EMINENT PERSONS WHO HAVE FLOURISHED IN GREAT BRITAIN AND IRELAND, vol. 4 (excerpt)

[Jonathan Goddard] did not . . . always labor for nothing, if it be true, which is very confidently affirmed, that he sold the secret of making the *Guttae Anglicanae*, or English Drops, to King Charles the second for 5000 *1.* of which precious receipt this is said to be a true copy:

"Take five pounds of human cranium of a person hanged, or dead of some violent death, two pounds of dried vipers, two pounds of harts horn [an ammonia compound, originally made from the horns of a male deer] and two of ivory, mince the whole small, put it in two or three retorts, and distil it in a reverberatory furnace, with the same precautions as are ordinarily used in distilling harts horn and vipers to extract their volatile salt. . . ."

The real composition of the *Guttae*, however, is somewhat controverted. Dr Lister assures us, that he had the secret communicated to him by King Charles the second, and that it is no other than the volatile spirit of raw silk rectified with oil of cinnamon, or other essential oil.

The fame author assures us, he had found by experience that the Guttae Anglicanae, were not in any respect preferable to the common volatile spirits of harts horn and sal ammoniac, except that the smell is more supportable. It will not always however be found expedient, to take the sentiments of one great man of the same faculty in prejudice to the prescription of another; and whoever considers what the honorable and learned Mr. Boyle has written upon subjects of the same nature, will be inclined to think, that if there be anything due to authority, it is at least equal on the *fide* of Dr. Goddard. Let us also add, that these drops were not calculated for the relief of persons in slow and chronic cases, but in violent and acute distempers, when if their operation had not been certain and apparent, it is not easy to conceive how they could have gained their author any credit; and if they were, why it would be taken from him.

§ 2.16.3. Martin Lister, English Doctor, reveals the real composition of Goddard's Drops, which was given to him personally by King Charles II

Martin Lister, A JOURNEY TO PARIS IN THE YEAR OF 1698 (excerpts)

April 14 [1698]. The Prince of Conty sent his Gentleman and Coach at midnight to fetch me to his Son, and to bring with me the late King Charle's Drops to give him. This was a very hasty call. I told the Messenger, I was the Prince's very humble Servant; but for any Drops or other Medicines I had brought nothing at all with me, and had used only such as I found in their Shops, for all the occasions I had had to use any. I desired he would tell him, that I was ready to Consult with his Physicians upon his Son's Sickness, if he pleased to command me, but for coming upon any other Account I desired to be excused; but I heard no more of the Matter, and the young Prince died. By this it is evident, there is as false a Notion of Physick in this Country, as with us; and that it is here also thought a Knack, more than a Science or Method; and little Chemical Toys, the Bijous of Quacks, are mightily in request. . . .

Those Drops were desired of me by other Persons of Quality, as the Princess d'Espinoy, the Duchess of Boullon, Monsieur Sesac, &c., and having bethought myself how my Master, the late King Charles, had communicated them to me, and showed me very obligingly the Process himself, by carrying me alone with him into his laboratory at Whitehall, while it was Distilling. Also Mr. Chevins another time showed me the Materials for the Drops in his Apartment newly brought in, in great quantity, that is, Raw Silk. I caused the Drops to be made here. Also I put Dr. Turnfort upon making of them; which he did in perfection, by Distilling the finest Raw Silk he could get. For my part I was surprised at the Experiment often repeated, having never tried it before. One Pound of Raw Silk yielded an incredible quantity of Volatile Salt, and in proportion the finest Spirit I ever tasted; and that which recommends it is, that it is when rectified, of a far more pleasant smell, than that which comes from Sal Armoniack or Hartshorne; and the Salt refined and cohobated with any well scented Chemical Oil, makes the Kings Salt, as it used to be called. This my Lord Ambassador gave me leave to present in his Name; and the Doctor now supplies those which want. Silk, indeed is nothing else, but a dry Jelly from the Insect Kind, and therefore very Cordial and Stomachick no doubt. The *Arabians* were wise, and knowing in the *Materia Medica, to* have put it in their *Alkermes*.

This must be said for the Honour of this King, that he has ever given great Encouragements for useful Discoveries in all Kinds, and particularly in Physick. 'Tis well known he bought the Secret of the Jesuits Powder, and made it public; as he lately did that of the Hipococana.[20]

---

20. This is another name for the tree from where quinine is extracted. *See* § 2.20, with sources indicating the reward paid to Helvetius, the Dutch doctor, by Louis XIV for his invention of a medicine based on quinine.

§ 2.16.4. Cristopher Merrett, physician, attacks the apothecaries on their greed and appoints Dr. Goddard as an example of the physician's honesty in charging fair prices for his drug

Christopher Merrett, A SHORT VIEW OF THE FRAUDS, AND ABUSES COMMITTED BY APOTHECARIES; AS WELL IN RELATION TO PATIENTS: AND OF THE ONLY REMEDY THEREOF BY PHYSICIANS MAKING THEIR OWN MEDICINES, 1670 (excerpt)

The last of any Fame with us, were Dr. Goddard's Drops, a good Medicine, but not so universal, and superlative as he would have made the World believe, and was nothing else but what some Physicians many years since enjoyed. . . . Furthermore, that this Medicine of his was Spirit of Harts-horn, some relations plainly argue; One whereof was the following:

> A certain person in Norfolk having sent for as much as came to a 11 l. and dying upon the 2d. dose of it, and by accident most part of the remainder being spilt; there comes in a friend to the House, of some skill, who supposing it to be Spirit of Harts-horn, told the Widow he would endeavour to gain back the money for her. And thereupon went to a Chymist, and bought as much of the said Spirit, as would make up the quantity purchased of Dr. Goddard, who after Tryal of it by smell, and taste, acknowledged it to be his, and honestly payed back the sum 't was first sold for; which I think few of the Mountebanks do. Sure I am that a Quack sold 21 Pills for 20 l. whereof the Patient took 4 at two doses, to the great hazard of his life, who then repairing to me for my advice, I by Tryal of one of them found them to be Mercurial, and wished him to return them back, but the Quack would not give him 10 *s*. for the 16 remaining.

The inference and sum of what hath been said, is to show briefly by what Artifices people are deceived in their Healths, and Purses, and how easily the ignorant are couzened, and such practices used, that Physicians, men of honesty and repute, would be ashamed to own, and must by using them in a short time be ruined and discredited.

§ 2.16.5. An anonymous group of apothecaries responds to Dr. Merrett's accusations

Lex Talionis, SIVE VINDICIAE PHARMACOPORUM: OR A SHORT REPLY TO DR. MERRETT'S BOOK, 1670 (excerpt)

A third abuse of the Apothecaries, relates to the Prices of their Medicines, and here the Doctor runs on to a seventh-Lie; as he says getting of a 11 *d*. in the Shilling; This is pretty well: Yet I think hardly so much as one of your selves, Doctor Goddard, might get by his drops, being nothing but Spirit of Harts-horn, as may appear by the Story he tells himself in his Book. A certain Gentleman in Norfolk having sent for as much as came to 11 *l*. (mark, a pretty round Sum) and dying upon the second dose; observe, it was likely for his own taking, which doubtless could not be above 2 or 3 Ounces, which is not worth above 5 *s*. the Ounce at most, as now sold; by this we may see we are like to pay for their new Inventions, and that they have the knack, as well as the Apothecaries. . . . This lies a little too wide, I pray lay it closer in the next Edition: these pretty facetious Stories were inserted (by the grave Doctor) I suppose for People to laugh at. But Sir, you have left out the main Ingredient in your Relation, which might well have been put in, causing the Apothecaries Bills to be sharp, which are these. . . .

§ 2.17. A TRADE SECRET CONCERNING A MEDICAL DEVICE: THE INVENTION OF THE OBSTETRICAL FORCEPS

1672

Having invented the obstetrical forceps, Dr. Peter Chamberlen kept it secret and transmitted it only to his brother and nephews, obstetricians like him. The family would go a long way in protecting the secret. The legend goes that when the Chamberlens were called for intervening in a difficult delivery, only those in possession of the secret would be allowed in the room. The forceps would be introduced in the room hidden inside an enormous wood box. The Chamberlens would then lock the doors, and while one of them carried the medical procedure, the others produced strange noises, including the ringing of bells.

Later, the secret was sold by Hugh Chamberlen to a Dutch practitioner, Roonhuysen. But it would not be revealed until 1818, by means of a report submitted to the Royal Medical and Chirurgical Society of London by H.H. Cawardine, based on findings in the Chamberlen's estate.

The text that follows consists of excerpts from the preface by Hugh Chamberlen, Senior, to his translation into English of Dr. Mauriceau's textbook on midwifery (first edition published in 1762), where he makes reference to his family's secret.

J.H. Aveling, THE CHAMBERLENS AND THE MIDWIFERY FORCEPS—MEMORIALS OF THE FAMILY AND AN ESSAY ON THE INVENTION OF THE INSTRUMENT (excerpts)

Courteous reader;

Having long observed the great Want of necessary Directions how to Govern Women with Child, and in Childbed, and also new-born Babes should be well ordered, I designed a small Manual to that purpose; but meeting sometime after in France with this Treatise of Mauriceau, (which, in my Opinion, far exceeds all former Authors, especially Culpeper, Sharp, Speculum Matricis, Sermon, &c., being less erroneous, and enriched with divers new Observations) I changed my Resolution into that of translating him; whom I need not such commend, because he is fortified with the Approbation of the Wardens of the Chirurgeons Company of Paris. . . .

In the 17th Chapter of the second Book, my Author justifies the fastening Hooks in the Head of a Child that comes right, and yet because of some Difficulty or Disproportion cannot pass; which I confess has been, and is yet the Practice of the most expert Artists in Midwifery, not only in England, but throughout Europe; and has much caused the Report, That where a Man comes, one or both must necessarily die; and is the reason of forbearing to send, till the Child is dead, or the Mother dying. But I can neither approve of that Practice, nor those Delays; because my Father, Brothers, and my Self (tho no one else in Europe as I know) have, by God's Blessing and our Industry, attained to, and long practiced a way to deliver Women in this Case, without any Prejudice to them or their Infans; tho all others (being obliged, for want of such an

Expedient, to use the Common Way) do, and must endanger, if not destroy one or both with Hooks. By this manual Operation a Labour may be dispatched, (on the least Difficulty) with fewer Pains, and sooner, to the great Advantage, and Without Danger, both of Woman and Child. If therefore the use of Hooks by Physicians and Chirurgeons, be condemned, (without thereto necessitated through some monstruous Birth) we can much less approve of a Midwife's using them, as some here in England boast they do; with rash Presumption in France, would call them in Question for their Lives.

In the 15th Chapter of this Book, my Author proposes the Conveying sharp Instruments into the Womb; to extract a Head; which is a dangerous Operation, and may be much better done by our forementioned Art, as also the Inconvenience and Hazard of a Child dying thereby prevented, which he supposes in the 27th Chapter of this second Book.

I will now take leave to offer an Apology for not publishing the Secret I mention we have to extract Children without Hooks, where other Artists use them, viz. there being my Father and two Brothers living, that practice this Art, I cannot esteem in my own to dispose of, nor publish it without Injury to them; and think I have not been unserviceable to my Country, although I do but inform them that the forementioned three Persons of our Family, and my Self, can serve them in these Extremities, with greater Safety than others. [...]

§ 2.18. THE INVENTOR OF A MEDICINAL OINTMENT (ANTIHEMORRHAGIC) SELLS HIS SECRET TO SEVERAL EUROPEAN KINGS—1673

In the second half of the seventeenth century, the acquisition by governments of secret formulations from inventors of medicines had become a generalized practice throughout Europe. The following documents concerning an antihemorrhagic ointment invented sometime around 1670 show how that medicine was offered by the inventor to several European kings and was acquired by at least three: France, England, and Denmark.

There is some uncertainty as to the real inventor of the ointment. The British Royal Society cites a certain physician Denis, who brought the medicine to England and was paid by Charles II for his knowledge of the secret composition. Johan Jacob Waldschmidt, a German physician who wrote on medicine and pharmacy, attributed the inventorship of the ointment to a certain Vivens. And the Portuguese physician, Dr. Silva Carvalho, who found this interesting episode on how the diplomacy of his country intervened in bringing the medicine to the hands of Charles II, noted that the diplomatic archives in Lisbon do not mention the inventor. But he added that later the ointment took the name of Weber, physician to the French king, who disseminated knowledge about the therapeutic qualities of the drug.

§ 2.18.1. Weber's styptic liquor by Dr. Silva Carvalho (excerpt)

The Portuguese Ambassador to London in 1673, D. Francisco de Mello, having learned from his colleague, the Portuguese envoy to Paris, Duarte Ribeiro de Macedo, that a surgeon from that city had composed a Styptic Essence with the power of stopping the hemorrhages of the wounds, information which had been followed by the dispatch of a few bottles of the elixir, praised this discovery at the court. Charles II had in his service a French apothecary very learned in chemistry, member of the Royal Society of London and to whom the title of doctor had been granted, Nicolas Lefèvre, but the king did not want to involve him and instructed the Portuguese ambassador to bring the person who knew the secret of the Essence to London to sell it, bringing a large quantity of the remedy to be sent to the fleet, where it would be very useful in the treatment of the wounds caused by harquebuses and bombards.

The king was offering a large sum of money for the purchase of the secret and was ready to send one of his yachts to find the person in charge of this mission.

D. Francisco de Mello has transmitted these offers by letter addressed to his colleague on June 5th. Soon three emissaries left for London in charge of selling the secret of the remedy and bringing several bottles of the famous Styptic Essence, a doctor, a surgeon and an apothecary, whose names do not appear in the letters that are in the Archives of the Ministry of Foreign Affairs in Lisbon, where we got this information. So we cannot know if the surgeon in question was the inventor of the remedy.

Naturally these emissaries will have made the experiment proposed by the inventor to demonstrate the effectiveness of the elixir and which consisted in cutting the paw of a dog and, by applying a compress soaked in the essence, fixed by a band, stopping the hemorrhage immediately.

The king was satisfied and offered one thousand pounds to the three French, but the division was not easy, each of the three believing that they had more rights than the others to the royal reward. . . .

The inventor tried to sell his secret to other countries, but only succeeded in Denmark, where the king gave him a large sum. The anti-hemorrhagic qualities of the product were highly praised by the king's first physician, Weber, and the liquor taking his name was celebrated in several treatises. . .

§ 2.18.2. Waldshmits appoints a French surgeon, Mons. Vivens, as the inventor of the antihemorrhagic liquor

Johan Jacob Waldschmidt, Opera Medico Practica, vol. 1 (excerpt)
Finally, a cure has been shared with a society of several famous physicians, chaired by a French Surgeon, Mons. Vivens, who received a large sum of money from the king of the Gauls, and later from the King of Denmark, for a styptic liquor; using a towel immersed in it, and applying the towel on the wound, the hemorrhage stops immediately: this remedy has been tested several times in dogs, from which the foot is taken off, and then the liquor applied to the resulting wound; the hemorrhage stopped and on the next day it was found that there was no inflammation.

§ 2.18.3. An Account of the Experiments promised at the end of the next precedent transactions concerning the wonderful effects of the Blood staunching liquor upon a Man and a Woman in St. Thomas's Hospital in Southwark London

July 21, 1673

Royal Society, PHILOSOPHICAL TRANSACTIONS, GIVING SOME ACCOMPT OF THE PRESENT UNDERTAKINGS, STUDIES AND LABOURS OF THE INGENIOUS IN MANY CONSIDERABLE PARTS OF THE WORLD (excerpt)

The King [Charles II] having in his presence caused some considerable Experiments to be made with the new Blood stopping liquor upon *Brutes*, and there remaining yet some persons here doubting, whether it would as well succeed upon Men, his Majesty gave order to his Chirurgions to go and see in the Hospitals whether there were not some wounded persons whose blood had need to be stopped. Hereupon there were found two very fit Patients in the Hospital of St. Thomas. The first was a Woman laboring under an inveterate Scurvy and the Kings Evil, Whose Leg was to be cut off because of a malignant ulcer, not suffering her to sleep day or night. The other was a Seaman, whose leg was also to be cut off because of a wound accompanied with a fracture made by a canon bullet in the left Sea-fight. . . .

The King easily concluding from these and the former Experiments [also reported in the Philosophical Transactions of May 30, 1673], how useful this medicine would be in his Armies and Fleets, and understanding that those who before opposed it, did now highly praise it, gave order that Monsieur Denis should be desired to communicate the secret of it; which being done, his Majesty commanded a quantity of it to be made in his own Laboratory of which trials were made upon three Calves in White Hall the 12th of July; a leg of each of them having been cut off, as high as was possible, and the blood of them stopped with this new liquor to the admiration of all the Spectators. For this Water having been prepared with more exactness than ever, the effect of it was so quick and effectual that the blood was stopped in four minutes of time, the Calves by their motion making the pledgets to fall off that had been put on the parts cut, and not a drop of blood appearing.

The King hereupon caused the quantities that had been thus prepared, which were very considerable, to be immediately dispatched away to his Majesties Fleet; and 'tis not doubted but that upon occasion all that shall happen to be wounded will receive great relief and benefit thereby.

§ 2.19. THE KING OF FRANCE, LOUIS XIV, ACQUIRES THE FORMULA OF A SECRET MEDICINE AND ORDERS ITS DISCLOSURE

Because in the seventeenth and eighteenth centuries, the compositions of many medicines were kept secret—to the point that the term "secret" has become synonymous with medicine—Louis XIV acquired and paid for the compositions of a number of them when they were deemed of particular interest and efficacy to treat common diseases. The king subsequently submitted the drugs to the examination of the Palace's physician. In the case the latter recommended their use, the formulae were made public, along with recommendations on how to employ them.

However, the king's motivations in acquiring the formulae of secret medicines were not always altruistic. Louis XIV, like Charles II, of England, his contemporary, ally, and cousin, entertained himself with chemical experiments. He had a laboratory at Versailles, where, in secrecy, he researched a cure for hernia. Fearing that someone could discover his secret composition, he ordered an infinity of ingredients that did not have any effect against the hernia, so as to create confusion. He intended to reveal his medicine only after he was fully satisfied with its efficacy. In this regard, Louis XIV might have learned from Pacchius, who, seventeen centuries earlier, had done the same to protect his secret hyera (see § 2.01). Louis XIV worked alone in his laboratory. It seems that his formulations smelled terribly. [*A. Baudot,* Etudes Historiques sur la Pharmacie en Bourgogne avant *1803, at 267-268 (A. Maloine, 1803). Source: <gallica.BnF.fr>.*]

The following texts tell about Louis XIV's acquisition of the formula of a medicine basically composed of an extract from quinine, whose invention was claimed by Robert Talbor, physician of Charles II of England. The drug was known in France as the "remède de l'anglais." The second text is an excerpt from a technical memoir that reveals the secret formula and uses of that medicine. In 1679, in exchange for the formula's revelation, Louis XIV ordered that Robert Talbor be paid a sum of 48,000 pounds. In addition, the inventor received a knighthood and a pension for life in the amount of 2,000 pounds.

§ 2.19.1. An account of Robert Talbor's secret medicine, its success in English and French kings' courts, and the purchase of its formula by Louis XIV

C.J.S. Thompson, The Mystery and Art of the Apothecary (excerpt)

[The] general introduction of quinine [extracted from cinchona, originally called, "Peruvian bark"] seems to have been largely due to Robert Talbor, who may be said to have made his name and fortune by exploiting it as a secret remedy.

Robert Talbor, or Talbot as he was sometimes called, had a remarkable and interesting career. He was born in 1642, and after leaving school, was apprenticed to Mr. Dear, an apothecary of Cambridge. Although entered as a sizar at St. John's College for five years, there is no evidence that he ever graduated.

About 1671 he settled in Essex to practice medicine, where he says, "I planted myself near the seaside where agues are the epidemical diseases." In the following year he published a little book called "Pyretologia, a rational account of the cause and cure of Agues," in which he makes reference to his secret remedy for the fever, and states that it consisted of four ingredients, " two indigenous and two exotic." He alludes to Peruvian bark as follows:—" Let me advise the world to beware of palliative cures and especially of that known as Jesuit's Powder, as it is given by unskillful hands. Yet this powder is not altogether to be condemned, for it is a noble and safe medicine, and if rightly prepared and corrected, and administered by a skillful hand, otherwise as pernicious a medicine as can be taken."

Talbor's reputation soon increased and he removed to London, where he set up his sign next door to Gray's Inn Gate in Holborn.

The results of his treatment brought him rapid success, and after having cured the daughter of Lady Mordaunt of an attack of fever, he was summoned to Windsor to see King Charles II, who had been seized with the same complaint.

He was fortunate in being able to restore the King to health, and so secured the Royal favor. Talbor was not a Licentiate of the College of Physicians and had no qualification to practice, so, to save him from attacks from that quarter, the King caused a letter to be written to the College, restraining that body from interfering with him in his practice in London.

On July 27th, 1672, he was appointed Physician to the King, and later on received the honor of knighthood at Whitehall. Under a patent issued under the Privy Seal dated August 7th, 1678, Sir Robert Talbor was granted an annuity of £100, together with the profits and privileges appertaining to a Physician-in-Ordinary to the sovereign.

Evelyn, in his Diary on August 29, 1679, states, that "he had conversed with the Marquis of Normanby concerning the Quinquina, which the physicians would not give the King (out of envy, because it had been brought into vogue by Mr. Talbor, an Apothecary) at a time when he was in a dangerous ague. It was the only thing that could cure him. Mr. Short, to whom the King sent to know his opinion of it, privately sent word to the King, that it was the only thing that could save his life, and then the King enjoined the physicians to give it to him, which they did, and he recovered."

From this it would appear that the active ingredient in Talbor's remedy was more than suspected at that time.

In 1679, Talbor visited Spain, and on his return through France, stayed for some time in Paris, where he soon became a prominent personage. Madame de Sevigne alludes to him several times in her "Letters" and remarks, "Nothing is talked of here but the English man and his cures." In November 1680, when the Dauphin was seized with an attack of fever, Talbor, who had made influential friends at the French Court, was called in and undertook to treat him. Madame de Sevigne says, "The King, Louis XIV, insisted on Talbor preparing his wine in his presence before giving it to the Prince."

The treatment was eminently successful and the Dauphin soon recovered. Talbor was made a Chevalier, but the King, determined to learn his secret, eventually induced him, for a sum of 2,000 *louis d'or* and an annuity of 2,000 livres, to reveal his method of treatment and the formulae for his remedy, which, however, was not to be published until after his death.

After a further visit to Spain, where he cured the Queen of an attack of fever, Talbor returned to London, where he died shortly afterwards in 1681, at the early age of forty. He was buried in Trinity Church, Cambridge.

The formula for his remedy was published in England in 1682 under the title, "The English Remedy, or Talbor's wonderful Secret for curing of Agues and Fevers."

§ 2.19.2. Supplement of the Journal of Medicine published by order of the King

January 15, 1681

Nicolas de Blégny, LE REMÈDE ANGLOIS POUR LA GUÉRISON DES FIÈVRES, 1683 (excerpt)

I have spoken to you several times of the liberalities of the King towards a large number of individuals, from whom his Majesty has drawn the secrets of Medicine, with the intention of devoting them to the common utility of his subjects; and you have been so much less surprised that no one knows better than you the greatness of this incomparable Prince; but will you believe it, Sir, all these rich presents, all his great rewards, this pension so considerable; in a word, all the good deeds that the English Doctor has received from him, have had for principle only the same paternal goodness of which we feel every day so many surprising effects.

Perhaps you have felt that he had bought so dearly the admirable Antipyretic of this Physician with the only purpose of reserving it for himself, and for the Princes and Princesses of His Royal Family; and I confess that any other Sovereign would have used it in this way; but such maxims are as much below the Character of the King, as he is above other men, by his virtue and glory; all these excellent medicines that he had published on different occasions, by the care and orders of his first Physician, are strong proofs of this; it is in this manner that this great Prince has found a sure means to spread over his subjects the most precious treasures of medicine, so that nothing is missing in their happiness; and it is on this same principle that he wishes to gratify the public of the English remedy, which I have just received by his order from the hands of Mr. Daquin, his first physician, to deduce from it the nature and the properties, to justify its goodness, and to prescribe its adequate use. . . .

Thus to return to my own duty, and for the execution of the orders of which I have just been honored, I am going to confine myself in the character of simple Naturalist, to give you an exact description of the English Medicine, with the judicious observations of the first Doctor on all his dependencies; to which I will add of my own the natural history of Quinquina, that of opium, several important remarks on fevers, and a new system on antipyretics, in which one will find some important reflections on the nature, on the proprieties and on the use of these kinds of medicines. . . .

§ 2.20. HELVETIUS (C. 1661-1724), A DUTCH PHYSICIAN AND INVENTOR IN THE MEDICAL FIELD, WAS REWARDED BY LOUIS XIV WITH SEVERAL FAVORS IN EXCHANGE FOR THE DISCLOSURE OF ONE OF HIS SECRET MEDICINES

Adrien Helvetius received several awards from Louis XIV in exchange for revealing the composition of a medicine he claimed to have invented, and which was effective in the treatment of dysentery and diarrhea. The first of the following texts, authored by a contemporary, gives a biographical account of Helvetius' life and successes.

*As it had already become a practice since his father's reign, Louis XIV asked Helvetius to reveal the composition and the method of using it, which he did in a leaflet published in 1688 (*METHODE DU SIEUR HELVETIUS, MEDECIN DE S.A.R.M. LE DUC D'ORLEANS, & INSPECTEUR GENERAL DES HÔPITAUX DE FLANDRES, POUR L'USAGE DE SES REMÈDES DANS LES DYSENTERIES, & DIFFERENTES ESPÈCES DE COURS DE VENTRE*). In exchange for the revelation of his secret, Helvetius received from the king a thousand louis d'or, citizenship status, the degree of doctor of medicine, and the permission of making and selling his medicines throughout the French kingdom. Later, he was hired as a physician to the Duke of Orleans, Louis XIV's nephew, and designated General Inspector of the Hospitals in Flanders.*

Helvetius was not only a pharmacist. He was also a surgeon and inventor of surgical devices and methods, as shown in another of his medical works: LETTRE DE MONSIEUR HELVETIUS, DOCTEUR EN MEDECINE, A MONSIEUR REGIS, SUR LA NATURE ET LA GUÉRISON DU CANCER *(Jean Cuisson, 1696). This booklet contains illustrations of a medical device whose invention Helvetius claimed: "I will only add that having noticed that the new instrument, in connection which some have already called me Tenette Helvétienne, because I invented it to hold the cancer and to be the master in the operation, had enough approval from everyone, especially yours in particular; I thought it was appropriate to send you here the figure and description, so as to share it with the public, with the illustration of the very cancer that it serves to extirpate; to which I add the method in which one must proceed for carrying this operation well; . . ."*

The first and third texts illustrate an interesting aspect that is linked to the granting of monetary awards to inventors: more than once, the inventors may see themselves involved in disputes because of conflicting claims filed by third parties. Above, we saw a reference to a similar dispute, concerning the invention of an antihemorrhagic ointment (see § 2.18.1.). This could serve as a lesson to those who today fight the patent system and propose a reward system in its stead. The fact that the market does not intervene by attributing to consumers the task of rewarding inventors, through their choices, does not eliminate conflicts.

The decision of the Parliament is also interesting because the challenger (apparently, a crook), besides alleging that he was coerced, also disputed Helvetius' entitlement to the secret ownership.

*The awards Helvetius received were partly described by himself in the Preamble of another book (*MÉTHODE POUR GUÉRIR TOUTE SORTE DE FIÈVRES SANS RIEN FAIRE PRENDRE PAR LA BOUCHE*), in which he revealed another of his inventions: a new method of using quinine to treat fevers.*

§ 2.20.1. A sketch of the life and the events surrounding Helvetius' invention and his rewards

De Vigneul-Marville, MÉLANGES D'HISTOIRE ET DE LITTÉRATURE, vol. 1, 1713 (excerpt)

Hipekakuana, Radix Brasiliensis, Root that is sovereign against the Flow of blood, comes to us from Brazil, where it is commonly used as well as in Portugal. . . .

Mr. Helvetius, father of [Adrien Helvetius], has practiced Medicine in Holland for more than 55 years, with a very great reputation. Today he is still Doctor of the General States, and enjoys a Pension attached to this Charge, which has been created expressly for him. . . .

The young man, known in France under the name of Dutch Doctor, after having studied Medicine at the Academy of Leyden, like his brothers, and having practiced under his Father himself, in Chemical Operations, and in the knowledge of Diseases, decided to travel at the age of 20, as his brothers had done, and as most foreign doctors usually do. He came to Paris without any intention of stopping there, and it was only because of unforeseen reasons that he decided to settle in there afterwards. Hardly had he arrived there when he avoided the death of Mr. de la Chabane, Counselor in the Parliament of Bordeaux, who had been already abandoned by four of the most famous Doctors of the Faculty. This dazzling cure, which can be attested to by Father de la Chabane, brother of this Magistrate, and priest of the Oratory in Saint Magloire, began to build Mr. Helvetius' reputation. It was followed by those he made with regard to Mr. Turet of the Seminary of Saint Sulpice, of Mr. Tronçon, Superior of the same Seminary, of Mr. Brisassier, Superior of the Seminary of Foreign Missions, and several others; but what finally made him known in Paris was the cure of Madame la Duchesse de Chaulne, who had vainly exhausted all the means of medicine. This lady, whose manners were extremely noble and generous, did not content herself with giving him a present of one thousand *écus*, she also granted him a very considerable pension, and procured him the protection of Mr. Colbert. Mr. Helvetius had been introduced to her by Mr. Marshal d'Estrade, who had had his father as his Doctor during his stay in Holland, and who, in recognition of the help he had received from him, honored the son with his trust and friendship.

It was around that same time that Monsignor having been attacked by Dysentery, Mr. d'Aquin, then First Physician, sent for Mr. Helvetius, to find out from him whether his remedy could be used with certainty. The latter offered to experiment it in Hospitals, and during the conversation confessed to him that it was the Hipekakuana, of which Mr. d'Aquin did not know the use yet; he had a box full of it, which had been given to him for Monsignor by Mr. de Guenegaud, formerly Ambassador to Portugal.

Shortly after Rev. Father de la Chaize, to whose protection M. Helvetius is partly indebted for his success, proposed to him to communicate his Remedies to Father Beize who was going on mission, with a promise that their secrets would not be revealed. The effects, and especially those of the Hipekakuana, were so surprising, that Father de la Chaize felt obliged to speak to the King. The Marquis of Seignelay was then ordered to send for M. Helvetius, and to indicate to him that the King, for the good of his Subjects, wished him to communicate the preparation of his Remedy against Dysentery to Mr. d'Aquin.

This First Physician, who has always favored Mr. Helvetius with his esteem, received him very pleasantly and consented without any difficulty, that the experiment be made at the Hôtel-Dieu in Paris. Mr. Helvetius was conducted there and introduced by the President of Novion himself. On the favorable report of Mr. Leger, Doctor of the Faculty of Paris, and of Mr. Gastelier, Surgeon of Mr. Colbert, who had examined for more than one month the effects of this remedy on various Patients, Mr. Helvetius was ordered to make it public, and was rewarded by the King with a sum of one thousand *Louis d'or*.

Several Doctors, jealous of this success, invoked against him [the testimony of] a certain Grenier, formerly Hatter, who had brought the Root of Hipekakuana and other Remedies from Cadiz and Lisbon, because there was some trade of it [in those cities], although very different from this one. This man dared to boast of having given this Remedy to Mr. Helvetius, claiming on this title to be entitled to the reward. The matter was clarified by Mr. de Louvoy himself. Grenier was accused of fraud by this Minister, and afterwards, much more formally, by Sentence of the Châtelet of Paris, and by Decision of the Parliament. . . .

§ 2.20.2. Letters Patent granting permission to Adrien Helvetius, Doctor of Medicine, naturalized French, to distribute alone throughout the Kingdom his specific against stomach colic, the flow of blood, and dysentery

Maurice Bouvet, Les laboratoires autorisés au XVII siècle (suite et fin) (excerpt)

At Versailles, August 24, 1688

. . . Having been informed that our beloved Adrien Helvétius, doctor of medicine, naturalized French, in addition to several beautiful discoveries that he made in his science to the great advantage of our subjects who every day receive considerable help in the most dangerous diseases, has recently found a specific to cure unfailingly and without return stomach colic, and the dysentery, we ordered that it be made various experiments at the general hospital and at the Hôtel-Dieu of our good city of Paris on all the sick affected by these kinds of evils, besides those tests that Mr. d'Aquin, our Counselor and first doctor, has made and ordered to be made, which had a happy result, and wishing that Helvétius be allowed to distribute his remedy in our Kingdom for the relief of our subjects, and that he be in some way rewarded for his care and dedication to his profession.

For these reasons, We have permitted, granted and bestowed upon him permission, grant and accord by the presents signed by our hand, to distribute his specific against stomach colic, the flow of blood and the dysentery, both in wholesale and in retail, in any the extent of our Kingdom, country. . . and domains of our obedience and have it sold and distributed in his name by such persons as he sees fit during the time and space of four years, starting on the day and date hereof. Counterfeiters will be punished with a fine of 3,000 pounds, a third for the king, a third for Helvétius, the rest for the Hôtel Dieu. However, the King reserves the right to have Helvétius' medicine distributed in civilian and military hospitals without being obliged to buy it from Helvétius.

Registered in the Parliament on September 6, 1688, and the Court of Currencies a few days later.

[It seems that between the registration of this letter at the Parliament and its registration at the Court of Currencies (*Cour des Monnaies*) there have been some changes. The latter document sets the price of sale of the medicine at 3 *louis d'or*; the duration of the privilege is extended to 15 years; and the authorization includes Helvetius' right to set his own furnaces and laboratories necessary for the making of its medicine. This last element is mentioned by Helvetius in the Preamble to his work MÉTHODE POUR GUÉRIR TOUTE SORTE DE FIÈVRES, as shown below.]

§ 2.20.3. Decision by the Parliament settling the dispute between Garnier Chapelier and Helvetius, concerning some alleged arrears by the latter in the payment of some quantities of ipecacuanha roots, which he used in preparing his famous medicine against dysentery

Nicolas Nupied, Journal des Principales Audiences du Parlement, depuis l'année 1685, jusqu'en 1700, vol. 4 (excerpt)

On Tuesday May 30, 1690, in the Hearing of the Great Chamber concerned, a judgment was issued on the question above.

The agreement was between a named Garnier Chapelier, and Mr. Helvetius, Doctor of Medicine from the Faculty of Reims, commonly called the Dutch doctor. Garnier appealed from a decision of the Châtelet rendered by default, which had rejected his request for the endorsement of Letters of termination by him of a contract that he said he had been obliged to sign under fear and violence, by which contract he was satisfied with a sum of 2,000 pounds for sixty pounds of a root that he had supplied to Mr. Helvetius and promised by the same contract to provide another twenty-five pounds. The decision under appeal condemned him to deliver the roots to Helvetius in eight days, at the rate of forty-two francs for each pound.

The appellant. . . with regard to the contract alleged that the fear and violence inflicted on him had obliged him to sign it. Because of this, he stated several facts, namely, that having made several trips to foreign countries, in India, in Spain, and in Portugal, he had been aware of a root called *Veguigulio* or *Vexecullo*, otherwise *Hipepocuana*, which grows in Brazil and Peru, usually on the steepest places of the areas where gold mines are found, and whose virtue is to cure dysentery; that he had taken a few pounds for him; that afterwards, being in Spain, he had made acquaintance with Helvetius, and had given him most of it; that Helvetius, on his return to France, had tested it, and he had found it marvelous and infallible, which had led him to ask the appellant, who was also back in France, to write to the correspondents he had in Spain that they sent him fifty or sixty pounds, and in that note Helvetius promised the appellant he would pay him the roots at the rate of thirty-seven francs per pound, that this root in Cadiz cost fifteen francs per pound for transportation expenses, and that for his profit, as he was an honest man, he would give him whatever he would ask.

That, moreover, he did not fail to ask his correspondent to write to him what name the root had in the country, its particular qualities, its different usage, and how much exactly corresponded to each dose; that the appellant had brought in sixty pounds, but having been imprisoned for debt, this root had arrived while he was in prison; that on this Helvetius had come to find him, and had promised him that if he wanted to allow him to have the roots delivered to his house, he would get the Appellant out of prison, and that afterwards they would agree on the price, with which the Appellant had consented, without even taking a receipt from Helvetius.

That, in the meantime, being in possession of these roots, he had made a large number of cures, he had cured the most desperate dysenteries, and thereby acquired credit, and had amassed much wealth; that in truth he had taken the Appellant out of prison, but without paying the sum of 2,000 pounds for which he was detained there, and without having full personal freedom, because he had only been released from prison under the custody of Bailiff Masson; that Helvetius, having acquired great reputation because of this specific, the rumor had reached the King's ears; so that in 1687 the latter had this remedy inspected by his first Physician, and had allowed it to be tested in Hospitals, and as the cures were infallible, he had made a gift of 10,000 pounds to Helvetius, and had accorded him a Patent permitting him alone to sell his remedy for fifteen years, at [the price of] three gold louis for each dose of one drachma; that after all this the appellant had asked Helvetius to pay the sixty pounds of the root that he had supplied him, but Helvetius, wishing to pay a very low price for it, had conceived a trick, and had brought Bailiff Master Masson to the appellant's house, with three or four Archers and a Sergeant of the Guards, whom he asked to remove him, and made him understand that he was to be taken to the Bastille as a money counterfeiter; but, however, instead, he had been taken to a low and very dark room at Master Masson's house; . . . that he has been presented with a previously prepared Contract, which he had been obliged to sign; that by this Contract he was made to agree to be satisfied with a sum of 2,000 pounds for the quantity of roots that he had brought in, and that he had been made to promise to deliver to Helvetius another twenty-five pounds of this root at the rate of thirty-seven francs a pound, given that in Cadiz the transportation expenses cost fifteen pounds; after which the Appellant had been sent home with threats, that if he pursued this affair further, the order which had been given to put him in the Bastille would be carried out. . . .

Basically, the contract in question having been extorted by fear and violence, it could not subsist because of the fear instilled, *ut posset cadere in constantem virum*, since he had been threatened with being taken to the Bastille, and that he had been removed because of that; that the violence was evident, having been in the hands of the Archers and in a prison; that an obligation made *in vinculis* was null; that what characterized the violence even more was the impossibility that he could be satisfied with such a modest sum, given that these roots were more in demand than he could sell, that it was not probable that he, who had been the cause of the reputation and the credit that the Dutch Doctor had acquired, would have been satisfied with forty-two francs per pound of this root, while Helvetius had obtained more than forty thousand francs at the beginning, at which time he did not made cures for less than thirty and forty *louis d'or*, and he did not put in each dose more than one drachma, which was the forty-eighth part of the pound; that he still made more than 4,000 pounds, although the King had limited [the price of] each dose to three *louis d'or*.

That the obligation to deliver twenty-five pounds was null, since it had no foundation; that Monsieur de Louvois had ordered him to bring as many roots as he could for the Army, with the prohibition of giving it to anyone else, and that even if he wanted to, he could not, since the war against Spain eliminated the hope of having access to the root, this Crown having under its domination Peru and Brazil, where this root grows.

Helvetius stated the opposite, that the acts of violence that the appellant alleged were a story of fantasy; that there was no reason for the termination of this contract passed between adults in the office of the Notary Arroüet; that it was not probable that two officers, like Arroüet and the bailiff Masson, would have agreed to engage in the acts supposed to have happened in 1687; that the appellant had confirmed the contract concluded in 1687 by a second one signed six months later, by which he had confirmed receipt for the 2,000 pounds in question owed to him for the sixty pounds of roots; that it was not true that it was the appellant who had given him the knowledge of this root, that he had obtained it from a Dutch doctor who had written a Treatise about it, printed more than twenty years ago; that he had cured the sick in 1684 and that he had only known the Appellant in 1686. He produced several certificates, and one among others from Mr. de Pontcarré, Counselor at the Court, whose son he had cured of the dysentery in 1684. That, moreover, the price he had paid for this root to the Appellant was considerable enough for what he had ordered him; and in respect of the twenty-five pounds that he had promised to deliver to the defendant, there was nothing to complain about, since the Appellant had them at his house.

The Court, disregarding the Letters obtained by Garnier, rejected his appeal; furthermore, it ordered that Garnier would be satisfied with the sum stipulated by the contract in question for the price of the roots delivered by him, and dismissed Helvetius from the demand for delivery of the twenty-five pounds of the same root promised to him, costs compensated. Mr. President de Nesmond decided.

§ 2.20.4. Prologue to Helvetius' treatise, Méthode pour Guérir toute Sorte de Fièvres—1694

To the King

Sire,

The new use that I discovered of Cinchona, to cure infallibly all kinds of Fevers without having anything taken by mouth, has been approved by Your Majesty with such obliging kindness and when I had the honor to present it to Him, that I would have every reason to believe that the public would not give it a less favorable reception when I offered it to Him. But in what way, Sire, will it not be expected from all your subjects, when they will know that it is Your Majesty yourself who gratifies them with this discovery, by the paternal care with which Your Royal very kindness wishes to look after their health?

Yes, Sire, it is this extreme kindness that, after Your Majesty having brought to all the needs of the sick who have found themselves among those who have the happiness of serving Him in his House, and who did the honor to put in my hands, has obliged Him afterwards to order me to publish my medicine, so that there was no one in his Kingdom who was deprived from the advantage of using it. I obey, Sire, not only with the very humble respect and the very deep submission that I owe to the orders of my King, but also with a very particular joy of being able to enrich and improve the Medicine for the benefit of France, which your heroic virtues rise so strongly above all the other countries of the world, and which is my true homeland since it has pleased Your Majesty to honor me with becoming Your subject, by naturalizing me.

But at the same time, Sire, I take the liberty that Your Majesty has allowed me to put under the protection of His august Name which I give to the public: being quite just that after the singular grace that He accorded me when I had the honor to offer Him my specific against the dysentery,[21] to grant me the right to hold Laboratories throughout the whole of the Kingdom, in the future there will be no fruit of my work that is not dedicated to Him as belonging to Him by right, and which does not serve me as a means of witnessing to Him the lively recognition of his blessings with which my heart is full, and the zeal with which I burn to sacrifice in His service throughout my life, with complete devotion, everything which will depend on my little lights, and on my weak forces. I am, . . .

§ 2.21. NEHEMIAH GREW OBTAINS THE FIRST ENGLISH PATENT FOR A MEDICINE UNDER THE STATUTE OF 1624—JULY 15, 1698

Although the granting of industrial privileges had become a common practice in England after the fifteenth century, inventive pharmacists would not apply for them—or if they applied, they were not successful in obtaining them. Instead, they resorted to secrecy as the preferred manner of appropriating inventions in their field. Things changed with the enactment of the Statute of Monopolies, in 1624. Because § 6 of the Statute promised patents for inventions concerning "new manufactures within this realm," and because new medicines were "manufactures" in the sense that their elaboration implied the manipulation of ingredients, there was no legal obstacle to their patenting. And yet, it took several decades for the first patent to be issued for a new medicine. After 1624, a few English pharmacists applied for patents under the Statute. They would not be many, however, because most inventors of new medicines would continue keeping their compositions secret, in particular after English patent law, more than one century later, incorporated the requirement of specification. In France, pharmacists would have to wait more than 150 years to have the same possibility of acquiring patent rights—and yet for a limited period, because in 1844, as we will see, a new law excluded pharmaceutical inventions from patentability.

The first English patent for a medicine was granted in 1698. The inventor was Nehemiah Grew (1641-1712), who was primarily a professional botanist (he is known as "the father of plant anatomy," according to Wikipedia). Grew's invention was related to the use of water for medical purposes—the famous Epsom Salts. Water and the salts extracted therefrom appear with certain frequency, as this book shows, in the literature

21. Helvetius here refers to another of his claimed inventions: a "poudre spécifique" (specific powder) against dysenteria and many other conditions of the digestive system. A leaflet authored by him explained in detail the composition and the method of using the medicine.

concerning intellectual property and medicines, starting with Dondi's industrial privilege, in 1255 (see § 2.04). The patent letter protecting Grew's invention does not include a specification, as noted in the document: "notwithstanding the not full and certain describing or mentioning of the said Invention, or of the materials, ways, or means of making, using, using, or exercising of the same" However, two years after obtaining the patent, Nehemiah Grew published, in Latin, a complete, detailed account of his invention in "A Treatise of the Nature and Use of the Bitter Purging Salt—Easily Known from all Counterfeits by its Bitter Taste." This text was published in London by the author himself, and, from the title's reference to counterfeits, it appears to be more than a scientific description of his findings and invention, but rather a piece of commercial advertisement.

And indeed the book, as well as his late patent application, were just episodes of Grew's struggle against counterfeiting and misappropriation. Two brothers, Francis and George Moult, not only claimed his invention as their own, and persistently counterfeited it, but also misappropriated the authorship of Grew's treatise on the salt. A detailed account of Grew's drama is found in Adrian Johns, PIRACY—THE INTELLECTUAL PROPERTY WARS FROM GUTENBERG TO GATES, *at 87* et seq. *(Univ. of Chicago Press, 2009).*

A.D. 1698. [Patent] N°354.

William the Third, by the grace of God, &c., to all whom these Presents shall come greeting.

Whereas our trusty and wellbeloved Nehemiah Grew, Doctor in Physic, had by his petition humbly represented unto us that he had with much study and great charge invented "The Way of Making the Salt of the Purging Waters Perfectly Fine in Large Quantities and Very Cheap, so as to Be Commonly Prescribed and Taken as a General Medicine in our Kingdom," and he having therefore prayed us to grant him our Letters Patents for the sole benefit of the said Invention for the term of fourteen years, and we are graciously pleased to gratify him in his request.

Know yee, therefore, that we being willing to cherish and encourage all laudable endeavours and designs of such our subjects as have by their industry found out useful and profitable arts, mysteries, and inventions, and that the said Nehemiah Grew may accordingly reap some fruit and benefit of his labour and charge in and concerning the premises, of our especial grace, certain knowledge, and mere motion, have given and granted, and by these Presents do give and grant unto the said Nehemiah Grew, his executors, administrators, and assignees, especial licence, power, privilege, and authority, that he and they, by him and themselves, and by his and their deputies, servants, agents, and workmen, and such others onely as he, the said Nehemiah Grew, his executors, administrators, and assignes, shall agree with, shall and may from time to time and at all times hereafter during the space of fourteen yeares next ensuing the date of these Presents, at his and their own proper costs and charges, erect, use, teach, exercise, and put in practice the said new Invention so by him contrived and found out as aforesaid in any place or places within our Kingdom of England, Dominion of Wales, and Towne of Berwick-upon-Tweed, and also shall and may receive, take, and enjoy all the benefit, profits, commodities, and advantages of and by the said new Invention to be had, made, acquired, or gotten to his and their own proper benefit, use, and uses, to have, hold, use, exercise, and enjoy the said licences, powers, privileges, and authorities, and all other the premises by these Presents granted or mentioned to be granted unto the said Nehemiah Grew, his executors, administrators, and assignees, for and during and unto the full end and term of fourteen years from the day of the date of these Presents next ensuing, and fully to be complete and ended according to the Statute in that case made and provided. And to the end the said Nehemiah Grew, his executors, administrators, and assignees, may the better enjoy the full and whole benefit, and the sole use and exercise of his said new Invention, we do by these Presents, for us, our heirs and successors, straightly charge, require, and command all and every person and persons, bodies politique and corporate, of what quality, degree, name, or condition soever they be, within our Kingdom of England, Dominion of Wales, and Towne of Berwick-upon-Tweed, that neither they nor any of them, during the said term of fourteen years hereby granted, either directly or indirectly, to use, exercise, or put in practice the said new Invention so by the said Nehemiah Grew invented and found out as aforesaid nor do nor shall counterfeit, imitate, or resemble the said new Invention, or any materials thereunto belonging, nor do nor shall make any addition thereunto or subtraction therefrom, whereby to pretend themselves the inventors or devisors thereof, without the licence, consent, or agreement of the said Nehemiah Grew, his executors, administrators, or assignees, in writing under his or their hand and seals first had and obtained in that behalf, under such pains and penalties as can or may be inflicted on the offender or offenders therein for the contempt of this our royal command; and further to be answerable to the said Nehemiah Grew, his executors, administrators, and assignees, according to the utmost rigor of the law, for his and their damages thereby sustained. And further, we do by these our Letters Patents, for us, our heirs and successors, will, authorize, require, and command all and singular justices of the peace, mayors, sheriffs, bailiffs, constables, leadboroughs, and all other officers and ministers whatsoever of us, our heirs and successors, now and for the time being whom it may concern, that they and every of them respectively be from time to time during the terme hereby granted in their respective offices, and according to their and every of their best skills and endeavors, aiding, helping, and assisting unto the said Nehemiah Grew, his executors, administrators, and assignees, deputies, agents, and servants in and by all things in and about the accomplishment of our royal will and pleasure hereinbefore declared, and in the execution of the several powers and privileges hereby granted as aforesaid. And moreover, wee do by these Presents, for us, our heirs and successors, will and command that our said respective officers and ministers before mentioned, or any of them, do not nor shall at any time hereafter during the term hereby granted in any wise molest, trouble, or hinder the said Nehemiah Grew, his executors, administrators, or assignees, deputies, agents, or servants, in or about the use or exercise of the aforesaid Invention, or any part thereof, or anything relating thereunto: Provided always, and these our Letters are and shall be upon this condition, that if at any time during the said terme of fourteen years hereby granted it shall be made appear to us, our heirs or successors, or any six or more of our or their Privy Council, that this our grant is contrary to law, or prejudicial or inconvenient to our subjects in general, or that the

Invention before mentioned is not a new invention as to the public use and exercise of the same, and not invented and found out by the said Nehemiah Grew as aforesaid, then, upon signification and declaration of such prejudice or inconveniency, to be made by us, our heirs or successors, under our or their signet or privy seal, or by the Lord or others of our or their Privy Council, or any six or more of them, under their hand, these our Letters Patents shall forthwith cease, determine, and be utterly void to all intents and purposes, anything hereinbefore contained to the contrary notwithstanding: Provided also, that these our Letters Patents shall forthwith cease, determine, and be utterly void to all intents and purposes, anything hereinbefore contained to the contrary notwithstanding: Provided also, that these our Letters Patents, or anything herein contained, shall not extend or be construed to extend to give privilege unto the said Nehemiah Grew, his executors, administrators, or assignees, to imitate any invention or work whatsoever which had been heretofore invented and found out by any other of our subjects whatsoever, and publicly exercised within our Kingdome of England, Dominion of Wales, and Town of Berwick-upon-Tweed, to whom we have already granted our like Letters Patents of privilege for the sole exercise and benefit thereof, it being our will and pleasure that the said Nehemiah Grew, his executors, administrators, and assignees, and all and singular other person and persons to whom we have already granted our like Letters Patent, shall distinctly use and practice their several Inventions by them selectively found out, according to the true meaning of such our Letters Patents and of these Presents. And lastly, wee do hereby, for us, our heirs and successors, grant unto the said Nehemiah Grew, his executors, administrators, and assignees, that these our Letters Patents, or the enrollment thereof, shall be and continue in and by all things good, valid, firm, and effectual in the law, according to the true meaning of the same, notwithstanding the not full and certain describing or mentioning of the said Invention, or of the materials, ways, or means of making, using, using, or exercising of the same, or of the certain use or benefit thereof, or any other defect, uncertainty, or imperfection in these Presents, or any other matter, cause, or thing whatsoever to the contrary in any wise notwithstanding.

In witness, &c. Witnesse our self at Westminster, the Fifteenth day of July [of 1698].

§ 2.22. A FRENCH DOCTOR ATTACKS THE PRIVATE APPROPRIATION OF MEDICINES THROUGH SECRECY ON ETHICAL AND RELIGIOUS GROUNDS—1708

Until the seventeenth century, secrecy, as already said, was practically the only legal mechanism that pharmacists resorted to for protecting their inventions. When carefully protected and enforced, secrecy could ensure ownership for very long periods. This would naturally give rise to some exasperation by physicians and by society at large. With the growth of the professions associated with health, as a result of the knowledge gains that stemmed from the Scientific Revolution, a generalized discomfort against certain practices by inventors of medicines grew. Pharmacists and physicians engaged in the making and selling of medicines were, therefore, the target of many attacks. The first texts defending the private appropriation of medicinal knowledge also emerged in that period. The text that follows, in the form of a letter, authored by a French physician, attacks those who invented new medicines and kept them secret, thus avoiding their dissemination.

Besides the motivations of a religious nature, the author relied on two arguments: (i) medicines at that time were still essentially formulations or combinations of natural ingredients (chemistry was just starting its influence on pharmacy); the ingredients being originated in Nature, they should not be the matter of appropriation; (ii) costs eventually incurred by the makers of medicines should not be taken into consideration because those physicians who prepared the best medicines could recover them by gains in reputation.

Of course, this text has to be seen in a historical context. But the second argument has not disappeared from today's debates involving patents on diagnostic, therapeutic and surgical methods. And the charitable tone behind the proposal concerning the public sharing of privately owned medicinal knowledge is not strange to the motives exposed in various international initiatives aiming at making all COVID-19 related treatment and cures freely available.

Brisseau, Pierre (1626-1717), *Lettre d'un médecin à un de ses amis, touchant les remèdes secrets*, 1708 (excerpts)

. . . It will not be difficult for me to prove that the concealment of a useful remedy is against Christian charity. We see nothing more common in the Holy Scriptures, that all good comes from God, that it must be shared charitably, and the talent that has been received should not be buried. Remedies are gifts from God, and whatever industry one adds to prepare them, they must always be reported back to that first Author, who created them for the relief of humans. . . .

For supporting this Doctrine it is not necessary to refer in detail the hundreds of places of the Gospel and the writings of the Apostles, and it suffices to say that charity is recommended all over them, as the soul of all the other virtues, and the basis of Christianity.

With regard to the Fathers of the Church, Saint Ambrose considers as a murder the one who lets a poor die of starvation, having enough to feed him, *non pavisti, occidisti*. From which it follows very naturally that he who hides some important medicine will be guilty of death, and of all the evils which he could have prevented, or cured by manifesting it: *non curasti potens curare, ergò occidisti*; and I see no difference there, except that it costs money to feed a poor person, and that it costs nothing to divulge a secret. This is the proposal that I have sent you so as to have it examined, and which would deserve to be approved by the Sorbonne, whose authority would be of great weight. . . .

The Doctrine that we have just exposed is pure Christianity. No matter how hard we try to elude it by human reasoning, and by ingeniously fabricated exceptions, the truth of the Oracles of Scripture and of the Fathers will always prevail. It is in vain that those who hide the remedies will say that they do not refuse them to anyone. To condemn them, it suffices that the most distant peoples be deprived of them since the Gospel of the Lord has extended the term neighbor beyond compatriots and neighbors, that is to say to all humans. So little thought was given to it that we have seen Priests and Religious until now to distribute secret medicines, and derive great tribute from them. This disorder went so far in France, that the Doctors often met Religious in their way, who, in order to assert their secrets, introduced themselves in the patients' houses, and diverted them from the good rules of Medicine. But the King has wisely dealt with that by the same Decree, art. 27, where he forbids Religious from making medicines, and administering any medicine under any pretext whatsoever, on the penalty of a fine of 500 pounds, or one year in prison for the Beggars, who have no means to pay it. . . . The concealment of remedies is not only contrary to Christian charity, but also to humanity. Humans are made for each other, and according to natural law they must communicate to each other everything that can be useful to society. Otherwise the arts and sciences would never have come down to us, and we would live like the Barbarians. Medicine, above all, needed this communication more, because it could only be formed through an infinity of discoveries and experiences transmitted from hand to hand, and it is mainly to the ancient Greeks that we owe the best part of what we have of it. . . . Among the laws of the Athenians there was one that expressly ordered that travelers be taught the way. If the times had preserved them all to us, I have no doubt that, on the same principle, we would find one which forbade the refusal to reveal a medicine, and one can say that it is comprised in the other. Not to show the way to a traveler who gets lost is a very blameworthy offense, and it is even a greater one to conceal from a sick person what nature has produced for his recovery. . . .

The most considerable exception, or rather the only one that I could accept, is that a person who is poor and responsible for a family, and who has made a discovery, would not be able to profit from it so as to extract himself from poverty. I answer that this exception can at most take place in the other arts, which concern only the comfort of the humans: but that an important medicine for their health and their life must never be hidden; that nothing can dispense with Christian charity, and that Providence will know how to reward him anyway; finally that the public good must be preferred to that of an individual, mainly when the supposed case can only be very rare, ... In addition to all these general reasons drawn from Divine and natural law, I will say moreover that if it is a Doctor who has found this important remedy, he is bound by his duty, and by the privileges and exemptions that have been attributed to his profession, to unveil it; and the honor of having added a good remedy to Medicine, will give him enough reputation to permit him to extract himself from poverty. . . .

We even see Doctors who have some name, and who nevertheless reserve specific remedies for themselves. They say that the invention of these remedies cost them and their Fathers a lot of study and work. But this is to impose on the ignorant, since as Hypocrates formally says, the remedies are only found by chance, and by experience; that reasoning and work can only add to them something better for their preparation, or by their mixing, and that the most skillful physicians today are of the same opinion as the illustrious Mr. Boyle, who proves very well that the preparations in which there is the most art, and the most sophisticated mixtures most often spoil the good medicines, instead of making them better. . . With regard to the expense that these Doctors with secrets say they have incurred, it is another falsehood; because it follows from what I have just told you, that good medicines cost nothing to find, and that the best ones are easier to prepare. . . .

I believe, Sir, to have sufficiently demonstrated that the concealment of medicines is contrary to humanity, and to Christian charity. I have even shown that nothing is more opposed to common sense than the faith that is attributed so lightly to the sellers of secrets. You can imagine that at my age I no longer have much interest in the thing, and it is only my zeal for the public good and for the honor of our profession that has led me to prepare these reflections for you, in order to reform, if possible, such a great abuse. I am sure that we would succeed if we could join the authority of the Sovereign to a good decision by learned theologians; and the occasion seems favorable to me, while the King is willing to take care to support the Medicine, and that we have with His Majesty the Illustrious Mr. Fagon, the support of the real Doctors, and the scourge of the Charlatans.

I fully anticipate that whatever I have the honor to tell you here will not be to the liking of many people. But since it is the truth, an honest man who is convinced of it, must never hide it, when it cannot do harm; and I myself would be sinning against my principles, if I concealed the remedy to the evil with which Medicine and the public are attacked. . . .

§ 2.23. CREATIVE PHARMACISTS FIND THE WAY TO THE BRITISH PATENT OFFICE: THE SECOND BRITISH PATENT FOR A MEDICINAL COMPOSITION WAS GRANTED IN 1711 TO TIMOTHY BYFIELD

Inventors of new medicinal compositions had, under the Statute of Monopolies, a choice: they could apply for patents, or they could keep their inventions under secrecy. In the first case, they were entitled to the right to exclude others from the making and using of their formulae. In the second case, exclusivity was a natural consequence of the fact that others would not have access to the recipes. However, these apparently straightforward rules had exceptions. In a few cases, the English King granted the privilege of exclusivity for secret medicines. This was a rare situation, but it occurred with some regularity in France. But in other cases, also rare, patentees would not be obliged to submit the specification with the description of their invention. We saw this with the patent granted to Nehemiah Grew (see § 2.21). In 1711, Timothy Byfield, a well-reputed physician, author of several medical treatises, was bestowed with the same favor in connection with his patent for another salt. The English patent system, actually, had to wait until 1778, when, in Liardet v. Johnson, *Chief Justice Lord Mansfield imposed enabling disclosure as a condition of patentability.*

Like Nehemiah Grew, Byfield also had problems with counterfeiters. And like Grew, he also revealed the manner of making and the composition of his salts. In the leaflet where he did so, he justified the disclosure with his wish to make the product cheaper to the poor families. Moreover, it seems that the patent he received from the Queen brought him a great reputation—which, in itself, gave him a greater competitive advantage than a much-infringed patent. In the digital Wellcome Library, where I have obtained it, the leaflet is accompanied with a note: "Apparently published soon after Byfield was granted a patent, 22 Oct. 1711."

This patent was the second to be granted in respect of a medicinal invention. It had taken 74 years (i.e., from 1624 to 1798) for the first patent to be granted under the Statute. It took only thirteen years for the second title to be issued. This time sequence reflects the beginning of a pattern, with the slow and gradual but firm increase in the granting of pharmaceutical patents in the UK. And yet, secrecy in medicines continued to be an available mechanism for inventors, until the twentieth century, when their advertisement and trade were definitively banned.

§ 2.23.1. Byfield's Patent – 1711, No. 388 (excerpts)

Anne, by the grace of God, &c., to all to whom these presents shall come, greeting.

Whereas our trusty and welbeloved Timothy Byfield, Doctor in Physick, has, by his petition, humbly represented unto us that he has, by his long study and great expence, found out and brought to perfection "A New and Most Useful Chemical Preparation and Medicine Publicly Known by the Name of Sal Oleosum Volatile, which by Abundant Experience Has Been Found very Helpful and Beneficial, as Well in Uses Medicinal as Others, and Will Very Much Tend to the Public Use and Benefit of All our Subjects," and having therefore humbly prayed us to grant him our Royal Letters Patents for the sole use and benefit of his said Invention, for the term of fourteen years:

Know Yee, that we, being willing to give encouragement to all arts and inventions which may be of public use and benefit, of our especial grace, certain knowledge, . . .

And lastly we do by these presents, for us, our heirs and successors, grant unto the said Timothy Byfield, his executors, administrators, and assignes, that these our Letters Patents, or the enrollment thereof, shall be in and by all things good, firm, valid, sufficient, and effectual in the law, according to the true intent and meaning thereof, and shall be taken, construed, and adjudged in the most favourable and beneficial sense for the best advantage of the said Timothy Byfield, his executors, administrators, and assignes, as well in all courts of record as elsewhere, and by all and singular the officers and ministers whatsoever of vs, our heirs and successors, within that part of our said kingdom of Great Britain called England, our dominion of Wales, and town of Berwick-upon-Tweed, and within our said kingdom of Ireland, and amongst all and every the subjects of vs, our heirs and successors whatsoever and wheresoever, notwithstanding the not full and certain describing the nature or quality of the said Invention, or of the materials thereto conducing and belonging.

In witnesse, &c., witnesse ourself at Westminster, the Twenty-second day of October.

By Writt of Privy Seale.

§ 2.23.2. Dr. Byfield's leaflet describing his invention—1712 (?)

Some Plain Directions for the Use of Our Sal Oleosum Volatile

Although great (and truly noble) Remedy has been public many years, with much Applause and good Success;

It is nevertheless Unknown to Multitudes, as to its Incomparable Nature, and Powerful Virtues,

The Knowledge, that belongs to it, is so very sublime, that it is next to impossible to convey it to common Understandings.

This has given Occasion to many to put off, under its Name, scurvy compounded Trash, only for filthy Lucres sake.

But the Method now taken will enlarge its Knowledge, in some degree, from mere Experience.

While it lay in a single hand, it was scarce and dear, by reason of the great Labour in Preparation, and many other Difficulties; so that it could be derived but to a Few.

But now in the Hands of expert and industrious Artists, it will be multiplied, and Universally obtained.

However, This Advantage it has gained by its slow Progress (which is observable) That it is now spread abroad with the bright *Authority of Her Most Gracious Majesty*'s Letters Patent, backed with the Knowledge and undoubted Experience of the Learned, Great and Rich, with whom it gained its first Reputation.

So that it descends (with much good Nature) to be Opened in a lower Price, and meanlier Represented too, on purpose to serve the Necessities of the less knowing, and lower Abilities. . . .

[A description of the composition and the manner of preparing it follows. Next, the leaflet contains a Postscript explaining how to distinguish the original salts from the counterfeit ones: "A Description of the True S. V. O. whereby it may be known from Counterfeits." The leaflet closes with the notice of the lowering of prices and the place where the salts could be acquired:]

Whereas this Medicine was formerly Sold only in Five Shilling Bottles, it is now sold in Half Crown, Crown, and Pint Bottles, at Sixteen Shillings the Pint for the Service of Families. They who buy the Pints will be Gainers.

To be had at Dr. Byfield's in Salisbury-Court near Fleetstreet.

§ 2.24. THE ROYAL ACADEMY OF SCIENCES OF FRANCE EXAMINES SEVERAL PATENT APPLICATIONS CONCERNING MEDICAL DEVICES—1741 AND 1754

In 1666, the French Royal Academy of Sciences (which until then was part of the Academy of Letters) became an independent entity and moved to a special room in the King's library, then sieged in a house owned by Jean-Baptiste Colbert, the Minister of Finance of Louis XIV. In 1699 Colbert moved the Academy to a gallery at the Louvre Palace, and on January 29 of that year, the king approved its by-laws, which included the task of examining patent applications as to novelty and utility. An excerpt from those by-laws can be found in FROM BABYLON TO THE SILICON VALLEY.[22]

The records of the examinations of inventions carried by the Academy do not show inventions concerning medicines, even if there was no law in place excluding them from patentability (until 1844, that is). The reason is that the submission of inventions to the Academy entailed their disclosure by the examiners, which inventors preferred to avoid. But several inventions concerning medical devices were submitted and examined by the Academy.

The following texts concern the first four of those examinations, one in 1741 (with a recommendation of approval), another in 1742 (with an undecided conclusion that might have led to the grant of the requested patent), another in 1748 (with a positive conclusion as to the invention's utility) and one in 1754 (with a negative report as to the novelty of the claimed inventions). The last two inventions are significantly pertinent to current times, under the COVID-19 pandemic, and the struggle of hospitals to acquire ventilators to treat those more severely affected by the virus.

§ 2.24.1. Bed for the Disabled, Invented by Mr. Hanot, Carpenter—1741

. . . [The Report includes a detailed description of the invention, including a number of drawings, whose details are indicated by numbers, the same way as in current patent specifications.]

Report of the Commissioners.

On Wednesday, August 9, 1741, Messrs. d'Ons-en-Bray, Petit, and Morand read the following report on a sickbed model, presented by Mr. Jean-Nicolas Hanot, Carpenter.

We have examined, by order of the Academy, a model of the bed presented by Mr. Hanot, in which we have found more conveniences for making beds for the disabled than any other we know of.

§ 2.24.2. Bandage for Hernias, Invented by Mr. Abeille, Engineer—1742

Report of the Commissioners.

On Wednesday September 5, 1742, Messrs. Bourdelin and Hunauld read the following report on the bandage of Mr. Abeille.

We have examined, by order of the Academy, the design of a new bandage for hernias, invented by Mr. Abeille, and the accompanying memorandum.

This bandage, generally considered, is made up of a spring-loaded instrument and a simple belt of leather. . . .

Mr. Abeille's new bandage seemed to us all the more happily imagined, as the efforts of the muscles of the lower abdomen which usually displace the other bandages, only making it firmer in its place, the Author knew to turn the accidents that are the

22. *See supra* note 2, at 29.

most frequent cause of the insufficiency of ordinary bandages to his advantage infinitely, and thus to the patients.

We therefore believe that this bandage can be usefully applied; but although the Author has already tried it, and, so to speak, put it to experience on himself last winter, for three months, that he was inconvenienced by a very violent cough, without, as he assures himself, his bandage showing any defects, we nevertheless leave it to time and use, to put the public in a position to appreciate the usefulness of this bandage, and to judge it definitively.

§ 2.24.3. Fan or Ventilator for renewing the air of the room of the sick, established by experiment at the Hotel Royal des Invalides—1748

The report of the Commissioners responsible for examining this machine explains the properties of the parts that form the ventilator: it also gives an account of the experiments they have made with it in the Room du Bon-Pasteur at Les Invalides, where it has been assembled for the trial. I will therefore limit myself to reporting fully, by letters of reference, how those same parties interconnected.

The Journal of Trévoux for the month of April 1771, page 806, mentions a Memoir on the corruption of the air in Vessels, by Mr. Bigot de Morogne, Captain of Vessels and Correspondent of the Academy. This Officer says in his treatise that he made use of Mr. Halés' ventilator on the vessel le Sorbay. This machine was only four feet long, twenty inches wide, twelve deep. With the work of two men, it shed more than twenty-five thousand cubic feet of air per hour, but this quantity was sufficient to renew, more than fifteen times during that time, the air of the provisions hold, in a vessel such as le Sorbay.

. . . [A description of the various components of the invention follows, with references, in the form of letters, to the drawings].

Report of the Commissioners.

On Wednesday March 27, 1748, Messrs. Ferrein, Morand, Duhamel du Monceau, and Camus read the following report.

We have examined, by order of the Academy, a fan or ventilator, which has been assembled at the Hotel des Invalides, to be tested, with the intention of subsequently using it to renew the air in the rooms of the sick persons.

As this fan is different, in a few respects, from those that Mr. Halés described in his Book, we will begin by giving the description of that of the Invalides: we will then talk about its assembling in the Room, the air of which we wanted to pump, and finally we will report the experiments we made to ascertain the effect of this machine.

Description of the Ventilator of les Invalides. . . .

Assembling the Ventilator. . . .

Details of the experiments. . . .

Conclusion.

We believe that if the ventilator had been assembled immediately at the ceiling level, the smoke would have been dissipated earlier; but the arrangement of the ventilator appeared to us to be very good, and preferable, on the present occasion, to the ventilator that Mr. Halés has described: we think therefore that the air renewal can only be advantageous to the sick and to those who attend them, especially in the event of contagious diseases, when the Rooms are very low, and small, etc.

[In 1752, a certain Pommier, engineer of the king for bridges and roadways, submitted an improved design of this ventilator to the Academy, and likewise received a favorable report.]

§ 2.24.4. Devices used to vaporize the chest, invented by Mr. Guignon, Surgeon—1754

Diseases, of whatever kind, have their particular remedy; but it is not always easy to apply them; the place where these diseases occur makes the difference: those that affect the nasal cavities, the lungs, i.e., all the parts exposed to the current of the air, usually have disastrous consequences, because of the difficulty of immediately applying medicines to them.

The property of either of the devices that Mr. Guignon proposes is to distribute in the chest, by means of inspiration, the vapors of the remedies suitable for calming the cough, for dissolving and destroying the ulcers of the bronchi, and finally for operating their effect without weakening the stomach, which is often only too weak by the great use of ointments, syrups, oily products in general, which decrease appetite, make digestion difficult, chylification of poor quality, which only increases the generation of complaints and aids the worsening of the disease, and even generates many other evils. . . .

Report on two Devices used to vaporize the chest.

The Academy has instructed us to examine a Memoir presented by Mr. Guignon, Surgeon, on two devices used to introduce vapors into the chest.

There are cases in which it is very useful to pass into the lungs, by means of inspiration, the air charged with certain vapors: one can thus distribute in the interior of this affected organ several remedies considered useful, and which operate as topicals: this practice, known to the ancients, cited in the Writings of Hippocrates, was especially recommended by Christophe Benoît, English doctor, in his excellent Ouvrage on the Phthysis (*Theatrum Rabidorum*).

He supports this with several interesting observations. Boerhaave [a famous Dutch physician, botanist and chemist—1668-1738] and other modern writers also praise it. Christophe Benoît's device is only a hollow cone, which serves to collect and direct the vapors that the patient inhales, by smothering the open top of the cone. Mr. Guignon shows some drawbacks of these instruments in several cases, where the patients could not place themselves in a suitable position, to inhale the vapors by this kind of funnel: he proposes two other devices; . . . There are several instruments already known and very similar to those of M. Guignon.

In Paris, August 7, 1754. Signed, Morand, Lasone.

Figure 20 Drawings that accompanied the patent application for the devices for vaporizing the chest, of Dr. Guignon, in 1754. Extracted from M. Gallon, MACHINES ET INVENTIONS APPROUVÉES PAR L'ACADÉMIE ROYALE DES SCIENCES DEPUIS SON ETABLISSEMENT, AVEC LEUR DESCRIPTION, [vol. 7], at 473 (Antoine Boudet, 1778).

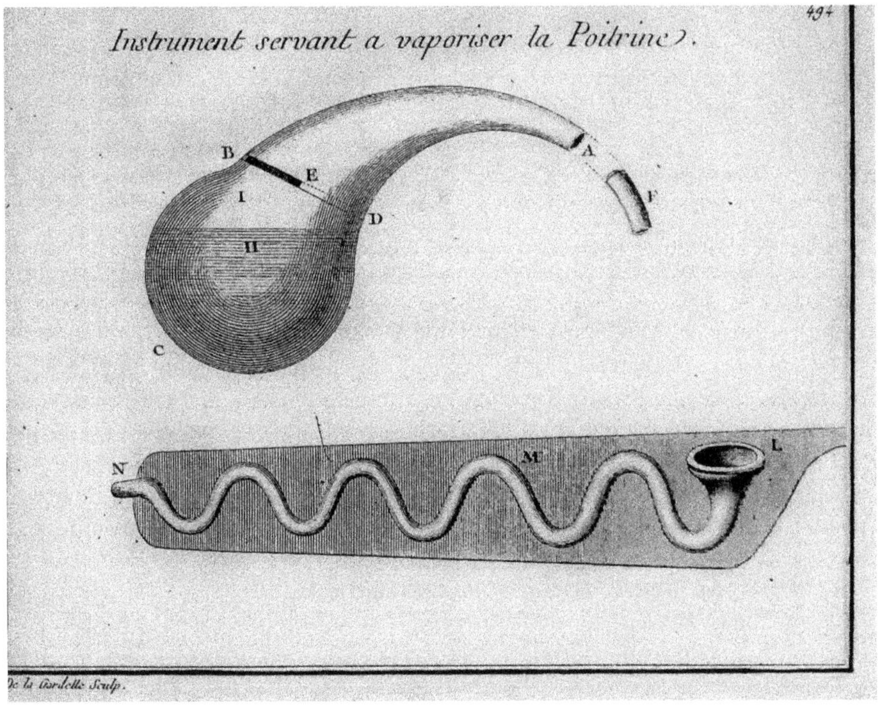

§ 2.25. THE DROPS OF GENERAL DE LA MOTTE: A SECRET MEDICINE PROTECTED BY SEVERAL PRIVILEGES; ADVERTISEMENT AND ENFORCEMENT—TYPICAL INTELLECTUAL PROPERTY OF MEDICINES IN THE EIGHTEENTH CENTURY

In 1730, King Louis XV acquired from General de la Motte the secret composition of a drug known as "gouttes du général de la Motte" ("General de la Motte's drops"), also known as "teinture de Bestucheff." The General was not the drug's inventor, but only the proprietor of its formula. He had acquired it from a Russian diplomat and inventor, earl Alexis Bestucheff-Rumin. The drops, or water, or elixir, of de la Motte were sold under two formulations: one was called "golden or yellow drops," because originally it contained some gold dust, and the other, white drops.

De la Motte received from the king a pension of 4,000 pounds and the exclusive privilege of making and selling the drug. Twelve years later, the privilege was renewed, after his death, to the benefit of his widow. This second privilege, with the duration of fifteen years, had several interesting points from a legal standpoint: (i) it renewed the exclusivity in the industrial and commercial exploitation of the secret composition; (ii) it prohibited others not only from making, using, and selling the secret medicine, but also from "s'immiscer," i.e., from interfering in any manner whatsoever with the exploitation of the secret—this eventually meaning that other druggists and pharmacists should even refrain themselves from trying to reverse engineer the drops' composition; (iii) the exclusion did not encompass the making and the distribution of the drug by the Maison Royale de St. Cyr (a boarding school for girls established by Louis XIV in 1684), limitation which was already set in the first privilege; (iv) it maintained another limitation that benefitted the military hospitals—these could prepare and administer the drug to internalized soldiers; and (v) the renewed privilege kept the same prices determined for the drug in 1730.

According to the recommendations on its use contained in a booklet prepared under the instructions of de la Motte's widow, the elixir could be taken at any time in the day, and even frequently, with an increase in dosage if need be. Both the gold and white elixirs had therapeutic effects against fevers, smallpox, stomach pains and cramps, attacks of apoplexy (in which cases their ingestion should be accompanied with the bleeding of several parts of the body), dysentery, the retention of urine, vapors of all kinds, etc. Moreover, the white elixir was especially recommended for melting any sorts of tumors, for curing inveterate obstructions, and in particular for treating venereal diseases.

Louis XV himself would become one of the main promoters of the curative properties of the drops because, in 1744, he was treated with them. According to the "Exact Journal of the Serious or Acute Disease by which was attacked, in the City of Metz, our very August King Louis XV, while he was heading towards the Rhine," the French sovereign, after spending three months conquering three very powerful fortresses in Flanders, had exhausted himself by painful labor of body and mind and had been subjected, when approaching Metz, to the influence of the rays of a scorching sun. [La France Médicale, *1913, at 82-84. Source:* <gallica.Bnf.fr>.].

Mrs. de la Motte's booklet also contains numerous depositions by physicians, apothecaries, civil servants, and patients, who claimed having been cured of an enormous quantity of medical conditions by using the drops of General de la Motte.

§ 2.25.1. Privilege granted to the widow de la Motte, confirming the one granted twelve years before to his late husband, on the occasion of the acquisition by the king of the secret composition of his Drops of de la Motte

May 3, 1742

Exclusive Privilege of the King.

Louis, by the grace of God, King of France and Navarre: to all who see these present Letters, Greeting. Our beloved Lady Widow of General de la Motte, had represented to us that by a Patent of January 1, 1730, we allowed her husband to continue composing his Water or Elixir, known under the name of *Drops of General de la Motte*, with the privilege and right of selling and distributing it alone, to the exclusion of all persons, for his lifetime, and under the terms and conditions set forth by said Patent: that her husband by his death left her no other resource to subsist, than the secret of its composition; but in addition to the fact that she cannot use them without our express permission, she is saddened to see that her Drops are counterfeited by different people, so that there is every reason to fear that the Public will suffer a considerable prejudice; that is why she begged us to kindly grant her the exclusive privilege of composing, selling and distributing them, with prohibitions for all people from interfering in their composition, under such penalties that we will wish to establish, providing nevertheless that such exclusivity shall comprise the composition and the distribution of the Drops that are made in the Royal House of St. Cyr.

For these reasons, and wishing to give the widow de La Motte new marks of satisfaction that we felt towards her husband's zeal in our service and public good; we have allowed her, and by these Presents, signed by our hand, we allow her to compose, sell and distribute the Water or Elixir, concurrently with our house of St. Cyr, and to the exclusion of all other persons, during the time of 15 consecutive years, counting from the day and date of these present, for the price and sum provided by our Patent of January 1, 1730: namely, Water or yellow Elixir, 25 pounds per flask, containing at least two and a half of weight of liquor; and Water or white Elixir, twenty pounds a vial, with the same quantity of liquor.

We prohibit all persons, of whatever quality and condition, from interfering in the composition, sale and distribution of the Water or Elixir, in whatever way and manner, under the penalty of a fine of 1,500 pounds against each of the offenders, of which one third shall be paid to us, a third to our House of St. Cyr, and the other third to the widow de La Motte, without prejudice to the reservation made by us by our Patent of January 1, 1730, which we do not intend to modify by these Presents, of having the Water or Elixir composed in our Hotel des Invalides, both for the use of that Hotel, and of the sick Officers and Soldiers therein, and for the use of our Military Hospitals.

Thus we order our Beloved and Loyal Counselors, the People belonging to our Court of Parliament in Paris, and other Officers to whom it will concern, that they register these Presents, and ensure that of their contents the widow de La Motte, her heirs, successors, or assigns, enjoy and use fully and peacefully, during the time that is established therein, without suffering any disturbance or hindrance to them. For such is our pleasure. Given at Fontainebleau, the 3rd day of May, the year of Grace 1742, and of our Reign the 27th. Signed, Louis, and below, Phelipeaux.

§ 2.25.2. Judgment confirming the conviction of an apothecary of Paris who counterfeited the drops of General de la Motte

April 22, 1751

Louis by the grace of God, King of France and Navarre, to the Premier of the Bailiffs, of our Court of Parliament, or any other of our Bailiffs or Sargeants, as required; We make known that, between Bertrand Couzier, Merchant Apothecary in Paris, Appellant of a Sentence of the Lieutenant General of Police of the Châtelet of Paris, of January 29, 1751, and Defendant on the one hand; and Mr. Antoine Calsabigi, Knight, in charge of the affairs of the King of the Two Sicilies, and Dame Simonne Dorcet, his Wife, previously widow of Mr. Antoine Dunut de la Motte, General-Major of Artillery, Respondent and Plaintiff in Request of March 8 also last, asking to receive written confirmation of the confessions and declarations made by Couzier, that he was selling the Water or Elixir in question; that he always has a small amount at home for his patients; consequently, to declare that the said Couzier, purely and simply, is dismissed from his appeal, to condemn him to a fine of 75 pounds, and to the expense of the Causes of appeal, pleas, costs and execution, and other conclusions, on the one hand; and again between the same Bertrand Couzier, Plaintiff in Request of April 6 this month, to be given written confirmation that he withdraws from the Appeal by him lodged from the Sentence of the Châtelet of Paris above-dated: and Antoine Calsabigi and his wife, Defendants on the other hand; and again between Calsabigi and his wife, Plaintiffs in Request of the 19th of the present month of April, to that they be provided with the record of such withdrawal by Couzier, by Request of the 6th of the month of April, of the Appeal of the Sentence of the Lieutenant of the Police of the Châtelet de Paris, above dated, made on April 29, 1751, as a result of the dismissal of the Appeal; that it has been ordered that the matter under Appeal would be accorded its full and entire effect, and that Couzier be condemned to a fine of 12 pounds, and to the expense of the Causes of Appeal, and pleas, costs and execution, and other conclusions on the one hand; and Bertrand Couzier, Defendant on the other hand, after hearing Babille, Lawyer of Antoine Calsabigi and his wife, and Virion, Lawyer of Armand Couzier: our Court confirms to the Parties of Babille the withdrawal made by the Part of Virion, of his appeal of the Sentence of the Châtelet of January 29, 1751.

As a result, [the Court] has dismissed and dismisses the Appeal; orders that the Judgment under Appeal shall come into full effect; condemns the said Party of Virion to pay a fine of 12 pounds, and all the expenses of the Causes of Appeal and pleas, costs and enforcement. Hereby We instruct the First Bailiff, or Sargent as required, to put this Judgment into execution, according to its form and content; to do so We give power. Done in Parliament on April 22, the year of Grace 1751, and our Reign the thirty-sixth.

§ 2.25.3. Advertisement of the Drops of General de la Motte

ANNONCES, AFFICHES, ET AVIS DIVERS, NEUVIÈME FEUILLE HEBDOMADAIRE, Wednesday, February 27, March 7, 1754 (the following ad appears on pages 35-36 of the publication—a weekly printed paper with small news and advertisements; the ad would be repeated in subsequent papers)

Miscellaneous Advertisements and Notices

The reputation of the *Drops of General de la Motte* has been established for a long time; but recent cures, attested by skilled Practitioners, have urged us to record, at least in our Columns, this Remedy, the excellence of which is already well known, and which advertises itself for its good effects. The King, by buying in 1730 the secret of the Drops, of the late General de la Motte, for a pension of 4,000 pounds, had granted him an exclusive Privilege. His Majesty, by Letters Patent of May 3, 1742, confirms the Privilege to his widow, who continues to compose the same Remedy. So we are now distributing it at Mrs. Générale de la Motte, at rue de Richelieu, opposite the Stables of the late H.R.H. It is known that these Drops consist of two Elixirs called the Golden Elixir and the White Elixir. [A long list of the therapeutic effects of the drugs follows].

§ 2.26. JUDGMENT BY THE STATE COUNCIL OF LOUIS XV, OF FRANCE, ACCORDING EXCLUSIVITY TO GUILLAUME ARNOULT, CONCERNING A SECRET RECIPE OF A MEDICINE AGAINST APOPLEXY

August 2, 1748

In the eighteenth century, in France, exclusivity in trade secrets was a settled matter, as this judgment shows. No special arguments or justifications were necessary for the State Council to acknowledge exclusivity in the secret formula of a medicine, not even the allegation that the owner of the secret was his inventor, and thus the acknowledgment of his rights would represent a sort of an incentive for the efforts and expenses in inventing—the verification of precedence was enough to persuade the Council to exclude the later comer from making and selling the medicine.

Indeed, as least as far as pharmaceutical inventions are concerned, the notion that the appropriation of knowledge should operate as an incentive to inventive activity is recent. Until the end of the eighteenth century, when that rationale was introduced by the patent statutes of the United States of 1790, and of France, of 1791, the main goal was to bring new medicines to the market, regardless of who their possessors were.

The exclusivity in the making and selling of this secret medicine—some mixture of herbs wrapped in a small bag that was to be worn pending from the neck, at the height of the stomach, which the Arnouf family claimed to have prodigious powers in preventing and curing apoplectic attacks—was the subject of bitter disputes within the Arnoult family for no less than three generations.

In spite of the harsh criticisms the composition and his owner received, including a very critical article in the famous and well-respected Encyclopedia (a major expression of the Enlightenment), edited by Denis Diderot (and published between 1751 and 1772), the medicine enjoyed large reputation and was praised by distinguished personalities.

The first Arnoult, who claimed to have received the formula from a non-identified Italian friend, and his successors were very protective of the secret. Not only they have not disclosed it outside the narrow family circle, but also they refused to put it in the normal distribution channels: they remained as the sole sellers of the sachet d'Arnoult, *the brand that designated the famous remedy, until the buyers disappeared, well beyond the beginning of the nineteenth century. In this manner, they were able to keep the secret as a commercial venture for more than one century.*

This had, of course, a price: the family had to spend time and many resources in keeping counterfeiters away—a struggle that they carried over for three generations.

The first four texts are excerpts extracted from DISSERTATION EN FORME DE LETTRE, SUR L'EFFET DES TOPIQUES DANS LES MALADIES INTERNES, EN PARTICULIER SUR CELUI DE M. ARNOULT CONTRE L'APOPLEXIE—ÉCRITE PAR UN MÉDECIN DE PARIS À UN MÉDECIN DE PROVINCE—1759 (Dissertation in the form of a Letter, on the effect of topicals in internal diseases, in particular on that of Mr. Arnoult, against apoplexy, written by a Doctor of Paris to a Doctor of the Interior) [Source: < gallica.BnF.fr >].

§ 2.26.1. Guillaume Arnoult explains how he has learned the secret composition of the medicine and assigns it to his son

In this manner Guillaume Arnoult expresses himself, in "a certificate written on a sheet of paper about an anti-apoplexy sachet [...] given to and filed with Michelin, one of the undersigned notaries . . . ." December 30, 1734

I, the undersigned, Guillaume Arnoult, merchant brewer in Paris, certify to all concerned that in 1701 I rendered a considerable service to an Italian citizen. The same year, I had the misfortune of falling twice in apoplexy; this same Italian, full of gratitude, came to see me and brought me a small sachet of powder which he then told me it would protect me from apoplexy, which remedy had to be hung on the neck and on the pit of the stomach. (And) then having no confidence in said remedy, I put the package in my pocket without giving any thought to it; eight days later, I had three more attacks of apoplexy at different, short intervals; the second attack was followed by paralysis of the mouth without however much pain; it made me turn my mouth to the left side.

(And) the Italian, having learned of my indisposition and always remembering the service I had rendered him, came to see me again and, finding me in such a sad state, asked me what I had done with the little bag he had given me. I showed it to him and told him that I had not had much confidence in it up to now; he replied that I would risk nothing, [the substance] not entering the body and only needing to carry it on the pit of the stomach; for this reason I surrendered and [since then] I have always worn it on my collar hanging on my chest. (And) I owe to the truth that within eight days, without resorting to any other remedy, my paralysis was dissipated and healed radically, and thus since then I have never found myself without having this remedy on my stomach [...] nor have I had any [new] stroke of apoplexy or paralysis.

This Italian, obliged to return to his country and always taking a particular interest in my health for the fear that I might be left without his remedy, regarded it as infallible by the quantity of experiments he had made both in Italy and in several other countries. He could not show me his gratitude better than by entrusting me with the recipe for his remedy, on the condition, however, that, under the seal of confession, I promised him never to make the remedy public because it was for him of great consideration, having always sold this remedy for 24 pounds—which I promised him.

But fearing death and knowing the virtue of this remedy without any doubt and desiring nothing but the public interest, I thought it was my duty, for the good of the state, to entrust it to Louis Arnoult, druggist, my son, who like me has been warned of the good effects that this remedy has produced to relieve the public in these needs, which I certify and affirm true for serving and supporting what is right.

§ 2.26.2. Judgment of the King's State Council of August 2, 1748

Which keeps Mr. Arnoult Merchant Pharmacist, on Cinq-Diamants Street, in Paris, with the right to compose, sell and distribute alone the Anti-Apoplectic Medicine and Specific against Apoplexy, of which he and his late father have been in possession since almost 50 years. Prohibits Ms. Rhodès, widow Arnoult, and all others to compose, sell and distribute the same Medicine, under the pretext that they would have Mr. Arnoult's Secret, under the penalty of a fine of 1000 pounds, and abolishes Ms. Rhodès, widow Arnoult's brochure, in the form of Advice.

Extract from the Records of the Council of State.

On the Motion presented to the King, present in his Council, by Louis Arnoult, Merchant Grocer-Wholesaler-Pharmacist, stating that since the year 1701, he is by him and by Guillaume Arnoult, his father, in the right and possession of composing and selling alone the true Specific against Apoplexy. Guillaume Arnoult himself has received the Recipe from an Italian who had brought it to France, and who presented it to him as a token of gratitude, but under the seal of secrecy, Mr. Arnoult having promised never to make the preparation of this medicine public. Faithful to this commitment, Guillaume Arnoult alone has composed and distributed the Specific in question, until, fearing death, and that the public was deprived of the great and inestimable advantages it derived from it, he confided it to the Plaintiff alone, who is the only person in France, and perhaps in Europe, who has the true secret of this Specific. The good effects it has produced in the Court and the City, in the Provinces of the Kingdom and among foreigners, are well-known and such that there is not one person who has used it that has not been cured of Apoplexy or preserved from its relapse. The late Cardinal de Polignac has dedicated it the greatest of appraisals at the Academy, even citing a dozen Lords, his relatives and friends, who were healed by the use of the said Medicine; the late Dame Princess of Guise spoke of it with the same advantages; the late Cardinal of Fleury and the late Hérault know and protect it; Messrs. Dukes of the Force . . . and others are in a position to certify the same to His

Majesty. The fact has been attested by non-suspicious testimonies of persons of every state and every country; in particular famous doctors both of His Majesty and of various Medical Schools, as well as skillful Surgeons who have seen the wonderful effects of the said Specific. The Gazettes and Newspapers have even mentioned it for several years; many people were very jealous of the progress of this Medicine, and spared nothing to take it from Mr. Arnoult, or to make him lose the high reputation he has acquired. The attacks he has suffered only served to strengthen this reputation. Among the false Imitators of this Specific, there is only one alleged widow of Mr. Arnoult who had the audacity to announce herself to the Public through brochures as having the real secret, having received it from her Ancestors, and always having distributed it successfully. Everything in this proposition is tainted with falsity. There is no widow Arnoult; the one who adorns herself with this quality is the wife of Mr. Rhodès. She has had actually for first husband a brother of the Plaintiff, but this brother has never had the secret of this anti-Apoplectic Specific: Mr. Arnoult father did not entrust it, as he declared on December 30, 1734, other than to the Plaintiff. Never his other son, let alone his widow, today Mr. Rhodès' wife, has had the said secret, hence she has not distributed it; it is therefore only for imposing herself on the Public and for confronting them that the wife of Mr. Rhodès announces herself as the widow of Mr. Arnoult, and attests to the Public that she has received from her Ancestors the anti-Apoplectic Medicine, and that she has always distributed it. . . . From such a bold action it follows not only that Ms. Rhodès does not possess the secret that she claims to have, but also that she makes a false Medicine capable of producing two dangerous effects: one of making the true secret, of which the Plaintiff is the only holder, to lose the Public reputation, which it has justly acquired; the other of causing much harm, either by not having the effect which is guaranteed on the part of the true Specific, or even by operating badly on those who would use it, who would never be compensated for the loss of their money, and moreover would run a clear risk of life. These misfortunes are more to be feared, that the Plaintiff, who has had one of her Sachets against Apoplexy collected in Ms. Rhodès' shop, dares to attest to His Majesty that at the only sight it is possible to judge the difference between this false Medicine and the true one. He speaks with all the more confidence, that in the end it is physically impossible for Ms. Rhodès to compose this Medicine in the same way as the Plaintiff, as well as the late Mr. Arnoult, his father. The public interest does not allow such an attempt to be tolerated. . . . If it were true that Ms. Rhodès had always and successfully composed and distributed her anti-Apoplectic Medicine, she would have proofs of it; she is challenged to produce only one.

Pleading on these grounds, the plaintiff [requests] that it please to His Majesty to maintain him in the right and possession, such as he and his late father have been since almost fifty years, of composing, selling and distributing alone the anti-Apoplectic Medicine and the Specific against Apoplexy, taking all the precautions he deems appropriate for its safety and that of the Public; To prohibit Ms. Arnoult, and all others of whatever quality, from composing, selling, or distributing any Medicine of the same quality and as if it came from Mr. Arnoult, for whatever cause and under any pretext whatsoever, under such penalty as His Majesty deems fit; To order that the Brochure by which the alleged widow of Mr. Arnoult has given notice that she has the secret of said Medicine, which she has received from her Ancestors, and which she has always distributed successfully, be and remain removed; To enjoin Ms. Rhodès, claiming to be widow Arnoult, to bring within twenty-four hours to the Police Court, at the Châtelet of Paris, all the copies she may have of the said Brochure, to be destroyed; to prohibit her and all others, from having others printed, and to all the Printers from printing them, also on such penalties as appropriate; Allow the supplicant to print, display, publish and distribute the Judgment that will be made on the Motion, together with such notice or instruction as he deems appropriate. [...]

Heard the Report, the King being in his Council, having regard to the Motion, has maintained and maintains the said Arnoult in the possession of the anti-Apoplectic medicine and Specific against Apoplexy, which he and his Father have been composing, selling and delivering alone for nearly fifty years; Prohibits Ms. Rhodès and all others, of whatever status and quality they are, from composing, selling and delivering the same Remedy on the pretext that they would have the secret of the said late Arnoult, under the penalty of a fine of one thousand pounds, half being due to the whistleblower, and the remaining to Arnoult, and all costs, damages and interests; Furthermore His Majesty orders that the Brochure by which the said widow Arnoult has given notice that she has the secret of the medicine and that she has received it from her Ancestors will be and will remain abolished; Enjoins the said Rhodès, widow Arnoult, to bring within twenty-four hours, from the date of the service of the present Judgment to the Police Court, at the Châtelet of Paris, all the copies she may have of said Brochure to be destroyed; Prohibits her, and all others, from having it printed, sold, and distributed; His Majesty permits the said Arnoult to print, publish and display the present judgment wherever necessary, together with such advice and instruction that he will consider appropriate for the use of the said Anti-Apoplectic medicine. Done at the Council of State of the King, His Majesty being present, held at Compiegne on the 2nd of August, one thousand seven hundred and forty-eight. Signed . . .

§ 2.26.3. Arnoult advertises the authenticity and the virtues of his secret medicine

The object of this Brochure is to prove the effect of topicals in internal diseases, to destroy the few accusations that have been made against Mr. Arnoult's sachet, and to increase the public's confidence in this famous remedy. It seems to us that the Author did well in all three points. He has especially insisted on the virtue of the sachet, and had produced in his favor the Certificates of the late Cardinal de Polignac, of Mr. the Duc of Gêvres, Governor of Paris, of Mr. Merault, Councilor of State, formerly Prosecutor General of the Great Council, of the Abbot Franquiny, formerly Envoy of Florence, etc. Whatever confidence these certificates deserve, those from the people in the trade are even more important: innumerable of those are found in the Brochure that we announce, among others those of Mr. Garnier, Doctor of the Faculty of Paris, today Doctor of Martinique; Mauran, Doctor in Bergerac; Mercier, also Doctor, and today the King's Doctor at the Calais Hospital; Woiler, Chief Physician of Emperor Charles VI; Gaulard, Ordinary Doctor of the King; Silva, Consultant physician to the King; Santeuil,

Doctor-Regent of the Faculty of Paris; the Archbishop, Doctor of Rouen; Desjours, Fevrier, Dubertrand, Sworn Surgeons in Paris; Desport, Queen's Ordinary Surgeon; Desormeaux, Surgeon of Paris, etc. The letters from Mr. Lecomte, Doctor at Rhetel Mazarin, from Mr. Delacroix, Doctor in Bailleul, in Flanders; and especially from Mr. Pels, Doctor and Mayor of the City of Schelestat, deserve special attention because of the wonders they tell of the sachet. However the most important part of the Brochure is a Certificate issued to Mr. Arnoult by the first Physician to the King; let us see what has happened: We use the words of the Dissertation itself.

Miss Rodesse [Rhodès] seeks to accredit, by the name of widow Mr. Arnoult, an anti-apoplectic sachet, which she claims to be the same as the one that Mr. Arnoult has been distributing for fifty-one years, both by his father and by himself, with successes that have never been denied since it has never been possible to prove that any apoplectic has had a relapse while wearing it, while we have examples known to the whole Court as that of Miss Rodesse does not prevent the relapses of this disease.

We will also see from the attached Certificate, that that of Miss Rodesse does not have the same composition as Mr. Arnoult's. It is therefore obvious that we should not expect that it has the same effects. It is now seventeen years since Mr. Louis Arnoult, by order of Cardinal de Fleury, has deposited a preparation of this remedy in the hands of M. Chicoyneau, First Physician to the King. He certainly did not foresee at that time that one should disturb the peaceful possession in which he must sell *alone* this medicine, of which he *alone* has the true preparation. If the deposit that Mr. Arnoult has made of his composition were subsequent to the lawsuit he has against Miss Rodesse, one might suspect the fidelity of the preparation he deposited; but could he guess seventeen years ago that he would draw from this deposit a victorious argument to prove that he is the unique, the *only* possessor of the remedy which he derives from his father's recognition?

Here is the copy of the Certificate of Mr. Chicoyneau, First Physician to the King:

> On the representation to us by Mr. Arnoult, Merchant Druggist, that the controversy between him and Miss Rodesse has been referred by the Council to the Judges to whom it belongs to decide, and that he would need the decision that we have already transmitted to the King's Council, concerning the quality and difference of the two Remedies or Sachets, for preventing or curing apoplexy, of which they claim to be in possession; We, the undersigned, Councilor of State, and First Physician to the King, certify that the composition of the anti-apoplectic sachet of the Mr. Rodesse's wife has been submitted to us, to compare it with that which had been submitted to us by Mr. Arnoult, Merchant Druggist in Paris, about sixteen years ago; this representation, having been ordered consequently by the Gentlemen of the Council, so as to have our opinion on the parity or disparity of the two Sachets, we have seen that that of Miss Rodesse contained only three of the drugs that go into the preparation of Mr. Arnoult, and that the five additional drugs that are found in the latter's composition can only significantly increase its effectiveness, which is moreover established by the submission of the originals of the Certificates of the Most Eminent Persons in Dignity, and especially by the attestations of the Masters of the Profession, very enlightened and of a well-established reputation, while none has been shown to us on the part of the Dame Rodesse, who has only been distributing her Sachet for a very short time, and that it is to our knowledge that Mr. Arnoult has been selling his own for about twenty

years, without his reputation or distribution having suffered the slightest reduction: in faith of which we have delivered this Certificate. At Versailles, April 26, 1750. Signed, Chicoyneau.

§ 2.26.4. Louis Arnoult advertises a Patent Letter he obtained from the King and announces his trademark as the only evidence of his Sachet's authenticity

Letters Patent of the King, ratifying and confirming the Order of the King's Council of State, of August 2, 1748, that maintains Mr. Louis Arnault, Merchant Druggist, rue Quincampoix in Paris, in the right to compose, sell and distribute alone the Anti-Apoplectic and specific remedy against Apoplexy.

On the first of March, one thousand seven hundred and seventy-two.

Registered in Parliament on the twenty-eighth of August, one thousand seven hundred and seventy-two.

Louis, by the grace of God, King of France and Navarre: To our beloved and loyal Councils and the People holding our Court of Parliament in Paris, and to all others our Officers and Justice to whom it will concern: Greeting. By Judgment of our State Council of the second of August, one thousand seven hundred and forty-eight, We have, for the causes contained therein, kept and maintained our beloved Louis Arnoult, grocer and druggist in Paris, in the possession (which he has been since nearly fifty years), [of the right], by him and by the late Mr. Arnoult his father, of composing, selling and distributing alone the anti-apoplectic and specific remedy against apoplexy, known under the name of *Sachet d'Arnoult*; and well informed of the virtue of this Specific, and wishing to increasingly promote its distribution for the benefit and conservation of our Subjects, We have deemed it appropriate to confirm again Louis Arnault in the exercise of this Privilege. For these reasons, and others that convince us, as well as upon the opinion of our Council, We have ratified and confirmed, and by these Presents signed by our hand, ratify and confirm the Judgment of August 2, 1748, which will be executed according to its form and content; we keep and maintain the said Louis Arnoult in the free possession of composing, selling and distributing alone the anti-apoplectic and specific remedy against apoplexy, and authorize him to print, publish and display wherever it sees fit, the necessary instructions for the use of this Remedy, and this notwithstanding any Edicts, Declarations, Decrees and Regulations to this contrary, which We have abrogated and abrogate by these Presents.

Therefore, we order you that these Letter you have registered and ensure that their content be enjoyed and used by Louis Arnoult fully and peacefully, ceasing and making cease all troubles and impediments, and notwithstanding all things contrary to this: For such is our pleasure; in witness of which We have caused our seal to be placed on these Letters. Given at Versailles on the first day of May, the year of grace one thousand seven hundred and seventy-two, and of our reign the fifty-seventh. Signed: Louis. . . .

Registered, with the consent of the King's Attorney General, to be executed in their form and content, and for the Applicant to enjoy the effect and content thereof, in accordance with today's Judgment. In Paris, in Parliament, on August twenty-eighth, one thousand seven hundred and seventy-two.

Notice

Mr. Arnoult, sole owner of the Sachet preservative against any kind of apoplexy, whose virtue is confirmed every day by new successes, certified by the greatest Doctors of Europe, warns the public that researches have been made in vain to find the occurrence of a single stroke of apoplexy, in the period of more than seventy-two years, to a single person provided with this preservative (truth of which the silence of its opponents is the best proof). At the same time he warns that such constant success has engaged many people, both in Paris and in the provinces, to counterfeit it; that the greed for gain makes them give these false Sachets, copied in their exterior, at low prices, without worrying about the lives of the Citizens they sacrifice to a sordid motivation; that the people of the Interior who order the purchase, for their own use, of Mr. Arnoult's true Remedy, are consequently often deceived, because their agents prefer the cheap one; that because of this abuse several accidents of apoplexy have happened to those who carried these pretended Sachets, and sold, although counterfeited, as having left the house of Mr. Arnoult; that to obviate such a prejudicial abuse, the King, on the report of Mr. Chicoyneau, his first Physician, has, by an Order of his State Council, forbidden all persons, of whatever condition and quality they may be, from counterfeiting, selling or distributing the said Remedy, on the penalty of a fine of 1,000 pounds, and kept Mr. Arnoult in the right to sell and distribute it alone; that by a second Judgment of the Council, rendered on the report of Mr. de Senac, State Councilor, and first Physician to the King, His Majesty has, subsequently, confirmed the previous one; and that lastly the King has stamped the Seal on both [judgments] by Letters Patent, the reason for which is that, well informed of the virtue of this Specific, he wishes to promote its distribution for the benefit and preservation of his Subjects. For greater security still, and to better fulfill the intentions of His Majesty, Mr. Arnoult declares that he does not appoint anyone, neither in Paris nor in the interior, for the distribution of his Remedy; that each of his anti-apoplectic sachets will be provided with a printed document signed and initialed by his hand, with the date on which it will have been delivered to him; and that without this handwritten signature, one should not have any faith in the Sachets that would be presented as being those of Mr. Arnoult, rue de Quincampoix, in Paris.

§ 2.26.5. The widow of Louis Lanfranc Arnoult, son and heir of Guillaume Arnoult, advertises her genuine secret sachet against a counterfeiter—November 24, 1800

JOURNAL DE PARIS, 3 Frimaire, IXme Année de la République [November 24, 1802]

Mrs. Widow Arnoult warns the public that a Dame Arnoult, living at the corner of Boucher street and Etienne street, falsely announces herself as the owner for more than a century of Arnoult's anti-apoplectic sachet. She never had the secret of this remedy, which has always belonged by direct succession to Cdr. Arnoult, former notary in Paris, living on Grenelle-S.-Honoré Street, no. 33, deceased three months ago. Dame Fournier therefore deceives the public by her announcements and posters, and consequently the family of the late Cdr. Arnoult is forced to have her sued for counterfeiting before the court of police. — The distribution of this precious Medicine is only made in the house of Cdr. Arnoult, located on Grenelle-S.-Honoré Street, no. 33, only store where it can be found.

§ 2.26.6. Leaflet explaining how to use the Sachet and warning against counterfeits

Mercure de France Dédié au Roi, July 1751.

The Specific Remedy against Apoplexy, which Mr. Arnoult, Merchant Druggist in Paris, Cinq Diamants Street, distributes, and of which he alone has the Secret, must be tied to the neck with a ribbon, so that the sachet goes down to the pit of the stomach: It is essential not to remain without this Preservative, and to place another Sachet as soon as it appears empty.

The virtue of this Specific is confirmed every day by new successes. For more than 37 years the public has been using it, no one has yet been seen of those who wear it, either as a preservative, or as a remedy, to whom the slightest accident of Apoplexy has happened; and the silence of the Opponents in this regard is the best proof that we can give.

As several people, both in Paris and in the Interior, have announced the same Secret, without any other proof than their only testimony, and without any other desire than to discredit Mr. Arnoult's Medicine, by deceiving the Public by a false imitation, and that it shall result in considerable inconvenience for those who would be abused, Mr. Arnoult believes himself obliged to inform the Public that his Remedy is only distributed at his house, and that he does not appoint or will appoint anyone to sell it elsewhere.

§ 2.27. JACOB DE CASTRO SARMENTO, A PORTUGUESE PHYSICIAN, ESTABLISHED IN LONDON, DEFENDS THE MERITS OF HIS SECRET IN THE METHOD OF PREPARATION OF A MEDICINE, AS OPPOSED TO THE SECRET IN THE NATURE OF THE INGREDIENTS—1758

Jacob de Castro Sarmento, as seen above (see § 1.19.), was the improver of an antipyretic medicine—known as Água de Inglaterra (Water of England)—that gained great popularity in Portugal and Brazil in the eighteenth and nineteenth centuries.

In a medical treatise he published in London, in 1792, he criticized the secrecy of previous formulations of the same medicine introduced by Talbot (see § 2.19) and

Fernando Mendes, in spite of those two pharmacists having been rewarded with considerable sums of money by the kings of England and Portugal, respectively.

Sarmento criticized the secrecy in medicines, claiming that such practice was unworthy of physicians. He was not, however, against secrecy in general, but against secrecy that concerned the ingredients used in the compositions of medicines. Indeed, he had no qualms with keeping secrecy in the methods of preparing those compositions—which he did.

The following text has two other important aspects. First, Sarmento criticized (to a certain extent only, be it said) the secrecy in remedies, as being unworthy of the medical profession. This same argument, as noted already, is used today as far as the patenting of diagnostic, therapeutic and surgical methods is concerned. Second, he raised a point that was also mentioned above: frequently the owners of secret formulae of successful medicines were rewarded without any consideration for inventorship—the justification of the reward was the possession of the formulae, not the inventive activity, as well as the risks, costs, and labor associated with it.

J. de Castro Sarmento, Da Quina, e em especial, das Minhas Agoas de Inglaterra (1758)

However, as the fate of all new Remedies is to meet with the opposition, instead of curiosity and examination by Doctors; although Cinchona was such an evident remedy, and had no less than a Cardinal for authority and a witness to its virtue, he did not, for that reason, get rid of the same unhappiness, and this prodigious bark remained, for over 30 years, buried, and forgotten, until Dr. Talbot put it to use, without naming it; and reserving its composition for himself, the Cures he did were so extraordinary that King Louis XIV gave him a royal gift to make the secret public, and then it was known that it was *Cinchona*.

At the same time, a strong cooking of the same bark began to flourish, with the title of *Agoa de Inglaterra*, with which Dr. Fernando Mendes had the same, and even better success, as he received a generous gift from *Sereníssimo* King D. Pedro [II], just for communicating the Remedy to him, with the condition of not making it public. And as Cinchona was not well known, and among some persons it was a crime to name it, there were many cures that *Water of England* did, and its Author hiding what he was composed of, made him gain a great fame, as well as the opinions of the same ones who were against Cinchona.

To Dr. Talbot, and to Dr. Mendes, it is fair to confess, that we owe, for the most part, the end of the aversion that some Doctors, and all the People, had conceived against the use of this excellent medicine, convinced by the strength of its same effects.

But even though success makes us owe a large part of it to the memory of these two Professors of Medicine, Dr. Talbot sinned against Doctors' laws and generosity in not immediately revealing, before receiving the award, his Remedy's composition, reserving for himself the way to prepare it. And Dr. Mendes sinned even more in covering up to the public what his water was made of (reserving also the method and preparation of it) even after the *Sereníssimo* King D. Pedro gave him such a generous gift.

Dr. Talbot won a great capital, and the Royal prize, just for making public that his Remedy was Cinchona (and the same that had been rejected before), and he did not even have to claim invention, work, or study. Dr. Mendes, I am positive, because of the great capital he won with *Water of England* (cloudy and poorly prepared), could not claim anything more than to use the same Cinchona (when everyone was against it) without saying what it was made of. And since both of them, without any work, received such huge prizes, it is not much that they did not make the observations they owed, of the extensive effects of this wonderful bark; and they forgot to look for the most exquisite way to prepare it, so as not to be offensive.

And this is what we have achieved through study and work, and what we keep secret; declaring to the Public that all the effects of our *Water of England* are due to Cinchona; but in particular the method of preparing it, or *Menstruum*, with which we extract equal parts of its salt and resin, as if they were weighed on a scale, rejecting the fibers, or the unchanging stick of the bark; which, when introduced into the [human] vessels, reaching the minimum, cannot pass, and forms the Obstructions, which the Sick experience.

And this is the kind of secret that is not unworthy of the Spirit and the profession of a Doctor; naming the Remedy and Virtue, so that others know if it is convenient or not; and reserving its preparation, as the famous Boerhaave suggests to us: And whoever covers up what his secrets are made of, is not as generous as he should be with the other Doctors, and gives occasion for the People to be suspicious.

On these Salt and Resin from the Peruvian bark all effects depend, and the way it works; and on the various combinations of the same Salt and Resin, the variety is found in its effects.

§ 2.28. LOUIS XV OF FRANCE GRANTS ANOTHER EXCLUSIVE PRIVILEGE FOR A SECRET MEDICINE—1762

The following text illustrates another exclusive privilege granted for a medicine's secret formula. The grant, as it had already become a standard, was preceded by the testing of the drug by the First Physician to the King, and invoked the King's concern with public health. Like other privileges, it did not require the disclosure of the secret formula or the manner of its preparation. However, this privilege shows a main difference as compared to a number of privileges inserted above—it states a public policy of fostering inventions in the pharmaceutical sector and of making them available to the public at lower prices. This policy may have been present before, but in this case, it is explicitly stated.

It should be noted that the brochure, which was written and published by the inventor, by King's order, and which was given to customers with the pills, described the various dosages and methods for their use, but did not disclose the composition. On this topic, the text did not go beyond saying that its active ingredient was mercury.

Prologue (excerpts)

Method by Mr. Keyser for the Administration of Dragées in the Treatment of Venereal Diseases, Printed by King's Order.

1762

Prologue (excerpts)

. . . Mr. Keyser, called from his youth to the practice of Surgery, and particularly devoted to the treatment of venereal diseases, learned early the imperfection of the different methods. Provided with a decided taste for chemistry, he applied himself mainly to working the mercury in all possible manners, to discover the most suitable one to develop and fully manifest its anti-venereal virtue.

He observed that this metallic substance, the most singular that has ever existed, so remarkable for its fluidity, for its divisibility, for the constantly globular shape of all its parts, and for its specific weight—the greatest of all, after that of gold—was almost always soiled by the mixture of other matter. He understood that these heterogeneous particles harmed its purity, they were like obstacles that opposed its distribution and its action in the body. . . .

What Mr. Keyser imagined with so much sagacity he carried out with the happiest success; but he only succeeded after redoubled efforts; only after long and arduous work. The first rays of light appeared to him, more than twenty years ago; and he then composed anti-venereal pills that deserved the praise of some enlightened persons, to whom they were shown, and who approved them; but the inventor was not so easy to satisfy, convinced that his remedy, although good, was still far removed from the degree of perfection to which it could be brought. He retired to the Interior to dedicate quietly and exclusively to this important work. He devoted several years to it, and his courageous steadfastness finally led him to the desired end; the views he had proposed were fulfilled; and the Anti-Venereal Dragées came out of his industrious hands. . . .

His Majesty was willing to accept the offer that Mr. Keyser made to him of the secret of his composition; and with a view to proportioning the reward to the usefulness of this remedy, either for Military Hospitals, or for the general good of humanity, He granted him an annual pension of ten thousand pounds, by a Patent from which we have just borrowed the terms. The King in his Letters Patent, according exclusive privilege in favor of Mr. Keyser, to compose and distribute his remedy alone, during his life, recalls the reasons which determined Him to acquire the secret, that is to say, the use which has been made of it, as much on a number of private individuals, as in military hospitals, under the eyes of enlightened persons, the usefulness which has been thus noted by a series of successes promised and achieved, and the repeated testimonies provided to Him.

His Majesty, justifying the grace in question, expresses himself as follows: "and considering that if it is worthy of our attention to perpetuate useful discoveries for the conservation of the life of the humans, it is of our justice to favor the Authors of these discoveries, when these are supported by recognized experience. For these reasons, etc." This grace is also grounded on reasons of public good; it was advisable to facilitate to everyone the possibility of obtaining, for a modest price, an excellent remedy and so often necessary, and not to permit that if fell into discredit by ignorance, inexperience, and perhaps by the bad faith of some of those who would prepare it.

There is no reason to fear that this important deposit will perish;[23] it could not be entrusted to safer and more skillful hands than to those of Mr. de Senac. The place he occupies, the confidence with which the King honors him, the extent of his knowledge in Medicine, his learned writings, and his particular knowledge in Chemistry, must give the greatest weight to the faithful report, which he made of it to His Majesty. . . .

So [the treatment] should start by using two Dragées on the first day, in two takes, and afterwards it will increase to 12, 16, 20, 24, and even to a larger number, if necessary. . . . It is also impossible to determine the number of Dragées necessary to operate a cure; this is also due to the respective gravity of the disease, as well as to the diversity of temperaments more or less susceptible to the action of Mercury. One Sick Person will be cured with one hundred or two hundred Dragées, while another will need five or six hundred and more; but Mr. Keyser has observed in the Hospital of French Guards, entrusted to his care, that the sick were healed there, one after another, with about six or seven hundred Dragées. . . .

Notice.

Mr. Keyser will be happy, if need be, to give advice, whenever required by any Person. They are requested to stamp their Letters and Memoirs exactly, and to be succinct in their presentations, otherwise it would be impossible for him to respond appropriately and as he wishes to correspond to the confidence of the Public.

He also believes he is justified in requiring all those who will be in the case of asking him questions, to consult with their Doctors or Surgeons about them, so that they are intelligible in all respects, and that he thus may be in a state of replying to them with more precision and utility.

Address.

Mr. Keyser, Privileged and Pensioner of the King, lives on St. Louis street, on l'Île, near the Red Bridge, in Paris.

§ 2.29. A FRENCH PHARMACIST PUBLICIZES THE TWO PRIVILEGES HE HAS GAINED FOR HIS SECRET MEDICINE: ONE PRIVILEGE FOR THE EXCLUSIVE SALE OF THE MEDICINE AND ANOTHER FOR PRINTING AND SELLING HIS BOOKLET—1769

As another illustration that some inventors (or mere possessors of secret formulae) would acquire reputation and financial gains not only from selling the medicines but also from selling the publications in which they described them, the following text invokes a privilege for the exclusive sale of a medicine and another for the exclusive printing and sale of a book that explained how to use the medicine in question, both granted by Louis XV, of France, to Barthelemi Agirony, botanist and pharmacist.

Agirony belonged to French nobility. Historical reports mention that he was a very rich man, with an acute sense of business.

By the King.

23. The reference to the deposit implies that, like Arnoult (*see* § 2.26.3), Keyser has also submitted a sample of his invention to the First Physician to the King, so that it could be tested.

By letters patent of June 21, 1769, registered in Parliament on July 9, 1770, it pleased the King to grant Mr. Agirony, botanist, an exclusive privilege to sell and distribute throughout the Kingdom his Antivenereal remedy, in order to offer, as it is said in those letters patent, to his subjects the help they need and that they must expect from this remedy, seen and recognized as useful.

His Majesty has confirmed the said letters patent by the following patent:

> Today, December 7, one thousand seven hundred and seventy-two, the King being at Versailles, Mr. Barthelemi Agirony has very humbly exposed to His Majesty that in order to satisfy his Declaration of last April 25, he had presented to his Royal Commission of Medicine the Letters Patent granted to him by His Majesty on June 21, 1769, registered in Parliament on July 9, 1770, bearing the exclusive privilege of composing, selling and distributing, having sold and distributed by him or by such persons as he would like to appoint, both in Paris and in the whole extent of the Kingdom, its odoriferous Balm for head flushes and his Antivenereal Remedy for the period of fifteen consecutive years, from the day of their registration; that the Royal Commission had given him notice of the representation made by him of the Letters Patent, as it resulted from the decree of their Deliberation of the 24th of last month, of which he reported the formal issuance, and that he therefore implored His Majesty to wish to grant him a Confirmatory Patent of those; he offered to comply with the provisions of the said Declaration of April 15. With regard to this, having regard to the formal issuance of the said Decree of Deliberation attached hereto under the seal of His Royal Commission of Medicine, His Majesty has confirmed and confirms the Letters Patent by Him previously granted to Mr. Barthelemi Agirony on 12 June 1769; registered in its Court of Parliament on July 9, 1770; . . .

Mr. Agirony warns the public that he continues to sell, distribute and administer his antivenereal remedy, in which he ensures that no mercury enters, [it is] composed solely of the juice of plants, for the treatment of all venereal diseases. This gentle, balsamic remedy purifies all the acridities of the mass of blood, and is easy to take, no one having to leave his business or to confine him/herself to the bedroom; and since it is palatable, several people from both sexes can even make use of it without having been attacked by venereal disease, but simply for purifying the blood and maintaining good health.

Mr. Agirony continues to send orders to the Interior, [upon commands addressed] to him at his house in Paris, Richelieu street, at the corner of that of Menards. You have to stamp the letters if you want an answer.

There is a book in his house that teaches how to use his remedy, which is printed with permission and privilege of the King. [The reference is to DES BONS EFFETS DU REMÈDE VÉGÉTAL ANTIVÉNÉRIEN DY SIEUR AGIRONY.]

[Mr. Agirony] is found in the morning from nine to one, and in the evening from eight to nine.

§ 2.30. FRANCE ENACTS THE FIRST REGULATION ON THE ACQUISITION OF SECRET MEDICINES BY THE KING—1776

We have seen that in France, in the eighteenth century, the administrative grants of privileges for secret medicines whose composition was acquired by the king had already reached a certain level of standardization. This was naturally the consequence of the increasing number of grants of privileges, which permitted the development of uniform legal criteria and formulae. But in 1776, a few years before the Revolution, French authorities moved further and enacted the regulation that follows.

This regulation had two striking aspects: it explicitly admitted that the compositions of medicines could remain secret during the lifetime of their inventors, or during another term that was eventually to be determined, on a case by case basis; and the inventors were entitled, during that period, to make and sell the medicines exclusively. And this in spite of the inventors in question having been paid for communicating the secret compositions to the Secretary of State.

From these two particularities, one concludes that the main purpose of the 1776 Regulation was not publicizing secret medicines, but rather having them submitted to the technical inspection of the First Physician to the King or of a Commission that he would appoint. Therefore, the main target of the Regulation was charlatanism. In this way, those drugs that were filed with the Secretary of State would be commercialized with the stamp of technical approval. This was not, however, an early sort of market authorization, because pharmacists, at that time, did not need it to put their medicines on the market. And actually, the regulation confirms this because, in its article VI, it provides for the only cause of prohibition of commercialization: the pharmacist's failure to publish information on the manner of using the medicine.

It seems that the regulation was not often applied. First, it had a short life because just thirteen years later, the French Revolution would start and would completely subvert all the laws in force. Second, and perhaps more importantly, the public resources to pay for the secret medicines—so many they were—were very scarce.

Ordinance of the King,

Which provides the rules concerning the acquisition that His Majesty deems advisable to make, of the composition and preparation of certain particular Remedies.

Of April 12, 1776.

By the King.

His Majesty, wishing henceforth to make as useful as possible the acquisition that He deems advisable to make, for the good of human kind, of the composition and preparation of certain particular remedies, according to the report of His First Physician, or such other Commissioners, if need be, chosen and appointed for this purpose; and wishing that these remedies acquired by His charity are no longer, as in the past, liable to be lost or altered, and that no abuse may result therefrom; His Majesty has ordered and orders the following:

First Article

When the acquisition of any remedy whatsoever has been made by His Majesty, without any reservation of secrecy for the benefit of the sellers, until after their death or after a certain limited time, then the original document containing its composition, the preparation, and the properties of the medicine will be handed over to the Secretary of State in charge of the department of the House of His Majesty, who will order the making of certified, exact, and faithful copies by the King's First Physician.

II.

One of the two copies will remain in the files of the Secretary of State; the other will be sent to the Royal Printing, which subsequently will distribute it to the public, in printed form: The original document will be sent to the Faculty of Medicine of Paris, with orders to keep it in its archives; and the Dean of the Faculty will immediately send to the Secretary of State, on behalf of his Company, a receipt of this writing, obliging himself to produce it if so requested.

III.

When His Majesty has purchased the composition and preparation of some particular remedy, previously unknown, and deemed effective, and granted the reservation of secrecy to the seller until after his death, or after a certain limited time, then the original document containing the composition and preparation of the remedy will be handed over, in a sealed envelope, to the Secretary of State, who will put it in a second envelope, by him similarly sealed: The name and special properties of the remedy, the time when this composition can be made public, and the date of the acquisition by the King, will be written on this second envelope

IV.

Thus, the document, under this double envelope, will be sent by the Secretary of State to the Dean of the Faculty of Medicine of Paris, who will immediately give receipt, in the name of his Company; and the said Dean, after having informed the assembled Faculty of Medicine, will immediately deposit the said writing, as it will have been handed over to him, in the archives of the Faculty, where it will be faithfully kept, without being allowed that it be trusted to any one, until it has to be made public.

V.

Within three months, from the day of the deposit made with the Faculty of Medicine, the Dean shall inform the Public through Newspapers and Gazettes, [of the deposit]: The Authors and Editors of these periodical works will be required to publish this notice given by the Dean, on behalf of the Faculty of Medicine, in a manner that the public knows that the secret has been deposited, and when it will be published.

VI.

The seller of the remedy, who will enjoy alone during his life, or for a certain limited time, the composition or preparation of the said remedy purchased by the King, under this granted condition, will be obliged to have it published by means of the Journals, or by such another way that he wishes, the precise rules of the use and the administration of the drug, by specifying the particular ailments and the circumstances in which it is advisable to use it; but this kind of warning and summary instruction may not be published and printed, in any way, unless it is approved by the King's First Physician, or such other Commissioners who will have been instructed to have, subject to secrecy, knowledge of the composition and preparation of the remedy, to examine it, to judge it, and to make their report subsequently: And if it happened that the possessor of the remedy still secret contravened this law that applies to him, then the sale of the remedy would be ceased and prohibited.

VII.

The possessor of the remedy sold, subject to secrecy, will be obliged to provide the Secretary of State in charge of the department of Paris and the Dean of the Faculty of Medicine every year with a certificate of life in good form, failing which, after six months from the date in which the certificate should have been provided, the following article shall apply.

VIII.

Immediately after the death of the possessor of the remedy purchased by the King is verified, or such other time limit set for the reservation of secrecy has expired, the Dean of the Faculty of Medicine will be required to send the writing containing the composition and the preparation of the remedy to the authors of the Newspapers and Gazettes, to publish it: And nevertheless the original text will still remain ten years pending in the archives of the Faculty.

IX.

As soon as the said remedies are made public, either through the Newspapers, or otherwise, all the Apothecaries will be obliged to record exactly their formulae and the preparation thereof in a register specially intended for this purpose, so that they can conform to it, and that there is never in this preparation, when it is prescribed for use, either variation, or innovation, or change; and they shall be obliged to communicate the said register whenever requested by some of the Members of the Faculty of Medicine, without possibility of refusal, under any pretext whatsoever. Done at Versailles on the twelfth day of April one thousand seven hundred and seventy-six.

§ 2.31. LOUIS XVI ESTABLISHES THE ROYAL SOCIETY OF MEDICINE, WHICH BECOMES VERY CRITICAL OF THE PRIVATE APPROPRIATION OF REMEDIES—1778 ONWARDS

In France, the concern of the authorities with the quality of medicines did not cease with the approval of the Regulation on the acquisition of the compositions of secret medicines, as seen in the previous section. And indeed, generalized charlatanism and quackery were a genuine problem of public health. Of course, there were good medicines being sold and administered to the sick, and not all pharmacists and self-proclaimed inventors of new medicines were dishonest and ignorant. But those were the exception rather than the norm.

So, the King established the Royal Society of Medicine, and, reviving a practice that was used in the Middle Ages, submitted drugs made and sold by apothecaries to the technical examination of physicians—thus, in a certain way, giving physicians professional ascendance over pharmacists.

The second of the following texts is particularly interesting. It reveals that the Royal Society of Medicine was established as a sort of a combination of a patent office and a sanitary authority. As a patent office, it should verify if the medicines under examination had novelty (art. 4, second sentence) and utility (art. 4, first sentence, and art. 5); as a sanitary authority, it had the competence of examining the safety and efficacy of medicines, and approving their commercialization (or not).

Two other striking features of the by-laws of the Royal Society of Medicine as far as the examination of secret medicines was concerned were that the Society was under the duty of keeping the confidentiality over the composition unless the inventor wished otherwise; and that it was up to the Society to determine the name under which the medicine would be sold. It is implied, however, that this determination concerned the technical or generic name of the drug. Pharmacists were not prevented from using their own trademarks.

Likewise importantly, the notion of secrecy does not disappear with these new rules: on the contrary, unless the inventor decides otherwise, the Society was bound to keep the confidentiality of compositions submitted to its examination.

Like the Regulation on the acquisition of the secret compositions of new medicines, these rules also had a very short life: eleven years later, the Revolution would arise in France, and with it, as we will see below, all laws concerning the supervision of the apothecaries were abrogated (even if, in the case of several of those, the abrogation was temporary). However, the Society itself, in the Report on its experience is presented to the National Assembly after the Revolution, admitted that the small number of patents issued was due to its strictness in examining the new medicines. A particularly important aspect of this Report is the harsh criticism against secrecy in pharmaceuticals as well as their private appropriation—which the Society considers "one of the innumerable evils that owe their birth to the greed and credulity of men."

The third text is perhaps the first source that refers to clinical tests. Today, the information obtained with those tests, while secret, is covered by a sui generis *regime of intellectual property set, on a global scale, by art. 39.3 of the TRIPS Agreement. The first country to introduce such protection was the United States in 1984. Before, protection already existed for test data, but only as far as agricultural chemical products were concerned. So, test data is not specific to pharmaceuticals but rather associated with regulated products, the commercialization of which depends on prior governmental approval. Anyway, the text is interesting in the sense that it reveals a procedure for the public revelation of new medicines, their effects and uses, while the Royal Society of Medicine promised to keep their formulations secret. Secrecy, be it said, was preserved as far as the formulae were concerned, not the data. Actually, it was the Society that took care of trying the medicines, not their makers. Nevertheless, we have here a document that associates the procedure for obtaining marketing approval with mandatory secrecy—a distant ancestor of the secrecy that art. 39.3 of the TRIPS Agreement has made mandatory for all the WTO Members that provide for such procedures.*

The fifth text is a strong reminder that the laws of the market, even if their operation is very often challenged because of the alleged insensitivity of proprietors, may be more effective than a mechanism of public prizes for inventions. Under trade secret and patent systems, inventors are rewarded (or not) by the market. The market may be a blind judge, insensitive to the needs of the poor, but at least it is not affected by the vested interests of those that are in charge of granting the prizes (and who are no less insensitive to social demands). A lesson about this comes from the prize never granted to John Harrison (1693-1776), the inventor of the maritime chronometer, the definitive solution for the longitude problem—because at least one of the members of the commission in charge of examining and granting the prize was also a candidate to the prize (but with a much worse solution)—and the other members could not be impartial because, after all, they were his colleagues. In the same token, when a society formed by physicians proposes to award a prize for a new method of curing rabies, one may wonder if in that commission there are no members with a personal interest in the solution found. That may not have been the case, but the question is still appropriate.

§ 2.31.1. Letters attributing to the Royal Society of Medicine the examination of new medicines

Versailles, August 1778. Registered in Parliament on September 1.

Louis, etc. However considerable the advantages that our dear and beloved eldest daughter the University of Paris, and, following its example, the other universities of our kingdom, have at all times provided to our subjects by the enlightenment that their teaching has never ceased to spread over all the sciences; nevertheless, the kings our predecessors thought that it was useful for the progress of letters and the fine arts to form particular societies of the most learned and the most recommendable persons, to hold conferences between them, in order to improve their own knowledge by the communication of their discoveries, and to be enriched even by those which could be collected in foreign countries where the sciences and the fine arts are not cultivated with less success. And yet the formation of these particular companies has been far from impinging on the rights and prerogatives of our universities or of some of the faculties that compose them; we have, on the contrary, always considered their establishment as adding to the glory and the splendor of these bodies, since antiquity destined to public education, given that the greater part of those who compose these literary societies have received the first elements of science in the universities, received with praise in our academies, have made of them one of their main ornaments. . . .

Led by such considerations, we have established a society of persons experienced in the science proper to the treatment of diseases of all kinds, and we have ordered them to assemble, with a view to gathering a collection, both of the observations that their personal experience has enabled them to bring together, and of those that would be obtained by the correspondences which we had proposed to maintain with the most famous doctors of the Interior and even of the foreign countries. . . .

As a result of the considerations that lead us to favoring this society, and to opening up a vast career to its research, it seems natural to us to attribute to it the examination of the so-called specific remedies and others of whatever species they may be, for the verification of which our very honored lord and grandfather had already thought it necessary to establish a special commission in 1772. A greater number of objects of the same kind, brought together in the hands of the same people, will give rise to a greater emulation between them, and we will succeed in a simpler way to put an end to the over-multiplied inconveniences of the distribution of unknown remedies, and mostly harmful to the health of our subjects. . . .

For these reasons, etc., we have hereby, signed by our hand, instituted and established, institute and establish, under the title of Royal Society of Medicine, the assembly and conference of physicians, who have already met by our orders since the month of April 1776, to take care of studying the history of nature of the various epidemics; accordingly we have ordered the following:

1. The Royal Society of Medicine will be under our special protection. . . .
10. We attribute to the society the examination of new remedies, both internal and external, of whatever nature they may be, for which we are asked to grant patents: we wish that none of those remedies be sold and distributed without a deliberation of the society admitting them, and regarding which patents in the ordinary form will be issued by the secretary of state in charge of the department of our house: we also revoke, as much as necessary, the declaration of April 25, 1772; and any other decision relating to these objects will remain with no effect, from the date of publication hereof. The lieutenant general of police of our good city of Paris, and all other judges or officers of our provinces, shall not give permissions to sell and distribute any remedy, without having been shown the mentioned patent, which will be quoted in the permissions that they will grant: we also remove and revoke all patents and permissions previously granted, except those granted to whom have obtained them from the mentioned society, in the form prescribed by this article.
11. We wish that, with regard to external and surgical remedies that will be submitted for the application of privileges, a special committee be formed, which will be held on the first Monday of each month, in the assembly hall of the society; which committee will be composed of the president of the society, or, in his absence, of the director or the vice-director, of the perpetual secretary, of the dean of the faculty of medicine of Paris, and of four other members of the society (which this society will always choose among the doctors of the faculty); of our first surgeon and five other surgeons of his choice. The members of this particular committee will be renewed each year, with the exception of the officers of the society, the dean of the faculty and our first surgeon. . . .

We thus give in mandate to our beloved and loyal counselors and the people holding our court of parliament in Paris, etc.

§ 2.31.2. The State Council defines the attributions of the Royal Society of Medicine concerning the examination of secret medicines

May 10, 1779

Art. 1. The Royal Society of Medicine shall examine not only all remedies for the distribution of which certificates or letters patent will be applied for to the Secretary of State in charge of the Department of His Majesty's House, but also the preparations, whether cosmetic or otherwise, that can affect health.
Art. 2. When the Society is required to examine any remedy or preparation, it will appoint at least two commissioners to report thereon, from the reading of which it will deliberate whether the remedy presented deserves its approval.
Art. 3. The Society will not pass judgment on the remedies presented to it, unless the commissioners appointed to examine them are instructed in their preparation, which must be done in their presence. The commissioners will keep the secrecy of these different procedures, until their authors consent to their being made public.

Art. 4. When the Society has approved a remedy submitted for its examination, it will itself determine under which particular name it must be announced and distributed; it will indicate the doses and, in its report, it will explain the main circumstances in which the said remedy may be useful and those in which it may be harmful.

The appointed commissioners will especially look with great care if remedies declared as new are not found prescribed in some dispensary.

Art. 5. The remedies which will be judged to be able of great effectiveness will be authorized by a patent, which will be issued, according to a deliberation of the Society, by the Secretary of State in charge of the department of His Majesty's house; but cosmetic or other preparations, the sale of which the Society believes can be tolerated, will only be distributed by simple tacit permission. . . .

§ 2.31.3. The Royal Society of Medicine establishes a procedure for the examination of secret medicines and the public exhibition of those approved—1778

Royal Society of Medicine, Notice to the Public on the examination of medicines for which permissions or patents are requested—1778

The Royal Society of Medicine, to which the King has attributed the examination of the medicines for which permissions or patents are requested, eager to respond appropriately to the confidence with which His Majesty has honored it, hastens to make its intentions known to the public.

It would be equally unfair to admit or proscribe all new remedies, but there are reasons that justify the belief that, among those who submit them and who extol their successes, most of them being very ignorant in Medicine, are not in a position to know the nature of the diseases they say they have cured, nor the properties and the combination of drugs that they use, as it is also certain that many add bad faith to ignorance, the Society has decided to spare neither time nor care in the research and care with which it intends to engage itself on this subject. . . .

The Company believes that it must report to the public to whom this review is of interest the manner in which it proceeds. Those in possession of the proposed remedies are obliged to submit a certain amount of their preparation with an account of the virtues they attribute to it and the circumstances in which they believe they should be used. They are required to communicate under seal their recipes and details of their processes. The Company appoints two Commissioners to whom this deposit is entrusted, who certify having received it under the authors' seal, and that they shall keep what it contains under the utmost secrecy. Those in possession of remedies must justify to the appointed Commissioners the truth of what they have put forward, by doing in their presence the preparation for which they are applying for a patent. These Commissioners will search if similar formulae are not found in the Pharmacopeias, which is very important, so as not to put the Government in the situation of buying the same remedy several times; they describe the good or bad effects that one can expect from their use, and after they have made their report to the assembled Society, this

Society deliberates whether the remedy should be subjected to experiments, or whether it deserves to be approved.

It is not necessary to say that the making of tests shall be allowed only in the case where one is assured that the remedy does not expose him/her to any danger. This is one of the reasons why it is required that the recipe be known to the Commissioners; but what is essential to observe is that, in addition to the trials which are carried out in hospitals, from which no one can ever flatter him/herself of warding off all kinds of fraud, the Company requires that a certain number of people of the art bear good testimony to the remedies proposed, after having employed them in their practice, on patients absolutely unknown to the authors of the remedies. The Society will always wait sufficient time to ensure the success [of the trials] and not to run the risk of passing judgment too hastily. . . .

The Society will not only give its attention to the remedies that are announced as having great virtues; convinced that nothing of interest in any way whatsoever to the health of men is indifferent, it will examine with great care all preparations, whether cosmetic or otherwise, which may have impact on the human body, and those of its members who have the most knowledge in Chemistry will not disdain to take care of these details, very tedious indeed, but of which they feel all the importance.

The Society did not believe that it should limit itself to announce this part of its work; it has imagined a means which could make the public in the situation of benefiting from it immediately. It has decided that henceforth there will be in its office a noticeable statement of the new remedies approved by it, and of the decisions that it will have made on the remedies previously authorized, and which will have been submitted to its examination. This statement can be consulted by all those who, before exposing themselves to employing secret remedies, want to know what degree of confidence these deserve. The office of the Company, located at rue du Sépulcre, Fauxbourg Saint-Germain, will be open from nine in the morning until one o'clock, and from four in the afternoon until eight in the evening; the public will find there all possible information on the reports and deliberations of the Society concerning the distribution of remedies and medicinal preparations throughout the Kingdom; it will be easy to know the true intentions of the Company on this subject and it will see the zeal, the exactitude and lack of self-interest it devotes itself to this work.

The Company has already reviewed a large number of preparations, among which it has thus far found only one that has deserved its approval. In addition, [the Society] asks Citizens of all classes, and especially the people of the art, to communicate to it their observations on the effects of the remedies to which it has given its approval, and it hopes that persons who may be dissatisfied with some of the matters entrusted to its supervision will not feel authorized to lodge complaints unless it has refused to listen to them and to give them satisfaction.

§ 2.31.4. The Royal Society of Medicine reports on its experience in examining patent applications for pharmaceutical inventions and requests the National Assembly to ban secrecy, as well as any sort of private property in new medicines

Nouveau Plan de Constitution pour la Médecine en France, présenté à l'Assemblée Nationale par la Société Royale de Médecine, 1790

Address to the National Assembly,
On the Examination of Secret Remedies.
The Society of Medicine was charged by Letters Patent of the King, of the month of August 1778, and by a Declaration of May 26, 1780, of the examination of the remedies presented as new, and for which their authors request Letters Patent, Certificates, or Permissions.

The Society has always believed that the most active vigilance and the most rigorous severity were the first of its duties in functions whose main purpose was to defend the health and life of the Citizens, against the endeavors of greed or the dangerous illusions of ignorance.

Consequently, it has imposed on itself a rule to regard as worthy those remedies that would receive its approval; only remedies which would meet the double condition of being absolutely new, and of having, at least in some circumstances, a marked superiority over all known remedies of the same kind.

This law, the Society has religiously observed it.

So in the fourteen years since it has been established, it has given only four approvals, only two of which are for new remedies, the other two for remedies formerly approved and generally used.

Experience of fourteen years has convinced it of several truths that it believes should be brought to the attention of the National Assembly. These truths will certainly deserve its attention, since they are of interest to humankind.

(1) Nothing is more dangerous than secrecy when it comes to medicine. The most useful often becomes fatal by the mere fact that it remains covered under the veils of mystery. This mystery excites enthusiasm and maintains the credulity of the people. It produces uncertainty in the discernment of the circumstances and inaccuracy in the application of a means that is employed without knowledge. The Society has in its Collections multiplied proofs of the unfortunate effects, and we are not afraid to say it, of the poisonings caused by remedies whose successes in some cases had been attested by well-known Doctors and by citizens of all ranks.

(2) As long as the dangerous privilege of secrecy is granted to the Authors of a small number of useful remedies, a host of others, jealous of the same advantages, but fearing the severity of the same trials, will appear on all sides. The Society has seen with sorrow, in spite of its complaints, a large number of secret remedies withdrawn from its scrutiny, approved without being

> known to their approvers, and yet vested in imposing authority. Let us not praise a few successes that have served to accredit its use: humanity has paid for them only too dearly by a host of victims.

Keeping a secret of some really useful remedies is therefore an obstacle to the destruction of Charlatanism, a scourge which, until now, like so many others, has been mainly fatal to the needy, the poor, and especially the poor in the countryside.

If one could suggest that, persuaded by these truths, the Society of Medicine had allowed itself to exaggerate, it would invoke the testimony of several Members of this august Assembly, who, closer than us to the inhabitants of the countryside, in providing them with their care, have witnessed their misfortunes.

The proposal that today we submit to the National Assembly is that in the future it shall be not issued Certificate, or Patent Letter by which a useful remedy can remain secret; that any new remedy, and of a utility superior to that of all known remedies in the same genre, be purchased by the Nation, and published immediately afterwards, so that people of the Art can apply it in the circumstances where it is appropriate, with the modifications that these circumstances require, and not blindly on the faith of an approval.

This is how Louis XIV bought and published the medicine of the Prior of Babrières for Hernias, and the powder of the Chartreux; this is how the Parliament of England bought and published that of Miss Stephens.

The prize given to the publication of a remedy must result from consideration of its usefulness and its superiority, and from the number of circumstances in which it may be used; because it is on these two bases only that we must estimate the legitimacy of the product, if the property were attributed to the Author.

We can assure, and the history of Medicine proves it, that the small number of new preparations that will be judged worthy of this distinction, can never form an object of considerable expenditure.

It is not for us, it is for the Lawmakers of France to examine what right a man can have to a property whose alienation matters for the health of all, and to what extent we owe to the good of the public the sacrifice of the particular interest.

We will confine ourselves to saying that if the Assembly adopts our proposal, it will have destroyed once again one of the innumerable evils that owe their birth to the greed and credulity of men. . . .

§ 2.31.5. The French Royal Society of Medicine proposes prizes for new therapeutic methods—1778

History of the Royal Society of Medicine

Year M. DCC. LXXIX.

The Society had proposed, in its first public meeting in the year 1778, as the subject of a prize in the value of 600 pounds, the following question: To determine what is the best treatment of rabies. The value of this prize having been increased to 1,200 pounds, it was announced again at the second public meeting of the same year. A period of three years did not seem too long to do research and collect observations on such an important subject: the term fixed for the end of the competition was January 1, 1781.

Their authors were to expect a severe examination: the Company had requested observations to serve as a basis for the methods that would be adopted. In order to make the work of the competitors easier, it had asked one of its members (Mr. Andry) to collect the facts relating to the treatment of rabies, scarce among the authors. Finally, it had recorded in its volumes the most accredited recipes against this terrible disease.

In order to have rights at the proposed prize, therefore, it was necessary to add some new knowledge to that which had already been acquired; to shed, by exact and authentic observations, a new light on the question; in short, to make the treatment of this disease safer than it was before. None of the competitors having fulfilled these conditions, the Company has not been able to award this prize, the distribution of which it felt it necessary to defer until the first public meeting in the year 1783.

§ 2.32. AN ATTACK AGAINST THE PATENT SYSTEM, AND PHARMACEUTICAL PATENTS IN PARTICULAR

1780

Although European countries and the United States gradually embraced the patent system as a mechanism to bring technical and economic progress, not all citizens would be happy with it. As a matter of course, they might have strong reasons to be suspicious of such a system: patents were still basically industrial privileges, and many of them—especially those granted for medicines—would not require the disclosure of the inventions. In England, as shown, the regular patenting of medicines started, albeit very slowly, after the passing of the Statute of Monopolies. However, the term "patent medicine" could also mean a medicine that received a patent letter authorizing its commercialization and advertisement. As it will be shown below, patents were seen by the public as a combination of an administrative permission for the making and sale of medicines and a certificate of merit. In that way, the term "patent medicines" also designated those products that, not being covered by a patent letter in regard to their novelty and utility, were the object of a permission of commercialization.

It is natural, therefore, that "patent medicines," in the broad meaning of the term, proliferated in England and in the United States, which could only give rise to a generalized suspicion as to the quality and effectiveness of medicines available on the market,

The text that follows is an interesting and funny expression of that suspicion.

The Patent, a Poem (excerpt), by W. Woty, 1780

Happy the Man, who duly pays his debts,
He still more happy, who a Patent gets.
This prose enlivens, and adorns the rhime,
Lifts the low thought, and stamps it with sublime;
Catches the eye, allures that erring sense,
Ere steady Judgment can her reign commence,
Like Copper-plates, at which Men-children look,
And praise the Prints, before they read the book.
Hail to the Patent! which enables Man
To vend a Folio—or a Warming-pan.
This makes the Windlass work with double force
And smoke-jacks whirl more rapid in their course;
Confers a sanction on the Doctor's pill,
Oft' known to cure, but oft'ner known to kill.
What man would scruple to resign his breath,
Provided he could die a Patent death! . . .
The time may come, when nothing will succeed,
But what a previous Patent hath decreed;
And we must open, on some future day,
The door of Nature with a patent Key. . . .

§ 2.33. IN ENGLAND, PATENT MEDICINES AND THEIR SECRECY—THE PARADOX EXPLAINED

Frequently English and American texts concerning medicines in the nineteenth century refer to "patent medicines," and yet they really meant medicines whose composition was kept secret. This, in today's terms, is an obvious paradox, in view of the rule established by English courts, at the end of the eighteenth century, that inventors had to fully disclose their inventions in order to be entitled to patent protection. Actually, the paradox does not come from the adjective "patent" itself, because, originally, this term was linked to the public nature of the royal letters granting the privilege. The letters might be "patent," i.e., *open to the public (as opposed to "closed letters"), but not necessarily its subject matter (*i.e., *in this case, the invention). Thus, strictly speaking, there was no contradiction in the granting of privileges, through patent letters, for secret medicines. The paradox, as said, results from the social deal imposed by British courts, requiring disclosure. After that doctrine was established, starting with* Liardet v. Jonhson, *in*

1778, to speak of the secrecy of "patent medicines," which was not out of the question, became an oxymoron indeed.

The term "patent medicines" had, actually, two meanings, regardless of their formulae being kept secret or disclosed. One was that they had been examined as to their novelty and utility, and their inventors and assignees were entitled to their exclusive making and selling for a certain period of time. The other was that the owner of the formula had submitted the medicine to a committee of physicians and had received their approval for its commercialization. This approval had been granted to him by letters patent signed by the King.

Soon the two meanings became entangled, and when the pharmacist in possession of the formula of a medicine claimed that it had received a patent, the public would take that reference as a certificate of the efficacy and safety of the product.

This has given rise to strong criticism of the patent system as applied to medicines, because, in order to take a patent for an invention, the inventor did not (and does not, still) need to prove security and efficacy. And many dishonest inventors would not be reluctant in resorting to that confusion to pursue gains in their trade. We will see that several courts would later step in to clarify the matter. But in the meantime, the criticism persisted. The following text is a report on the mentioned paradox provided for by a British medical specialized magazine, "Health News."

Editor of HEALTH NEWS, Exposures of Quackery: Being a Series of Articles Upon, and Analyses of, Various Patent Medicines, vol. 1 (excerpts)

For the sake of realizing an annual sum of money—about £ 250,000—the British Government perpetrates a gross wrong on the community by giving a fictitious value and importance to the myriad quack remedies which are sold throughout the country. We refer, of course, to the amount raised by issuing Government Stamps for articles of this class, designated as Patent Medicines; but, as we are in the habit of calling a spade a spade, we prefer to use the shorter name. The injury done to the community by this system of protecting quack medicines is incalculable. "Oh!" say the artisan, the small tradesman's wife, and many others in a higher position in society, "this must be a good remedy, it is protected by Royal Letters Patent." And so they go on, swallowing the bait as well as the physic, whilst the proprietor reaps a golden harvest. Government officials are always slow in making any changes involving them in additional trouble or new arrangements; and, consequently, succeeding Chancellors of the Exchequer leave the question of the Patent Medicine Stamp alone. Of late years there has been—and very properly, too—considerable public agitation concerning the adulteration of articles of food and drink, and it has been enacted that various admixtures of this character can only be sold with a distinctive label showing their composition. But there is no provision of this nature on behalf of the purchasers of quack medicines, for which the term "Patent" is a misnomer, and also misleading, as the only protection afforded by the Government stamp is to the manufacturer of the nostrum, all information concerning the ingredients that enter into its composition being withheld.

Patents for new and useful inventions carry with them the sole right of making, using, or selling such inventions for a limited period only, namely fourteen years, and before they can be obtained the person seeking the patent must deposit at the Patent Office a description of the invention. Moreover, he has to make large and frequent payments, otherwise the patent lapses. In the case of "Patent" medicines, nothing is required by way of proving either novelty or utility, while the composition remains a mystery. All that the manufacturer has to do is to pay for a given number of stamps, only three-halfpence each, and he can dose as many people as he can induce to buy the stuff with the most noxious drugs, or he can make a pile of money by selling colored water, soap, or any other commodity, very cheap when purchased in bulk, and capable of being disguised in appearance or taste before it is passed on to the consumer in smaller quantities. . . .

One of our colonial subscribers asks us how, having regard to the origin of the word "patent," that term came to be applied to preparations of which the composition is kept secret. The misnomer arose in this way.

During the reign of George III., whose obstinacy and incompetence lost our fairest colony, America, and raised the National Debt from £138,000,000 to £794,000,000, the Ministers were frequently much exercised in their minds as to the means of raising money. The Chancellor of the Exchequer of that period bethought him of quack medicines, and an Act of Parliament was passed (23rd George III., cap. 62) "to grant to His Majesty a stamp duty on licenses to be taken out by certain persons uttering and vending medicines, and certain stamp duties on medicines sold under such licenses, or under authority of His Majesty's Letters Patent." A subsequent Act, in 1785, designated these medicines as "prepared or compounded by any person or persons whatsoever" who had or claimed to have "any occult or secret or unknown art, or some exclusive right or title to their manufacture," the same being advertised or recommended as "specifics or otherwise for the cure or relief of any ailment or malady incident to, or in any way affecting, the human body." The otherwise in this definition applies quite as much to quack medicines at the present day as it did then.

. . . [T]he term " patent " applied to these secret quack compounds is used in the sense of "privileged " (by letters patent), and not of "open or divulged."

In 1875 an act was passed reducing the medicine license duty, which previously had ranged from five shillings to forty shillings in different localities, to the uniform amount of five shillings throughout the United Kingdom. The consequence of this reduction was to greatly increase the number of patent medicine vendors. In 1874, the year before the passing of the new Act, the licenses taken out were 12,430; now the annual number is about double that—considerably over 20,000. . . .

The ease with which [secret medicines] can be procured—we refer now more particularly to the opiate and other narcotic preparations—has led to a widespread system of home-drugging, while it is undoubtedly responsible for many deaths, especially of children, not invariably arising from mere misadventure, but always very difficult to detect and bring to light. . . .

But the great reform necessary is to take a leaf out of the legislature of Continental countries, and to make it unlawful to sell any patent medicine without previously placing on the bottle or box in which it is issued to the public a legible description of the contents. By law the sale of certain articles of food, such as chicory and margarine, is prohibited without a label apprising the purchaser of the nature of the substance which he is buying. How much the more is it desirable, in the interests of the purchasers of patent medicines, that they should be duly warned as to the composition of articles which contain potent drugs inimical to health and often dangerous to life?

Further, if a stamp duty be continued, it should be clearly made known that it is to be regarded as of the nature of a tax, and not—as now commonly supposed—as an authoritative guarantee of the quality or value of the preparation. "Protected by Her Majesty's Royal Letters Patent" is a statement which has deluded hundreds of thousands of purchasers of quack remedies.

But if the manufacturers of quack medicines are silent concerning the actual ingredients of the stuff concocted by them, they cannot be charged with similar reticence respecting the assumed virtues of such components. Bold assertion is their sheet anchor, and equally bold advertisement is the talisman with which they conjure the coin out of the pockets of their credulous customers.

§ 2.34. THE FRENCH REVOLUTIONARY ASSEMBLY REVOKES ALL LAWS AND STATUTES CONCERNING THE GUILDS, INCLUDING THOSE OF APOTHECARIES—AND REINSTATES THE MANDATORY INSPECTION OF MEDICINES JUST ONE MONTH LATER—1791

The following texts show the practical implementation of the idea of economic freedom pushed to the extreme and its almost immediate abrogation: in 1791, in the wake of the libertarian revolution of 1789, pharmacists, along with all other professions, were freed by the French Assembly from any administrative supervision. Competition on the market would be the only constraint upon those who invented, made and distributed medicines. In such a scenario, intellectual property would be even more important than it was before because the more the economy is free, the more every difference introduced in products counts for enticing customers.

However, the idea of pharmacists being totally free to sell medicines, without the need for any examination as to their professional ability, or for any testing of the products, did not work—even under the Revolution's radical philosophy. In view of alleged abuses, just one month later, the supervision on the profession of pharmacists would be reestablished.

§ 2.34.1. March 17, 1791—Decree abolishing all rights of assistance, all masteries and *jurandes*, and the establishment of patents

. . . 2. As from the same period [next April 1], the offices of wig makers-barbers-bathers steamers, those of stockbrokers, and all other offices for the inspection and works of arts and commerce, patents and master's letters, the fees collected for the reception of master's degrees and *jurandes*, those of the college of pharmacy, and all professions' privileges, under any name whatsoever, are also abolished. . . .

7. From next April 1, it will be free for anyone to do such business, or to exercise such profession, art or trade as they see fit; but he/she will be required to provide

him/herself beforehand with a patent, to pay the fee thereof according to the rates determined below, and to conform to the police regulations that are or may be made.

. . .

12. The fees of the annual licenses for business, arts, crafts and professions, other than those that will be hereinafter exempted, will be paid at the rate of the rental price, or of the rental value of the housing of the shops, stores and workshops occupied by those who request them, and in the following proportions:. . .

§ 2.34.2. April 17, 1791—Decree relating to the practice of pharmacy, and the sale and distribution of drugs and medicines

The National Assembly, after having heard its health committee on an abuse that is introduced into the practice of pharmacy, considering the object and utility of this profession, decrees:

That the laws, statutes and regulations existing on March 2, relating to the practice and teaching of pharmacy, for the preparation, sale and distribution of drugs and medicines, will continue to be executed according to their form and content, under the penalties imposed by the said laws and regulations, until, on the report that will be made about this matter, it has been ruled definitively in this respect: consequently, patents cannot be issued for the preparation, sale and distribution of drugs and medicaments throughout the kingdom, except to those who are or may be authorized to practice pharmacy, according to the statutes and regulations concerning this profession.

§ 2.35. FRANCE GRANTS THE FIRST UTILITY PATENT (BREVET D'INVENTION) FOR AN INVENTION WITH THERAPEUTIC USES—26 AUGUST, 1791

On January 7, 1791, the French National Assembly enacted a statute on patents that had no limitations to the subject matter of protection. Thus, from 1791 onwards, there were no restrictions as to the patentability of medicines. In reality, such limitations did not exist before either, but industrial privileges with medicines for their subject matter were very rare. Pharmacists preferred secrecy, whose protection was unconditioned and unlimited.

So, although hesitantly, if not reluctantly, some inventors in the pharmaceutical area filed patent applications under the 1791 Act. Between 1791 and 1844, when a statute excluding pharmaceutical products from patentability was enacted, a few patents were granted for medicines—the first one on August 26, 1791 (the text that follows). The records of French patents granted after 1791 show that a few more patents on medicines and on ingredients with a medicinal application were granted. Still, in 1791, a patent was granted to Le Blanc, an inventor from Paris, for a method of extracting soda from sea salt. In 1837 another patent was granted for an analeptic. In 1840, two patents more were issued, one for an antibilious product and the other for an antirheumatic balsam. [PATENTS FOR INVENTIONS (BREVETS D'INVENTION) GRANTED IN FRANCE

FROM 1791 TO 1876 INCLUSIVE, at 505 (Government Printing Office, 1883). Source: < archive.org >].

Of course, these figures are very low when compared with the number of patents granted in France for mechanical and chemical inventions. Inventors of medicines continued preferring secrecy for many years to come, which led the French government to take measures against "secret remedies," as we will see next. In 1832, even before the patentability of medicines was excluded under the statute of 1844, a French court had already held that medicines could not be patented because of the inherent conflict between the granting of patents without prior examination and the requirement that medicines should be examined in order for their commercialization to be authorized. This was an explicit statement about the paradox mentioned in § 2.33.

*The following text concerns the first French utility patent (*brevet d'invention*) for a medicine granted to Jean-Baptiste Daguin. The grant, dated August 26, 1791, was confirmed, jointly with the other 21 patents issued before October 31, 1791, by a royal proclamation of November 16 of the same year. Source: < gallica.BnF.fr >. It appears from the text itself that the patent was not granted for a genuine invention because, as Daguin himself admits, he did not invent anything, given that the salt of Glauber had been known for more than one hundred years, his inventor being the Dutch chemist Johann Rudolf Glauber (1604-1670), who called it SAL MIRABILIS, having in view its effectiveness as a solvent.[24] What Daguin did, actually, was to find a piece of land in the Parish of Montoir, in Bretagne, from where he extracted the raw material (ashes) used in making the salt of Glauber.*

Daguin also claimed that the ashes, from which he extracted the salt, had a second use—as an agricultural fertilizer.

Patent No. 11. Department of Maine et Loire. August 26, 1791

Louis, by the grace of God and by the Constitutional Law of the State, King of the French, to all present and to come, Greeting.

Mr. Jean-Baptiste Daguin, citizen of the town of Seiches, District of Bauge, in the Department of Maine et Loire, having exposed to me that he wishes to enjoy the property rights guaranteed by the Law of January 7, 1791, to the authors of inventions and discoveries in all kinds of industry, and consequently to obtain a patent for an invention that will last the term of ten years, to manufacture, sell and distribute throughout the Kingdom, sulphate or vitriol of soda, commonly called *Glauber's salt,*

24. "First, it is to be noted, that not only Metals, but also all Stones, and Bones themselves, refusing the solution of all corrosive Salts, may be radically dissolved by my Sal Mirabilis, and most things so dissolved, whether they be Metallic, Vegetable, or Mineral, put on a green colour, of some of which the greeness remaineth, but of others, in process of time, is changed into a yellow or red colour.

 Concerning this wonderful mutation and solution, I could write a great Volume, if I had not designed this Labour for another place, intending here only to describe the solution of Gold because another better cannot be found."

 Christopher Packe (transl. and ed.), THE WORKS OF THE HIGHLY EXPERIMENTED AND FAMOUS CHEMIST JOHN RUDOLPH GLAUBER: CONTAINING GREAT VARIETY OF CHOICE SECRETS IN MEDICINE AND ALCHEMY, at 264 (Thomas Milbourn, 1689). *Source*: < archive.org >.

and improperly *salt of Epsom*, of which he has declared to be the inventor, the improver and the wholesale importer, as it results from the report elaborated at the time of the filing with the Secretariat of the Directorate of the Department of Maine and Loire, dated August 12, one thousand seven hundred and ninety-one, of the request of Mr. Daguin, together with the explanatory memorandum, addressed by the applicant to the Directorate of Patents for Invention, the contents from which memorandum follow:

I, the undersigned, have the honor, by virtue of the decree of the National Assembly of December 30, one thousand seven hundred and ninety, to certify to the administrative body that the discovery envisioned in my request, presented to the secretariat of the Directorate of the Department of Maine et Loire, on the twenty-third of May, one thousand seven hundred and ninety-one, consists of the tests explained below on the materials, the description of which follows along with the way of operating; which materials are located in the Parish of Montoir, near Saint Nazaire, in Brittany, which the inhabitants extract to heat themselves, from a very well large neighboring piece of land, which they call Étiès; they produce a lot of ashes, which alone contain the interesting salt, and especially those from the Towns and Villages of Saint Joachim, Cameurin, Les Illes, Guersac, Vedrin, Mazin, Trignac, and other villages located in the parish of Montoir, and other places, where these materials are transported to burn, even as far as Nantes. It is by leaching these ashes in barrels or vats, prepared as if to leach saltpetered substances, which they carefully fill well, that these matters are produced at the first leaching, up to twenty degrees at the hydrometer; when one has a sufficient quantity of these waters, they are heated and passed over new ashes, and as soon as they reach twenty-five to thirty degrees, which is about all that the water can contain in salts in dissolution; they are then placed in barrels, and after they are cooled, which takes place after a few days in winter, they are taken out of the barrels to be passed again over new ashes; by continuing to leach the ashes in this way, the salts formed naturally in the barrels will be found. . . .

As the materials that produce these ashes are transported to burn in different places, where Daguin buys and has them collected, he begs and asks that these ashes from where he draws his salts cannot be taken away from him by any of those who seek and would try against the law, discover and counterfeit his salts.

Angers, twenty-third of May one thousand seven hundred and ninety-one. Signed Jean Daguin.

We have, in accordance with the mentioned Law of January 7, 1791, conferred by these presents, grant to Mr. Daguin a patent for invention to manufacture, sell and distribute throughout the kingdom, for the time and term of ten full and consecutive years from the date hereof, sulphate or vitriol of soda, commonly called *Glauber's salt*, and improperly *Epsom salt*, obtained by the means described above, and on the barrels containing it a stamp or label shall be affixed bearing these words: Patent for Invention, and the name of the author, so that, he and his successors enjoy the patent throughout the Kingdom, during the time provided above, all in accordance with the provisions of the Law of January 7, 1791.

We make very express inhibitions and prohibitions to all people from imitating or counterfeiting the mentioned salt, by whatever means and under whatever pretext. We wish that, for securing to Mr. Daguin the enjoyment of his Patent, a proclamation be made about it, so that no one can ignore it.

We command and order all Courts, Administrative Bodies and Municipalities to make Mr. Daguin and his heirs enjoy and use fully and peacefully the rights conferred by these presents, ceasing and making cease all disturbances and impediments to the contrary. We also command that, upon the first requisition that the Patentee presents, they have it transposed to their registry, read, published and displayed in their respective jurisdictions and departments, and executed during their term, as law of the Kingdom. In witness whereof the seal of the State will be affixed on the issuance of these present letters, in Paris, on the twenty-sixth day of August, one thousand seven hundred and ninety-one.

§ 2.36. A BRITISH INVENTOR, WILLIAM BODRUM, OBTAINS A PATENT FOR TWO OF HIS MEDICINES AND ADVERTISES THEIR QUASI-MIRACULOUS POWERS—1799

Adopting a market strategy that would become a common practice until the end of the nineteenth century in many countries, William Bodrum, after obtaining a patent for two medicines: Doctor Brodum's Botanical Syrup *and* Doctor Brodum's Nervous Cordial, *engaged in intensive advertisement through the publication and distribution of leaflets and placing of posters in various places in the city.*

The fact that Brodum's patent covers two different medicines should not come as a surprise. The rule of unity of invention, according to which patents should not protect more than one single inventive concept, was introduced in France later, at the beginning of the nineteenth century, as a fiscal measure, i.e., *as a way of ensuring higher revenues for the governmental agency in charge of examining and granting patents. Before the rule of inventive unity spread through the world (which happened fast because, as Adam Smith wrote, "There is no art which one government sooner learns of another than that of draining money from the pockets of the people."), patents could cover several inventions unrelated to each other. A famous patent granted in 1606 by Felipe III of Spain to Jerónimo de Ayanz y Beaumont, covered no less than fifty inventions on very different topics, such as devices applied to high furnaces, machines for desalination of seawater, diving equipment, and submarine vessels, among others.*

Brodum's patent specification

1799—Patent No. 2303

To all whom these presents shall come, I, William Brodum, of the Parish of Christ Church, in the County of Surry, Doctor of Physic, send greeting.

Whereas His most Excellent Majesty King George the Third did, by His Letters Patent under the Great Seal of Great Britain, bearing date at Westminster, the Tenth day of April, in the thirty-ninth year of His reign, give and grant unto me, the said William Brodum, His especial licence that I, the said William Brodum, during the term of years therein mentioned, should and lawfully might use, exercise, and vend, within England, Wales, and the Town of Berwick-upon-Tweed, my Invention or Discovery of a Medicine which I denominate "Doctor Brodum's Botanical Syrup" for the Cure of Scorbutic, Leprous, and Scrofulous Complaints, and various other Diseases to which the Human Body is subject; and also a Medicine which I denominate "Doctor Brodum's Nervous Cordial," for the Cure of Consumptive, Nervous, and Debilitated Constitutions, and People who have been in Hot Countries, and many other Complaints to which the Human Body is likewise subject in which said Letters Patent there is contained a proviso obliging me, the said William Brodum, by an instrument in writing under my hand and seal, to cause a particular description of the nature of my said Invention, and in what manner the same is to be performed, to be enrolled in His Majesty's High Court of Chancery within one calendar month after the date of the said recited Letters Patent, as in and by the same (relation being thereunto had) may more fully and at large appear.

Now know ye, that in compliance with the said proviso, I, the said William Brodum, do hereby declare that my said Invention or discovery is described in manner following, that is to say:—

To prepare my botanical syrup, take five pounds of sassafras, five pounds of guaiacum chips, ten pounds burdock roots, three pounds liquorice roots, five pounds red bark in roots, five pounds elm bark, one ounce cochineal, twelve middle-sized beetroots; boil them in sixteen gallons of river water until it evaporates to eight, then add to it one gallon steel wine.

To prepare my nervous cordial, take tincture of bark four gallons, tincture of cardamom two gallons, tincture aromatic two gallons, nutmeg water four gallons, spirit of lavender two gallons, and mix them together.

In witness whereof, I, the said William Brodum, have hereunto set my hand and seal, this Twenty-seventh day of April, in the year of our Lord One thousand seven hundred and ninety-nine.

Figure 21 A leaflet advertising Dr. Brodum's "nervous cordial and botanical syrup." Besides the list of drugstores where the two medicines could be found, and a list of cures obtained by their use, the leaflet contains a notice of a book authored by Dr. Brodum, entitled "A Guide to Old Age, Or a Cure for the Indiscretions of Youth," in which he advertises the antivenereal effects of his medicines. Printed in 1801.

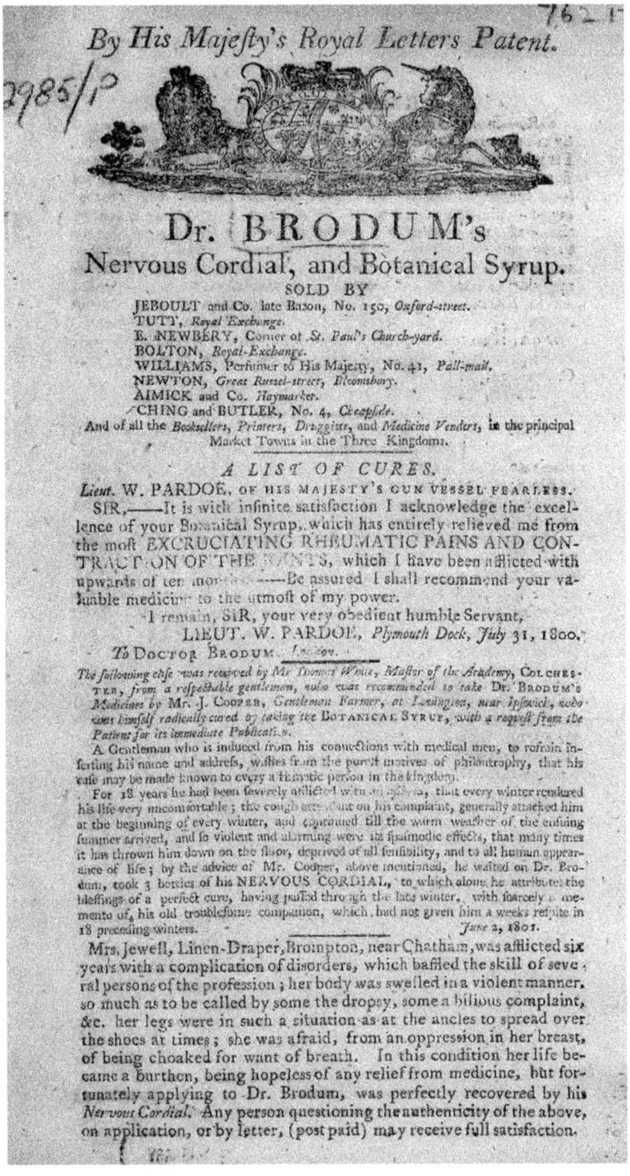

By His Majesty's Royal Letters Patent.

Dr. BRODUM's
Nervous Cordial, and Botanical Syrup.

SOLD BY

JEBOULT and Co. late Bazon, No. 150, *Oxford-street.*
TUTT, *Royal Exchange.*
E. NEWBERY, Corner of *St. Paul's Church-yard.*
BOLTON, *Royal-Exchange.*
WILLIAMS, Perfumer to His Majesty, No. 41, *Pall-mall,*
NEWTON, *Great Russel-street, Bloomsbury.*
AIMICK and Co. *Haymarket.*
CHING and BUTLER, No. 4, *Cheapside.*
And of all the *Booksellers, Printers, Druggists,* and *Medicine Venders,* in the principal Market Towns in the Three Kingdoms.

A LIST OF CURES.

Lieut. W. PARDOE, OF HIS MAJESTY'S GUN VESSEL FEARLESS.

SIR,——It is with infinite satisfaction I acknowledge the excellence of your Botanical Syrup, which has entirely relieved me from the most EXCRUCIATING RHEUMATIC PAINS AND CONTRACTION OF THE [illegible], which I have been afflicted with upwards of ten [illegible]——Be assured I shall recommend your valuable medicine to the utmost of my power.

I remain, SIR, your very obedient humble Servant,
LIEUT. W. PARDOE, *Plymouth Dock, July* 31, 1800.

To DOCTOR BRODUM, [illegible]

The following case was received by Mr [illegible]*, Master of the Academy,* COLCHESTER, *from a respectable gentleman, who was recommended to take* DR. BRODUM's *Medicines by* MR. J. COOPER, *Gentleman Farmer, at* [illegible]*, near Ipswich, who was himself radically cured by taking the* BOTANICAL SYRUP, *with a request from the Patient for its immediate Publication.*

A Gentleman who is induced from his connections with medical men, to refrain inserting his name and address, wishes from the purest motives of philanthropy, that his case may be made known to every asthmatic person in the kingdom.

For 18 years he had been severely afflicted with an asthma, that every winter rendered his life very uncomfortable; the cough attendant on his complaint, generally attacked him at the beginning of every winter, and continued till the warm weather of the ensuing summer arrived, and so violent and alarming were its spasmodic effects, that many times it has thrown him down on the floor, deprived of all sensibility, and to all human appearance of life; by the advice of Mr. Cooper, above mentioned, he waited on Dr. Brodum, took 3 bottles of his NERVOUS CORDIAL, to which alone he attributes the blessings of a perfect cure, having passed through the late winter, with scarcely a memento of, his old troublesome companion, which had not given him a weeks respite in 18 preceding winters. *June* 2, 1801.

Mrs. Jewell, Linen-Draper, Brompton, near Chatham, was afflicted six years with a complication of disorders, which baffled the skill of several persons of the profession; her body was swelled in a violent manner, so much as to be called by some the dropsy, some a bilious complaint, &c. her legs were in such a situation as at the ancles to spread over the shoes at times; she was afraid, from an oppression in her breast, of being choaked for want of breath. In this condition her life became a burthen, being hopeless of any relief from medicine, but fortunately applying to Dr. Brodum, was perfectly recovered by his *Nervous Cordial.* Any person questioning the authenticity of the above, on application, or by letter, (post paid) may receive full satisfaction.

§ 2.37. IN FRANCE, PHARMACISTS ARE REQUIRED TO EXPERIMENT AND DISCLOSE THEIR SECRET MEDICINES TO THE INSPECTORS, WHO WERE BOUND TO KEEP THEIR CONFIDENTIALITY—1802

In spite of the enactment, in 1791, of a patent statute that did not create obstacles to the patenting of medicines, in the early 1800s, there was no public discontent about their being kept in secrecy. Actually, the statute explicitly permitted that some patented inventions be kept secret. However, it seems that in the early nineteenth century, apparently the reaction was against abuses, which discredited honest pharmacists themselves, to the point that it was the College of Pharmacists that asked the Mayor of the Seine to put an end to those abuses by requiring that secret medicines be examined by the municipal inspectors (most probably pharmacists and/or physicians) before they could be advertised. It results from the following text that those medicines should not have their compositions revealed. On the contrary, the sample would be submitted for the record under a seal, which would preserve secrecy.

It should be noted that this statute, apparently of limited geographical scope, did not impose the prior approval of secret medicines for their commercialization, but rather for their advertisement. This particular measure was taken a few years later, on a national level, as we will see next.

L. André-Pontier, Histoire de la Pharmacie, Origine, Moyen Âge, Temps Modernes (excerpt)

. . . on 15 Frimaire (6 December 1801), the College of Pharmacy that had. . . the responsibility over and the right of supervision of pharmacy, realizing that the secret remedies devised by certain pharmacists, members of the College, with an aim of profit and speculation on public health, tended to become more numerous, obtained from the Mayor of the Seine a deliberation, as follows:

> Article 1. — No member of the College of Pharmacy may in the future have printed, published, distributed, or inserted in newspapers notices or posters that would have the purpose of announcing to the public the sale of drugs or medicines of any kind, both internal and external, without having been submitted to the committee for examination and obtained their prior approval. The author will be required: 1st to communicate the recipe of the secret to the commissioners, 2nd to prepare, under their eyes, the remedy or medicine in accordance with the recipe presented, 3rd to submit to the committee a sealed sample of the medicine to serve, if necessary, as an object of comparison, and in the event that the committee declares that the drug can be advertised to the public through newspapers, it will indicate the form of the advertisement, with which the author will be required to comply exactly.
>
> This deliberation, due to the initiative of pharmacists, has become the decision of Mayor Frochot, dated of the 6 Germinal An X (27 March 1802), on secret remedies.

§ 2.38. FRANCE REQUIRES THE PRIOR EXAMINATION OF SECRET MEDICINES, SETS A MECHANISM OF ACQUISITION AND DISCLOSURE OF SOME OF THEM, AND BANS THE TRADE OF THOSE THAT WERE NOT APPROVED—AUGUST 18, 1810

A Decree of 1810 attempted to put some order in the business of secret medicines in France, eliminating the risks that frequently their uncontrolled trade caused to public health.

The system required the examination of secret medicines as a precondition for the authorization of their commercialization. The secret compositions, therefore, had to be communicated to a special committee. In the case, the committee approved the medicine concerning both their safety and efficacy, a patent (i.e., *an administrative authorization) would be issued authorizing its commercialization. In some cases, the committee could recommend the acquisition of the secret by the government, in which case the composition would be disclosed and all registered apothecaries would be authorized to sell it.*

As said above, the system of acquisition of secret formulae was not very successful because of a lack of money. So, in practice, it did not aim at putting an end to the trade of secret medicines, but to the trade of medicines, secret or not, whose advertisement and sale were not previously approved. Therefore, in legalistic terms, a medicine ceased to be secret when its composition was communicated to the committee and approved—even if that communication did not mean the public disclosure of the composition.

However, as one of the following texts shows, the Court of Rouen has given another interpretation to this rule and has given immunity from the provisions of the 1810 Decree to a pharmacist who had advertised and sold a medicine without the committee's prior approval (hence, he had infringed the rule), because its composition had been published and its ingredients were well known. To oppose the sale of such medicines was illogical and raised an obstacle to the technical progress of pharmacy, the Court said.

By contrast, the owner of a patent for a medicine who offered it for sale in advertisements published in the written press was not excused from infringing the statute, as the Court of Liège (Belgium) decided in 1854. A report of this case can be found below. It is worth noticing that the Belgian statute of March 12, 1818, which the Court applied, did not employ the term "secret remedies" by contrast with the French regulations that extended to the Low Countries and were abrogated by the 1818 Act. Nevertheless, the Court of Liège used that term. The reason was that, after the 1810 Decree entered into force in France (and applied to the Low Countries until 1818), the term "secret remedies" meant medicines not previously approved by the competent authorities, regardless of their really being secret or not. The specific provision (art. 17 of the 1818 statute) that the Court of Liège applied reads:

> *No compound drug, under any name whatsoever, may be sold or offered for sale except by persons who are authorized thereto by law or by us [the king] and in accordance with the instructions to be issued on this matter, under the penalty of a fine of 50 florins.*

The 1810 Decree was not, in reality, a consolidation of the practices established after Louis XIII, which consisted of the acquisition of secret compositions from pharmacists. Indeed, in several cases, the pharmacists, in addition to the financial and dignitary awards they received, were granted a privilege to continue making and selling them with exclusivity for a certain period. These were industrial privileges for all effects, several examples of which can be seen above. The 1810 Decree did not provide for that exclusivity.

§ 2.38.1. The French statute concerning the examination and acquisition of secret medicines

Imperial Decree of August 18, 1810

Napoleon, etc. . . .

Several inventors of scientific remedies for various diseases, or of substances useful in the art of healing, have obtained permission to sell them, keeping the secret of their composition.

Others still ask for similar authorizations for such cases.

From the account that we have ordered, we have recognized that, if these remedies are useful in the relief of diseases, our constant care for the good of our subjects must lead us to spread their knowledge and use, by purchasing from inventors the recipe for their composition; that it is for the possessors of such secrets a duty to lend themselves to their publication, and that their eagerness should be the greater the more they have confidence in their discovery.

Consequently, wishing on the one hand to spread the light and increase the means useful for the art of healing, and on the other to prevent charlatanism from imposing a tribute on credulity, or causing fatal accidents, by distributing drugs without virtue or unknown substances, and of which one can, for this reason, make a use harmful to the health or dangerous to the life of our subjects;

Our State Council having been heard,

We have decreed and decree the following:

Title I.

Remedies whose sale has already been authorized.

Art. 1. The permissions granted to the inventors or owners of remedies or compositions of which they alone have the recipe, for selling and distributing these remedies, will cease to have their effect as of January 1st next.

Art. 2. In the meantime, the inventors or owners will deliver, if they deem it appropriate, to our Minister of the Interior, who will communicate it only to the committees mentioned below, the recipes of their remedies or compositions, with a notice of the diseases to which they can be applied, and of the experiments that have already been made.

Art. 3. Our minister will appoint a committee composed of five people, three of whom will be chosen among the professors of our medical schools, for the purpose: 1st of examining the composition of the remedy and to recognize if its administration cannot be dangerous or harmful in certain cases; 2nd if this remedy is good in itself, if it has produced and still produces useful effects for humanity; 3rd what price should be paid, for his secret, to the inventor of the remedy recognized as useful, by proportioning this price: 1—to the merit of the discovery; 2—to the benefits that have been obtained from it, or that can be expected for the relief of the humankind; 3—to the personal advantages that the inventor has derived from it or could still expect to derive.
Art. 4. In the event of a complaint from the inventors, a committee of review will be appointed by our Minister of the Interior, for the purpose of examining the work of the first committee, hearing the parties and giving a new opinion.
Art. 5. Our Minister of the Interior will submit to us, according to the account that will be provided to him by each committee, and after having heard the inventors, a report on each of these secret remedies, and will take our orders on the sum to be granted to each inventor or owner.
Art. 6. Our minister will then make a contract with the inventors. The contract will be approved by our State Council, and the secret published without delay.

Title II

Remedies whose distribution has not yet been authorized.

Art. 7. Anyone who has discovered a remedy and wants it to be used, will give the recipe to our Minister of the Interior, as provided in art. 2. Afterwards, the same procedure sated in arts. 3, 4, and 5, shall apply to it.

Title III.

General provisions.

Art. 8. No permission will henceforth be granted to the authors of any remedy, simple or compounded, the composition of which they would like to keep secret, except under the procedure provided for in Titles I and II.

§ 2.38.2. Case law setting the definition of "secret remedies" for the purposes of the application of the statute of 1810

Public Prosecutor v. Blancard and others

Royal Court of Rouen

January 27, 1852

The public prosecutor appealing from a judgment delivered by the Criminal Court of Rouen, on December 9, 1841, in the case against: Hypolyte Blancard, aged 31, pharmacist, residing in Paris, Seine St.-Germain street, no. 49, born in Sens; . . .

Regarding Blancard:

> Whereas he is being prosecuted only for having sold secret remedies; this, in fact, is the textual prohibition of the law of 21 Germinal Year Eleven (April 11, 1803) and of the decree of August 18, 1810;
>
> That if these laws and decree did not say what is meant by secret remedies, it is obvious, from the natural and rational sense of the words, from the very definition of the DICTIONNAIRE DES SCIENCES MÉDICALES, finally according to the text of the preamble and of articles one and eight of the aforementioned decree, that by that we must understand the remedies whose composition has not been disclosed, whose composition the inventors *keep secret*, and of which they *alone* have the recipe;
>
> Given that the medicines seized in Blancard's drugstore, and which are known under the name *Le Roy medicine*, have long since become *public*, that their composition, as regards each of its elements, with the doses that constitute it, was published and printed in 1813, by surgeon Le Roy in a work that has been reproduced since, until the fourteenth edition; that it has been deposited with its formulae, since 1819, with the Ministry of the Interior for the sole purpose of its greater publicity; that thus made known and accessible to all, it could be sold by any pharmacist; that in fact it was ordered in Paris or elsewhere by doctors who have approved its recipe; that it has been inserted in several formularies of pharmacy, in particular in that published by Mr. Bouchardat and in that of Doctor Jourdan; that it has frequently become the subject of Dissertations publicly defended before the Faculty of Medicine of Paris; in short, that it has fallen into the *public domain*;
>
> Whereas in such a state of affairs the medicines in question cannot be qualified as secret remedies; that it does not matter for the penal application of the law of germinal year eleven and of the decree of August 18, 1810, that this composition has not been inserted in the Pharmaceutical Codex, published under the authority of the Faculty of Medicine of Paris, since the mentioned laws do not ban the sale of the remedy not listed in the Codex, but the sale of the *secret remedy*, and that finally it is impossible to maintain that a published remedy, disclosed by all possible means, is a *secret remedy*, otherwise one would throw into the law the strangest confusion of words and ideas; that the lack of approval by the School of Medicine of a remedy whose composition has been made public can never make it a *secret remedy*; that in this regard the aforementioned legislation does not grant

any jurisdiction to the Academy of Medicine; that it is restricted by the decree of 1810 to *secret remedies* only;

Whereas the inclusion of a new formula in the Codex required as a condition of the lawful sale of that formula would be nothing less than a violent obstacle placed on the thought and the constantly progressive genius of men of science; that a kind of line drawn, to forbid him, under penalty of a fine, from going beyond the known formulas, at least until a new publication of the Codex; that such a claim, which is neither of our time nor of our civilization, would no less harm the interests of humanity, than it would be rejected by the impossibility of its execution, by the immense number of culprits it would create in the person of the very leaders of science, of those who honor it the most by the discoveries of their genius, unceasing discoveries, of every day, and of which a multitude, as the numerous examples cited attest it in oral argument, does not appear in the Codex formulae; that such consequences would suffice to ruin this interpretation of the law;

Whereas it is not a question here of appreciating the merit or the usefulness of the drug in question, that this question is solely within the domain of those skilled in the art; that moreover, subjected several times to the experiments of skillful chemists, and in particular of the famous Vauquelin, this drug has been recognized, not only as *not containing any substance harmful to health, but even as consisting of all the elements recorded in all the works of pharmacy*;

Whereas, sued, it is true, with great perseverance, before several courts, Le Roy and his adherents have always obtained from justice the recognition and protection of their right, just as it had been formally recognized by the Minister of the Interior in a circular of July 19, 1823, addressed to all the mayors; that it is thus that it was confirmed by various sovereign decisions, in particular by a judgment of the Royal Court of Orleans of May 18, 1819, then by a judgment of the Criminal of appeals of the Seine, which did not even undergo the challenge of an appeal; that in such a state of affairs and in view of the acts of the administrative and judicial authorities, the conviction of Blancard would have something more than rigorous; that it would in some way injure the public faith, the respect and the faith due to the judgments of justice;

Whereas, moreover, during the seizure of the medicines in question, and afterwards, during the enquiry, it was declared by Blancard that he sold this composition only upon the prescription formulated by a doctor, among others of Doctor Signoret; that this assertion, confirmed by the latter, has not been denied by any of the elements of the procedure, that this mode of operating is in conformity with the rules set by the law of 21 germinal year eleven, article 32;

The court, accepting the appeal, confirms the judgment of first instance. . .

.

This judgment is in accordance with the case law adopted by a large number of Courts and Tribunals. In fact, the Advocate General said in 1821:—"Any medicinal preparation must be considered as a secret remedy, the real name of which, if it is simple, or whose names and doses, if it is composed, are not known; whose formula is not part of the formulary drawn up by the Faculty, or which, not being printed in any formulary, treaty or medical journal, remains the property of its inventor, is not available to other doctors or surgeons, and cannot be performed by all pharmacists indiscriminately. "

(L'Officine, at 529).

"One cannot classify in the order of secret remedies those that are composed of known elements, otherwise medical science would be deprived of the means of improvement."

(Montpellier Court of First Instance, August 16, 1831).

"Artisanal remedies whose existence the printed brochures reveal cannot be considered secret in the legal sense."

(Civil court of Blois, June 18, 1831).

"A remedy whose formula has been published is no longer a secret."

(Tribunal de Lyon, February 5, 1828).

§ 2.38.3. According to a Belgian court, the offer for sale of a secret medicine was, in itself, an unlawful act

Demanet v. Public prosecutor's office

Court of Liège, 1854

Secret Remedies.—Offer for Sale.—Publication by newspapers.

The law of March 19, 1818, on the art of healing, which prohibits any unauthorized person from offering a secret remedy for sale, applies to the offer for sale through newspapers as well as to that made verbally.

The laws of *2l germinal an xi* (April 11, 1803) and *29 pluviôse an xiii* (February 18, 1805) cannot be applied in this case because they have been implicitly repealed.

Mr. Demanet has obtained a patent for a stomach liquor.

He had certificates printed in the Journal de Liège, by which various people attest that the use they have made of this liquor cured them or relieved them of the diseases they were suffering from. He was brought on this charge and two others (unnecessary to indicate) before the court of Neufchâteau, which condemned him for the following reasons:

Whereas by having the certificates in question printed in a newspaper, the defendant's aim was obviously to create in the public the reputation that the liquor of which he is the inventor is a remedy for several ailments, which assuredly had been ignored until then and could not be suspected from the name of *stomachic liquor* that was given to it in the patent;

That therefore, by the fact of this publication by printed advertisements, the accused has announced a secret remedy and committed the offense provided for by article 56 of the law of April 11, 1803 and incurred the penalty determined by the law of February 18, 1805;

For these reasons, the court condemns. . . . "

- Appeal by the accused.

Judgement.

The Court;—Whereas the law of 1818 (article 17), while forbidding any unauthorized person from offering a secret remedy for sale, applies to the offer for sale by way of newspapers as well as to that made verbally; that thus the defendant's act is envisaged and punished by this law, and not by those of 21 germinal an xi (article 56) and 29 pluviôse an xiii, which the law of 1818 has implicitly repealed;

For these reasons, confirms.

May 5, 1844.—Court of Liège.

Chamber of appeals—Lecocq.

§ 2.39. SEIDLITZ POWDERS—THE PATENT FOR THE INVENTION OF THE SEIDLITZ POWDERS, A VERY SUCCESSFUL MEDICINE, HELD INVALID BECAUSE OF THE DECEPTIVE NATURE OF ITS SPECIFICATION

In the specification of his invention patented in 1815 (patent no. 3,954), Thomas Field Savory (? -1847), an English pharmacist and druggist, designated his medicine as "Seidlitz powders." The powders gained so much commercial success that their name became synonymous with a mild laxative.

But Savory's success did not result from the patent only. Actually, several years before the end of its term, the patent was held unenforceable by an English court because of the misleading nature of its specification. The reason was that the specification mentioned a number of processes for making the product, which, after all, were not necessary.

Thus, Savory had to rely on advertisement and reputation. The patent, nevertheless, has given him some competitive advantage. It is undisputable that the head start Savory gained during those years before his patent was challenged served him in acquiring that reputation.

In 1797, Savory joined Paytherus, a London apothecary, in partnership, and the two constituted the firm Paytherus, Savory, & Co. Their drugstore was located in Bond Street—a very prestigious London address. Paytherus retired in 1811, and Savory associated with Thomas Moore. The society was renamed as Savory and Moore Ltd. The business soon expanded and opened two other branches in London. In subsequent years, they merged with other drugstores, thus acquiring considerable business dimension. An article on the history of the society published in 1928 in the magazine The Chemist and Druggist *starts by saying: "Though healthy competition is an excellent stimulant in business affairs, there are times where greater success is obtained by amalgamation of interests." The article made particular reference to the 1928 merger of Savory and Moore Ltd. with John Bell & Croyden Ltd., two of the most successful drug firms of London, but it mentions other acquisitions that the company made soon after the death of Thomas Field Savory. ["A Chapter of History — Some particulars relating to the amalgamation of two old-established London houses,"* The Chemist and Druggist, *vol. 108, January 28, 1928, at 104, 105* [*Source:* < *wellcomelibrary.org* >].

§ 2.39.1. Specification of Thomas Field Savory's patent on the Seidlitz powders

August 23, 1815 AD—No. 3954.

Savory, Thomas Field.—The combination of a neutral salt or powder which possesses all the properties of the medicinal spring of Seidlitz, in Germany, under the name of the Seidlitz powders.

To all to whom these presents shall come, etc. Now know ye, that in compliance with the said proviso, I the said Thomas Field Savory do hereby declare that the nature of my said invention, and the manner in which the same is to be performed, is described and ascertained in the following explanation thereof.

The process for making the Seidlitz powders, as invented and sold by me the said Thomas Field Savory, at No. 136, New Bond-street. — Recipe No. 1.—Take of subcarbonate of soda twenty pounds, of supertartrate of potash, twenty-four pounds; dissolve the subcarbonate of soda in twenty-five gallons of boiling water, and add supertartrate of potash; filter the solution through paper, and evaporate it in a gentle heat until a pellicle appears on the surface; then set it by to crystallize; redissolve these crystals thus formed in six times their weight of boiling water: the solution must again be filtered, evaporated, and crystallized, and afterwards reduced to a fine powder.

Recipe No. 2.—Take of subcarbonate of soda one hundred pounds, carbonate of ammonia twenty-five pounds; expose the subcarbonate of soda to a heat sufficiently strong to liquefy it; then add the carbonate of ammonia in powder, and with a heat of 212° dry the salt, and pass it through a fine sieve.

Recipe No. 3.—Take of supertartrate of potash one hundred pounds, mix it with thirty pounds of finely powdered chalk, and add it by degrees to one hundred and sixty gallons of boiling water; stir it for some time, and when the tartrate of lime has subsided pour off the supernatent liquor, and wash the residuum repeatedly with cold water. To the tartrate of lime thus formed add thirty pounds of sulphuric acid, previously diluted with eight times its weight of water; stir the mixture frequently stir during twenty-four hours; and, after having separated the acid from the sulphate of lime, by means of strong pressure, evaporate it in Wedgwood's dishes, over a sand heat, till a pellicle appears on the surface; then set it by to crystallize: these crystals are to be dissolved in boiling water, filtered through white filtering paper, and again crystallized.

Each dose of the Seidlitz powders consists of two scruples of Recipe No. 3, finely powdered, and dissolved in half a pint of spring water; to which are added two drachms of Recipe No. 1, and two scruples of Recipe No. 2 (previously mixed): they must be stirred together, and taken while effervescing.

In witness whereof, &c.

§ 2.39.2. Decision of the Court of King's Bench holding that Savory's patent was unenforceable due to its flawed specification

Savory v. Price

In the Court of King's Bench.—December 17, 1823

This was an action to recover damages for the infringement of a patent granted to the plaintiff, on the 23rd day of August, 1815, for a combined neutral salt, or powder, which possesses all the properties of the medicinal spring at Steidlitz, in Germany, and which invention is sold under the name of Seidlitz powder. It was objected to the specification, that it described processes which were well known, producing articles which were well known, and then combined the products in making "Patent Seidlitz Powders;" that any person reading the specification would imagine that these complex processes must be gone into in order to produce the result desired. And it was stated by the plaintiff's witnesses, that the modes pointed out in the specification for making the articles described in the first, second, and third, recipes, were not the best for that purpose, nor those which were usually followed. That a person might purchase the separate articles at any chemist's shop cheaper than he could make them by the processes described. The result of the first recipe would be Rochelle salts; the result of the second recipe would be carbonate, formerly called supercarbonate, of soda; and the result of the third recipe would be tartaric acid; but before the date of the patent it was not usual to mix an acid and an alkali to produce an effervescent draught. It was the mixture of these articles which ought to have been claimed, without misleading people by making it appear that three difficult processes were first to be carried on, and which were not the best for making the three articles, which were well known, and separately could not form any right under the patent.

Lord Chief Justice Abbott.—It is the duty of any one to whom a patent is granted, to point out in his specification the plainest and most easy way of producing that for which he claims a monopoly; and to make the public acquainted with the mode which he himself adopts. If a person, on reading the specification, would be led to suppose a laborious process necessary to the production of any one of the ingredients, when, in fact, he might go to a chemist's shop and buy the same thing as a separate simple part of the compound, the public are misled. If the results of the recipes, or of any one of them, may be bought in shops, this specification, tending to make people believed an elaborate process essential to the invention, cannot be supported. The plaintiff must be nonsuited.

§ 2.40. A CHARITABLE NORTH AMERICAN PHYSICIAN FELL IN CONTRADICTION: IN A BOOK, HE OFFERED THE SECRET RECIPES OF SEVERAL MEDICINES EFFECTIVE AGAINST THE EPIDEMIC OF CHOLERA FOR FREE BUT CLAIMED COPYRIGHT EXCLUSIVITY IN THE WORK

Confirming that in times of epidemics, it is not common for inventors to claim ownership in new medicines or methods of treatment, in the eighteenth and nineteenth centuries, a significant number of physicians published recommendations and advice on how to treat some sorts of medical conditions resulting from infections acquired during epidemics. Just to mention two works that dealt especially with medical conditions associated with epidemics, having been widely circulated: in 1721, in London, an alchemist, Eugenius Philaletes (generally accepted as being the pseudonym of Thomas Vaughan) published A Treatise of the Plague, *containing "A rare Collection of a great many Recipes of very valuable Medicines, made use of in the Plague by the greatest Physicians in the World, and published for the General Good of Mankind, especially the meaner Sort." (James Holland, 1721); and, in the same year, in Paris, Jean Adrien Helvetius, physician to the Queen, by instructions of Colbert, published* Remèdes contre la Peste *(Pierre-Aug. Le Mercier, 1721), in which he described a number of medicines that had been tested and used by several physicians of Marseille, where the Great Plague had erupted one year earlier.*

Following these examples, almost one century later, a North American author, Lewis Merlin, took the initiative of publishing a book containing recipes of medicines that could be helpful to treat diseases resulting from the cholera epidemic that in 1817 affected the entire United States. Indeed, the book contains a chapter entitled "Of the Plague and other Contagious Diseases, and many Sovereign Remedies, always used with the greatest success; as well preventives against the contagion, at to cure it whenever the disease has taken place." On the cover page, the author claims that the publication was made "for the benefit of humanity." One might expect that there would be no pecuniary interest in such endeavors.

This topic is of great interest in the times of pandemic in which we live today. Making medicines (or the information about them) available costs money. Moreover, it is the operation of commercial businesses that makes such availability possible. So the element of profit can never be completely eliminated unless the medicines are distributed by governments. However, this governmental distribution also entails costs, which must be covered through taxes. As the old saying goes, "There ain't no such thing as a free lunch." The difference is that both governments and charitable organizations will not impose mark-ups or capture profits.

And yet Lewis Merlin did claim copyright exclusivity, in spite of his pledge of working in favor of "the benefit of humanity." The author has offered a somewhat strange explanation for that, alleging that the profits obtained with the publication would be used in printing a special edition, which would be sent to remote settlements (in 1818, the United States was in full expansion westwards). Merlin said that the recipes contained in the book had been collected in Europe by a "Benevolent Society," but did not provide for any information about the nature of that organization. Did it really exist?

THE TREASURE OF HEALTH, by Lewis Martin (excerpts)

[Copyright notice]

District of Pennsylvania, to wit:

Be it remembered, That, on the sixth day of February, in the forty-third year of the Independence of the United States of America, A.D. 1819, Lewis Merlin, of the said district, hath deposited in this office the title of a book, the right whereof he claims as proprietor, in the words following, to wit:

> The Treasure of Health, or a wonderful Collection of the most valuable Secrets in Medicine, for the cure of all diseases, wounds, and other accidents to which the human body is subject, with the method of preparing, and instructions for using the necessary remedies. Also, the best preservatives against the plague, pestilential fevers, small pox, and other kinds of contagious diseases. Discovered after much research and experience, by the most skillful physicians in Europe, and employed with the greatest success, and unknown till the present time in the United States. Carefully collected by a benevolent Society in Europe. Faithfully translated from the French and other foreign languages, and published for the benefit of humanity, by Lewis Merlin.

In conformity to the act of the congress of the United Sates, entitled "An act for the encouragement of learning, by securing the copies of maps, charts, and books, to the authors and proprietors of such copies, during the times therein mentioned." And also to the act, entitled "An act supplementary to an act entitled 'An act for the encouragement of learning, by securing the copies of maps, charts, and books, to the authors and proprietors of such copies during the times therein mentioned,' and extending the benefits thereof to the arts of designing, engraving, and etching historical and other prints."

Caldwell, Clerk of the District of Pennsylvania.

[Publisher's preliminary note]

Mahy's Approved Plaster Cloth.

If we have not made mention in our proposals of this plaster, it is because we have deemed it unnecessary to distinguish it from the other secrets of this nature, of which are far superior to it on account of the great virtues they possess, and which were unknown to this present lime in the United States of America. It will only be necessary to prepare and try them, to be convinced of this truth.

Nevertheless, in order to deserve the confidence that an enlightened public has been willing to place in this work, the great usefulness of which cannot be too much appreciated by the heads of families; and to satisfy at the same time the request of many of our subscribers on account of this wonderful remedy; we can positively assure, without fear of being contradicted, that amongst the extraordinary secrets of balsams, ointments, and plasters contained in this inestimable collection, will be found the true and genuine receipt known within the United States under the name and denomination of Approved Mahy's Plaster Cloth, but called in France by its real name, Divine Plaster Cloth.

In giving to the public a receipt so well known, so recommended by its virtues, so salutary to suffering humanity, and so much approved and recommended by the most skillful physicians on this continent, we hope to put a stop to that spirit of self-interest, which those who are in possession of it exercise over all the community generally, by selling this Mahy's Plaster Cloth at an exorbitant price, considering the trifling expense that will cost to procure the drugs for its composition, and the little trouble it requires to prepare it.

The original receipt was published in France, for the benefit of all mankind, in the year 1713. This wonderful remedy has never been in that country an object of a pecuniary speculation.

The Publisher.

N. B. We have been informed, that several persons in easy circumstances have declined subscribing to this work, in expectation of borrowing it from some of their friends, who might be in possession of it, and copy put of it the receipt of Mahy's Approved Plaster Cloth, and others that might be useful to them. We hope our subscribers will be so good as not to countenance such a stinginess, because by refusing to lend it, they will not only do a charitable act towards suffering humanity, but aid us moreover, in fulfilling the benevolent views of the society, which are to appropriate the profit arising out of this publication, in printing a particular edition of a sufficient number of copies of this work, to be sent and distributed, gratis, to poor families residing in the new settlements on this continent, who, owing to their local situation, are entirely deprived of all medical assistance.

- The receipt of this plaster was sold in the year 1802 or 1803 by Mr. Mahy, alias Favras, to some persons in this city for a sum of 400 dollars, and some time after this same receipt was likewise sold to T. W. Dyott, by another person, by the name of Bouchony Lordonet, for a like sum.

[Final paragraphs of the Introduction]

We will conclude by recommending this rare and precious work to the heads of families, to be kept as a valuable treasure, and particularly to farmers, and those who reside in the country, who, owing to their situation, are often deprived of medical assistance in cases of the most urging necessity. It is, likewise, of the greatest utility to physicians, surgeons, apothecaries, ministers and pastors of congregations, who are by their profession obliged to visa the sick; it is also strongly recommended to captains and masters of vessels, seafaring men, and other travelers who frequent hot climates, where pestilential fevers very often prevail, and are always dangerous to strangers; in fine, to all those persons who wish to preserve their own health.

This work is intended entirely for the benefit of all mankind; no pecuniary speculation is the object of its publication. The benevolent society that gives it to the public, animated with a desire to relieve suffering humanity, and wishing as much as possible to attain the end of its laudable purpose, has directed that the profits which may arise out of this publication, shall be employed in printing a particular edition of a sufficient number of copies, to be sent and distributed, gratis, to poor families residing in the new settlements within the United States of America, who, owing to their local situations, are deprived of all medical assistance.

Figure 22 The cover page of Merlin's book, containing the "best preservatives against the plague," "published for the benefit of humanity." Philadelphia, 1819. Source: < archive.org >.

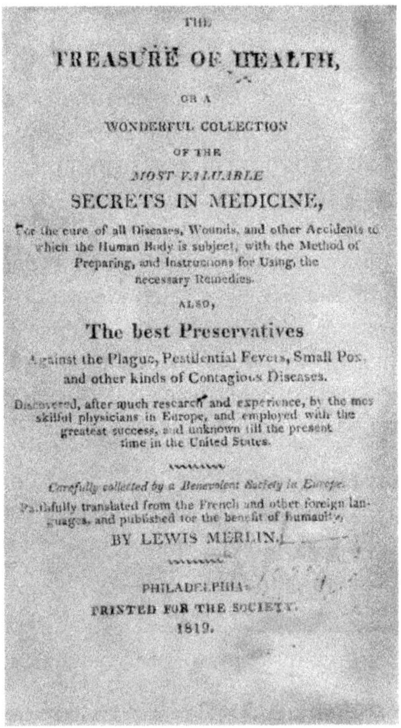

THE

TREASURE OF HEALTH,

OR A

WONDERFUL COLLECTION

OF THE

MOST VALUABLE

SECRETS IN MEDICINE,

For the cure of all Diseases, Wounds, and other Accidents to which the Human Body is subject, with the Method of Preparing, and Instructions for Using, the necessary Remedies.

ALSO,

The best Preservatives

Against the Plague, Pestilential Fevers, Small Pox, and other kinds of Contagious Diseases.

Discovered, after much research and experience, by the most skilful physicians in Europe, and employed with the greatest success, and unknown till the present time in the United States.

Carefully collected by a Benevolent Society in Europe.

Faithfully translated from the French and other foreign languages, and published for the benefit of humanity,

BY LEWIS MERLIN.

PHILADELPHIA:

PRINTED FOR THE SOCIETY.

1819.

§ 2.41. THE KING OF PORTUGAL, JOÃO VI, GRANTS A BRAZILIAN APOTHECARY A PRIVILEGE FOR THE EXCLUSIVE IMPORTATION AND SALE OF MEDICINAL WATER IN THE PROVINCE OF RIO DE JANEIRO

As noted in FROM BABYLON TO THE SILICON VALLEY,[25] *in 1809, the Prince Regent of Portugal and Brazil (future João VI), then residing in Rio de Janeiro, approved a statute, clearly inspired and influenced by the British Statute of Monopolies, providing for the grant of patents with the term of fourteen years. Besides machines, the patents also covered "invention in the arts," a term which would comprise pharmaceutical inventions. However, during the period the decree of 1809 was in force*—i.e., *until 1830—no patent for a medicine appears in the records of the Court in charge of examining patent applications.*

But in 1820, the king granted a patent for the importation of Água das Caldas, a medicinal water then in much vogue. Today the water is still extracted in Caldas da Rainha, with therapeutic applications in the respiratory system and some other ailments, such as rheumatism. Significantly, the patent does not mention the Decree of 1809, which implies that it was an isolated measure.

Decree—March 7, 1820

It grants José Luiz Mendes & Co., Apothecaries resident in this Court, the privilege for selling water from Caldas.

In view of what José Luiz Mendes & Co., licensed apothecaries residing in this Court, represented to me and how convenient it is to public health that the water of Caldas da Rainha be sold in this Court and in the Province [of Rio de Janeiro]: I am pleased to grant them the exclusive privilege for a period of 10 years, so that during that term, only in this Province, they can order, with the purpose of selling, water from Caldas, under the duty of selling it to the public at a reasonable price, and giving them the assistance they need to be well packed and transported regularly. The Desk of Affairs of the Palace having so understood, have it executed with the necessary orders. Palace of Rio de Janeiro, on March 7, 1820.

With the signature of the King, Our Lord.

§ 2.42. JOSEPH METTEMBERG (17?-1840), FRENCH PHYSICIAN AND INVENTOR OF A MEDICINE AGAINST SCABIES, STRUGGLED TO SECURE PROPRIETARY INTERESTS IN HIS INVENTION

Around 1795, Joseph Mettemberg, military surgeon, responded to a request from the leaders of the French army to find a solution for alleviating scabies that was afflicting hundreds of thousands of soldiers every year. He developed a composition to be applied as a cosmetic on the skin, which, he claimed, completely cured the condition. After leaving the army, he dedicated his time to pursue a business around the making of his

25. See *supra* note 2, at 43-44.

medicine, which he named "Quintessence Antipsorique" or "Eau the Mettemberg," and its commercial distribution in glass vials.

Even though the French patent law of 1791 did not exclude pharmaceuticals from patentability, as noted above, rarely would inventors apply for patents for ensuring exclusivity in the making and selling of medicines. Instead, the majority of them relied on the mechanism that had been successfully used by French pharmaceutical inventors for several centuries—secrecy. As such, secret medicines might be eligible for the benefits created by the 1810 Decree, which provided that, for those approved, the government might pay a determined sum in exchange for the disclosure of their formulae (see § 2.38).

The problem was that, in order to be eligible for that reward, the medicine should go through an examination as to its efficacy and safety by a technical committee—which, in the case of Mettemberg's water, issued a negative recommendation. The reason, it seems, was that the Medical School of Paris, having been requested to examine the medicine, asked Mettemberg to communicate to it the medicine's formula, which the inventor refused to do. Consequently, Mettemberg's request for remuneration was turned down, and, worse, he was prohibited from continuing making and selling the product. Nevertheless, because Mettemberg had never revealed the product's secret composition, he was able to circumvent that prohibition by offering his medical services to those who wished to use his cure for scabies. This is something similar to what we call today, in patent terms, product-by-process protection, i.e., *having exclusivity in the process, the exclusive proprietor of that process indirectly acquires exclusivity in the product.*

Moreover, with obstinate enthusiasm, Mettemberg did not spare efforts to ensure the commercial, if not medical, success of his invention. On the one hand, he would author a number of booklets defending the scientific merits of Mettemberg's water and attacking his detractors. He even sued one of those detractors, who had accused him of being a "charlatan." Mettemberg won the case because charlatans, under the law, were those that sold secret medicines without submitting them to the rules set by the 1810 Decree—which Mettemberg did, albeit unsuccessfully.

Mettemberg would also seek the administrative permission to sell his product in other countries, where, it seems, he had no enemies. Accordingly, he got permissions in Spain (1809) and Prussia (1814).

*Moreover, Mettemberg would engage in a vast advertisement campaign for his product, which has led to the notoriety of his brand (*i.e., *his own name).*

And finally, Mettemberg applied for and obtained a patent for his invention in a country where, as also noted above, there were no restrictions, legal or practical, to the patentability of medicines: Great Britain. On February 26, 1825 (about thirty years after the making of the invention), Mettemberg was issued a patent for his medicine as well as for a method of using it as a cosmetic (Patent no. 5,112). However, under British law, Mettemberg was required to disclose his invention, which he did by filing the complete specifications on July 31, 1825.

Importantly, the British patent mentioned the medicine's trademark: "Mettemberg's water."[26] *Moreover, following the general formula employed in British patents at that time—with a still strong reminiscence of the Middle Ages—Mettemberg's patent granted him the right to make and sell the medicine in England for the term of fourteen years. More than the exclusivity in the making, Mettemberg was particularly interested in that right, which allowed him to have access to the British market.*

So here we have a case of an inventor who had to work around the absence of patent protection in France in the nineteenth century for a medicine he invented, and who, moreover, was unable to secure a financial reward. His strategy around the exploitation of a trade secret gave him a very extended period of exclusivity—much more extended, indeed, than if he had applied for a patent.

§ 2.42.1. Extract from the Report on the Public Experiments Made in Paris, with the Antipsoric Quintessence, known as *Eau de Mettemberg*, renewed in the Hospices de Lille, and confirmed in the Hospitals of Lyon, by order of the Government

1800

This Water is tawny in color, it becomes frothy when stirred; it is cloudy and slowly allows a reddish sediment to settle. Its smell is slightly aromatic; its bitter taste approaches that of absinthe, associated with a very pronounced metallic flavor. Its specific weight is 1,027, etc. etc. The vials [containing the samples of the medicine] have been recognized as having a round seal on the stopper, with the initials of Mr. Mettemberg in the center, and as legend, *Eau de Mettemberg*; on the body of the vase itself, another stamp having as legend around the initials, these words *Experientia judex*, and that of the Municipality, both affixed on an Label indicative of the liquor contained in the vial.

26. We saw before that mentioning the trademark in the patent specifications in England at a later stage would create a problem in connection with securing its exclusivity. See § 1.25.2.

Figure 23 Poster advertising the Eau de Mettemberg in France.

§ 2.42.2. Observations on the safety of the use of *Eau de Mettemberg*

Découverte Importante pour la Santé Publique, ou Méthode Particulière Pour guérir les Métastases de la Gale, par METTEMBERG (de Sainte-Marie-aux-Mines) (excerpt)

Besides finding my Property guaranteed by the Imperial Decree of 25 Prairial year 13 [July 13, 1804], inserted in the Bulletin of Laws, n ° 48, which assures the Medical Ingenuous his/her reward in his/her own labors' fruit, I have the honor to observe, 1st That the *Secret* of the composition of my Specific is necessary for a certain time, that is to say, for the safety of the Doctor and of the Patient who use this Specific, the same hand must prepare it, until its identity and effects have been sufficiently ascertained. 2nd That we only know mineral waters, plants and all medicinal products through chemical analysis and experience of their effects on the health of animals. 3rd That the analysis is also very sufficient to legitimize the application, especially reasoned and methodical, that I make of my remedy, whose application is always limited to being *external*.

§ 2.42.3. Two pieces of advertisement of *Eau de Mettemberg*, the first in France, the second in Spain

Affiches, Annonces, et Avis Divers, ou JOURNAL GÉNÉRAL DE FRANCE DU DIMANCHE 13 Brumaire (November 4, 1804)

Small Notices

Eau de Mettemberg. The merit of this remedy is to cure, by cutaneous absorption, the scabies and all the psoriatic diseases in general: its successes are noted by public experiments authorized by the government. The address is at Mr. Mettemberg's, former major surgeon, rue d'Enfer, no. 734, opposite the Luxembourg garden gate, where he continues his verbal and written consultations. For the convenience of the public, bottles of Eau de Mettemberg can be found at Mr. Didiaux, pharmacist, rue Beauregard, no. 211, near the Bonne Nouvelle Church.

Diário de Madrid of Tuesday, January 1, 1811

With Government approval.

New method of curing Scabies with Mr. Mettemberg's water, unknown until now in Spain, and approved by the Government.

Experientia judex. Mr. Mettemberg, as a result of the public experiments that, under a higher order, has made with his water in the Hospital of the Real Hospicio of Madrid, has had the honor of obtaining the following decree:

> Considering the report of the doctors appointed by the Supreme Board of Medicine for examining the advantages of the Method and Remedy invented by Doctor Mettemberg, House Doctor and Guard of the Senate of France, for the cure of Scabies, I have granted him the free use and sale in these Kingdoms of the anti-psoriatic Remedy.—Madrid, June 5, 1869.—The Minister of the Interior, Signed—Manuel Romero.

The water is sold at the Royal Customs of Madrid, entering through Calle Angosta de San Bernardo, at the Office of the Purgative Salt, Mercury, Wax and other effects, where its general warehouse for Spain is sieged, and where the Prospectus of the advantages and utilities that it carries in the practice of medicine will be given for free.

In France, the general warehouse of Mettemberg's water is in Paris, at the Inventor's home, rue d'Enfer, no. 11. A warehouse has been established in Bayonne, at the home of Mr. Barroilhet, merchant on the street and near the Mayou Bridge.

§ 2.42.4. Specification of Mettemberg's British Patent—February 26, 1825

Medicinal Compound.

De Mettemberg's Specification (excerpts)

To all to whom these presents shall come, I, the Chevalier Joseph de Mettemberg, of Foley Place, in the Parish of Saint Marylebone, in the County of Middlesex, Physician, late Surgeon Major in the French Armies, send greeting.

Whereas His present most Excellent Majesty King George the Fourth, by His Letters Patent under the Great Seal of Great Britain, bearing date at Westminster, the Twenty-sixth day of February, in the sixth year of His reign, did, for Himself, His heirs and successors, give and grant unto me, the said Joseph De Mettemberg, His especial licence, that I, the said Joseph De Mettemberg, my executors, administrators, and assigns, or such others as I, the said Joseph De Mettemberg, my executors, administrators, and assigns, should at any time agree with, and no others, from time to time and at all times during the term of years therein expressed, should and lawfully might make, use, exercise, and vend, within England, Wales, and the Town of Berwick-upon-Tweed, and also in His said Majesty's Colonies and Plantations abroad, my Invention of "A Vegetable, Mercurial, and Spirituous Preparation which I denominate *Quintessence Anti-psorique*, or Mettemberg's Water, and also a particular Method of employing the same by Cutaneous Absorption as a Specific and Medical Cosmetic;" in which said Letters Patent there is contained a proviso obliging me, the said Joseph De Mettemberg, by an instrument in writing under my hand and seal, particularly to describe and ascertain the nature of my said Invention, and in what manner the same is to be performed, and to cause the same to be enrolled in His Majesty's High Court of Chancery within six calendar months next and immediately after the date of the said in part recited Letters Patent, as in and by the same, reference being thereunto had, will more fully and at large appear.

Now know ye, that in compliance with the said proviso, I, the said Joseph De Mettemberg, do hereby declare that the nature of my said Invention, and the manner of making, producing, and compounding my aforesaid quintessence anti-psorique, or Mettemberg's water, and of using and applying the same when so made and produced, are herein-after particularly set forth and described, that is to say:—. . .

And be it remembered, that on the Thirtieth day of July, in the year of our Lord 1825, the aforesaid Joseph De Mettemberg (through the interpretation of Charles Drewry, the said interpreter being first sworn, that he had truly, distinctly, and audibly interpreted the contents of the above 5 Specification to the said Joseph De Mettemberg, and that he would truly interpret the acknowledgment of the same) came before our said Lord the King in His Chancery, and acknowledged the Specification aforesaid, and all and everything therein contained and specified, in form above written. And also the Specification aforesaid was stamped according to the tenor of the Statute made for that purpose.

Enrolled the Thirtieth day of July, in the year of our Lord One thousand eight hundred and twenty-five.

[A French version of an excerpt from this patent (granted with the usual conditions and a term of 14 years) can be found in one of the many booklets that Mettemberg wrote in defense of his invention—LETTRES-PATENTES ROYALES RÉCEMMENT ACCORDÉES EN ANGLETERRE PAR S. M. BRITANNIQUE LE ROI GEORGE IV POUR UNE INVENTION EN MÉDECINE PRATIQUE, at 7 (self-publication, 1825).]

§ 2.43. THE SUPREME COURT OF OHIO DELINKS PATENTS FROM ADMINISTRATIVE PERMISSIONS, THUS ACCORDING PATENTS THEIR CURRENT LEGAL MEANING—THE RIGHT TO EXCLUDE, RATHER THAN THE RIGHT TO USE—1830

For the opponents of the grant of patents for pharmaceutical inventions, the major barrier was the administrative permission embedded in them for the inventors to make and sell the inventions. Therefore, utility patents were used (or, rather, misused) by inventors to circumvent the existing mechanisms of supervision of the quality and safety of medicines. This explains the opposition that English and American physicians expressed against the patentability of medicines. France, as we will see next, on that same ground excluded pharmaceutical products from patentability. In the United States, a bill was proposed to Congress in the same sense (see § 2.47), and that same exclusion was enacted in a few European countries, such as Germany, where, according to a report elaborated by the English Parliament in 1914, only processes used in the production of medicines were patentable, not the products themselves.

That misunderstanding of the patent system had to wait until the middle of the twentieth century to disappear. Otherwise, given the impossibility of resorting to secrecy, as they had done until the nineteenth century, the inventors had no meaningful way to appropriate the results of their inventive work.

And yet, in 1830, the Supreme Court of Ohio had already made it clear that utility patents did not replace or overlap the analysis and testing of drugs by health authorities for the purposes of their commercial distribution. Later, a Belgian court held the same understanding (see § 2.49).

Jordan v. The Overseers of Dayton

Decision in Bank, 1831

The overseers of the poor, brought an action of debt before a justice of the peace, against Jordan, to recover certain penalties, for practicing physic, in violation of the statute, regulating the practice of physic and surgery. The case was appealed to the court of common pleas, and judgment was there rendered in favor of the overseers of the poor; to reverse which, this writ was prosecuted.

The facts were agreed between the parties as follows:

> It was admitted, that Jordan, not being a member of any medical society of the state, and not being qualified to practice medicine, as required by the statute, did administer to, and prescribe for one William Sullivan, and one William Prigg, and received fees and rewards therefor. That on the 25th of January, 1823, a patent was regularly issued, from the United States to Samuel Thompson, granting to him, his heirs and assigns, for the term of fourteen years, the exclusive right of making, constructing, using, and vending to others to be used, a certain new and useful improvement, being a mode of preparing, mixing, compounding, administering and using, the medicine described in certain specifications thereto annexed, in the manner, and in the diseases set forth in said specification. It was also further admitted, that Jordan was the assignee of Thompson, and vested with all the rights and privileges conferred upon Thomson by the patent, and that the medicines prescribed and used by Jordan in his treatment of Prigg and Sullivan, were the same set forth in the patent and specifications, and were administered for the diseases therein mentioned. Also, that on the . . . day of . . . 1813, a patent was granted to the same Samuel Thompson, with specifications substantially the same as those attached to the patent of 1823, and conferring the same rights and privileges.

Opinion of the Court, by Judge Lane.

The case presents two questions: 1. whether the evidence sufficiently shows that the defendant practiced medicine, and 2. whether the eleventh section of the statu[t]e, imposing a penalty for practicing medicine, by persons not members of the medical society—is inoperative on him, by reason of Thompson's patent.

On the first point, the case shows that Jordon prescribed and administered medicines to two sick persons, for fees. The stipendiary character of the service forbids the belief that it was an act of neighborly kindness, or the execution of a moral duty. Administering medicine may be the office of a nurse; but prescribing medicine to the sick implies the exercise of skill, in the discrimination of diseases, and the selection of fit remedies; to acquire which skill is the object of medical education, and to exercise which, for fees, is but another name for the practice of medicine. In the absence of explanation, we believe the statement sufficiently shows that Jordan, in these cases, acted in the character of a physician.

In discussing the second question, I choose to divest the case of all matters except those arising from its simplest merits. For present purposes, therefore, I assume that the right of prescribing and administering medicines is a proper subject for a patent, and that the patent of 1823 is to all purposes regular and effective. I proceed to consider, whether the patent conveys such a right, that the authority of the State may not control its exercise.

A large portion of the duty of the lawgiver, in every civilized community, consists in regulating the conduct of individuals, in different matters, for purposes of general welfare. Some acts of this nature are the objects of penal legislation. There is moral turpitude, in vending tickets of lotteries from other States, or in selling spirituous liquors to Indians: yet the good of society demands their prohibition. Other and the larger class are in various forms regulated by law. Thus, the act of keeping tavern is a lawful trade: yet, because it is of public concern, that the convenience of travelers be secured, and because it is conducive to public morals that intemperance be suppressed, the legislature have forbidden its indiscriminate practice, and have placed those engaging in it under the watch of a court. And for reasons, in some respect similar, peddlers and ferrymen are placed under the same supervision. The exercise of police powers by municipal corporations, the laws concerning the inspection of provisions, and the fixing rates of toll for turnpikes and bridges, are examples of similar powers. So the business of grinding grain, a work strictly private, interests so many persons, that the legislature have deemed it proper to fix a price for labor. So the profession of law is of so public a nature, that its practice is wholly forbidden, until after a reasonable demonstration of ability, and until after an opportunity has been offered, to learn the morals of the practitioner. And the profession of medicine is regarded, by the legislature, as of similar character, so that policy requires an examination should be instituted into the professional capacity of the practitioner, before he shall be permitted to operate upon the health of citizens. In all these cases, the interpretation of the law given, is justified by the obvious principle, that although a man's rights to his own are absolute and indefeasible, yet these rights must be so used, as not to infringe the rights of others, and may be so regulated as to promote the general good.

But the plaintiff in error, without denying these matters, to be the suitable and ordinary subjects of legislation, insists the power of the legislature is limited, in this case, so used, as not to infringe the rights of others, and may be so regulated as to promote the general good.

But the plaintiff in error, without denying these matters, to be the suitable and ordinary subjects of legislation, insists the power of the legislature is limited, in this case, because the patent, securing to Thompson the exclusive right of preparing and mixing medicines, emanated from the general government, under the authority of the constitution: and that its full effect cannot be had, unless it be holden altogether exempt from State control. This leads us to consider the nature and extent of such rights as accrue from letters patent, for useful discoveries. Although the inventor had, at all times, the right to enjoy the fruits of his own ingenuity, in every lawful form of which its use was susceptible, yet, before the enactment of the statute, he had not the power of preventing others from participating in that enjoyment, to the same extent with himself; so that however the world might derive benefit from his labors, no profits ensued to himself. The ingenious man was therefore led, either to abandon pursuits of this nature, or to conceal his results from the world. The end of the statute was to encourage useful inventions, and to hold forth as inducements to the inventor, the exclusive use of his inventions for a limited period. The sole operation of the statute, is to enable him to prevent, others from using the products of his labors, except with his consent. But his own right of using is not enlarged or affected. There remains in him, as in every other citizen, the power to manage his property, or give direction to his labors, at his pleasure, subject only to the paramount claims of society, which requires that his enjoyment may be modified by the exigencies of the community to which he belongs, and regulated by laws, which render it subservient to the general welfare, if held subject to State control. If the State should pass a law, for the purpose of destroying a right created by the constitution, this court will do its duty; but an attempt, by the legislature, in good faith, to regulate the conduct of a portion of its citizens, in a matter strictly pertaining to its internal economy, we cannot but regard as a legitimate exercise of power, although such law may sometimes directly affect the enjoyment of rights flowing from the federal government.

Judgment affirmed.

§ 2.44. FRANCE EXCLUDES MEDICINES FROM PATENTABILITY

July 5, 1844

In 1844, France introduced a new statute on patents. One of its main features was the exclusion of pharmaceutical inventions from patentability.

But the 1844 statute excluded products only, not the processes for their making. Therefore, some patents relating to the pharmaceutical sector continued being granted. That number increased after 1920, under the pressure of French chemical industries, and with the support of the Academy of Medicine, concerned with the domination of European and international markets of chemical products by the German industry. But it was only in 1959, with the enactment of a regulation, that "special patents" started being granted in France for medicines. With the new law of 1968, pharmaceuticals were treated as any other subject matter for the purposes of patentability.

This long delay in granting patents may explain in part why countries like the United States, England, and Switzerland are ahead of France in the research and development of pharmaceutical inventions (and therefore, in the number of patent applications).

The 1844 law provided that the exclusion from patentability did not supersede any administrative requirements concerning authorizations for the commercialization of pharmaceuticals, including secret medicines, the commercialization of which was, under the Decree of 1810 (see § 2.38.1), dependent on a technical examination as to their safety and efficacy.

Law of July 5, 1844, on patents for inventions

Title I

General provisions

Article 1. Every new discovery or invention in every kind of industry confers on its author, under the conditions and for the term herein determined, the exclusive right of exploiting for his own benefit such discovery or invention.
This right is established by titles issued by the Government under the name of *patents for invention*. . . .
Art. 3.—[The following] Are not patentable:

(1) Pharmaceutical compositions or medicines of any kind, said objects remaining subject to special laws and regulations on that matter, and in particular to the decree of August 18, 1810, concerning secret medicines.
(2) Plans and combinations of credit or finance.

§ 2.45. A FRENCH INVENTOR OBTAINS A PATENT IN ENGLAND FOR A DEVICE FOR PURIFYING THE AIR—1848

It was said above that rarely inventors have claimed ownership in new solutions developed exclusively or mainly to be applied in times of epidemics. The trend has been that those new solutions are made available for free. This does not mean that certain medicines and medical devices useful to prevent or treat diseases arising from plagues have never been patented. Actually, a good number has been. See, for example, the inhaler device, patented by Stanislas Limousin (see § 2.51), which could be of great utility for treating patients of pulmonary illnesses resulting from viral infections (such as more than 150 years later, the infection caused by the COVID-19 virus). But it is not common to see in patent specifications a reference to epidemics.

One exception, however, concerns a patent for a medical device whose inventor's name was not designated in the specification, as it was the practice in England at that time. The name that appeared was that of the patent attorney, Fontaine Moreau, who had two offices, one in Paris, the other in London.

1849—No 12,385—Hygienic Apparatus and Process for Curing Diseases.

Fontaine Moreau's Specification.

To all to whom the presents shall come, I, Pierre Armande Lecomte de Fontaine Moreau, of No. 4, South Street, Finsbury, in the County of Middlesex, English and Foreign Patent Agent for Inventions, send greeting.

Whereas Her present most Excellent Majesty Queen Victoria, by Her Royal Letters Patent under the Great Seal of Great Britain, bearing date at Westminster, the Twenty-first day of December, One thousand eight hundred and forty-eight, in the twelfth year of Her reign, did, for Herself, Her heirs and successors, give and grant unto me, the said Pierre Armand Lecomte de Fontaine Moreau, my ex^{ors}, adm^{ors}, and assigns, Her especial licence, full power, sole privilege and authority, that I, the said Pierre Armand Lecomte de Fontaine Moreau, my ex^{ors}, adm^{ors}, or assigns, should at any time agree with, and no others, from time to time and at all times during the term of years therein mentioned, should and lawfully might make, use, exercise, and vend, within England, Wales, and the Town of Berwick-upon-Tweed, and in the Islands of Guernsey, Jersey, Alderney, Sark, and Man, and in all Her said Majesty's Colonies and Plantations abroad, the Invention of "Certain Hygienic Apparatus and Processes for Preventing and Curing Chronical and other Affections, and to Prevent or Stop certain Epidemic Diseases," communicated to me from abroad; in which said Letters Patent is contained a proviso that I, the said Pierre Armand Lecomte de Fontaine Moreau, should cause a particular description of the nature of the said Invention, and in what manner the same is to be performed, by an instrument in writing under my hand and seal, and to be enrolled in Her said Majesty's High Court of Chancery within six calendar months next and immediately after the date of the said in part recited Letters Patent, as in and by the same, reference being thereunto had, will more fully and at large appear.

Now know ye, that in compliance with the said proviso, I, the said Pierre Armand Lecomte de Fontaine Moreau, do hereby declare that the nature of the said Invention communicated to me, and the manner of performing and carrying out the same, are particularly described and ascertained by the following statement thereof, reference being had to the Drawing hereunto annexed, and to the figures therein contained, in which the same letters of reference indicate similar parts, that is to say:—

The Invention communicated to me consists—

Firstly, in treating certain diseases and affections of the human body by the application of cold dry heat or water on the diseased part without humectant it; and in effecting these infections by means of waterproof garments with which I envelope the part or parts to be operated upon,

Secondly, in the construction of certain apparatus, such as beds, sofas, couches, &c., and for affording relief, and to treat diseased invalids and other persons I construct garments of all sizes, made of calico, silk, ticking, linen, netting, or any tissue rendered waterproof by means of caoutchouc, India rubber, gutta percha, collodion, or any other suitable substance producing a similar effect. I will here observe that it is competent for me to employ one or more waterproof surfaces as herein-after described for the construction of my garments in order to protect the patient from all chance of humidity during a long-continued operation, although the simple surface will be found adequate for the majority of cases. These garments serve as a mode of conveying or administering local or general baths at any desired temperature in the ordinary bathing machine without the water being in immediate contact with the person of the patient. I have constructed for that purpose a paletot sack. . . .

Double Waterproof Garments.—As I have hereinbefore stated, I also construct garments with double surfaces. They consist merely of a second surface superposed on a first. They have a shape exactly similar to the garments or apparatus I have already described, but they are nevertheless a little wider to allow room for the liquid which is to be introduced between the two surfaces composing them. . . .

Secondly, Calefactor Apparatus, for the use of persons having rheumatism, women lying in, patients attacked of the cholera, &c., &c., &c. . . .

And having now described the nature of the Invention communicated to me, and the manner the same is to be performed, I wish it to be understood that I do not confine myself to the use of the several substances and materials employed, nor to the precise form and size of the apparatus herein-before described, nor do I lay claim to the said substances and materials, or *modi operandi*, beyond their application for obtaining the end of my Invention. But what I claim as the Invention communicated to me, and intended to be protected by Her Majesty's Letters Patent, is,—

Firstly, the treatment of certain diseases and affections of the human body by the application thereon of cold dry heat and water, without humidity, as therein-before described in reference to the Figures- in Drawing I.

Secondly, the application of waterproof garments having the shape of the several parts of the body, made of any dimensions, as media for operating upon the human body, as hereinbefore described in reference to the Figures of Drawing I. . .

Thirdly, the construction of an apparatus having the form of a bed, sofa, or couch, for affording relief, repose, and heat to afflicted and other persons, as herein-before described in reference to Drawing II.

In witness whereof, I, the said Pierre Armand Le Comte de Fontaine Moreau, have hereunto set my hand and seal, this Twenty-first day 5 of June, in the year of our Lord One thousand eight hundred and forty-nine.

Figure 24 Some of the drawings included by Fontaine Moreau in the specifications of his client's patent, one of the possible uses of which is during an epidemic (of cholera, as mentioned), for cooling down the body's temperature.

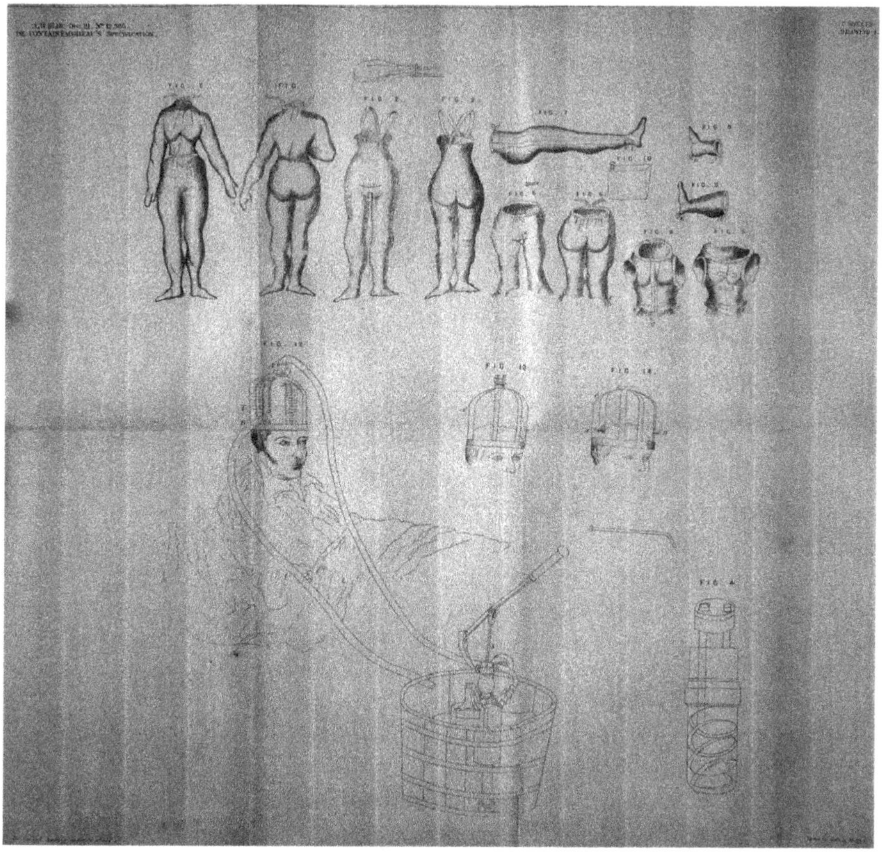

§ 2.46. THE PHILADELPHIA COLLEGE OF MEDICINE TAKES A CRITICAL STANDING AGAINST SECRETS MEDICINES OR NOSTRUMS—1848

Following a movement that had started in France, one century earlier, and continued in the United Kingdom, also in the United States, physicians, worried with the flooding of secret medicines and quackery practices, voiced their opposition to such a system. In this token, the Philadelphia College of Medicine introduced in its Code of Ethics rules that discouraged its members from dealing with secret medicines.

Joseph W. England (edit.), The First Century of the Philadelphia College of Pharmacy (excerpt)

Philadelphia College of Medicine

Code of Ethics

March 31, 1848

Pharmacy being a profession which demands knowledge, skill and integrity on the part of those engaged in it, and being associated with the medical profession in the responsible duties of preserving the public health, and dispensing the useful though often dangerous agents adapted to the cure of disease, its members should be united on some general principles to be observed in their several relations to each other, to the medical profession, and to the public.

The Philadelphia College of Pharmacy being a permanent, incorporated institution, embracing amongst its members a large number of respectable and well-educated apothecaries, has erected a standard of scientific attainments, which there is a growing disposition on the part of candidates for the profession to reach; and being desirous that, in relation to professional conduct and probity, there should be a corresponding disposition to advance, its members have agreed upon the following principles for the government of their conduct: . . .

3d. As the practice of pharmacy can only become uniform by an open and candid intercourse being kept up between apothecaries, which will lead them to discountenance the use of secret formulas, and promote the general use and knowledge of good practice, and, as this College considers that any discovery which is useful in alleviating human suffering, or in restoring the diseased to health, should be made public for the good of humanity and the general advancement of the healing art, no member of this College should originate or prepare a medicine, the composition of which is concealed from other members, or from regular physicians.

Whilst the College does not at present feel authorized to require its members to abandon the sale of secret or quack medicines, they earnestly recommend the propriety of discouraging their employment, when called upon for an opinion as to their merits. . . .

§ 2.47. IN THE UNITED STATES, THE HOUSE OF REPRESENTATIVES DEBATES AND REJECTS A BILL THAT AIMED AT EXCLUDING MEDICINES FROM PATENTABILITY—1849

The movement against patents for pharmaceutical inventions, which in France had resulted in their prohibition, in 1844, reached the United States. In that sense, a bill was submitted to Congress. The concern of the House was the same that had arisen in other countries: patents were being used by dishonest inventors as being the equivalent to administrative market authorizations, thus allowing them to circumvent the rigors of the technical examinations of new medicines. Quackery was a natural consequence of that situation. But, unlike other countries, the entrepreneurial spirit that has always been behind the way that American people have seen the patent system has prevailed, and the temptation to ban patents for pharmaceuticals was overcome.

It is my personal opinion that the world has only to be grateful to the United States Congress for that.

30th Congress, session of February 6, 1849

Mr. Edwards, by leave, from the select committee on the subject of adulterated medicines and drugs, reported a bill to prevent the patenting of medicines, accompanied by a report in writing; which bill was read twice.

The bill (said Mr. E.) contained but one section. It would not take the House five minutes to act upon it. It asked that it be read.

The bill was read, as follows:

A Bill, to prevent the patenting of medicines

Be it Enacted by the Senate and the House of Representatives of the United States of America assembled, That from and after the passage of this act, letters patent shall not be granted for any article or preparation whatever as a medicine; and that the use, as a medicine, of any article or preparation, for which letters patent may hereafter be granted shall not be held to be an infringement of such patent; *Provided,* that no patent granted prior to the passage of this act shall, by reason thereof, be held to be void; and this act shall not be so constructed as to deprive an inventor or discoverer of the right to letters patent for a new and improved process for preparing or manufacturing any medicinal article, whether simple or compound; *And provided,* also, that the prohibition contained in this act shall not apply to machines, instruments or apparatus pertaining either to surgery or medicine.

He said Congress had, at the last session, passed a bill to prevent the importation of adulterated drugs and medicines. That act had worked well. This was another step in continuation of the same system for the protection of the public health. He moved that the bill be put upon its passage.

At the suggestion of Mr. Nicoll, however, who stated that he desired an opportunity to look into the bill before it was passed, by general consent the bill was passed to the Speaker's table and was ordered to be printed.

Session of March 3, 1849

On motion of Mr. Edwards, the bill to prevent the patenting of medicines was taken up; and the question being on the third reading thereof—

Mr. Edwards moved the previous question; which was nor seconded.

After some debate by Mr. Edwards and Mr. Hall, of Missouri,
Mr. Edwards again moved the previous question; which the House again refused to second.
Mr. Duer moved that the bill be laid on the table; which motion was agreed to.

§ 2.48. THE LAW OF TRADE SECRETS, WHICH WAS THEN IN DEVELOPMENT IN ENGLAND, ASSISTS A PHARMACIST TO HOLD THE SECRET IN HIS INVENTED MEDICINE—1851

In the nineteenth century, English courts started building the law of trade secrets, initially grounded on the notion of breach of confidence. Curiously, in that period, most of the cases brought to courts seeking a remedy for the infringement of trade secrets concerned medicines. See, e.g., Williams v. Williams, *High Court of Chancery, 817, March 14;* Newbery v. James and Others, *March 27, 1817;* Yowatt v. Winyard, *High Court of Chancery, 1820, May 15 [see in* FROM BABYLON TO THE SILICON VALLEY *excerpts from those opinions*[27]*]. But perhaps the best-known opinion was delivered by the Privy Council of the House of Lords in* Morison v. Moat, *in 1851, an excerpt from which follows.*

Morison v. Moat

House of Lords, Privy Council

August 5, 6, and 20, 1851

The facts, arguments, and authorities cited in this case are fully detailed in his honor's judgment. . . .

Sir George Turner, V.C. This was a motion for an injunction to restrain the defendant, William Crofton Moat, from making, compounding, or selling any medicine as "Morison's Universal Medicine," or as "Morison's Vegetable Universal Medicine," or from in any manner using the name of Morison in the manufacture or sale of any medicine; and from using the secret of compounding the said medicines, or any part thereof; and from communicating to any person or persons whomsoever the knowledge of the "ingredients whereof the said medicines are compounded, or the secret, or any part of the secret, of compounding the said medicines." The facts of the case, so far as they are undisputed, are these: James Morison was the inventor and sole proprietor of the medicine or medicines in question. By an indenture bearing date the 23d of June, 1830, and made between James Morison of the one part, and Thomas Moat of the other part, reciting that James Morison was the inventor and sole proprietor of the medicine called or known by the name of "Morison's Vegetable Universal Medicine," the secret of making which he, Mr. Morison, had communicated to his son John; and then reciting "that James Morison, in consideration of the past services of the said Thomas Moat, and in further consideration that the said Thomas Moat should

27. *See supra* note 2, at 174 *et seq.*

devote his whole time and attention to the conduct and promotion of the manufacture and sale of the said medicine or medicines, had agreed to take the said Thomas Moat into partnership with him in the manufacture and sale of such medicine or medicines upon the terms after mentioned;" it was witnessed that Morison and Moat were to be the partners in the profession and business of manufacturers and venders of the medicines for the term of twenty years and three quarters of a year, to commence and be computed from the 24th of June next ensuing, the day of the date of the indenture, upon the terms and under the provisions thereinafter contained; and the style of the firm was to be "Morison, Moat, & Co., Hygeists." The profession or business of the partnership was to be carried on certain terms, in certain premises, which are mentioned in the deed, where alone (save and except the foreign establishments) the medicines were to be compounded, and whence alone, save as aforesaid, the said medicines so made and compounded might be issued to any part of the world, through the respective agents of the copartnership; with a proviso that it should be lawful to and for the partners for the time being of the partnership to cause the establishment to be removed to and carried on at such other place or places as he or they should or might from time to time judge most convenient. The deed then witnessed that the premises in which the business was to be carried on were to be called "The British College of Health," and that Morison and Moat were to be considered to be entitled to the gains and profits of the business, and liable to the losses, in the proportion of two thirds to Morison and one third to Moat, and upon no account was any partner to draw more than two thirds of the share of the annual profits; and that if Moat should die before the 25th of March, 1851, then the interest, share, or proportion of Mr. Moat of and in the copartnership was not to devolve, as by law it would, upon the personal representatives of Moat, but it should go and belong to such person, not being a female, as Thomas Moat should by any instrument under seal, with or without power of revocation, to be by him sealed and delivered, and to be attested by James Morison, his appointee or appointees, direct or appoint; and in default of such direction or appointment, then the interest, share, or proportion of him, Moat, of and in the partnership, should devolve upon James Morison, his appointee or appointees, executors, administrators, or assigns.

Then the deed witnessed that Moat was to devote and employ his whole time and attention in the conduct and promotion of the manufacture and sale of the medicine or medicines, or in such other manner as should best conduce to the advantage or benefit of the partnership. Morison was not to be obliged to devote any more time or attention to the manufacture and sale of the medicine or medicines, or otherwise, in and about the premises, than he should think proper; and might, if he should think proper, introduce into the copartnership any person or persons whomsoever, such person or persons not being a female or females, upon the same terms and conditions as Moat was thereby subjected to. That James Morison should, on or before the commencement of the partnership, communicate to Thomas Moat a full and true knowledge of the mode of making and compounding the medicines, and should be at liberty to communicate such knowledge to such person or persons as he was thereby empowered to introduce into the partnership. That Morison, notwithstanding anything contained to the contrary, should be at liberty to form an establishment in any part of the world, except the United Kingdom of Great Britain, Ireland, and America, for the manufacture and sale of the medicines; and that all the medicines which he might order or receive from the partnership should be charged to him at a certain price. In case Thomas Moat should live to the expiration of the partnership, a new partnership for a further term of years was to be agreed upon between the parties before the expiration of the partnership, on terms similar to those in the indenture contained;

but if Morison or Moat should happen to die before the expiration of the partnership, then an account in writing should be made and taken, under the signature of the partners for the time being, of the state of the partnership, and a balance struck between the partners and the representatives of the party so dying, for the purpose of ascertaining what then might be due from the partnership to the estate of Morison, or to the estate of Moat, as the case might be. . . .

On that part of the case it is sufficient, therefore, to observe that there might be difficulty in maintaining it; at all events, until the plaintiffs should have established their right at law. The true question is, whether, under the circumstances of this case, the court ought to interfere by injunction on the ground of breach of faith or of contract. That the court has exercised jurisdiction in cases of this nature does not, I think, admit of any question. Different grounds have been assigned for the exercise of that jurisdiction. In some cases it has been referred to property, in others to contract, and in others, again, it has been treated as founded upon trust or confidence; meaning, as I conceive, that the court fastens the obligation on the conscience of the party, and enforces it against him in the same manner as it enforces, against a party to whom a benefit is given, the obligation of performing a promise on the faith of which the benefit has been conferred. But upon whatever ground the jurisdiction is founded, the authorities leave no doubt as to the exercise of it. The case of *Green v. Folghamb*, 1 Sim. & S. 398, which was cited for the plaintiffs, and where the court decreed an account against a party to whom a secret of this nature had been entrusted, might perhaps be accounted for upon the ground that the defendant in the case had expressly admitted himself to be a trustee of the secret. But there are other cases in which the court has interfered without any such admission. In *Williams v. Williams*, 3 Mer. 159, Lord Ellon, dealing with a case in which a father had divulged a secret like the present to a son, and had delivered to him a stock of medicines upon the faith of a future partnership being formed between them when the son should come of age, puts the case, as to confidence, in these terms: "If, on a treaty with the son while an infant, for his becoming a partner when of age, the plaintiff had, in the confidence of a trust reposed in him, communicated to him this secret, and at the same time given him the possession of the articles mentioned in the bill; and, instead of acting according to his trust, the son had taken to himself the exclusive dominion over these articles, and begun to vend them without permission, it must be said that he had no right in any case so to act, and that he was bound either to abide by or to waive the agreement. If, then, he had intended to abide by the agreement, the injunction was so far right." That was an injunction that had been granted by the vice chancellor. "And if to waive it, he was bound to return the articles; and so far the injunction was also right in that case. Upon the plaintiff's affidavit, therefore, the injunction was properly granted as to this part of the case. But so far as the injunction goes to restrain the defendant from communicating the secret, upon general principles I do not think that the court ought to struggle to protect this sort of secrets in medicine. The court is bound, indeed, to protect them, in cases of patents, to the full extent of what was intended by the grant of the patent, because the patentee is a purchaser from the public, and bound to communicate his secret to the public at the expiration of the patent. Then, whether the principle can be extended to such a case as this—whether a contracting party is entitled to the protection of the court, in the exercise of its jurisdiction to decree the specific performance of agreements, by restraining a party to the contract from divulging the secret he has promised to keep—that is a question which would require very great consideration. But the present case is not one which calls for the determination of it. If the defendant has already disclosed the secret, the injunction can be of no use; if he only threatens to disclose, it then becomes necessary to look at his affidavit; and by that he insists that what he has to disclose is no secret at all." In that case, the son said he had a right otherwise than from the father, and that it came to him from his mother. "Then," continued his lordship, "how is the court to try this question?" Here Lord Eldon, I think, distinctly lays down the doctrine—it does not carry that case farther—it does not go very far— that articles delivered over upon the faith and in the confidence of a future arrangement cannot be used for a purpose different from that for which they were delivered over. The cases, however, do not stop here. In *Yovatt v. Winyard*, 1 Jac. & W. 395, Lord Eldon, upon the express ground of breach of trust and confidence, granted an injunction to restrain the defendant, who had been the plaintiff's assistant in his business, from using or communicating recipes which he had surreptitiously copied whilst in the plaintiff's service. There, there was a motion, "upon certificate of the bill filed, and affidavit, to restrain the defendant from making use of, or communicating, certain recipes for veterinary medicines, and from printing and publishing certain papers of directions for the mode of administering them, and of managing the animals while taking them."

The motion was put upon the ground of its being "a breach of confidence towards an employer, in the manner of acquiring the knowledge." Sir Charles Wetherell contended, "that though the court might not protect a secret from disclosure by one to whom the proprietor had himself communicated it, yet it would when the person sought to be restrained had clandestinely possessed himself of it." In those cases," (referring to *Newberry v. James*, 2 Mer. 447, and *Williams v. Williams*,) his lordship says, "in those cases the knowledge was communicated for a particular purpose, and it was attempted to prevent the party from using it for any other; but here the first discovery was obtained by a breach of duty, and in violation of a positive agreement."

The lord chancellor "granted the injunction on the ground of there having been a breach of trust and confidence; but confined it so as not to prevent the defendant from administering the medicine to any animals then under a course, it being stated in the papers of directions that a sudden discontinuance would be prejudicial." The question again came before Lord Eldon in Mr. Abernethy's case, (*Abernethy v. Hutchinson*, 3 L. J., Ch., 209.) in which Mr. Abernethy had filed a bill to restrain the publication of the lectures delivered by him at St. Bartholomew's Hospital, and I well remember that upon the first argument he refused to grant the injunction on the ground of copyright, Mr. Abernethy not being able to swear that the whole lecture was written; but that afterwards, on a second argument, he granted it on the ground of breach of confidence.

We have also Lord Eldon's opinion referred to by Lord Cottenham in *Prince Albert v. Strange*, as contained in a note, with which he had been furnished by Mr. Cooper, of the case of *Wyatt v. Wilson*, before Lord Eldon, in the year 1820, in which Lord Eldon is reported to have said, "If one of the late king's physicians had kept a diary of what he heard and saw, this court would not, in the king's lifetime, have permitted him to print and publish it." And in the case of *Prince Albert v. Strange*, Lord Cottenham very decidedly expresses his own opinion upon the subject. What he says, after going into the right of Prince Albert to the etchings,—the mode in which it came before Lord Cottenham being upon motion to dissolve an injunction which had been granted to restrain the publication of the catalogue of the etchings which had been prepared,—is this: His lordship, after dealing with the question as a subject of property, says, "But this case by no means depends solely upon the question of property; for a breach of trust, confidence, or contract would, of itself, entitle the plaintiff to an injunction." . . .

And upon the evidence on behalf of the plaintiff, and in the absence of any explanation on the part of the defendant, I am bound to assume that the possession of the etchings by the defendant or Judge has its foundation in a breach of trust, confidence, or contract, as Lord Eldon did in the case of Mr. Abernethy's lectures; and upon this ground, also, I think the plaintiff's title to the injunction sought to be discharged fully established. The observations of Vice Chancellor Wigram in *Tipping v. Clarke*, 2 Hare, 393, are applicable to this part of the case. He says, "Every clerk employed in a merchant's counting-house is under an implied contract that he will not make public that which he learns in the execution of his duty as clerk. If the defendant has obtained copies of books, it would very probably be by means of some clerk or agent of the plaintiff; and if he availed himself surreptitiously of the information, which he could not have had except from a person guilty of a breach of contract in communicating it, I think he could not be permitted to avail himself of that breach of contract." He approves, therefore, of what fell from Vice Chancellor Wigram in *Tipping v. Clarke*.

Vice Chancellor Knight Bruce appears also to have concurred in opinion with Lord Cottenham in *Prince Albert v. Strange*. There is, therefore the concurrent opinion of Lords Eldon and Cottenham and of Vice Chancellors Knight Bruce and Sir James Wigram upon the question. By those authorities, in which I most fully concur, and which appear to me to agree in principle with many other cases to be found in the books, I must hold myself to be bound. It was much pressed in argument on the part of the defendant, that the effect of granting an injunction in such a case as the present would be to give the plaintiffs a better right than that of a patentee; and the case of *Cunham v. Jones*, 2 W. & B. 218, was cited on the defendant's behalf. But what we have to deal with here is, not the right of the plaintiffs against the world, but their right against the defendant. It may well be that the plaintiffs have no title against the world in general, and may yet have a good title against this defendant; and the case of *Cunham v. Jones* does not appear to me to touch the question. In that case the allegation was, not that the defendant was compounding the syrup according to the recipe, but that he did not know the recipe, and was compounding and selling a spurious preparation, falsely describing it under the title by which the true preparation was known, and thereby damaging the character of that preparation. The case, therefore, did not depend on any breach of confidence, for there was no confidence reposed, but depended wholly upon a supposed right of property in the medicine; . . .

Such being the state of the authorities upon this subject, I have now to consider whether the circumstances of this case bring it within the range of those authorities, and whether the court ought not to interfere by injunction, for which purpose it is necessary to examine the case as it has stood at several different periods. . . .

The true effect of these instruments appears to me to be this: that Morison reserved to himself the secret against all the world except Thomas Moat. Morison had power to introduce partners into the concern; Moat had the like power, with the concurrence of Morison, but not otherwise. It was entirely at the option of Morison whether he would communicate the secret to any partner, introduced either by himself or by Moat. Moat was absolutely bound not to reveal the secret to any person whomsoever. At this stage of the case, therefore, there was, according to the authorities to which I have referred, a perfect right on the part of Morison, against Moat, to restrain him from divulging the secret. It is to be seen whether what has since passed has destroyed that right; and if not, whether the plaintiffs are entitled to enforce it against the defendant. The next stage in the case which we have to consider is the transaction of 1835.

. . . And in this state of the evidence I am bound, I think, to conclude, that if the defendant did, in fact, after he became a partner in the concern, acquire by practice the knowledge of the mode of mixing these medicines, (but which I do not believe he did,) he acquired that knowledge surreptitiously, and without the sanction of his partners. The case, then, in this stage stands thus: The defendant admits that the secret was communicated to him by Thomas Moat. His allegation, that he acquired a knowledge of it by acting as partner in the concern, is disproved; and it is shown that, if he did so, he did so surreptitiously. The question then is, whether there was an equity against him; and I am of opinion that there was. It was already a breach of faith and of contract on the part of Thomas Moat to communicate the secret. The defendant derives it under that breach of faith and of contract, and I think he can gain no title by it. . . .

The deeds were executed for carrying into effect this compromise, and each of those deeds recited the will of Morison, with the recital contained in it that he was the inventor and sole proprietor of the medicine, and with the trusts for sale of the secret declared by it, and by one of those deeds the annuity was secured in the manner above mentioned. The defendant was a party to each of those deeds; and it is clear, therefore, that he did not claim any right or interest in the secret adverse to the title under the will of Morison. . . . And besides, the defendant had clearly the right to sell the medicines and use the labels allotted to him at the termination of the partnership. Upon the whole, therefore, I am of opinion that the plaintiffs have made out their case for an injunction. I think, however, that the injunction cannot go to the extent which is asked for by the notice of motion. It should, I think, go to the extent of restraining the defendant from selling, under the title or signature of "Morison's Universal Medicine," any medicine made or manufactured by him—proceeding to this extent, not upon the mere use of the name, but because this is clearly the mode in which the defendant is availing himself of the breach of faith and contract. And upon the authorities, and particularly upon *Yovatt v. Winyard*, I think it should also go to the extent of restraining the defendant from making or compounding any medicines according to the secret in the bill named, and from in any manner using the secret of compounding the said medicines, or any part thereof; but I cannot grant it to restrain the defendant from in any way or manner using the name of Morison in the manufacture or sale of any medicine, as, in my view of the case, it would very much depend on the purpose for which, and the mode in which, the name may be used, whether the injunction would be due or not. Nor can I grant it to restrain the communication of the secret, there being no evidence, or even allegation, of an intention to communicate it. The order, therefore, that I shall make will be for an injunction to restrain the defendant, his agents, servants, and workmen from selling, or causing or procuring to be sold, under the title or designation of "Morison's Universal Medicine," any medicine made or manufactured by him, the said defendant, or by and under his order or direction; and also to restrain the defendant, his agents, servants, and workmen from making or compounding any medicines according to the secret in the said bill mentioned, and from in any manner using the secret of compounding the said medicines, or any part thereof. . . .

§ 2.49. A BELGIAN COURT DELINKS THE EXCLUSIVE RIGHTS OF MAKING AND USING MEDICINES THAT RESULT FROM A PATENT FROM THE NOTION OF ADMINISTRATIVE PERMISSION TO EXERCISE THE MEDICAL PROFESSION—1857

Above we saw a decision by the Supreme Court of Ohio (see § 2.43) holding that the exclusive right to make and to use the invention that results from the grant of a patent does not imply an administrative permission to carry out the medical profession. One thing is the right to exclude. Another is the right to use. Those rights are independent and may be granted independently one from the other. Therefore, in the absence of a marketing authorization accorded by the competent authorities, the patentee may still prohibit others from using the invention, but he/she may not make and sell the medicine in question.

A similar idea, but in a different context, was some thirty years later acknowledged by one Belgian court. The Belgian patent had granted to the inventor not only the right to exclude but also the right to make and sell the medicine. The court said that such patent, which had been taken in pursuit of a private interest, could not prevail against the special laws that ruled the "art of healing," which had been enacted for the sake of the health and the well-being of citizens.

In this manner, the Belgium court set quite an interesting balance between private and public interests.

The view of both courts corresponds to the doctrine that prevails today: it is not the fact that an inventor depends on a permission issued by the authorities to manufacture and sell a patented product that makes the patent automatically invalid. The patent corresponds to a certificate of novelty, inventiveness, and utility or susceptibility of industrial application. The latter, as far as medicines are concerned, are usually analyzed by patent examiners, whereas the safety and efficacy of the medicines are determined by the sanitary authority. The difference between a medicine's utility for patent purposes, and efficacy, for sanitary purposes, is a matter of evidence. Patent examiners are satisfied with a promise, stated in reasonable terms, that the medicine, as described and claimed in the patent specifications, works. But sanitary authorities ask for more than that: they require evidence that the invention really works and that it complies with minimum standards of safety and efficacy, and only when satisfied of these, they release the authorization for commercialization.

In some countries, however, things are more blurred. In Brazil, in 1999, for political reasons, Congress amended the patent law that it had passed just three years earlier, in order to implement TRIPS obligations, and gave the sanitary agency the attribution of granting "prior approval" to the issuance of patents for pharmaceutical inventions by the Patent Office. The main concern of the proponents of the new statute was with patents for second uses and other incremental inventions, which the Patent Office was granting. Regrettably, the scheme was a disaster and had long-standing repercussions, having given rise to a conflict among the two agencies. In 2017, the General Attorney's Office had to intervene and determined that the sanitary agency's role should confine to looking at matters of public health. As a matter of course, this is still a mistaken view because matters of public health are to be considered during the review that precedes the granting (or refusal) of market authorization, not that of grant of patents. This is what Article 4quater *of the Paris Convention for the Protection of Industrial Property and Article 27.2 of the TRIPS Agreement establish.*

Public Prosecutor's Office v. Maya

Court of Appeals of Brussels, on December 28, 1854

Art of healing—Medical preparations—Sale—Authorization—Patent.

Whereas it results from the discovery that the defendant, through advertisements published in various Brussels newspapers, offered for sale hides, which he described in these advertisements as feline hides and magneto-electric hides, prepared for the cure of rheumatisms;

Whereas these hides, offered for sale to be applied on rheumatic limbs, are coated with a kind of ointment composed with various ingredients and essences, constituting a remedy or compound medicine;

Whereas a drug of this type may only be offered for sale subject to compliance with the conditions and provisions prescribed by the laws and regulations on the art of healing, and that this drug, in any case, may only be sold or offered for sale by persons duly qualified and authorized for that purpose;

Whereas the accused was neither qualified nor legally authorized to offer for sale, as he did, the remedy or compound in question;

That if a royal decree, of December 13, 1852, grants the defendant a patent for the improvement of these feline hides, with the right to make and sell these patented hides, this decree, granted in contradiction with the decree of August 18, 1810, and with the provisions that rule the art of healing, should not be applied by the courts, according to art. 107 of the Constitution, and cannot therefore exempt the defendant from the application of art. 17 of the law of 12 March 1818.

For these reasons, the court condemns . . . -

Appeal.

The Court — Whereas if the royal decree of December 13, 1852 grants the defendant a patent for an improvement of feline hides, with the right to make and sell these hides thus patented, this decree, taken in a private and individual interest, has not had and could not have the effect of derogating from the laws and regulations on the art of healing, laws and regulations which were introduced in a general interest, to promote the salutary influence of this art on citizens' life and health;

That if the defendant wishes to use his patent, he must comply with the laws and regulations on the art of healing;

For these reasons and adopting for the rest the reasons of the trial judge, confirms . . . .

July 11, 1856.—Brussels Court—4th Chamber—De Behr.

§ 2.50. PORTUGAL REGULATES THE EXAMINATION AND THE LICENSING OF SECRET MEDICINES—1863

Building on the experience acquired by France in struggling with charlatanism and the commercialization of ineffective, unauthorized with secret medicines, upon a royal decision of 1863, Portugal, in 1893, adopted a system of mandatory examination and approval of secret medicines. In 1899 the respective regulations were amended.
The royal decision of 1863 had two interesting aspects. First, it required the disclosure of the secret as soon as the term of the license ended. The second aspect was that it made it clear that the approval of commercialization was not the same as a patent because it did not grant exclusivity. Implicitly the decision provided that exclusivity resulted from secrecy only, i.e., *it was a factual matter. But if a competitor somehow learned the licensed composition (or reinvented it him/herself), the authorization "did not guarantee ownership of the licensed medicines, not even during the term for which they are granted."*

§ 2.50.1. Royal decision granting authority to the kingdom's public health council concerning the licensing of secret medicines

August 3, 1863

A consultation has been presented to His Majesty the King in which the kingdom's public health council asked to be clarified on whether it could limit the term of the licenses it grants for the sale of the secret medicines, and impose on the sellers the condition of disclosure of the secret once the term of those licenses expires; and His Majesty, having heard the assistant to the Crown's Attorney General with the ministry of the kingdom, . . . orders the Council to declare that. . . it is clear that the council can establish all those [conditions] that it deems to be of public convenience and indispensable for the performance of the mission of supervision attributed to it, and consequently make those licenses temporary and tentative.

And because remedies and medicines cannot be the subject of privilege of invention or introduction, in view of the final provisions of article 4 no. 2 of the decree of December 31, 1852, the council must not only impose on all licenses for the sale of secret medicines the condition that, after the expiry of its term, it will be disclosed by the individual who has obtained the license, or by the council, where an exact description of the preparation of the remedy must be filed, under secrecy, and that it must state in those licenses, very explicitly, that they do not guarantee ownership of the licensed medicines, not even during the term for which they are granted.

Palace, July 24, 1863

§ 2.50.2. New regulations on the marketing approval of secret medicines

May 10, 1899

Having become convenient to modify the license procedure for the sale of medicines of secret composition, in order to facilitate its prosecution without prejudice to the indispensable health guarantees: I am pleased, after hearing the public health advisory board, to approve the regulation annexed to this decree and that is part of it, signed by the president of the council of ministers, minister and secretary of state for the affairs of the kingdom, who having so understood, [shall] have it executed. Palace, on May 10, 1899.—King.

Regulations on the licensing process for the sale of secret medicines, referred to in the decree of this date

Article 1. Whoever wants a license, so that they can sell some remedy of secret composition, must, by themselves or by an attorney sufficiently qualified to comply with the provisions of this regulation, request it through the secretariat of state for the affairs of the kingdom, adding to the application a detailed exposition of the effects and usefulness of the same remedy, a note of the respective formula and preparation, signed and sealed by the interested party or by his/her attorney, a portion of the drug to be licensed, and the receipt of the deposit of the amount of 753,000 reis with *Caixa Geral de Depósitos*.[28]

Art. 2. Once these conditions and the legality of the power of attorney, if there is one, have been verified, the professor of pharmacy, extraordinary member of the public health advisory board, will be appointed for the necessary examinations and tests, and the note of the formula or composition and the portion of the drug, referred to in the preceding article, will be made available to him

Art. 3. The mentioned professor will call for the interested party, or his/her attorney, as soon as possible, for the day, time and place when the note of the formula or composition will be opened, and the examination and tests, directing these works in such a way that no extraneous person can discover or know the mentioned formula or composition.

Art. 4. The author or inventor of the secret remedy, or his attorney, will present to the mentioned professor the components designated in the respective note, and the devices, tools and indispensable material, in order to verify the quantities, qualities and additional conditions required, and subsequently the preparation will be carried out in the presence of the same professor, . . .

Art. 5. The preparation obtained will be placed in an appropriate container, in whose opening paper strips are attached, sealed and initialed by the professor and by the author or inventor, or by his/her attorney.

Sole § The container will then be sent to the secretariat of state for the affairs of the kingdom, with the confidential note on the formula of the preparation, accompanied by a declaration, also confidential, signed by the interested party or by his/her attorney, and initialed by the professor of pharmacy, reporting the circumstances that occurred during the examination, and whether or not all the necessary precautions to guarantee the inviolability of the secret have been given to the interested party.

Art. 6. Subsequently, the note with the formula and preparation will be confidentially presented to the public health advisory board, to which the extraordinary member, professor of pharmacy, will be summoned and who will give an opinion on the grant and term of the license and on the price of the drug, in the case

28. A state-owned bank, still existing today.

it is admitted for sale, and for this hypothesis, the main therapeutic indications that the preparation may serve, its method of administration and doses, will be indicated by the Board, of which everything must be declared always, in a label, in the packages of the same medicine.

Sole § The formula note, well-sealed, will be presented, with the respective opinion of the public health advisory board, to the general directorate of political and civil administration, where it will be filed, under secrecy, with the license application file.

Art. 7. Once the medicine is approved by the government, an ordinance granting the requested authorization will be issued and published in the official journal. . . .

§ 1. The licenses obtained by the authors or inventors of remedies of secret composition will be personal and temporary, but may be renewed, when, upon request by the interested parties, and after hearing the public health advisory board, the government deems it convenient.

§ 2. The minimum term for granting the license will be five years, and after fifteen years from that grant the drugs' formulae will be published in the official journal.

§ 3. To the heirs or successors . . ., of the author or inventor of a secret medicine, deceased within the period of the license, this license may be granted for the time remaining, if under the terms of the present regulation they give evidence of knowing the respective formulas and manipulations, and of knowing how to execute them. . . .

Art. 10. Secret remedies of notorious fame, which have already obtained approval from several foreign medical academies, authenticated by those in charge of affairs in Portugal in the respective countries, may, upon affirmative consultation of the public health advisory board, be admitted in the kingdom, without more formalities than those of Article 1. . .

Palace, May 10, 1899.

§ 2.51. A FRENCH PHARMACIST AND INVENTOR, STANISLAS LIMOUSIN, USED VARIOUS MANNERS OF CAPTURING REVENUE FROM HIS INVENTIONS: PATENTS, EXPOSURE IN SCIENTIFIC ARTICLES, ADVERTISING, PARTICIPATION IN INTERNATIONAL EXPOSITIONS, TRADEMARKS (AND THEIR ENFORCEMENT), AND LOBBYING FOR A MORE BENEFICIAL PATENT LAW—1866 ONWARDS

Stanislas Limousin was a pharmacist and prolific inventor of devices and machines useful in providing medical care and dispensing medicines. The following texts concern two of his most celebrated inventions, for which he obtained patent protection in France and in the United States: the oxygen inhaler and the press for making medicinal cachets—the first invention being of particular interest in these times of COVID-19 pandemic because when it first erupted, many hospitals struggled with the insufficient availability of ventilators.

In the United States, Limousin patented the cachets and the process of making them (patent no. 173,226, of February 8, 1876), and, three years later, some improvements (patent 216,197, of June 3, 1879). Although initially a very successful invention, medicinal cachets—a sort of a double wafer, as the following texts will describe—was abandoned soon, as a result of the introduction of more convenient ways of dispensing medicines in powder, such as pills and capsules.

Limousin was not an industrialist, but a pharmacist, owner of a drugstore in Paris. He sold the inhaler, but in his drugstore, he also provided services of renting the use of the machine, charging for it. The inhaler also had other applications, some of which the inventor would not expect: for example, it was employed by balloonists for compensating for the air's rarefaction at high altitudes.

Limousin, besides patents, secured his commercial enterprises through intensive publicity in all sorts of magazines and periodicals, including some of a religious inclination. He submitted some of his inventions to international fairs, as several of his pieces of publicity inform, and was even designated commissioner in some of them. In a number of those fairs, his invention on the device and method of encapsulating medicines was awarded medals. At that time, the laws of some countries, such as France and the United Kingdom, protected those rewards as special industrial property rights.[29]

Two of the following texts show that Limousin would not disdain in pushing the borders of intellectual property to some length. In one episode of his life as an entrepreneur, he attempted to claim exclusivity in the use of the words "cachets médicamenteux" (medicinal cachets), which a French court refused, because the expression had not been registered as a trademark, but just as a part of one. However, the fact that the term, when considered in isolation, was purely descriptive, may have had a strong influence on the decision. In another episode, Limousin joined the first debates on a future international treaty on industrial property, which would lead to the adoption of the Paris Convention for the Protection of Industrial Property, in 1883. Sitting at the international conference on industrial property in 1878, in Paris, Limousin opposed the idea that the granting of patents concerning pharmaceutical inventions should be subject to prior examination. Stanislas, satisfied with the absence of examination in France, argued that pharmacists should not be treated differently from other professions. Limousin also opposed the adoption of a special provision on the expropriation of patents. This, in his view, would be a shortcut for establishing compulsory licenses—thus implying his disagreement with this mechanism.

Eventually, he might have one personal reason for supporting a patent system without examination. It seems that he was accused that his invention on the press for making medicinal cachets was not original, and he was confronted in that regard by the allegedly true inventor. Moreover, the first patent he obtained in the United States was invalid for lack of novelty under Section 6 of the Patent Act of 1836, then in force: not only it had been patented three years earlier in France but also Limousin was using the invention publicly.

29. *See* From Babylon to the Silicon Valley, *supra* note 2, at 135 *et seq.*

§ 2.51.1. Specification of French patent no. 71,176, of April 15, 1866, for 15 years, concerning a "appareil inhalateur pour respirer de l'oxygène ou tout autre gaz ou vapeur," ["inhaler device for breathing oxygen or any gas or vapor"], granted to Stanislas Limousin

Stanislas Limousin, Notes sur l'Inhalation d'Oxigène (excerpt)

Inhaler device

The inhaler device shown below consists, as seen, of a rubber balloon and a wash bottle functioning like a hookah. Here is, moreover, how it is operated:

The quantity of oxygen gas, pure or mixed with air, which is to be inhaled, is introduced into the rubber balloon, and its closed valve is adapted to the copper fitting that ends the first tube that plunges to the bottom of the bottle.

The patient introduces the kind of pipe end that terminates the other tube into his/her mouth. The balloon valve is opened, the gas escapes through the water with which the bottle has been filled, a little below the beginning of the neck, and goes into the mouth with each movement of inspiration. When this movement is complete, the rubber tube below the mouthpiece is compressed between the thumb and the forefinger to prevent the gas from escaping and being lost. The patient then retains for a moment in the interior of the lungs the inhaled gas and releases it gently when the movement of expiration occurs. This continues until the balloon is completely empty.

Care must be taken, when exhaling, of removing the tube from the mouth, because the insufflation in the inside of the flask would cause water to rise up in the tube and even in the balloon. By operating in this way, one always allows to enter the lungs, along with the oxygen, a small amount of atmospheric air that penetrates through the nasal cavities. If one wishes, in certain special cases, to breathe completely pure gas, it would suffice to pinch the nose so as to prevent the introduction of air.

Whenever possible, when inhalation has started, one should not breathe outside the device, so that the oxygen, penetrating continuously into the lungs, can produce the hematosis of the blood in a continuous manner.

Figure 25 Cover of Limousin's NOTES SUR L'INHALATION D'OXIGÈNE*, with an illustration of the inhaler. Limousin, subsequently, used this same image in all advertisements of the device.*

§ 2.51.2. Specification of the Patent Limousin obtained in France for his medicinal cachets

Patent no. 97,304, of November 27, 1872

To Mr. Limousin, for a new process used for the dosage, storage and administration of powders and medicated pills.

This process consists in hermetically enclosing medicinal powders or pills between layers of unleavened bread, or any other substance easily solvable in the stomach.

By the aid of appropriate mechanism, similar to that used in the industry for stamping sheets of metal or paper, I stamp on one side of my envelope the name and dose of the medicine, and on the other my trademark. The matrix is arranged to give to these envelopes a slightly concave form in the central portion, so as to obtain the cavity necessary to receive the medicine. With the help of a graduated spoon, the quantity of the medicinal substance that one wishes to administer is introduced between the two envelopes.

These two envelopes are rigorously of the same size, and have in their circumference a round flat space, which has been reserved and reproduced by the matrix. This margin, slightly moistened, serves in soldering the two envelopes by means of a press having a prominence corresponding with this circular portion. By this means, the medicinal substance, accurately dosed, is protected from the causes of deterioration that may result from the contact with varying atmospheric influences.

Each packet bears on its center the name and dose of the substance, which avoids the possibility of an error, when the paper is taken from the box in which it is delivered to the customer.

Finally the patient has only to moisten the medicinal cachet in a spoon with water in order to allow its easy swallowing it as soon as the envelope is sufficiently softened.

§ 2.51.3. Extract from the specification of Limousin's patent on the medicinal cachets issued by the United States Patent Office in 1876

United States Patent Office

Stanislaus A. A. Limousin, of Paris, France

Improvement in Processes of Capsuling Medicaments.

Specification forming part of Letters Patent No. 173,226, dated February 8, 1876; application filed on September 17, 1875.

To all whom it may concern:

Be it known that I, Stanislaus A. A. Limousin, of Paris, in the Republic of France, have invented a new and useful Improvement in Capsuling Medicaments, of which the following is a specification:

My invention relates to an improved mode of capsuling medicaments by which druggists may furnish them in a neat and readily made up form to the public, to be taken in an easy and convenient manner; and the invention consists of capsules made of two concaved disks of wafer that are joined by being moistened at the circumference, the cavity of the wafers being filled with the required quantity by means of measuring, moistening, and edge compressing devices. . . .

The wafer capsules form thus an elegant and convenient means of taking medicaments of all kinds, with the advantage of having them made up in the exact quantities required, so that the taking of greater or lesser doses by the spoon or knife may be avoided, and a neat and cheap mode of furnishing them to the public be provided.

Having thus described my invention, I claim as new and desire to be secured by Letters Patent—

1. A capsule for containing medicaments composed of two concaved wafers or disks joined at their edges, substantially as and for the purpose set forth.
2. The process herein described of capsuling medicaments consisting in placing the exact quantity into a dished or concaved wafer, moistening the edges of the closing wafer, and pressing them firmly together at the edges, substantially in the manner and for the purpose described.

The above specification of my invention signed by me this 6th day of August, 1875.

S. A. A. Limousin.
Witnesses:
E.J. Brunot,
D.F.S. Fuller.

§ 2.51.4. A French Court rejects Limousin's attempt to enforce exclusive rights in the term *medicinal cachets*

Trademarks—Designation—Various Elements of the Mark—Medicinal cachets.

The names used to distinguish the products of an industry or a trade are protected by the law of June 23, 1857 only insofar as they have been registered as a trademark.

When the name is only one of the elements of the registered trademark which consists of a certain number of signs, all of which constitute the property of the manufacturer, the use of this name alone may not constitute a counterfeit or a fraudulent imitation of a trademark.

Rejection of the appeals of Stanislas Limousin and Charles-Gustave Toiray, civil parties at the trial, against a Judgment rendered on May 7, 1879, by the Paris Court of Appeal, revision chamber, in the case between them and the named Vie, Serres and Cruet.

On December 19, 1879.

The court, . . .

On the sole ground of appeal, based on the alleged violation of articles 1, 7 and 8 of the law of 23 June 1857, to the extent the challenged judgment refused to protect a manufacturer against the misappropriation of the name of its product, as specified in the initial brief:

Whereas if the law of June 23, of 1857, protects, as trademarks, the names used to distinguish the products of an industry or a trade, it is only on the condition that the name has been registered as a trademark;

Whereas it follows from the findings of fact in the judgment under appeal that the plaintiffs' trademark, filed on September 16, 1876, consists, not in the name of *medicinal cachets* taken in isolation, but in a set of indications that the judgment enumerates in detail; that it bases this assessment, having examined the samples filed and the filing certificate, on the multiplicity and diversity of the external signs that are found in such certificate, and that, from this examination, the judgment draws the conclusion that Limousin and Toiray have intended to reserve the exclusive ownership of all of these indications and not that of the special name of medicinal cachets;

Whereas, as a consequence of this assessment, which is sovereign, the challenged judgment has been able to decide, without violating the articles of the law of 1857 invoked by the appeal, that there was no manner of attributing to

Messrs. Vié and others, because of the use of the two words "medicinal cachets," either a counterfeit or a fraudulent imitation of a trademark;

Whereas, moreover, that the challenged judgment is regular in form;

Rejects,

Thus decides and concludes, etc. — Criminal Chamber.

Figure 26 Advertisement of Limousin's medicinal cachets. JOURNAL DE PHARMACIE ET DE CHIMIE, *May 15, 1896.*

§ 2.51.5. At the International Congress on Industrial Property, of 1878, Limousin defends a patent system that better serves the interests of inventors in the pharmaceutical sector

Exposition Universelle de 1878—Palais du Trocadéro—Congrès International de la Propriété Industrielle, Tenu à Paris en 1878 (excerpt)

The opening session of the International Congress of Industrial Property took place on September 5, in one of the halls of the Trocadero Palace, under the chairmanship of Mr. Teisserenc de Bort, Minister of Agriculture and Trade, one of the honorary chairs of the congress. Mr. de Chlumetzky, Minister of Commerce and Public Works of the Austrian Empire, also one of the Honorary Presidents of the Congress, had taken place in the office next to Mr. Teisserenc de Bort. . . .

The opening session of the International Congress of Industrial Property took place on September 5, in one of the halls of the Trocadero Palace, under the chairmanship of Mr. Teisserenc de Bort, Minister of Agriculture and Trade, one of the honorary chairs of the congress. Mr. de Chlumetzky, Minister of Commerce and Public Works of the Austrian Empire, also one of the Honorary Presidents of the Congress, had taken place in the office next to Mr. Teisserenc de Bort. . . .

Session of September 9
Patents for Inventions

. . . The congress adopts *question no. 1* of the agenda: "All inventions, processes or products are patentable, other than combinations or plans of finance and credit or inventions contrary to public order or good morals." . . .

Mr. Léon Lyon-Caen asks for the patentability of pharmaceutical products. Quinine sulfate, he said, to cite just one example, did not deserve a patent? Is not it doing enough service? Today, the pharmacist, who cannot have a patent, takes a trademark, and the infringement, prosecuted, is no longer that of the product, but that of the bottle! . . .

The discussion continues on the patentability of pharmaceuticals.

Mr. Turquetil opposes the patentability of these products; he would like the Faculty of Medicine alone to take care of it. There has been mention, says Mr. Lecoq, of the interests of pharmacists. It seemed to him that whoever made a medicine with a particular substance would deserve to obtain a patent. In addition, by replacing specialties with patented medicines, we will be able to serve the less well-off classes. Who pays the industry's multiple ads? It is the public. When the product is patented, there will no longer be the same expense. With a patent, the product will fall into the public domain after a certain period of time, to the great benefit of society.

Mr. Genevoix, speaking on behalf of the pharmacists' union, rejects the patentability of pharmaceutical products. The patent grant, in his opinion, would only increase the scourge of the secret remedy. . . .

46 members against 38 decide that patents should be granted to inventors of "pharmaceutical products."

The agenda brings the discussion of question no. 2 concerning the grant of patents for inventions "after or without prior examination."

Mr. Barrault points out the importance of the question. In the United States, the previous examination mechanism has been in operation for ninety years. In 1877, 23,000 patents were applied for and 17,000 granted. Prior examination there has become impossible; patents were issued for inventions patented thirty years previously. So, despite the enormous expense of the Patent Office, the examination is lacking in certainty. In France, the prior examination regime has not been adopted. After one year, half of the patents are no longer valid. As a result, without administrative error, the public domain was enriched by 50 percent of patents.

In England, after the seventh year, only 7 percent of patents are left.

Prior examination is therefore not necessary, since the best result is obtained without any inconvenience.

Mr. Klostermann, from Berlin, supports the following amendment which he submits together with a number of his foreign colleagues:

Patent applications are subject to prior examination. This examination cannot lead to the rejection of the application by the body of examiners, but the right of objection must be granted to both the administration and to third parties, by means of suitable publicity. The oppositions made in the terms fixed by the law will be settled by the courts.

Mr. Pieper, from Dresden, says that prior examination is excellent, in his opinion. The country that adopts it will have *better inventors* than countries under another regime. He adds that French members of congress are too busy creating a law for France; he asks them to worry more about international issues. . . .

Session of September 10.

Patents for inventions.

. . . The discussion continues on the need for pre-grant examination or non-examination of patents for inventions. . . .

The resolution is definitively adopted in the following terms:

The invention patent should be granted to any applicant, at their own risk and peril. However, it is useful for the applicant to receive prior and secret notice, especially on the novelty issue, so that he/she can, at his/her option, maintain, modify or abandon the application. (Agenda item no. 2)

Mr. Genevoix, on behalf of the pharmacists' union, proposes the following restriction:

"Pre-grant examination will apply to pharmaceutical preparations." . . .

Mr. Stanislas Limousin states that, albeit a pharmacist, he could not vote for the proposal of his colleague, Mr. Genevoix. He requests that the pharmaceutical profession be subject to the common rules. . . .

Session of Friday, September 13. . . .

The discussion turned to matters relating to the expropriation of patents.

Mr. Pouillet explains that, in some cases, the private interest must give way to the public interest. This is a principle recognized by all laws. In France, we did it for the daguerreotype. . . .

Mr. Limousin: "If expropriation is to be accepted in principle, it should not be under special laws for an individual; it is dangerous to include a principle of this kind in our resolutions. In matters of invention, as in real estate, society only takes back what belongs to it. That will be opening the way to compulsory licenses." . . .

§ 2.52. A PORTUGUESE PHARMACIST OBTAINS A PATENT FOR A SYRUP AGAINST COUGH—1869

The following texts concern a patent and advertisements for a pectoral syrup allegedly invented by Pedro Augusto Franco (1833-1902), a Portuguese pharmacist, politician and banker.

In 1852 Portugal amended its industrial property law of 1837 and, following the example of France, excluded medicines from patentability. However, the Civil Code, enacted in 1867, revoked the substantive provisions of the industrial property act of 1852 and reinstated the patentability of all sorts of inventions, except those "related to unlawful industries or objects." Thus, Franco benefited from a significant change in the law.

What is striking in Franco's invention is the name he attributed to his medicine: "James pectoral syrup." Why James, an English name, in a medicine allegedly invented by a Portuguese pharmacist? The reason may be that Franco, in creating his syrup, may have been inspired by a passage of a famous medical book authored by Robert James (1705-1776), an English physician—A MEDICINAL DICTIONARY, published in London in several volumes, between 1745 and 1747. The work was translated by Diderot, Eidous and Toussaint, and published in France, in 1748, with similar success. Digressing on the various types of cough and the manners of treating them, Robert James described the composition and the manner of preparing a syrup against cough:

> *"For example: Take sweet almond oil, and maidenhair fern syrup (one ounce of each); whale white, three drachms of white of whale; fifteen grains of saffron. Mix it all together and administer it. The same indication will still be filled very well with veronique infusions." (A number of variations of the same formula follows)." [Extracted from the French version, DICTIONNAIRE UNIVERSEL DE MÉDECINE, DE CHIRURGIE, DE CHYMIE, DE BOTANIQUE, D'ANATOMIE, DE PHARMACIE, D'HISTOIRE NATURELLE, &C., vol. 6, at columns 459-460 (Briasson, David and Durand, 1748). Source: < gallica.BnF.fr >.]*

Like other medicinal inventors of his time, Franco also exhibited his medicines at international fairs and included in his advertisements the notice of the medals received. Thus, following the same marketing model of other inventors, Franco resorted to a combination of intellectual property tools to secure significant commercial success for his medicines.

Interestingly, the patent letter clarifies an issue that had been subject to legal debate, as seen above, namely that the patent did not represent a permission to commercialize the medicine, which was dependent on previously obtaining the necessary sanitary certificates.

Ministry of Public Works, Commerce and Industry

Directorate-General for Trade and Industry

Section of Trade and Industry—1st Section

> In response to what Pedro Augusto Franco, a pharmacist based in Belém, exposed to me, asking for a privilege for fifteen years as the inventor of a remedy called *James chest syrup, with application to the treatment of toxicological diseases*.
>
> . . . Whereas the applicant has fulfilled all the formalities required by law:
>
> I am pleased to grant Pedro Augusto Franco a patent for invention for the object indicated above for the term of fifteen years, during which his rights to the property of that invention will be placed under the custody and defense of the law, the patent being granted without prior examination, not guaranteeing the reality or

merit of the invention it concerns, and that by this privilege the inventor should not consider himself exempt from the respective health laws, and therefore the rights of third parties and the applicant subject to the laws in force and to the previous payment he owes are safeguarded, the corresponding certificate being issued to him by the appropriate ministry.

The Minister and Secretary of State for Public Works, Commerce and Industry, having so understood it and had it done. Palace, June 22, 1869.

Figure 27 Advertisement of the James Pectoral Syrup, against cough and chest ailments. The text goes like this: "Sole approved and legally authorized by the Public Health Council of Portugal. Prepared by Pedro Augusto Franco, Commander of the Order of Christ, a pharmaceutical supplier to the Royal House of His Faithful Majesty King Luis I, honorary member of the Lusitan Pharmacist Society, and other scientific and industrial societies, awarded at the Exhibition of Porto, etc., etc. The efficiency of this syrup, evidently proven in many observations in hospitals and in the private clinics of the most distinguished doctors in that country, led the kingdom's public health council to approve it (a distinction that other preparations have not deserved) and to consider it a true specific against bronchitis, both acute and chronic, reflux, rebellious coughs, convulsive and asthmatic coughs, chest pain, blood sputum, and against all nervous irritations. Each bottle is accompanied by a printout with the observations of the main doctors in Lisbon, acknowledged by the consuls of Brazil. General Warehouse in Pará [Brazil]." Extracted from O Liberal do Pará, no. 67, 23 de março de 1879.

Figure 28 The same advertisement published in a Portuguese newspaper. This ad, however, brings an important, intellectual property-related note: in its bottom, it displays the saying: "On the sealed part of the envelope is my signature in blue ink." And next to it, the signature (and trademark) of the inventor. VIMARANENSE, *No. 343, July 2, 1894.*

§ 2.53. AN APPRAISAL OF THE U.S. PATENT SYSTEM AS APPLIED TO MEDICINES IN THE LATE NINETEENTH CENTURY

A historian of pharmacy gives, in the following text, an impartial appraisal of how inventors in the pharmaceutical sector used the patent system in the nineteenth century. The final evaluation is quite positive, in spite of some problems detected—which, however, one can find in the system in general, and not only in the context of medicines.

John S. Billings, American Inventions and Discoveries in Medicine, Surgery, and Practical Sanitation, 1891 (excerpts)

> . . . The application of the patent system to medicine in this country has had its advantages for certain people, has given employment to a considerable amount of capital in production (and to a much larger amount in advertising), has contributed materially to the revenues of the government, and has made a great deal of work for the medical profession.
>
> So far as I know, but one complete system of medicine has been patented in this country, and that was the steam, Cayenne pepper and lobelia system—commonly known as Thomsonianism— to which a patent was granted in 1836. The right to practice this system, with a book describing the methods, was sold by the patentee for twenty dollars, and perhaps some of you may have some reminiscences of it connected with your boyish days. I am certain I shall never forget the effects of "Composition Powder," or of "Number Six," which was essentially a concentrated tincture of Cayenne pepper, and one dose of which was enough to make a boy willing to go to school for a month.
>
> From a report made by the Commissioner of Patents in 1849, it appears that eighty-six patents for medicines had been granted up to that date; but the specifications of most of those issued before 1836 had been lost by fire. The greater number of patents for medicines were issued between 1850 and 1860. The total number of patents granted for medicines during the last decade (1880-1890) is 540.
>
> This, however, applies only to "patent medicines," properly so-called, the claims for which are, for the most part, presented by simple-minded men who know very little of the ways of the world. A patent requires a full and unreserved disclosure of the recipe, and the mode of compounding the same, for the public benefit when the term of the patent shall have expired; and the Commissioner of Patents may, if he chooses, require the applicant to furnish specimens of the composition and of its ingredients, sufficient in quantity for the purpose of experiment. The law, however, does not require the applicant to furnish patients to be experimented on, and this may be the reason why the commissioner has never demanded samples of the ingredients. By far the greater number of the owners of panaceas and nostrums are too shrewd to thus publish their secrets, for they can attain their purpose much better under the law for registering trade-marks and labels, designs for bottles and packages, and copyrights of printed matter, which are less costly, and do not reveal the arcanum.
>
> These proprietary medicines constitute the great bulk of what the public call "patent medicines." The trade in patent and secret remedies has been, and still is, an important one. . . .
>
> According to the Census of 1880 there were in the United States 592 establishments devoted to the manufacture of drugs and chemicals, the capital invested being $28,598,458, and the annual value of the product $38,173,658, while there were 563 establishments devoted to the manufacture of patent

medicines and compounds, the capital invested being $10,620,880, and the annual value of the product $14,682,494. . . .

From the commercial and industrial point of view the great importance of patent and proprietary medicines is connected with advertising. The problem is to induce people to pay twenty-five cents for the liver-encouraging, silent-perambulating, family pills, which cost three cents. Someday I hope that the modern professional expert in advertising will favor us with his views as to the nature and character of those people who were induced to buy Jones's liver pills or Slow's specific by means of the huge display of these names on the sides and roofs of barns and outbuildings, which display forms such a prominent feature in many of our American landscapes, as seen by the traveler on the railway. I suppose there must be such people, for I have a high estimate of the business shrewdness of the men who pay for these abominations. I should also like to know how much a farmer gets for allowing his buildings to be thus defaced. He must be hard-up; indeed such a display indicates that the place is probably mortgaged and that the poor man is heavily in debt. . . .

Upon the whole I should think that the number of people who would take some trouble to avoid purchasing an article which is thus advertised must be rapidly increasing, so that such displays will soon be no longer profitable. The great importance of advertising does not relate to the placard or chromo business, but to its relations to periodical literature, —to the daily and weekly press and the monthly magazines and journals. To the establishment and support of some of our newspapers and journals, medical as well as others, these proprietary and secret medicines, cosmetics, food preparations, etc., have no doubt contributed largely.

I am sorry to say that I have been unable to obtain definite information as to the direct benefits which inventions of this kind have conferred on the public in the way of cure of disease or preventing death. Among the questions which were not put in the schedules of the last census were the following, namely: Did you ever take any patent or proprietary medicine? If so, what and how much, and what was the result? Some very remarkable statistics would no doubt have been obtained had this inquiry been made. I can only say that I know of but four secret remedies which have been really valuable additions to the resources of practical medicine, and the composition of all these is now known. These four are all powerful and dangerous, and should only be used on the advice of a skilled physician. Most of such remedies have little value as curative agents, and some of them are prepared and purchased almost exclusively for immoral or criminal purposes. . . .

In 1849 a special committee of the House of Representatives reported to the House a bill to prevent the patenting of medicines, accompanied by a report. This bill provided that after the passage of the act, letters patent shall not be granted for any article whatever as a medicine, provided that this shall not apply to machines, instruments or apparatus. When the matter came before the House for consideration the bill was laid on the table. . . .

As you know, the law prescribes that a patent may be given for a "new and useful art, machine, manufacture, or composition of matter." I used to think that the word " useful " in this law had its ordinary meaning, and, therefore, wondered exceedingly as to why the Patent Office examiners allowed patents to certain things which came under my notice. One day, however, I received an article from the Patent Office, with the request for a report as to whether it was useful in the sense in which that word was used by the Office, namely, "not pernicious or prejudicial to public interests—capable of being used "—and then for the first time I understood one of the first principles of the patent law of the United States, that is, that it does not take into consideration the degree of utility in the device, or, in other words, that " useful" means " harmless."

If a patent is granted to a medicine, it must be as a composition of matter as a special article of manufacture. The practice of the Patent Office in these matters is not generally understood. It does not now consider that medical prescriptions are inventions within the meaning of the law, or that a mere aggregation of well-known remedies to obtain a cumulative effect is a patentable composition of matter. A certain number of claims for government protection in the form of patents or trade-marks are made for medical compounds or for apparatus, under false pretenses; that is to say, the claim is for a new remedy for rheumatism or dyspepsia, or displacement, with a warning against their use under certain conditions, the real design being that they are to be used under precisely these conditions in order to procure abortion, etc. These are sometimes difficult cases for the Patent Office to treat properly, for the law does not allow a large discretion for refusal on mere suspicion, and where there is ostensible and possible utility (in the Patent Office sense) it can hardly reject the claim on the ground that the invention might be used for immoral purposes.

§ 2.54. IN 1914, THE BRITISH PARLIAMENT, DISCUSSING ABUSIVE PRACTICES IN CONNECTION WITH THE SALE OF SECRET MEDICINES, DID NOT RECOMMEND THE PROHIBITION OF THEIR COMMERCIALIZATION, BUT RATHER THAT INVENTORS PROVIDED THEIR COMPOSITIONS TO THE AGENCY IN CHARGE OF AUTHORIZING THEIR COMMERCIALIZATION—WHICH SHOULD KEEP THAT INFORMATION SECRET

We saw above that in 1914, the British Parliament elaborated a report that was very critical of the marketing practices of pharmacists as regards the sale and the advertisement of medicines (see § 1.29). The same Committee has also looked at those same practices concerning patent and proprietary medicines in particular. According to the Report, in 1912, 312 patents were in force for medicines, and medicinal preparations.

House of Commons, Report of the Select Committee on Patent Medicines—August 4, 1914 (excerpts)

The Select Committee appointed to consider and inquire into the question of the sale of Patent and Proprietary Medicines and Medical Preparations and Appliances, and Advertisements relating thereto; and to report what amendments, if any, in the Law are necessary or desirable:

Have agreed to the following Report:—

. . .

Class B. — Secret Remedies.

In consequence of the great variety of remedies of this class, it is difficult to give an adequate classification of them without entering into excessive detail. For practical purposes, however, they may be divided into three general groups.

Group 1. *Simple household remedies.*—This group consists of a number of household remedies, often originally manufactured from a doctor's family prescription, and undoubtedly beneficial for uncomplicated ailments. They have in most cases been sold for many years, and as their retail price is out of all proportion to their cost, large fortunes have often been amassed by their proprietors. Except for the fact that often the advertisements of them recommend their use for cases they cannot benefit, thus causing the purchaser to run the risk of serious injury by delay in securing proper medical treatment, there is little or nothing to criticise in their sale. We cannot, of course, give examples of these, as our remarks would at once be used for advertising purposes.

Group 2. *Dangerous remedies, and drugs for improper purposes.*—This is a small class of drugs which should not be sold at all, of which acetanilide is possibly an example; which should not be sold except on a doctor's prescription; or which should not be sold for the purpose for which they are offered—as, for example, an unsuitable drug as a general medicine for young children.

Group 3. *Fraudulent remedies.*—This is a large class, having an extensive sale, often at high prices, consisting of abortifacients, of alleged cures for cancer, consumption, diabetes, paralysis, locomotor ataxy, Bright's disease, lupus, fits, epilepsy, rupture (without operation or appliance), deafness, disease of the eye, syphilis, etc., together with electric belts, apparatus for supplying oxygen to the system (other than by inspiration), "ionised" waters and the like. The discovery of radium will probably add a number of remedies to this group. There should be little difficulty in identifying remedies of this class, and their treatment in the public interest need involve no doubt or hesitation. They are, and are known by their makers to be, cruel frauds; and the sale and advertisement of them should be prohibited under drastic penalties.

Group 4. *Remedies making grossly exaggerated claims.*—This is a final large class. Genuine simple remedies making exaggerated claims are included in Group 1, as the exaggeration in their case is usually of the nature of the "trade puff." Those we have in view in this group are remedies depending for their sale largely or wholly upon the extravagant promises they hold out to the purchaser. This, under the name of "misbranding," is now prohibited by law in the United States, and many cases came before us in which the advertisements of proprietary remedies in this country were refused admission into Australia. This group presents obviously great difficulties in drawing the line between claims which are merely "puffs" and claims which are fraudulent, but we regard it as beyond question that the public is defrauded on a large scale by promises which cannot possibly be fulfilled. As an example of the profits made by the sale of this class of remedies, George Taylor Eulford, the proprietor of "Dr. Williams' Pink Pills for Pale People," left a fortune of £1,111,000.

§ 2.55. THE AMERICAN MEDICAL ASSOCIATION ALERTS AGAINST THE ABUSIVE USE OF THE PATENT SYSTEM TO ENDORSE FAKE MEDICINES AND IN ONE PARTICULAR CASE, HAS ASKED FOR THE INVALIDATION OF ONE PATENT—1917

In an editorial in its own journal (dated June 23, 1917), the American Medical Association (AMA) called the attention for the risks that resulted from the frivolous patenting of quack medicines. Those risks arose from the fact that, as discussed above (see § 2.43), patents were at that time seen as administrative authorizations for the commercial exploitation of the patented inventions. Thus, the issuance of a patent for a medicine could be taken as the equivalent to a public recommendation of its therapeutic value. The AMA, in this text, claims that the Patent Office was not paying due attention to the frivolous claiming of quack medicines, which would never be able to meet the curative promises of the self-proclaimed "inventors."

Actually, this debate raises an issue that has been (and continues being) associated with pharmaceutical patents: because the patents are granted only for those inventions that reach the results described in the applications, should the Patent Office perform the role of the Food and Drug Administration and check whether the alleged therapeutic effects are indeed met? If not, what is the purpose of examining patent applications for pharmaceutical inventions as to their utility? The answer was given above: it is all a matter of evidence. While the Patent Office looks for a mere appearance of utility, the sanitary agency requires effective evidence, grounded on test data, of utility.

Anyway, the AMA did not object to the patent system per se, but rather to its abuse. However, the association has asked for the special nullification of the patent protection for a medicinal composition, known as asphernamine, and trademarked as Salvarsan. As a powerful medicine against syphilis, Salvarsan was in great demand, particularly during the Great War. Under the authority given to it by the "Trading with the Enemy Act," the Federal Trade Commission confiscated and licensed four patents owned by asphernamine's German inventors to four US companies. Because the trademark Salvarsan was owned by a US company, the FTC also ordered that the product be designated by its generic name "asphernamine."

AMA, The Propaganda for Reform in Proprietary Medicines, vol. 2—1922 (excerpts)

"Patents"

Patent Laws and Patent Office Practice

The inequity of our patent laws, or possibly it would be more correct to say, of the interpretation of our patent laws, has been commented on many times in The Journal [of the American Medical Association]. The Journal also has had occasion to call attention to patents that have been issued for obviously unscientific and quackish devices and preparations. The cases of the preposterous gas-pipe fake "Oxydonor" and the creatinine mixture for the alleged conferring of immunity against diphtheria, pneumonia, scarlet fever, syphilis, tuberculosis, etc., are cases in point.

In a patent issued the early part of this year for the "discovery" of a method of flavoring Epsom salt, the patent office has, in fatuity, piled Pelion on Ossa. The "inventor" declares that his invention relates to a pharmaceutical preparation and a special method of treatment of the medicinal agents whereby said agent will be rendered much more efficient in character. He further avows that the "prime object" of his "invention" is to "disguise the normal taste and impart an agreeable odor or smell to salts commonly employed as a cathartic." Parenthetically it may be said that probably not a day passes that some physician in the United States does not do substantially the same thing when writing a prescription. The "inventor" further claims that the object of his "invention" is to utilize the salts as a vehicle to carry an antiseptic and anesthetic agent whereby the salts when administered as a cathartic "will also act beneficially on the entire digestive tract" and "whereby cramped and pasmodic conditions are at once relieved with a resulting cure of flatulency, indigestion, sick and sour stomach, colic and the destruction of worms, etc."

Such claims are so absurd that the only excuse for commenting on them is the effect they have on the public mind. The layman reading the specifications of this patent would naturally conclude that an invention of great importance had been made—of such importance as to warrant the government in rewarding its inventor by granting him a seventeen-year monopoly on the sale of his invention.

The law requires that, to be patentable, inventions shall be new and useful and shall show a higher degree of skill in their inception than is naturally to be expected from those who are skilled in the arts to which the inventions belong. It has been decided again and again that physicians' prescriptions are not patentable because it is assumed that an educated physician will utilize his knowledge of pharmacy in devising proper compounds of medicines to meet the indications of disease. When a physician prescribes a dose of Epsom salt to be taken in one of the official aromatic waters, he does not produce or create a new invention by so doing. Of course, in one sense every prescription is an invention—an invention to meet the conditions presented by the patient—but such inventions are not patentable, because they represent the ordinary skill of a physician in carrying on his vocation.

If the patent office goes on granting patents for such "inventions" as flavored Epsom salt, and it should be found financially profitable to secure such patents and place the products on the market, it will only be a matter of time before the materia medica will be so restricted that a physician will be unable to write a prescription without infringing on somebody's patent.

The splendid conception of the framers of our constitution in providing a plan for promoting progress in science and useful arts by granting to inventors for a limited time the exclusive use of their inventions, in exchange for the publication of full knowledge thereof, is being debased. No branch of our government is of greater importance to the progress of the country than the patent office, provided that office is intelligently administered. When the patent office is used, however, for an extension of the nostrum business, founded on the abuse of patent and trade-mark laws, it becomes a menace to the public health. The objects of the patent law are being defeated by the practices of the patent office. (Editorial from The Journal A. M. A., June 23, 1917.)

Salvarsan: Abrogate the Patent

The Journal [of the American Medical Association] has already commented on the difficulty in securing salvarsan, on the moral and ethical question as to whether or not it is justifiable for one person to control the output of a drug necessary to public health. This week we publish an account of the action of the St. Louis and Chicago medical societies, which are calling on the medical profession to appeal to their senators and congressmen to abrogate this patent. The Journal believes that this patent should be abrogated, not alone because the patentees have not supplied the demand, not alone because they have dictated to the medical profession who should have the drug and how much a physician might have, not alone because of the war with Germany, not alone because of the special needs of the government at this time for the control of venereal diseases, not alone because, as some claim, the patent at Washington does not correctly describe the product, but also because the people who are supplying this product are charging prices that are exorbitant compared to the price at which others in this country can supply it. The fact is that the salvarsan one can obtain today costs $4.50 per ampule of 0.6 gram, whereas the same dose of arsenobenzol a preparation identical with, if not better than, salvarsan costs $2.00 at retail, and as Dr. Schamberg says: "If we are permitted to continue marketing the same drug after the war, we can sell it at $1.00 or less per tube." To abrogate this patent would be doing an injury to no one. Certainly the patentees of salvarsan have already reaped their harvest and a pretty rich one. The supply of salvarsan at a reasonable price in proportion to its actual cost of production is in the interest of the health of the entire population of the country, whereas to let matters rest as they are, is to the benefit of one man. While we are emphasizing here the cost, there is after all a greater question, and that is the supply necessary to help control the ravages of one of the most serious diseases which afflict humanity today. It is the duty of Congress to abrogate the patent on this preparation and, incidentally, on all medicinal preparations of importance. (Editorial from The Journal A. M. A., April 21, 1917.)

End the Monopoly

The Adamson Bill, known as the "trading with the enemy act," has recently been passed by the House of Representatives, is now before the Senate, and will doubtless be enacted into a law. One of its clauses confers authority on the Federal Trade Commission to grant licenses to citizens of this country to operate patents owned by enemy aliens. Physicians are interested in the bill primarily because it includes the salvarsan situation. The manner in which salvarsan has been supplied in this country has been so arbitrary and the prices charged so tremendously above the actual cost, that we should not be satisfied unless the monopoly is ended so that the drug can be supplied at least at a fairly moderate figure, and the old methods eliminated. It is to be hoped therefore, that the Federal Trade Commission will not grant exclusive control that is, exclusive license to any one person or firm. To do so would simply perpetuate the old monopoly and the old conditions. England has adopted a law, which, in principle, is similar to the Adamson Bill, and there several concerns have been licensed to manufacture the product. The same should be done here. The Dermatologic Research Laboratories of Philadelphia announce that they can supply arsenobenzol at $1.50 a tube, and that there is immediately available a supply sufficient for any demand that may be made. The same laboratories have announced also that in a few months they will be able to supply hospitals for $1.00 a tube. Considerable responsibility rests on the Federal Trade Commission in this matter, for it is not only a question of monopoly, but also a question of scientific qualifications and ability to make the product on the part of some who may make application. Undoubtedly the commission will secure the cooperation of the United States Public Health Service, under whose supervision these drugs should be manufactured no matter who shall be licensed to make the product. (Editorial from The Journal A. M. A., July 21, 1917.)

§ 2.56. BRAZIL EXCLUDES PHARMACEUTICAL INVENTIONS FROM PATENTABILITY—1971

Until the middle of the twentieth century, the opposition against the patentability of pharmaceutical inventions continued prevailing in a large number of countries, keen to profit from the highly risky investment made in that field in a relatively small number of developed countries. A certain level of harmonization of national laws obtained as a consequence of the Paris Convention did not work as far as pharmaceutical inventions were concerned. In that regard, the Paris Convention, for historical reasons, was neutral. But such scenario changed, first in parallel with the development of the legal framework of the European Communities (first France, then Italy, then Spain and Portugal, were induced to adopt patent protection for pharmaceuticals), and a few decades later, after the adoption of the TRIPS Agreement, an Annex to the Agreement that Established the World Trade Organization, of 1994, and its special provision against discrimination in the granting of patents as to the field of technology. In this case, the mandatory protection of pharmaceutical inventions extended to countries of all levels of development, conditioned to some transitional periods.

Before the entry of the TRIPS Agreement into force, some large developing countries have tried to use the exclusion of pharmaceutical inventions from patentability as a tool for the promotion of a national generic industry, as some arguments went, and as a matter of social ethics, for others.

There is a thin line between the exclusion of pharmaceuticals from patentability as a mechanism for promoting the generic industry and that same exclusion as a matter of social conscience—as misguided the latter may be. The former is opportunistic and unethical and discourages private investment in research and development. It rarely works, moreover, because its effectiveness depends on a significant number of factors, which, thus far, have only been found, to a certain extent, in India. Indeed, in the early 1970s, the Indian government excluded pharmaceutical products from patentability, and, at the same time, prohibited foreign companies from selling new drugs on the Indian market. The combination of these two factors, along with the large size of domestic demand for pharmaceuticals, opened a window of opportunity for national generic manufacturers, who were therefore legally insulated from foreign competition in the making and selling of new drugs. In this way, Indian generic pharmaceutical companies felt confident in investing in the reverse engineering of the newest drugs and manufacturing them. Benefiting from the fact that in other countries the same exclusion from patentability had been introduced, those companies also had opportunities for exporting. Of course, needless to say that India does not have the capacity to invent advanced, sophisticated drugs. Every policy based on copying is a disincentive for inventing.

At about the same time, Brazil also excluded pharmaceutical products from patentability. Brazil went even further than India because it denied patentability not only to the products but also to the processes. And yet, twenty-five years later, when the TRIPS Agreement entered into force, Brazil, unlike India, had not been able to establish a generic sector with the capacity to manufacture the most recent pharmaceutical active ingredients. The reason was that, unlike their Indian competitors, Brazilian generic manufacturers were not protected against competition from imported drugs. Therefore, they converted into assemblers of drugs: they would import the active ingredients from India and assembled them in Brazil. Assembling requires, in fact, a much lower technological level than making those ingredients—let alone than inventing them.

Brazil tried to change the course of things a few decades later. Like India, the country simply ignored its obligation under the TRIPS Agreement of protecting test data concerning chemical entities against unfair commercial use. Under Article 39.3 of the Agreement, the sanitary agency should not rely on the data submitted by the inventor or introducer of a new medicine for approving the marketing of a generic product. This measure, of course, is a powerful obstacle to the early introduction of generic pharma ceuticals, and Brazil, like India, has simply ignored it. Another step was the approval of the law of generics, in 1999, which included the provision that we saw in the first chapter, concerning trademarks (see § 1.33). Of course, this not being enough, Brazil, in 2012, established a mechanism designated as Partnerships for Productive Development (PDP), with the intent of encouraging technological joint-ventures between national manufacturers and foreign research-based pharmaceutical companies (see § 2.61).

Law No. 5,772, of December 21, 1971

Enacts the Industrial Property Code, and establishes other provisions.

Article 9. The following are not patentable: . . .

b) substances, materials or products obtained by chemical means or processes, excepted the patentability of the respective processes for their acquisition or modification;
c) food substances, materials, blends or products, chemical-pharmaceutical and medicinal products, of any kind, as well as the respective processes for their acquisition or modification; . . . .

§ 2.57. THE BIRTH OF THE BOLAR EXEMPTION—THE ROCHE CASE AND THE STATUTE—1984

The so-called Bolar exemption was introduced in the patent statute of the United States as a reaction by Congress to the holding of a Federal Court in Roche Products, Inc. v. Bolar Pharmaceutical Co. Inc.*—hence the name of the legal clause.*

In that case, the court held that the use of a patented pharmaceutical invention for the purpose of gathering data necessary to obtain marketing approval from the Food and Drug Administration (FDA) was an infringement of the patent. In the United States, the research exemption is permitted with serious restrictions. In general, the exemption is admitted when the use of the invention concerns purely scientific inquiries. But, also in general, any use that may have indirect commercial applications—such as the use of the invention for obtaining data that will be used in the submissions to the FDA—is not permitted (or, rather, was *not permitted). Significantly, it seems that the Court of Appeals for the Federal Circuit did not agree with the legal commandment, and, although it could not avoid finding an infringement in Bolar's actions, it nonetheless refused to issue an injunction that would make it destroy the data already obtained.*

The Bolar opinion naturally has raised some commotion within certain circles. Indeed, if the generic manufacturer had to wait for the end of the patent term to begin doing the testing of its generic molecule or compound, in order to acquire information on its bioequivalence and bioavailability, the granting of marketing approval would be delayed for one or two years. Consequently, the entry of the generic medicine on the market would be delayed too. Sensitive to that commotion, the United States Congress amended the patent statute and introduced the Bolar exemption.

In a demonstration of what this book has been asserting from the beginning—that the intellectual property that applies to pharmaceuticals is not the same that applies to other areas of business—the United States Supreme Court, in 2005, in Merck KGaa v. Integra Lifesciences, Ltd. *(545 U.S. 193 (2005)), pushed the Bolar exemption even further, and extended it to all tests and experiments "reasonably related" to the submission of data to the FDA, including those unsuccessful tests and experiments that end in nothing, and which do not generate any new relevant data for the purposes of obtaining marketing approval—and which, therefore, are not submitted to the FDA.*

> *The statutory text does not require such a result. Congress did not limit § 271(e)(1)'s safe harbor to the development of information for inclusion in a submission to the FDA, nor did it create an exemption applicable only to the research relevant to filing an ANDA for approval of a generic drug. Rather, it exempted from infringement* all *uses of patented compounds "reasonably related" to the process of developing information for submission under* any *federal law regulating the manufacture, use, or distribution of drugs. See* Eli Lilly, *496 U.S., at 674. We decline to read the "reasonable relation" requirement so narrowly as to render § 271(e)(1)'s stated protection of activities leading to FDA approval for all drugs illusory. Properly construed, § 271(e)(1) leaves adequate space for experimentation and failure on the road to regulatory approval.*

In other countries, which have adopted more flexible research exemptions, that would not be a very serious problem. In this sense, under the Dispute Settlement Mechanism of the WTO, a panel, settling a dispute between the European Community and Canada, held that the "Bolar exemption" did not infringe the norms of the TRIPS Agreement, provided that any act leading to the making and selling of the product in question be done after the end of the patent term only. So, products eventually made for the purposes of obtaining marketing approval should be destroyed. [See Canada—Patent Protection for Pharmaceutical Products, *Report of the Panel adopted on 7 April 2000 (WT/DS114/R, of 17 March 2000. [Source: < www.wto.org > .] Nevertheless, perhaps with the purpose of staying on the safe side, many WTO Members, after the publication of this Panel Report, amended their laws for also introducing the Bolar exemption, thus making it explicit.*

§ 2.57.1. The opinion that has originated the Bolar exemption

Roche Products, Inc. v. Bolar Pharmaceutical Co., Inc.

U.S. Court of Appeals for the Federal Circuit

733 F.2d 858 (Fed. Cir. 1984)

April 23, 1984

Nichols, Senior Circuit Judge.

This is an appeal from a judgment entered on October 14, 1983, in which the United States District Court, 572 F. Supp. 255, for the Eastern District of New York held United States Patent No. 3,299,053 not infringed and denied relief. We reverse and remand.

At stake in this case is the length of time a pharmaceutical company which has a patent on the active ingredient in a drug can have exclusive access to the American market for that drug. Plaintiff-appellant Roche Products, Inc. (Roche), a large research-oriented pharmaceutical company, wanted the United States district court to enjoin Bolar Pharmaceutical Co., Inc. (Bolar), a manufacturer of generic drugs, from taking, during the life of a patent, the statutory and regulatory steps necessary to market, after the patent expired, a drug equivalent to a patented brand name drug. Roche argued that the use of a patented drug for federally mandated premarketing tests is a use in violation of the patent laws.

Roche was the assignee of the rights in U.S. Patent No. 3,299,053 (the '053 patent), which expired on January 17, 1984. The '053 patent, which issued on January 17, 1967, is entitled "Novel 1 and/or 4-substituted alkyl 5-aromatic-3H-1,4-benzodiazepines and benzodiazepine-2-ones." One of the chemical compounds claimed in the '053 patent is flurazepam hydrochloride (flurazepam hcl), the active ingredient in Roche's successful brand name prescription sleeping pill "Dalmane."

In early 1983, Bolar became interested in marketing, after the '053 patent expired, a generic drug equivalent to Dalmane. Because a generic drug's commercial success is related to how quickly it is brought on the market after a patent expires, and because approval for an equivalent of an established drug can take more than 2 years, Bolar, not waiting for the '053 patent to expire, immediately began its effort to obtain federal approval to market its generic version of Dalmane. In mid-1983, Bolar obtained from a foreign manufacturer 5 kilograms of flurazepam hcl to form into "dosage form capsules, to obtain stability data, dissolution rates, bioequivalence studies, and blood serum studies" necessary for a New Drug Application to the United States Food and Drug Administration (FDA).

On July 28, 1983, Roche filed a complaint in the United States District Court for the District of New Jersey against three parties: Bolar, Bolar's principal officer, and the importer of the infringing flurazepam hcl. Only Bolar remains a party defendant. Roche sought to enjoin Bolar from using flurazepam hcl for any purpose whatsoever during the life of the '053 patent. When Bolar stated during discovery, on August 30, 1983, that it intended immediately to begin testing its generic drug for FDA approval, Roche moved for and was granted a Temporary Restraining Order, on September 2, 1983.

On September 26, 1983, Bolar was granted a change of venue and the case was transferred to the United States District Court for the Eastern District of New York. That court consolidated Roche's motion for a preliminary injunction with the trial on the merits pursuant to Fed. R. Civ. P. 65(a) (2) (both parties had stipulated to all the pertinent facts so no testimony was necessary) and on October 11, 1983, issued a Memorandum and Order denying Roche's application for a permanent injunction. The court held that Bolar's use of the patented compound for federally mandated testing was not infringement of the patent in suit because Bolar's use was *de minimis* and experimental. The court entered judgment for Bolar on October 14, 1983, and Roche filed its notice of appeal that same day.

II

The district court correctly recognized that the issue in this case is narrow: does the limited use of a patented drug for testing and investigation strictly related to FDA drug approval requirements during the last 6 months of the term of the patent constitute a use which, unless licensed, the patent statute makes actionable? The district court held that it does not. This was an error of law.

III

When Congress enacted the current revision of the Patent Laws of the United States, the Patent Act of 1952, ch. 950, 66 Stat. 792 (codified at 35 U.S.C.), a statutory definition of patent infringement existed for the first time since section 5 of the Patent Act of 1793 was repealed in 1836. Title 35 U.S.C. § 271(a) incorporates the disjunctive language of the statutory patent grant which gives a patentee the "right to exclude others from making, using, or selling" a patented invention, 35 U.S.C. § 154. Congress states in section 271(a):

> [W]hoever without authority makes, uses or sells any patented invention, within the United States during the term of the patent therefore, infringes the patent.

It is beyond argument that performance of only one of the three enumerated activities is patent infringement. It is well-established, in particular, that the use of a patented invention, without either manufacture or sale, is actionable. . . . Thus, the patentee does not need to have any evidence of damage or lost sales to bring an infringement action.

Section 271(a) prohibits, on its face, any and all uses of a patented invention. Of course, as Judge Learned Hand observed in *Cabell v. Markham*, . . .:

> [I]t is true that the words used, even in their literal sense, are the primary, and ordinarily the most reliable, source of interpreting the meaning of any writing: be it a statute, a contract, or anything else. But it is one of the surest indexes of a mature and developed jurisprudence not to make a fortress out of the dictionary; but to remember that statutes always have some purpose or object to accomplish, whose sympathetic and imaginative discovery is the surest guide to their meaning.

Because Congress has never defined use, its meaning has become a matter of judicial interpretation. Although few cases discuss the question of whether a particular use constitutes an infringing use of a patented invention, they nevertheless convincingly lead to the conclusion that the word "use" in section 271(a) has never been taken to its utmost possible scope. . . .

Bolar argues that its intended use of flurazepam hcl is excepted from the use prohibition. It claims two grounds for exception: the first ground is based on a liberal interpretation of the traditional experimental use exception; the second ground is that public policy favors generic drugs and thus mandates the creation of a new exception in order to allow FDA required drug testing. We discuss these arguments seriatim.

B

The so-called experimental use defense to liability for infringement generally is recognized as originating in an opinion written by Supreme Court Justice Story while on circuit in Massachusetts. In *Whittemore v. Cutter*, . . ., Justice Story sought to justify a trial judge's instruction to a jury that an infringer must have an intent to use a patented invention for profit, stating:

> [I]t could never have been the intention of the legislature to punish a man who constructed such a machine merely for philosophical experiments, or for the purpose of ascertaining the sufficiency of the machine to produce its described effects.

Despite skepticism, see, *e.g.*, *Byam v. Bullard*, . . . (opinion by Justice Curtis), Justice Story's seminal statement evolved until, by 1861, the law was "well-settled that an experiment with a patented article for the sole purpose of gratifying a philosophical taste, or curiosity, or for mere amusement is not an infringement of the rights of the patentee." *Peppenhausen v. Falke*, . . .

The Court of Claims, whose precedents bind us, on several occasions has considered the defense of experimental use. . . . Bolar concedes, as it must, that its intended use of flurazepam hcl does not fall within the "traditional limits" of the experimental use exception as established in these cases or those of other circuits. Its concession here is fatal. Despite Bolar's argument that its tests are "true scientific inquiries" to which a literal interpretation of the experimental use exception logically should extend, we hold the experimental use exception to be truly narrow, and we will not expand it under the present circumstances. Bolar's argument that the experimental use rule deserves a broad construction is not justified.

Pitcairn, the most persuasive of the Court of Claims cases concerning the experimental use defense, sets forth the law which must control the disposition of this case: "[t]ests, demonstrations, and experiments . . . [which] are in keeping with the legitimate business of the . . . [alleged infringer]" are infringements for which "[e]xperimental use is not a defense." . . . We have carefully reviewed each of the other Court of Claims cases, and although they contain some loose language on which Bolar relies, they are unpersuasive. The *Ordnance Engineering* case provides no guidance concerning the boundaries of an appropriately applied experimental use rule other than flatly stating that a device must have been "built for experimental purposes." In *Chesterfield*, the court's flat declaration that "experimental use does not infringe" is pure *obiter dictum*. See *Pitcairn*, 547 F.2d at 1125, 192 USPQ at 625. Douglas has no precedential value here since the Court of Claims never affirmed the part of the trial judge's opinion dealing with experimental use; moreover, Trial Judge Cooper's well-reasoned analysis of the experimental use rule concluded that no case had permitted a pattern of systematic exploitation of a patented invention for the purpose of furthering the legitimate business interests of the infringer. The authority of Trial Judge Cooper's views rests on his reputation as a fine patent lawyer, and on their own intrinsic persuasiveness.

Bolar's intended "experimental" use is solely for business reasons and not for amusement, to satisfy idle curiosity, or for strictly philosophical inquiry. Bolar's intended use of flurazepam hcl to derive FDA required test data is thus an infringement of the '053 patent. Bolar may intend to perform "experiments," but unlicensed experiments conducted with a view to the adaption of the patented invention to the experimentor's business is a violation of the rights of the patentee to exclude others from using his patented invention. It is obvious here that it is a misnomer to call the intended use *de minimis*. It is no trifle in its economic effect on the parties even if the quantity used is small. It is no dilettante affair such as Justice Story envisioned. We cannot construe the experimental use rule so broadly as to allow a violation of the patent laws in the guise of "scientific inquiry," when that inquiry has definite, cognizable, and not insubstantial commercial purposes.

C

Bolar argues that even if no established doctrine exists with which it can escape liability for patent infringement, public policy requires that we create a new exception to the use prohibition. Parties and amici seem to think, in particular, that we must resolve a conflict between the Federal Food, Drug, and Cosmetic Act (FDCA), 21 U.S.C. § § 301-392 (1982), and the Patent Act of 1952, or at least the Acts' respective policies and purposes. We decline the opportunity here, however, to engage in legislative activity proper only for the Congress.

The new drug approval procedure which existed between 1938 and 1962 was relatively innocuous and had little impact on the development of pioneer prescription new drugs. Section 505 of the FDCA, ch. 675, 52 Stat. 1052 (1938), required the manufacturer of a pioneer new drug to submit to the FDA a New Drug Application (NDA) containing information concerning the safety of the drug. If the FDA did not disapprove the new drug within 60 days after it received the NDA, marketing could begin.

The provisions of the Drug Amendments of 1962, Pub. L. No. 87-781, 76 Stat. 780, caused a substantial increase in the time required for development and approval of a pioneer new drug. Beginning in 1962, the amended Section 505 (codified at 21 U.S.C. § 355 (1982)) required an NDA to contain proof of efficacy (effectiveness) as well as safety, and required the FDA affirmatively to approve the NDA rather than just to permit marketing by inaction. A recent study indicated that it now can take on average from 7 to 10 years for a pharmaceutical company to satisfy the current regulatory requirements. National Academy of Engineering, *The Competitive Status of the U.S. Pharmaceutical Industry*, 79-80 (1983).

Because most FDA-required testing is done after a patent issues, the remaining effective life of patent protection assertedly may be as low as 7 years. *Id.*, citing Statement of William M. Wardell to the Subcommittee on Investigations and Oversight of the Committee on Science and Technology, U.S. House of Representatives, Feb. 14, 1982, at 14. Litigation such as this is one example of how research-oriented pharmaceutical companies have sought to regain some of the earning time lost to regulatory entanglements. They gain for themselves, it is asserted, a de facto monopoly of upwards of 2 years by enjoining FDA-required testing of a generic drug until the patent on the drug's active ingredient expires.

Bolar argues that the patent laws are intended to grant to inventors only a limited 17-year property right to their inventions so that the public can enjoy the benefits of competition as soon as possible, consistent with the need to encourage invention. The FDCA, Bolar contends, was only intended to assure safe and effective drugs for the public, and not to extend a pharmaceutical company's monopoly for an indefinite and substantial period of time while the FDA considers whether to grant a pre-marketing clearance. Because the FDCA affected prevailing law, namely the Patent Act, Bolar argues that we should apply the patent laws to drugs differently.

Simply because a later enacted statute affects in some way an earlier enacted statute is poor reason to ask us to rewrite the earlier statute. Repeals by implication are not favored. . . .Thus, "courts are not at liberty to pick and choose among congressional enactments, and when two statutes are capable of co-existence, it is the duty of the courts, absent a clearly expressed congressional intention to the contrary, to regard each as effective." *Morton v. Mancari*, 417 U.S. 535, 551, . . . (1974). There is no affirmative obligation on Congress to explain why it deems a particular enactment wise or necessary, or to demonstrate that it is aware of the consequences of its action. . . . . Rather, because "laws are presumed to be passed with deliberation, and with full knowledge of all existing ones on the same subject," T. Sedgwick, . . . we must presume Congress was aware that the FDCA would affect the earning potentiality of a drug patent, and chose to permit it. Although arguably Title 21 and Title 35 are not laws on the "same subject," we note that during Congress' deliberations on the 1962 amendments to the FDCA, it considered the relationship and interaction of the patent laws with the drug laws. See S.Rep. No. 1744, 87th Cong., 2d Sess., reprinted in 1962 U.S. Code Cong. & Ad. News 2884, 2911-2915.

It is the role of Congress to maximize public welfare through legislation. Congress is well aware of the economic and societal problems which the parties debate here, and has before it legislation with respect to these issues. . . . No matter how persuasive the policy arguments are for or against these proposed bills, this court is not the proper forum in which to debate them. Where Congress has the clear power to enact legislation, our role is only to interpret and apply that legislation. "[I]t is not our job to apply laws that have not yet been written." *Sony Corp. of America v. Universal City Studios, Inc.*, _ U.S. _, _, 104 S. Ct. 774, 796, 78 L. Ed. 2d 574, 220 USPQ 665, 684 (1984). We will not rewrite the patent laws here.

IV

The district court refused to grant a permanent injunction against Bolar because it believed the law did not require that it find infringement of the '053 patent. Since we hold that there is infringement, Roche is entitled to a remedy. We are not in a position, however, to decide the form of that remedy.

Roche requested us, at first, to remand this case to the district court with instructions to enter a permanent injunction against infringement by Bolar. After the main briefs were filed, but before oral argument, the '053 patent expired. This case is not moot, however, because although the initially requested order no longer is necessary, other remedies can be fashioned to give Roche relief against Bolar's past infringement. Roche requests, for example, an order to confiscate and destroy the data which Bolar has generated during its infringing activity, citing, *Pfizer, Inc. v. International Rectifier Corp.*, 217 USPQ 157 (C.D. Cal. 1982) (granting an injunction of that nature to remedy infringement done in contempt of a court order).

Statute provides the basis for Roche's request for injunctive relief, 35 U.S.C. § 283:

The several courts having jurisdiction of cases under this title may grant injunctions in accordance with the principles of equity to prevent the violation of any right secured by patent, on such terms as the court deems reasonable.

Section 283, by its terms, clearly makes the issuance of an injunction discretionary: the court "may grant" relief "in accordance with the principles of equity." The trial court thus has considerable discretion in determining whether the facts of a situation require it to issue an injunction. The scope of relief, therefore, is not for us to decide at the first instance, nor is this the time or place for a discourse on the "principles of equity."

Whether an injunction should issue in this case, and of what form it should take, certainly depends on the equities of the case. Bolar, Roche, and amici Pharmaceutical Manufacturers Association and Generic Pharmaceutical Industry Association, each detail the "catastrophic" effect our decision for either party will have on the American public health system. It is true that it "is a principle of general application that courts, and especially courts of equity, may appropriately withhold their aid where the plaintiff is using the right asserted contrary to the public interest," *Morton Salt Co. v. Suppiger Co.*, 314 U.S. 488, 492, . . . (1941), . . . Since "the standards of the public interest, not the requirements of private litigation, measure the propriety and need for injunctive relief in these cases," *Hecht Co. v. Bowles*, 321 U.S. 321, 331, . . . (1944), rev'g *Brown v. Hecht Co.*, 137 F.2d 689 (D.C. Cir. 1943), we remand this case to the district court for further proceedings to consider what this interest is and what measures it calls for.

There are other aspects here that might make a tribunal reluctant to select, within the scope of its discretion, relief along the harsher side of the possible scale. The case clearly was regarded by both sides as a test. The good faith with which Bolar acted is undisputed, at least before us. Bolar says it did nothing clandestine, but notified Roche what it was going to do at all times before doing it, so Roche could act promptly to defend what it believed to be its rights. The case may be unlike *Pfizer, Inc.*, supra, in that Bolar scrupulously obeyed all court orders while they were in effect, or so it says, whereas in *Pfizer, Inc.*, the infringer acted in defiance of court decrees. The destruction of material in *Pfizer, Inc.*, was ordered after everything milder had proved useless. If other measures can be made sufficient, one might well be reluctant to order destruction of the records of research and tests that may embody information that would contribute to the health and happiness of the human race. All this is, of course, for the district judge to consider so far as he finds the factual predicates established.

The actual infringing acts are said to have all occurred in the relatively brief period between vacation of the lower court's restraining order and the expiration of the patent. Counsel for Roche was candid in explaining that he pushed so hard for the harsh relief he did because he thought any money damages would have to be nominal. The correctness of this belief has not been briefed or argued, and we hesitate to state a firm position, but tentatively, at least, we are skeptical. It is clear that the economic injury to Roche is, or is threatened to be, substantial, even though the amount of material used in the tests was small. If the patent law precludes substantial damages, there exists a strange gap in the panoply (in its proper meaning, a suit of armor) of protection the patent statutes place around an aggrieved and injured patentee. The district judge, before getting into the issue of equitable relief, must determine if he can deal with the case by adequate money damages. If he can, the predicate for equitable relief of a harsh, or even a mild, character is gone.

Counsel are equally mistaken in their apparent belief that once infringement is established and adjudicated, an injunction must follow. In *Hecht Co. v. Bowles*, *supra*, the statute, unlike the one we have here, was seemingly mandatory by its language that once a violation was shown, an injunction must follow, and the D.C. Circuit had so held. But the circumstances made an injunction somewhat repugnant. Hecht Co., an unquestionably legitimate and long-established District of Columbia retailer, had got tangled up in the price control regulations of World War II, and its employees had in good faith unwittingly committed some violations. The situation was ironic in that the Hecht Co. had been a leader in extending the patriotic cooperation of the retail trade in application of the unpopular but necessary retail price controls, and had itself offered its own operation for study as illustrating the problems and how they could be solved.

After discovering some loopholes in the statute, in light of the legislative history, Justice Douglas continued at 329, 64 S. Ct. at 591-592:

> We are dealing here with the requirements of equity practice with a background of several hundred years of history. Only the other day we stated that "An

> appeal to the equity jurisdiction conferred on federal district courts is an appeal to the sound discretion which guides the determinations of courts of equity." *Meredith v. Winter Haven*, 320 U.S. 228, 235 .... The historic injunctive process was designed to deter, not to punish. The essence of equity jurisdiction has been the power of the Chancellor to do equity and to mould each decree to the necessities of the particular case. Flexibility rather than rigidity has distinguished it. The qualities of mercy and practicality have made equity the instrument for nice adjustment and reconciliation between the public interest and private needs as well as between competing private claims. We do not believe that such a major departure from that long tradition as is here proposed should be lightly implied.

While two justices declined to join in the opinion, none expressed themselves in favor of affirming the D.C. Circuit. In short, if Congress wants the federal courts to issue injunctions without regard to historic equity principles, it is going to have to say so in explicit and even shameless language rarely if ever to be expected from a body itself made up very largely of American lawyers, having, probably, as much respect for traditional equity principles as do the courts. If an injunction was not mandatory in *Hecht Co. v. Bowles*, the more permissive statutory language here makes it *a fortiori* that an injunction is not mandatory now.

The application of historic equity principles to the case at bar is in the first instance for the district court.

V

Conclusion

The decision of the district court holding the '053 patent not infringed is reversed. The case is remanded with instructions to fashion an appropriate remedy. Each party to bear its own costs.

Reversed and remanded.

§ 2.57.2. The amendment to the United States Patent Act (Title 35, USC) that introduced the Bolar exemption

Sec. 202. Section 271 of title 35, United States Code, is amended by adding at the end the following:

> (e)(1) It shall not be an act of infringement to make, use, or sell a patented invention (other than a new animal drug or veterinary biological product (as those terms are used in the Federal Food, Drug, and Cosmetic Act and the Act of March 4, 1913)) solely for uses reasonably related to the development and submission of information under a Federal law which regulates the manufacture, use, or sale of drugs.
>
> (2) It shall be an act of infringement to submit an application under section 505(j) of the Federal Food, Drug, and Cosmetic Act or described in section 505(b)(2) of such Act for a drug claimed in a patent or the use of which is claimed in a patent, if the purpose of such submission is to obtain approval under such Act to engage in the commercial manufacture, use, or sale of a drug claimed in a patent or the use of which is claimed in a patent before the expiration of such patent.

§ 2.58. THE CONTROVERSY OVER PATENTS FOR SURGICAL METHODS—THE CASE OF DR. PALLIN AND HIS INVENTION OF A METHOD TO OPERATE CATARACTS

One of the most controversial areas concerning access to health is undoubtedly that of the possibility of obtaining patents for diagnostic, therapeutic and surgical methods. If, for a long period, physicians complained of their colleagues' obtaining patents for medicines, that reason of discontent has vanished with the evolution of the pharmaceutical industry and the role of medical professionals. Indeed, for a certain period, physicians had an active role in the composition and making of pharmaceuticals. That was a time when the professions of physicians and apothecaries would coexist under the same corporations. In the Middle Ages, some by-laws and norms would even explicitly refer to the existing commercial societies between doctors and pharmacists. Old illuminations show doctors within the shops of pharmacists, giving them indications on the making of drugs. But this was a long time ago. Today, if it is for medical doctors to prescribe medicines in general, it is no longer their role to create their compositions and make them. Today, this is a matter for large and sophisticated pharmaceutical companies, research-based or not. So, in general, physicians tend to not to take a collective position against the private appropriation of pharmaceuticals through patents or trade secrets.

But when it comes to diagnostic, therapeutic and surgical methods, the problem changes. Unlike medical devices, which are frequently invented by individual medical practitioners, but whose design and make depend on industrial facilities, those methods are directly applied by the doctors in their offices. This means that, when a doctor applies for a patent for a therapeutic method, he/she is directly restricting the way his/her colleagues operate in the confined spaces of their offices. In general, medical doctors tend to receive this idea very badly. To them, the tradition and professional ethics dictate that any new method developed by an individual physician is to be shared with the colleagues for their peer-review—and use, in the case it is approved. So, doctors' general repulse against those colleagues who claim exclusivity in medical methods should not come as a surprise. The economic argument against the patenting of therapeutic, surgical and diagnostic methods has already been mentioned (§ 2.22): the reputation acquired by the creative doctor would allow him/her to charge higher prices and/or to have more clients/patients.

And indeed, the patentability of diagnostic, therapeutic and surgical methods is such a difficult theme that the TRIPS Agreement, in its art. 27.3(a), permits WTO Members to exclude it.

To the best of my knowledge, today, there are two countries where the patentability of those methods is accepted: the United States and Australia[30]*—not coincidentally, two*

30. The patentability of therapeutic methods was discussed (and accepted) by the High Court of Australia in *Apotex Pty Ltd v Sanofi-Aventis Australia Pty Ltd*, [2013] HCA 50, of December 4, 2013. In this case, the Court engaged in a profound debate on how to draw the line between inventions concerning concrete substances ("manner of new manufactures," as termed in the Statute of Monopolies) and inventions of an abstract nature. Interestingly, several times the judges, discussing case law, referred to "non-economical inventions," meaning with this term

countries whose wealth has been built on private entrepreneurship and individual economic freedom. But the case of the United States is worthy of particular notice: once more proving that the intellectual property of access to health is not the same as the one that applies to other areas of human inventiveness, and following a bitter debate on the patent obtained by a certain Dr. Pallin for a method of operating cataracts and the news that he was willing to sue those colleagues that used his method unless they accepted to pay him a given fee for every surgery they performed, the United States Congress intervened. However, it did not intervene to exclude that kind of inventions from patentability, but rather to annihilate the enforceability of the respective patents. It is debatable whether this measure is TRIPS compatible: art. 1.1 of the Agreement says that when WTO Members provide for more protection than is required, they should comply with all other provisions in respect of that additional protection. So, if the United States accepts the patentability of surgical methods, it should not prevent their enforcement, for that is a discrimination against a particular field of technology—which art. 27.1., drafted with the pharmaceutical field in the mind of those who wrote it, prohibits.

Anyway, in the course of the very first lawsuit Dr. Pallin launched against a colleague, he had his patent invalidated (in an unreported opinion). Actually, as evidence that United States courts do not appreciate that kind of patents very much, where inventors have tried to enforce patents on therapeutic, diagnostic or surgical methods, they have been invariably invalidated whenever their validity has been challenged on the grounds of lack of novelty, or of obviousness, or of absence of utility. See, e.g., Morton v. New York Infirmary, *17 F. Cas. 879, Case No. 9,865 (S.D.N.Y. 1862);* Martin v. Wyeth, *193 F.2d 58 (4th Cir. 1951);* In re Stanley, 1992 U.S. App. LEXIS 2361 (Fed. Cir. 1992).

In this manner, patents for therapeutic, diagnostic and surgical tests in the United States have become nothing more than a piece of paper, displaying the country's seal, vertical blue and white stripes, and a red ribbon. They may be pleasant to the view (the design of contemporary patent letters being, for some unclear reason, inspired by the old royal letters granting titles of nobility), but they are meaningless.

---

inventions whose performance did not result in a product, and thus are not patentable. In qualifying those inventions as "non-economical," they demonstrated a bias against inventions that may not handle concrete substances, but produce nevertheless new and sellable services, such as those that pertain to skilled surgeons and doctors. An extensive discussion on this theme can be found in Nuno Pires de Carvalho, PATENTLY OUTDATED: PATENTS IN THE POST-INDUSTRIAL ECONOMY—THE CASE FOR SERVICE PATENTS (Wolters Kluwer, 2012).

§ 2.58.1. Dr. Pallin's patent

United States Patent 5,080,111

January 14, 1992

Method of making self-sealing episcleral incision

Background of the invention

This invention relates, in general, to surgery of the eye, and more particularly to a self-sealing episcleral incision useful in scleral tunnel surgery for the removal of cataracts and the implantation of artificial lenses.

It is well known to those in the ophthalmology arts that microsurgery may be used to remove cataracts and implant artificial lenses to partially or wholly restore vision. Initially, a conjunctival incision is made to partially remove the conjunctiva and expose the limbus and sclera. The most conventional microscopic surgery method currently employed includes making an incision in either the limbus or the sclera directly posterior to the limbus. The incision is either linear or approximately follows the curvature of the limbus and extends into the anterior chamber directly in front of the iris.

A capsulorhexis is performed wherein a window is cut into the anterior of the crystalline lens capsule. Once the crystalline lens is opened, phacoemulsification is performed wherein the nucleus is removed using ultrasonic frequency and aspiration. The cortex is then removed by aspiration only. Once the nucleus and cortex have been removed, the empty lens capsule remains.

Following removal of lens material which includes the cataract, an artificial lens is implanted. The artificial lens is inserted through the incision, disposed in the empty lens capsule and stabilized therein. The artificial lens implant may be either a solid implant or a flexible folded implant. Both these types of implants are well known in the art. Once the lens implant has been successfully inserted into the lens capsule and stabilized, the incision is sealed with sutures so that the eye may be inflated.

A common problem with the described conventional microsurgery is suture induced astigmatism. The cornea is a potentially toric structure. The use of sutures in the limbus to seal the incision maximally alters the toricity of the cornea often creating an astigmatism which impairs vision. Additional suture induced complications include irritation of the eye, suture abscesses, suture extrusion and foreign body reaction. Further, the fine sutures employed in ophthalmic surgery are subject to breakage thereby exposing the wound to separation and dehiscence.

Scleral tunnel surgery greatly reduces the effect of sutures and suture induced astigmatism because the sutures are not disposed in the limbus, are much further away from the cornea and any material gathered by the sutures is sclera and not cornea. Standard scleral tunnel surgery includes making an incision in the sclera approximately 1 to 2 millimeters posterior to the limbus. This incision is also linear or approximately follows the curvature of the limbus. Following the scleral incision, a pocket or tunnel is formed through the sclera that extends into the anterior chamber of the eye.

Capsulorhexis, phacoemulsification and removal of the cortex to leave the empty lens capsule are performed in the same manner as described above. The artificial lens implant is inserted through the episcleral incision, transits the scleral tunnel and is properly positioned and stabilized in the empty lens capsule. The episcleral incision is then sealed with sutures and the eye inflated. Although the sutures sealing the scleral incision are not as detrimental as sutures disposed in the limbus, it is still possible for them to detrimentally effect the toricity of the cornea and cause an astigmatism.

In view of the above, it would be highly beneficial to have an episcleral incision that may be employed with scleral tunnel microsurgery that is substantially self-sealing, will admit solid or folded lens implants and greatly reduces or eliminates the probability of astigmatism.

Summary of the invention

Accordingly, it is an object of the present invention to provide an episcleral incision that is self-sealing.

Another object of the present invention is to provide a self-sealing episcleral incision that greatly reduces or eliminates the probability of astigmatism.

Another object of the present invention is to provide a self-sealing episcleral incision which does not rely on sutures for wound integrity.

Another object of the present invention is to provide a self-sealing episcleral incision having reduced incisional stress associated with lens implantation.

Another object of the present invention is to provide a self-sealing episcleral incision that will admit solid or folded lens implants of various sizes therethrough.

A further object of the present invention is to provide a self-sealing episcleral incision having a variable cord length.

The foregoing and other objects and advantages are achieved in the present invention by one embodiment in which, as a part thereof, includes a substantially self-sealing episcleral incision wherein the approximate central point of the incision is 1.5 to 3.0 millimeters posterior to the limbus. Portions of the incision extending from the approximate central point extend laterally away from the curvature of the limbus. The configuration of the self-sealing incision allows the incision to seal as the eye is inflated following surgery and therefore requires no sutures for sealing. Accordingly, the probability of astigmatism is eliminated or greatly reduced.

Figure 29 Drawings that were part of the specification of Dr. Pallin's patent.

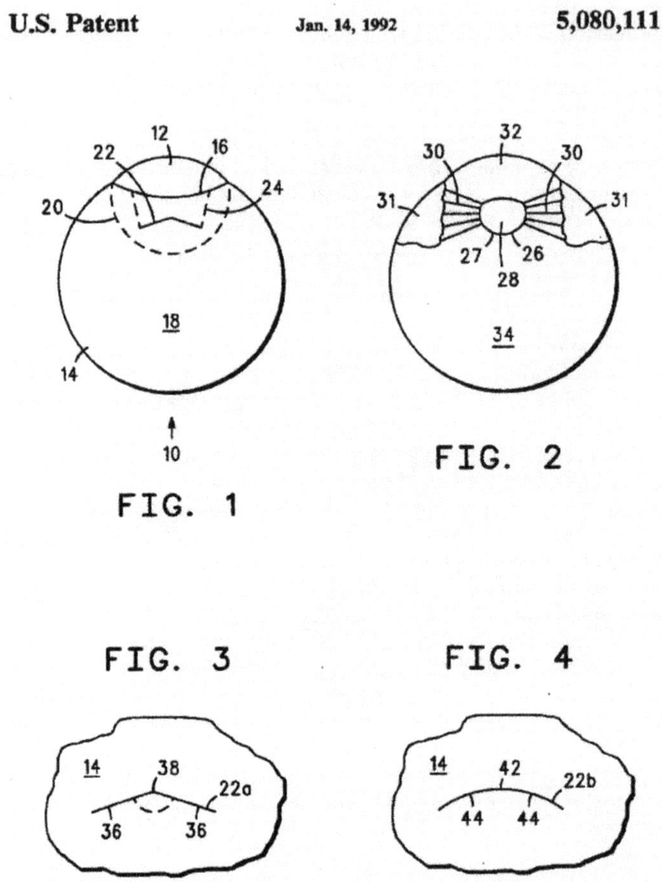

§ 2.58.2. The amendment to the United States Patent Act (United States Code, Title 35) that eliminated the enforceability of patents for therapeutic and surgical methods

35 U.S. Code § 287. Limitation on damages and other remedies; marking and notice

(c) (1) With respect to a medical practitioner's performance of a medical activity that constitutes an infringement under section 271(a) or (b), the provisions of sections 281, 283, 284, and 285 shall not apply against the medical practitioner or against a related health care entity with respect to such medical activity.

(2) For the purposes of this subsection:

(A) the term "medical activity" means the performance of a medical or surgical procedure on a body, but shall not include (i) the use of a patented machine, manufacture, or composition of matter in violation of such patent, (ii) the practice of a patented use of a composition of matter in violation of such patent, or (iii) the practice of a process in violation of a biotechnology patent.

(B) the term "medical practitioner" means any natural person who is licensed by a State to provide the medical activity described in subsection (c)(1) or who is acting under the direction of such person in the performance of the medical activity.

(C) the term "related health care entity" shall mean an entity with which a medical practitioner has a professional affiliation under which the medical practitioner performs the medical activity, including but not limited to a nursing home, hospital, university, medical school, health maintenance organization, group medical practice, or a medical clinic.

(D) the term "professional affiliation" shall mean staff privileges, medical staff membership, employment or contractual relationship, partnership or ownership interest, academic appointment, or other affiliation under which a medical practitioner provides the medical activity on behalf of, or in association with, the health care entity.

(E) the term "body" shall mean a human body, organ or cadaver, or a nonhuman animal used in medical research or instruction directly relating to the treatment of humans.

(F) the term "patented use of a composition of matter" does not include a claim for a method of performing a medical or surgical procedure on a body that recites the use of a composition of matter where the use of that composition of matter does not directly contribute to achievement of the objective of the claimed method.

§ 2.59. BRAZIL INTRODUCES THE EXAMINATION OF PATENT APPLICATIONS BY THE MINISTRY OF HEALTH—2001

In 2001, Brazil introduced a number of changes into its patent statute. At that time, the country had already implemented the obligations it accepted under the WTO framework, including those in the TRIPS Agreement. In 1996, in a gesture of good faith to its trading partners, Brazil had anticipated such implementation and went even beyond the basic standards it had promised to comply with in 1994.

But eventually, the Brazilian government seems to have realized that compliance with TRIPS obligations may have had more significant costs than those the country's diplomats had anticipated when they engaged in Uruguay Round negotiations, particularly in the field of pharmaceuticals. It is true that the WTO Agreement was negotiated as a "package," this meaning that concessions made in a certain field—say, agriculture—should have been compensated by gains in another field—say, intellectual property. And vice-versa.

However, these logics have not prevented Brazil, which left the Uruguay Round as a true winner (because of the enormous gains in access to new markets for its commodities—the reason for Brazil's fleeting prosperity in the first decade of 2000) from feeling harmed with the weight that the mandatory respect for intellectual property in the field of pharmaceuticals imposed on its national generics sector and its national and state public health systems.

As a reaction, Brazil, in 2001, changed its patent law and gave its national sanitary agency (ANVISA) the role of examining patent applications for pharmaceutical inventions (both products and processes). This has already been mentioned, as well as the problems it has caused. (see § 2.49). The main purpose was for ANVISA to step into the patent office's criteria for patentability and to exclude pharmaceutical incremental inventions, such as second medical uses, from patentability.

The first of the following texts is the statutory provision that has given ANVISA the attribution of looking at pharmaceutical inventions not only from a sanitary perspective but also from a patent perspective. The second text is a combination of excerpts from three administrative regulations of 2017 that tried to solve the problems caused by the conflicting roles of the two agencies involved. A simple reading shows that the problems have not been solved. It is true that the regulations make it clear that the patent office (INPI) regained the final word on patentability, but the sanitary agency has gained a role that has nothing to do with the examination of patent applications because it involves matters of sanitary nature, as well as of access to pharmaceuticals through the National Health System. The "subsidies" elaborated by ANVISA may be used—and they have been, indeed—by judges unfriendly to pharmaceutical patents to revert INPI's decisions.

§ 2.59.1. Law no. 10,196, of February 14, 2001

Modifies and adds provisions to Law no. 9,279, of May 14, 1996, which deals with rights and obligations related to industrial property, and establishes other provisions

> I make known that the President of the Republic has adopted Provisional Measure no. 2,105-15, of 2001, which National Congress has approved, and that I, Antonio Carlos Magalhães, President, for the purposes of the provisions of the sole paragraph of art. 62 of the Federal Constitution, enact the following Law:
>
> > Art. 1 Law no. 9,279, of May 14, 1996, is in force with the following amendments:
> > Art. 229-C The grant of patents for pharmaceutical products and processes shall depend on the prior approval by the National Agency of Sanitary Vigilance (ANVISA).

§ 2.59.2. Coordination of the work of the patent office with that of the sanitary agency

> Interministerial Ordinance MS/MDIC/AGU [Ministry of Health; Ministry of Development, Industry and Commerce; and General Attorney of the Union], and Joint Ordinance Anvisa/INPI no. 01/2017, and RDC no. 168/2017 (excerpts)
>
> Second Step—Anvisa analyzes the [patent] applications in the light of public health, checking whether the pharmaceutical product or process contained in the patent application presents a health risk. In cases where the application is

considered to be of interest for the policies of medicines or pharmaceutical assistance within the scope of SUS [Single Health System], an additional assessment is carried out regarding compliance with the patentability requirements and other criteria established by Law No. 9,279/1996 (Industrial Property Law)), for the purpose of subsidizing INPI's examination.

Third step—The applications considered to be of interest for drug policies or for pharmaceutical assistance are submitted for analysis for subsidy purposes, before the final decision. In these cases, the opinion on which Anvisa's decision is based, in addition to the risk analysis to which they all are subject, may contain an assessment of the patentability criteria, as well as additional conditions provided for in the Industrial Property Law, which will serve as subsidies for INPI's examination.

Fourth step—After Anvisa's final decision, the application returns to the INPI, for the conclusion of the administrative procedure, and may be accepted or rejected by the Institute.

§ 2.60. THE TRIPS COUNCIL HOSTS DEBATES ON ACCESS TO PHARMACEUTICAL PRODUCTS THAT LEAD TO THE FIRST AMENDMENT OF THE TRIPS AGREEMENT

June 12, 2001

*When implementing their obligations under the TRIPS Agreement, once the transitional period they received was exhausted, a significant number of developing countries have been led to believe that they had made excessive concessions in the field of intellectual property, and in particular of patents for pharmaceutical inventions, as compared to those they had received as regards tariffs on agricultural and industrialized products. Even before such a transitional period had finished, some countries had already started raising concerns over the impact of patent protection for pharmaceuticals in their territories and the access of their poor populations to health. The European Union (then the European Communities) has lent a sympathetic ear to those concerns (in spite of the major business interests of France, Germany and the United Kingdom on the patent protection of innovative medicines), and produced a paper that was the origin of long debates in the TRIPS Council (and around the world). Ultimately, that paper, excerpts from which follow, led to the adoption of the 2003 Decision of the WTO General Council, setting a mechanism of compulsory licenses for exporting pharmaceutical products for WTO Members that meet certain criteria, and to the 2015 adoption of an amendment to the Agreement, with the inclusion of its Article 31*bis.

Communication from the European Communities and Their Member States

IP/C/W/280, of June 12, 2001

The following communication, dated 11 June 2001, has been received from the European Communities and their member States with the request that it be circulated to Members.

The Relationship between the Provisions of the TRIPS Agreement and Access to Medicines

Background

1. At the last session of the TRIPS Council (2-5 April 2001), the Africa Group proposed that one day be set aside at the June session to clarify the interpretation and/or application of certain provisions of the TRIPS Agreement. The discussion is intended to examine the relationship between intellectual property and access to medicines and will seek to bring clarity regarding the interpretation and the application of the provisions of the Agreement which provide scope for Members to address public health concerns. The European Communities (EC) and their member States, together with most other delegations, welcomed and supported this initiative. It is an important development, since it will be the first time that the TRIPS Council discusses intellectual property issues in the context of public health. . . .
6. The EC and their member States recognise that the lack of affordable pharmaceuticals is a serious problem in many developing countries and especially for the poorest people.

Relevance of Intellectual Property

7. The EC and their member States consider that intellectual property rights provide an essential stimulus for creativity and innovation. These rights need to be adequately protected in order to encourage, for example, investment in research and development of new medicines, and particularly those targeted at the major communicable diseases.
8. The Agreement on Trade-Related Aspects of Intellectual Property Rights (TRIPS), which emerged from the Uruguay Round negotiations has, however, sometimes been criticised as limiting policy options in relation to public health concerns. In the view of the EC and their member States, the Agreement's objectives, principles and purpose (set out in Articles 7 and 8), special transitional arrangements and other provisions give these countries a sufficiently wide margin of discretion in implementing it. This margin enables them to set up an intellectual property regime that meets their policy needs and is capable of responding to public health concerns. The EC and their member States have declared their willingness—most notably in the Programme for Action—to promote discussions, within the WTO, WIPO and WHO, to address the link between the Agreement and public health protection issues.

This Communication summarises the views of the EC and their member States on some of the relevant provisions of the Agreement.

Compulsory Licensing . . .

13. Article 31 has been further criticised for requiring that goods manufactured under a compulsory licence be 'predominantly for the supply of the domestic market of the Member authorising such use.' This provision is sometimes said to prevent a small country that has no production facilities of its own from obtaining cheap medicines from abroad under a compulsory licence. This is an important argument as the Agreement does not appear to offer any legal certainty on the issue. What can be said is that a WTO Member is free to grant a compulsory licence for the importation of goods which are under patent in its own territory, as long as the imported goods have been produced in a country where they are not patented, or where the term of protection has expired. However, the EC and their member States also point to another possible interpretation of the Agreement . . . that would allow a Member to issue a compulsory licence to a manufacturer in another country, provided the

government of that other country recognised the licence (which it would not be obliged to do under the Agreement), and provided that all the goods manufactured under the licence were exported to the country granting the licence. It should be noted, however, that it is far from certain whether such a 'permissive' reading of the Agreement would stand scrutiny by a panel or the Appellate Body. The EC and their member States are ready to discuss this matter in order to reach consensus on this issue among all WTO Members. . . .

Conclusion

17. The TRIPS Agreement represents a delicate balance between the interests of right-holders and consumers. The EC and their member States stand ready to contribute constructively to any debate concerning the interpretation of its provisions.
18. Moreover, the spiraling health crisis in the developing world has underlined the need for rapid action. The TRIPS Agreement has increasingly come under fire for allegedly standing in the way of developing countries' efforts to implement an effective public health policy. The EC and their member States take such criticisms seriously and stand ready to engage in a positive manner in the discussion, leading where necessary to clarification, of certain of the Agreement's provisions. This paper has focused on Articles 7, 8, 30, 31 and 39, but Members may wish to discuss other provisions they consider to be relevant. The EC and their member States are also ready to discuss to what extent technical assistance can take into account health concerns.
19. Improving health at the same time as combating poverty requires a mix of complementary social, economic and health policies and practices. Health gains largely depend on using available resources in productive and efficient ways, as shown by the great strides made by some middle and low-income countries. Intellectual property rights play a role with regard to access to medicines. However, the TRIPS Agreement cannot be held responsible for the health crisis in developing countries, while it must not stand in the way for action to combat the crisis. The EC and their member States will continue to constructively and positively take part in the expanding global effort to develop a coherent and effective response to the health problems of the developing world.

§ 2.61. WITH THE AIM OF OBTAINING TECHNOLOGY CONCERNING THE MAKING OF MEDICINES NECESSARY FOR ITS NATIONAL HEALTH SYSTEM, BRAZIL INTRODUCES A MECHANISM OF PDPs (PARTNERSHIPS FOR PRODUCTIVE DEVELOPMENT)

In 2012, Brazil introduced the mechanism of Partnerships for Productive Development (the acronym of which, in Portuguese, is PDPs), aiming at encouraging foreign research-based pharmaceutical companies to transfer to national public research institutions and manufactures as well as private companies, technology concerning those medicines considered essential to the national health system. Those medicines are acquired through the national centralized purchase system of SUS (in Portuguese, the Brazilian acronym for the Unified Health System), which means bulk, large acquisitions.

The mechanism was introduced in 2009, through a Regulation of the Ministry of Health. It was modified several times, the most recently in 2018. But the main provisions that dictate the structure and operation of PDPs were introduced in 2014.
Very detailed, complex and bureaucratic, the mechanism of PDPs has nevertheless important aspects, from the perspective of the inventors: its voluntary character and the stated intent of respecting intellectual property (considering that those inventors are mostly foreigners, residents in countries that are Brazil's trading partners in the WTO—they are, therefore, protected by the principles and rules of the TRIPS Agreement). The voluntary cooperation of these inventors is naturally sparkled by the large size of Brazil's internal market. But this does not mean that they can be forced into it. Compulsory licenses to compel a particular owner of a particular technology, for example, are absolutely out of the question. Furthermore, one should not forget that a great deal of the technical knowledge of research-based pharmaceutical companies is composed of trade secrets rather than patents. In the pharmaceutical sector, these are just the tip of the iceberg. Therefore, unless Brazil wished to engage in a massive learning program on how to research and develop new medicines, which would take many years and consume unavailable human and financial resources, it must count on the willing participation of pharmaceutical research-based entities.
The PDP mechanism has been successful to a large extent, not in the sense that has permitted Brazil to build a sustainable pharmaceutical generic sector, let alone a national research-based industry—and that is not even its immediate target—but it has permitted easier and cheaper access to a number of medicines that are listed as essential to the national health system.

Ordinance No. 2,531, of November 12, 2014

> Redefines the guidelines and criteria for the definition of the list of strategic products for the Unified Health System (SUS) and the establishment of Partnerships for Productive Development (PDP) and regulates the respective submission, instruction, decision, transfer and absorption processes of technology, the acquisition of strategic products for SUS under the PDP and the respective monitoring and evaluation.
>
> The Minister of Health, using the powers conferred by items I and II of the sole paragraph of art. 87 of the Constitution, . . . decides:
>
> Chapter I
>
> General Provisions . . .
>
> Art. 2. For the purposes of this Ordinance, the following concepts are adopted:
>
> I—Partnership for Productive Development (PDP): partnerships that involve cooperation by agreement between public institutions and between public institutions and private entities for the development, transfer and absorption of technology, production, productive and technological training in the country in strategic products to respond to the needs of SUS; . . .
>
> Art. 3. The objectives of PDPs are:
>
> I—to expand the population's access to strategic products and reduce the vulnerability of the SUS;

II—reduce the productive and technological dependencies to meet the health needs of the Brazilian population in the short, medium and long terms, following the constitutional principles of universal and equal access to health actions and services;
III—to rationalize the purchasing power of the State, through the selective centralization of expenditures in the health area, with a view to the sustainability of the SUS and the expansion of production in the country of strategic products;
IV—protect the interests of the Public Administration and society as regards sound economics and advantages, considering prices, quality, technology and social benefits;
V—foster technological development and the exchange of knowledge for innovation within the scope of public institutions and private entities, contributing to the development of CEIS [*Complexo Econômico-Industrial da Saúde*—Economic and Industrial Health Complex] and making them competitive and capable;
VI—to promote the development and manufacture in Brazil of strategic products for SUS;
VII—seek SUS's technological and economic sustainability in the short, medium and long terms, with the promotion of structural conditions to increase the country's productive and innovation capacity, contribute to reduce CEIS's trade deficit and guarantee access to health; and
VIII—encourage the development of the public production network in the country and its strategic role for the SUS. . . .

Art. 9. The participants in the PDP may be:

I—a public institution, individually or jointly with other public institutions, with a view to enabling security, technological portability, agility and dynamism in the research, development, technological absorption and innovation process; and
II—a private entity, individually or jointly with other private entities, with a view to enabling security, technological portability, agility and dynamism in the technology transfer process. . . .

Art. 14. The preparation of a PDP project proposal will observe the following guidelines:. . .

III—regarding intellectual property:

a) the research, development and manufacture of the products to be acquired within the scope of the PDP shall follow the current legislation; and
b) the numbers of the patents granted or pending in the country, related to the production and transfer of technology of the product covered by the PDP, must be informed, indicating their respective holders and their term of protection;

Art. 22. The following criteria will be considered in the analysis of the merit of the PDP project proposal:. . .

VIII—compliance with intellectual property laws in force; . . .

§ 2.62. THE EUROPEAN UNION SUBMITS TO THE WTO DISPUTE SETTLEMENT MECHANISM A COMPLAINT CONCERNING TURKEY'S REQUIREMENT OF TECHNOLOGY TRANSFER AND NATIONAL PRODUCTION OF MEDICINES—2019

Recently, Turkey introduced a mechanism that is vaguely similar to that of Brazil's PDPs (see the previous section) and has the same objectives, but with a striking, if not shocking, difference: Turkey's program seems to be mandatory. At least this is what one can read in the request for consultations filed by the European Union with the WTO Dispute Settlement Mechanism (DSM) in 2019.

If the EU is right, and Turkey's requirement that medicines acquired by the national system of health be mandatorily manufactured in the national territory is indeed what it appears to be, then it is difficult to see how such a mechanism can resist the scrutiny under the WTO DSM. The Turkish scheme does not involve GATT-related matters only, but TRIPS matters also, because the requirement of local manufacture will inevitably lead to the impossibility of complying with the patent exploitation requirement by foreign manufacturers of medicines (Art. 130 of the current law of Turkey), which will make their patents automatically subject to compulsory licenses.

As the popular saying goes, you catch flies with honey, not with vinegar. It seems that Brazil has decided to use the first method, while Turkey may have opted for the second.

WT/DS583/1—April 10, 2019

Turkey—Certain Measures Concerning the Production, Importation and Marketing of Pharmaceutical Products (Request for Consultations by the European Union)

My authorities have instructed me to request consultations with the government of the Republic of Turkey (Turkey) pursuant to Articles 1 and 4 of the Understanding on Rules and Procedures Governing the Settlement of Disputes (DSU), Article XXII:1 of the General Agreement on Tariffs and Trade 1994 (GATT 1994), Article 8 of the Agreement on Trade Related Investment Measures (TRIMs Agreement), Article 64 of the Agreement on Trade-Related Aspects of Intellectual Property Rights (TRIPS Agreement), and Article 4.1 of the Agreement on Subsidies and Countervailing Measures (ASCM) with regard to various measures concerning the production, importation and marketing of pharmaceutical products.

1. The Measures at issue

a. The localisation requirement

The Turkish authorities have adopted plans to achieve progressively the localisation in Turkey of the production of a substantial part of the pharmaceutical products consumed in Turkey. In order to achieve that objective, Turkey requires foreign producers to commit to localise in Turkey their production of certain pharmaceutical products. If such commitments are not given, are not accepted by Turkish authorities, or are not fulfilled, the pharmaceutical products concerned are excluded from the scheme for the reimbursement of the pharmaceutical products sold by pharmacies to patients operated by Turkey's social security system (the "reimbursement scheme"). That scheme covers the vast majority of sales of pharmaceutical products by pharmacies to patients. Consequently, if an imported pharmaceutical product is excluded from the reimbursement scheme, its competitive opportunities in the Turkish market are significantly impaired, as compared with domestically produced like products.

In order to comply with the above described localisation requirement (the "localisation requirement"), certain producers of pharmaceutical products commit to localise their production of certain pharmaceutical products in Turkey. In those cases where foreign producers do not give the required commitments to localise (or where their offered commitments are rejected, or are considered not to be fulfilled, by the Turkish authorities), the pharmaceutical products concerned are no longer reimbursed. The localisation requirement is designed to apply on an ongoing basis, or at least until the localisation objectives established by the Turkish government are achieved. The localisation requirement is periodically adapted, modified, updated or extended with respect to, *inter alia*, the products it applies to and/or the extent of localisation sought.

The specific commitments to be implemented in order to comply with the localisation requirement are established for each foreign producer in a non-transparent manner and may differ from producer to producer.

b. The technology transfer requirement

As part of the localisation requirement, or closely connected to it, foreign producers may be required, in particular, to transfer technology, including patent rights, to a producer established in Turkey (the "technology transfer requirement"). This requirement does not apply to Turkish producers of pharmaceutical products. The type of technology transfer may also differ from producer to producer

c. The import ban on localised products

It appears that where the production of a pharmaceutical product has been localised in Turkey in accordance with the localisation requirement, applied in conjunction with the Turkish rules for approving the importation and marketing of pharmaceutical products, the importation of that pharmaceutical product is no longer permitted ("the import prohibition").

d. The prioritization measure

As part of the localisation requirement, or closely connected to it, foreign producers may be required, in particular, to transfer technology, including patent rights, to a producer established in Turkey (the "technology transfer requirement"). This requirement does not apply to Turkish producers of pharmaceutical products. The type of technology transfer may also differ from producer to producer.

It appears that where the production of a pharmaceutical product has been localised in Turkey in accordance with the localisation requirement, applied in conjunction with the Turkish rules for approving the importation and marketing of pharmaceutical products, the importation of that pharmaceutical product is no longer permitted ("the import prohibition").

Lastly, it appears that, even in certain cases where imported products are not excluded from the reimbursement scheme by virtue of the localisation requirement, the Turkish authorities give priority to the review of applications for inclusion of domestic pharmaceutical products in the list of products covered by the reimbursement scheme, as well as with respect to any pricing and licensing policies and processes, over the review of the applications of imported products (the "prioritization" measure). This measure is also administered in a non-transparent manner. . . .

3. Legal basis for the complaint

The various measures at issue described above appear to be inconsistent with Turkey's obligations under the covered agreements, in particular: . . .

- Article 3.1 of the TRIPS Agreement, because the technology transfer requirement does not apply to domestic producers of pharmaceutical products, and therefore it accords to the producers of other Members treatment less favourable than that accorded to domestic producers with regard to the protection of intellectual property;
- Article 27.1 of the TRIPS Agreement, because the technology transfer requirement may cover patent rights and does not apply to domestic producers of pharmaceutical products, and thus patents are not available and patent rights are not enjoyable without discrimination as to whether products are imported or locally produced;
- Article 28.2 of the TRIPs Agreement, because the technology transfer requirement may cover patent rights and because it restricts or infringes on the right of patent owners to assign, or transfer by succession, the patent and to conclude licensing contracts;
- Articles 39.1 and 39.2 of the TRIPS Agreement, because the technology transfer requirement may require foreign producers of pharmaceutical products to transfer undisclosed information protected by those provisions to a Turkish producer; . . .

The various measures relating to pharmaceutical products identified in this request appear to nullify or impair the benefits accruing to the European Union directly or indirectly under the covered agreements.

The European Union reserves the right to address additional measures and claims under other provisions of the covered agreements regarding the above matters during the course of the consultations.

§ 2.63. INTELLECTUAL PROPERTY RIGHTS UNDER THE COVID-19 PANDEMIC

The private appropriation of technology and reputation in the field of pharmaceuticals has almost always been a matter of controversy. But in times of a pandemic, the controversy becomes more acute.

Since March 2020, the world has attentively, if not anxiously, accompanied the search for treatments for the diseases that result from COVID-19 infection, as well as, with much hope and expectation, the development of a vaccine. The urgent nature and the superior necessity of both solutions have also given rise to a certain level—actually, a high level—of anxiety as to their availability.

Current international law contains provisions that may contribute to that availability—that is, as far as intellectual property is concerned. The TRIPS Agreement allows for compulsory licenses in the case the proprietors of important medicines do not meet the demands of the public interest. The TRIPS Agreement even permits that countries ignore all of its rules, in situations of emergency that put national security in jeopardy.

Nevertheless, perhaps with the main intent of giving a political response to the demands that intellectual property owners should not stand in the way of access to important medicines for COVID-19, many governments, international organizations, academics, and entities of a very diversified nature have called for measures that, in their view, help pave the way for an easier and cheaper access to those medicines.

One measure is compulsory licenses. That is a reasonably known and experimented mechanism. As said, it exists already in the TRIPS Agreement and most national laws. Another proposed measure is less clear in scope: vaccines for COVID-19 should be considered a "public good," hence insusceptible of being appropriated. This second measure has the same moral roots—and the same lack of rationality—as the calls for excluding medicines from patentability, based on the alleged immorality of the private appropriation of something that is essential to health. But some countries have reacted very quickly—and thoughtlessly, be it said—to these claims, and have enacted laws that in one or other way put those ideas in practice. A few will be reflected in the following texts.

A third measure has been proposed by India and South Africa to the TRIPS Council: the Council should recommend to the WTO General Council a waiver from all the intellectual property rights contained in the TRIPS Agreement that have a connection with the prevention, containment or treatment of COVID-19, except the protection of Performers, Producers of Phonograms (Sound Recordings) and Broadcasting Organizations. The waiver should operate for an undetermined period, until the pandemic is over.Obviously, there is a political tone in this proposal because, as said, WTO Members are already authorized to ignore TRIPS provisions for protecting their national security interests. Indeed, there is no need to debate whether the deadly worldwide spread of the virus constitutes an emergency in international relations, which justifies the national security exception under Article 73 of the TRIPS Agreement. But India seeks a multilateral approval for the (mis)appropriation by its huge generic industry of the inventions made by research-based pharmaceutical companies. Worse, by proposing a waiver from almost all intellectual property rights covered by the TRIPS Agreement, India wishes to have access not only to patented technology but also to the trademarks and trade names of those companies that may have already become well-known worldwide, in connection with COVID-19 treatments and prevention. If the TRIPS and the General Councils approved this proposal, other WTO Members would not be able to stop imports of generic products, even if these contradicted the rights of their national companies. The only exception mentioned in the proposal concerns an area of intellectual property in which the Indian industry has a strong interest. This suggests that India's proposal may be based on the cherry-picking of TRIPS-related intellectual property rights.

Unfortunately, all the debates on the protection through patents or other intellectual property rights of the inventions related to the COVID-19 arise from two completely wrong starting points. The first one is that the medicines and vaccines are still not available, nor have the companies that are now creating them manifested any intentions to behave in an antisocial manner. The fear is that they may charge prices different from those that correspond to the economic realities of the market, or that they refuse to license the respective technologies. The licensing of these technologies is of the essence, of course, in the face of the obvious impossibility of those companies to produce treatments and vaccines enough to attend the (worldwide) demand. In other words, most of the proposals so far aiming at diminishing the intellectual property rights of the companies that are making and will make the medicines for treating COVID-19 related diseases (including the so much desired vaccines), are based on the assumption that, when the time comes, those companies will behave in a socially irresponsible manner.

The second debate, which is linked to morals and ethics, is actually misguided. Simply eliminating intellectual property in essential medicines—for COVID-19 or any other disease—is the same as prohibiting the inventors from going to the market in search of a reward that pays them the costs of inventing, making and distributing the products, and that pay also the investment made by shareholders in the companies. The alternative is for governments to take the role of those private companies—which some countries are doing now, but with mitigated success, thus far. So, calls that have been made for COVID-19 vaccines to be treated as "global public goods," and for the poor nations to receive the vaccine at the same time as the rich ones, as well as other calls based on similar charitable motivations, unfortunately, tend to ignore the sound advice that Adam Smith has left us: "It is not from the benevolence of the butcher, the brewer, or the baker that we expect our dinner, but from their regard to their own self-interest. We address ourselves not to their humanity but to their self-love, and never talk to them of our own necessities, but of their advantages."

This entire book has revealed expressions of the absolute truth of that. Both the existing medicines and the future ones, as well as the vaccines, will reach all those in need, through the operation of a combination of market forces—the market is blind but tends not to be completely stupid—and the intervention of governments—which inevitably will put their hands in the pockets of taxpayers—and—why not?—the social conscience and prudent behavior of pharmaceutical research-based companies. There is no free lunch, as the saying goes, but there are lunches more expensive than others.

At the end of the day, intellectual property shall survive to the COVID-19 pandemic, even if its role may be temporarily adulterated. But that is inevitable—after all, the intellectual property that applies to pharmaceuticals is not the same that applies to children's toys, luxury cars, or office furniture. This is the essential message that comes from innumerous historical testimonies, as shown in this book.

§ 2.63.1. France—Emergency Law no. 2020-290 of March 23, 2020 to deal with the COVID-19 epidemic

Art. L. 3131-15.—In the territorial districts where the state of health emergency is declared, the Prime Minister may, by regulatory decree grounded on the report of the Minister responsible for health, for the sole purpose of guaranteeing public health: . . .

(7) Order the requisition of all goods and services necessary for the fight against the health disaster as well as of any person necessary for the operation of these services or the use of these goods. Compensation for these requisitions is governed by the Defense Code;

(8) Take temporary measures to control the prices of certain products made necessary to prevent or correct the tensions observed on the market for

certain products; the National Consumer Council is informed of the measures taken in this direction; . . .

(9) As necessary, take any measure allowing the provision of patients with appropriate drugs for the eradication of the health disaster;

(10) As necessary, take, by decree, any other regulatory measure limiting the freedom of enterprise, for the sole purpose of putting an end to the health disaster mentioned in article L. 3131-12 of this code.

The measures prescribed in application of paragraphs 1 to 10 of this article are strictly proportionate to the health risks incurred and appropriate to the circumstances of time and place. They shall be terminated without delay when they are no longer needed.

§ 2.63.2. Canada—An Act respecting certain measures in response to COVID-19, March 25, 2020

Statutes of Canada, Chapter 5

Bill C-13

First Session, Forty-third Parliament,

Patent Act

51. The Patent Act is amended by adding the following after section 19.3:

Application by Minister

19. 4 (1) The Commissioner shall, on the application of the Minister of Health, authorize the Government of Canada and any person specified in the application to make, construct, use and sell a patented invention to the extent necessary to respond to the public health emergency described in the application.

Contents of application

(2) The application must

(a) set out the name of the patentee and the number, as recorded in the Patent Office, of the patent issued in respect of the patented invention;

(b) include a confirmation that the Chief Public Health Officer, appointed under subsection 6(1) of the Public Health Agency of Canada Act, believes that there is a public health emergency that is a matter of national concern;

(c) include a description of the public health emergency; and

(d) specify a person, if any, that is to be authorized to make, construct, use and sell the patented invention for the purposes of responding to the public health emergency.

Cessation of effect

(3) The authorization ceases to have effect the earlier of

(a) the day on which the Minister of Health notifies the Commissioner that the authorization is no longer necessary to respond to the public health emergency set out in the application, and

(b) one year after the day on which it is granted.

Notice
(4) The Commissioner shall notify the patentee of any authorization that is granted under this section and provide them with the information referred to in subsection (2).

Payment of remuneration
(5) The Government of Canada and any person authorized under subsection (1) shall pay the patentee any amount that the Commissioner considers to be adequate remuneration in the circumstances, taking into account the economic value of the authorization and the extent to which they make, construct, use and sell the patented invention.

Authorization not transferable
(6) An authorization granted under this section is not transferable.

For greater certainty
(7) For greater certainty, the use or sale, in relation to a public health emergency, of a patented invention that is made or constructed in accordance with an authorization granted under this section is not an infringement of the patent.

Power of Federal Court
(8) On the application of the patentee, the Federal Court may make an order requiring the Government of Canada or any person authorized under subsection (1) to cease making, constructing, using or selling the patented invention in a manner that is inconsistent with the authorization granted under this section.

Restriction
(9) The Commissioner shall not make an authorization under subsection (1) after September 30, 2020.

§ 2.63.3. United Nations—International cooperation to ensure global access to medicines, vaccines and medical equipment to face COVID-19

A/74/L.56

General Assembly, April 8, 2020

The General Assembly,

Recalling its resolutions 74/270 of 2 April 2020 and 74/2 of 10 October 2019,

Noting with concern the threat to human health, safety and well-being caused by the coronavirus disease 2019 (COVID-19) pandemic, which has spread all around the globe, as well as the unprecedented and multifaceted effects of the pandemic, including the severe disruption to societies, economies, global trade and travel and the devastating impact on the livelihoods of people, . . .

Reaffirming the right of every human being, without distinct ion of any kind, to the enjoyment of the highest attainable standard of physical and mental health, . . .

Underscoring that equitable access to health products is a global priority and that the availability, accessibility, acceptability and affordability of health products of assured quality are fundamental to tackling the pandemic,

Recognizing the importance of international cooperation and effective multilateralism in helping to ensure that all States have in place effective national protective measures, access to and flow of vital medical supplies, medicines and vaccines, in order to minimize negative effects in all affected States and to avoid relapses of the pandemic,

Recognizing also that the COVID-19 global pandemic requires a global response based on unity, solidarity and multilateral cooperation, . . .

2. *Requests* the Secretary-General, in close collaboration with the World Health Organization and other relevant agencies of the United Nations system, including the international financial institutions, to identify and recommend options, including approaches to rapidly scaling manufacturing and strengthening supply chains that promote and ensure fair, transparent, equitable, efficient and timely access to and distribution of preventive tools, laboratory testing, reagents and supporting materials, essential medical supplies, new diagnostics, drugs and future COVID -19 vaccines, with a view to making them available to all those in need, in particular in developing countries;

3. *Encourages* Member States to work in partnership with all relevant stakeholders to increase research and development funding for vaccines and medicines, leverage digital technologies, and strengthen scientific international cooperation necessary to combat COVID-19 and to bolster coordination, including with the private sector, towards rapid development, manufacturing and distribution of diagnostics, antiviral medicines, personal protective equipment and vaccines, adhering to the objectives of efficacy, safety, equity, accessibility, and affordability;

4. *Calls upon* Member States and other relevant stakeholders to immediately take steps to prevent, within their respective legal frameworks, speculation and undue stockpiling that may hinder access to safe, effective and affordable essential medicines, vaccines, personal protective equipment and medical equipment as may be required to effectively address COVID-19; . . .

§ 2.63.4. A wide group of well-known, influencing personalities call for the public, free-for-all COVID-19 vaccine: "a people's vaccine"

Thursday, May 14, 2020

Uniting Behind A People's Vaccine Against COVID-19

Humanity today, in all its fragility, is searching for an effective and safe vaccine against COVID-19. It is our best hope of putting a stop to this painful global pandemic.

We are calling on Health Ministers at the World Health Assembly to rally behind a people's vaccine against this disease urgently. Governments and international partners must unite around a global guarantee which ensures that, when a safe and effective vaccine is developed, it is produced rapidly at scale and made available for all people, in all countries, free of charge. The same applies for all treatments, diagnostics, and other technologies for COVID-19. . . .

Now is *not* the time to allow the interests of the wealthiest corporations and governments to be placed before the universal need to save lives, or to leave this massive and moral task to market forces. Access to vaccines and treatments as global public goods are in the interests of all humanity. We cannot afford for monopolies, crude competition and near-sighted nationalism to stand in the way.

We must heed the warning that "Those who do not remember the past are doomed to repeat it." We must learn the painful lessons from a history of unequal access in dealing with disease such as HIV and Ebola. But we must also remember the ground-breaking victories of health movements, including AIDS activists and advocates who fought for access to affordable medicines for all.

Applying *both* sets of lessons, we call for a global agreement on COVID-19 vaccines, diagnostics and treatments—implemented under the leadership of the World Health Organization—that:

1. Ensures mandatory worldwide sharing of all COVID-19 related knowledge, data and technologies with a pool of COVID-19 licenses freely available to all countries. Countries should be empowered and enabled to make full use of agreed safeguards and flexibilities in the WTO Doha Declaration on the TRIPS Agreement and Public Health to protect access to medicines for all.
2. Establishes a global and equitable rapid manufacturing and distribution plan—that is fully-funded by rich nations—for the vaccine and all COVID-19 products and technologies that guarantees transparent 'at true cost-prices' and supplies according to need. Action must start urgently to massively build capacity worldwide to manufacture billions of vaccine doses and to recruit and train the millions of paid and protected health workers needed to deliver them.
3. Guarantees COVID-19 vaccines, diagnostics, tests and treatments are provided free of charge to everyone, everywhere. Access needs to be prioritized first for front-line workers, the most vulnerable people, and for poor countries with the least capacity to save lives.

In doing so, no one can be left behind. Transparent democratic governance must be set in place by the WHO, inclusive of independent expertise and civil society partners, which is essential to lock-in accountability for this agreement.

In doing so, we also recognize the urgent need to reform and strengthen public health systems worldwide, removing all barriers so that rich and poor alike can access the health care, technologies and medicines they need, free at the point of need.

Only a people's vaccine—with equality and solidarity at its core—can protect all of humanity and get our societies safely running again. A bold international agreement cannot wait.

[More than 140 signatures of well-known persons follow]

§ 2.63.5. World Health Organization—COVID-19 response

Seventy-Third World Health Assembly

A73/CONF./1 Rev.1 Agenda item 3

May 18, 2020

The Seventy-third World Health Assembly, . . .

Recognizing the need for all countries to have unhindered timely access to quality, safe, efficacious and affordable diagnostics, therapeutics, medicines and vaccines, and essential health technologies, and their components as well as equipment for the COVID-19 response; . . .

Calls for the universal, timely and equitable access to and fair distribution of all quality, safe, efficacious and affordable essential health technologies and products including their components and precursors required in the response to the COVID-19 pandemic as a global priority, and the urgent removal of unjustified obstacles thereto; consistent with the provisions of relevant international treaties including the provisions of the TRIPS agreement and the flexibilities as confirmed by the Doha Declaration on the TRIPS Agreement and Public Health; . . .

Calls on international organizations and other relevant stakeholders to: . . .

Work collaboratively at all levels to develop, test, and scale-up production of safe, effective, quality, affordable diagnostics, therapeutics, medicines and vaccines for the COVID-19 response, including, existing mechanisms for voluntary pooling and licensing of patents to facilitate timely, equitable and affordable access to them, consistent with the provisions of relevant international treaties including the provisions of the TRIPS agreement and the flexibilities as confirmed by the Doha Declaration on the TRIPS Agreement and Public Health; . . .

Requests the Director-General to: . . .

Rapidly, and noting OP2 of RES/74/274 and in consultation with Member States, and with inputs from relevant international organizations civil society, and the private sector, as appropriate, identify and provide options that respect the provisions of relevant international treaties, including the provisions of the TRIPS agreement and the flexibilities as confirmed by the Doha Declaration on the TRIPS Agreement and Public Health to be used in scaling up development, manufacturing and distribution capacities needed for transparent equitable and timely access to quality, safe, affordable and efficacious diagnostics, therapeutics, medicines, and vaccines for the COVID-19 response taking into account existing mechanisms, tools, and initiatives, such as the Access to COVID-19 Tools (ACT) accelerator, and relevant pledging appeals, such as "The Coronavirus Global Response" pledging campaign, for the consideration of the Governing Bodies; . . .

§ 2.63.6. The United States responds to WHA's "COVID-19 Response" Resolution

WHA 73

United States of America

Explanation of Position

"COVID-19 Response" Resolution

May 19, 2020

Written Statement

The United States thanks the European Union and the other co-sponsors for their leadership in preparing the COVID-19 Response resolution for adoption at the virtual 73rd World Health Assembly (WHA). That we are meeting in virtual session, at a time when more than 300,000 people have lost their lives and the global economy has been deeply affected, is a testament to the need to come together in response to this pandemic. This resolution makes an important contribution to that global response, immediately calling for whole-of-government and whole-of-society approaches to fighting the pandemic with the best available evidence, and by urging the international community to come together around all aspects of the response.

Most importantly, the terms of this resolution take the first critical steps necessary to ensure that, when we face the next pandemic, we will have a World Health Organization (WHO) and an international system capable of responding effectively and decisively to save lives and protect the vulnerable. We applaud the call for an impartial, independent, and comprehensive review of the WHO's response, to be undertaken in consultation with Member States, and we urge that work to begin now. This will help ensure we have a complete and transparent understanding of the source of the virus, timeline of events, early discussions, and the decision-making process for the WHO's response to the COVID-19 pandemic. We must reform the WHO and supporting entities to be fully capable of fulfilling their core and crucial mission moving forward. We further appreciate the mandate given by the resolution to the WHO to investigate the origins of the virus, and we are confident that through this knowledge, researchers and medical practitioners around the world will be empowered in the pursuit of vaccines and other countermeasures.

Finally, we wholeheartedly endorse the call in the resolution for all Member States to provide the WHO with timely, accurate, and sufficiently-detailed public health information related to the COVID-19 pandemic, as required by the International Health Regulations (IHR 2005). We stand ready to work with all partners to implement this resolution. If we are to fully realize the promise contained in the IHRs of a safer world for everyone, changes must be made within the WHO to hold Member State accountable to address and reduce risks that threaten public health.

Unfortunately, despite our best efforts at working toward consensus language in all areas of this resolution, we regret that the United States must disassociate itself from a few paragraphs due to the following issues: . . .

The United States must also disassociate from operative paragraphs 4, 8.2 and 9.8 because the language in these operative paragraphs does not adequately capture all of the carefully negotiated, and balanced, language in the World Trade Organization (WTO) Agreement on Trade-Related Aspects of Intellectual Property (TRIPS) and the Doha Declaration of 2001 and instead presents an unbalanced and incomplete picture of that language at a time where all actors need to come together to produce vaccines and other critical health products. The United States recognizes the importance of access to affordable, safe, high-quality, and effective health products and the critical role that intellectual property plays in incentivizing the development of new and improved health products. However, as currently drafted, paragraphs 4, 8.2 and 9.8 send the wrong message to innovators who will be essential to the solutions the whole world needs.

We are concerned that a misinterpretation of international trade obligations in non-WTO multilateral fora may negatively affect countries' abilities to incentivize new drug development and expand access to medicines. We would also like to clarify our understanding of the reference in 8.2 to "existing mechanisms for voluntary pooling ... of patents." The United States interprets this reference as limited to voluntary mechanisms existing before the COVID-19 pandemic, not new or proposed "patent pooling" mechanisms created in response to the pandemic. It is critical that any such voluntary mechanisms as applied to COVID-19 related technologies be narrowly tailored in scope and duration to the medical needs of the current crisis, and that the World Intellectual Property Organization (WIPO), as the UN agency with technical expertise on intellectual property issues, play an appropriate role in their operation and evolution.

The United States is leading global efforts for the development of vaccines, for therapies and treatments for COVID-19, including providing significant funding and leading other initiatives to accelerate innovation in this space, for example the ACTIV Partnership recently unveiled by the United States National Institutes of Health. We applaud other global efforts as well and are committed to supporting a collaborative approach to ensuring that all efforts support one another and that we are truly accelerating progress toward a vaccine.

Going forward, given the need for innovation incentives in the development of new health products, the U.S. Government encourages member states to engage with innovators to find mutually-acceptable solutions that achieve increased access to affordable, safe, effective, and high-quality COVID-19 health products. By taking an unbalanced and incomplete approach to the issue of access to medicines and TRIPS, this resolution misses an opportunity to galvanize the world, beyond bureaucracy and UN bodies, toward the critical goal of accelerating research, development, distribution and access to affordable, safe, quality and effective COVID-19-related products. We remain committed to working with all partners toward that goal.

§ 2.63.7. India and South Africa seek in the TRIPS Council a general waiver from the obligation to protect intellectual property rights, October 2, 2020

IP/C/W/669 2 October 2020

WAIVER FROM CERTAIN PROVISIONS OF THE TRIPS AGREEMENT FOR THE PREVENTION, CONTAINMENT AND TREATMENT OF COVID-19

COMMUNICATION FROM INDIA AND SOUTH AFRICA

. . . 3. Given this present context of global emergency, it is important for WTO Members to work together to ensure that intellectual property rights such as patents, industrial designs, copyright and protection of undisclosed information do not create barriers to the timely access to affordable medical products including vaccines and medicines or to scaling-up of research, development, manufacturing and supply of medical products essential to combat COVID-19.

4. The COVID-19 pandemic is now widespread, affecting most WTO Members. . . .

5. An effective response to COVID-19 pandemic requires rapid access to affordable medical products including diagnostic kits, medical masks, other personal protective equipment and ventilators, as well as vaccines and medicines for the prevention and treatment of patients in dire need. . . .

7. As new diagnostics, therapeutics and vaccines for COVID-19 are developed, there are significant concerns, how these will be made available promptly, in sufficient quantities and at affordable price to meet global demand. Critical shortages in medical products have also put at grave risk patients suffering from other communicable and non-communicable diseases.

8. To meet the growing supply-demand gap, several countries have initiated domestic production of medical products and/or are modifying existing medical products for the treatment of COVID-19 patients. The rapid scaling up of manufacturing globally is an obvious crucial solution to address the timely availability and affordability of medical products to all countries in need.

9. There are several reports about intellectual property rights hindering or potentially hindering timely provisioning of affordable medical products to the patients. [note omitted] It is also reported that some WTO Members have carried out urgent legal amendments to their national patent laws to expedite the process of issuing compulsory/government use licenses.

10. Beyond patents, other intellectual property rights may also pose a barrier, with limited options to overcome those barriers. In addition, many countries especially developing countries may face institutional and legal difficulties when using flexibilities available in the Agreement on Trade-Related Aspects of Intellectual Property Rights (TRIPS Agreement). A particular concern for countries with insufficient or no manufacturing capacity are the requirements of Article 31*bis* and consequently the cumbersome and lengthy process for the import and export of pharmaceutical products.

11. Internationally, there is an urgent call for global solidarity, and the unhindered global sharing of technology and know-how in order that rapid responses for the handling of COVID-19 can be put in place on a real time basis.

12. In these exceptional circumstances, we request that the Council for TRIPS recommends, as early as possible, to the General Council a waiver from the implementation, application and enforcement of Sections 1, 4, 5, and 7 of Part II of the TRIPS Agreement in relation to prevention, containment or treatment of COVID-19.

13. The waiver should continue until widespread vaccination is in place globally, and the majority of the world's population has developed immunity hence we propose an initial duration of [x] years from the date of the adoption of the waiver.

14. We request that the Council for TRIPS urgently recommends to the General Council adoption of the annexed decision text.

ANNEX

DRAFT DECISION TEXT

WAIVER FROM CERTAIN PROVISIONS OF THE TRIPS AGREEMENT FOR THE PREVENTION, CONTAINMENT AND TREATMENT OF COVID-19

The General Council

Having regard to paragraphs 1, 3 and 4 of Article IX of the Marrakesh Agreement Establishing the World Trade Organization ("the WTO Agreement");

Conducting the functions of the Ministerial Conference in the interval between meetings pursuant to paragraph 2 of Article IV of the WTO Agreement;

Noting that the coronavirus disease 2019 (COVID-19) is a new infectious disease caused by severe acute respiratory syndrome coronavirus 2 (SARS-COV-2);

Recalling that on 11 March 2020, the World Health Organization (WHO) declared the 2019–20 coronavirus outbreak to be a pandemic, and it continues to be a very high risk across the globe in all WTO Members;

Noting with concern the threat to human health, safety and well-being caused by the COVID-19 pandemic, which has spread all around the globe, as well as the unprecedented and multifaceted effects of the pandemic, including the severe disruption to societies, economies, global trade and travel and the devastating impact on the livelihoods of people;

Recognising the need for unimpeded and timely access to affordable medical products including diagnostic kits, vaccines, medicines, personal protective equipment and ventilators for a rapid and effective response to the COVID-19 pandemic;

Recognizing also that the COVID-19 global pandemic requires a global response based on unity, solidarity and multilateral cooperation;

Noting that, in the light of the foregoing, exceptional circumstances exist justifying waivers from the obligations of the Agreement on Trade-Related Aspects of Intellectual Property Rights (TRIPS Agreement);

Decides as follows:

1. The obligations of Members to implement or apply Sections 1, 4, 5 and 7 of Part II of the TRIPS Agreement or to enforce these Sections under Part III of the TRIPS Agreement, shall be waived in relation to prevention, containment or treatment of COVID-19, for [X] years from the decision of the General Council.

2. The waiver in paragraph 1 shall not apply to the protection of Performers, Producers of Phonograms (Sound Recordings) and Broadcasting Organizations under Article 14 of the TRIPS Agreement.

3. This decision is without prejudice to the right of least developed country Members under paragraph 1 of Article 66 of the TRIPS Agreement.

4. This waiver shall be reviewed by the General Council not later than one year after it is granted, and thereafter annually until the waiver terminates, in accordance with the provisions of paragraph 4 of Article IX of the WTO Agreement.

Credits and Sources of Texts and Illustrations

Texts

§ **1.01.** Andres de Laguna (transl.), Pedacio Discorides Anarzabeo, Acerca de la Materia Medicinal y de los Venenos Mortíferos, at 543 (Mathías Gastón, 1570). Source: <gallica.org>; Jean Cannape (transl.), Deux Livres des Simples de Galien, C'est à savoir, le Deuxième, et le Neuvième, at 96-98, 100 (Etienne Dolet, 1542). Source: Google Books; Jean de Renou, Les Oeuvres Pharmaceutiques, at 134, 387 (Nicholas Gay, 1638) (Louis de Serre, translator from Latin). Source: <www.bhv.univ-tous.fr>., 2–6

§ **1.02.** A. Héron de Villefosse and H. Thédenat, *Notes sur quelques cachets d'oculistes romains*, in Bulletin Monumental ou Recueil de Documents et Mémoires relatifs aux différents branches de l'Archéologie, 5th series, vol. 11, at 309 *et seq.* (1883). Source: <gallica.BnF.fr>., 6–10

§ **1.03.** Cesare Foucard, Lo STatuto dei Medici et dei Speziali in Venezia scritto nell' anno 1258 (Tipografia del Commercio, 1859). Source: <archive.org>., 10–11

§ **1.04.** Decrusy, Isambert and Jourdan, Recueil Général des Anciennes Lois Françaises depuis l'an 420 jusqu'à la Révolution de 1789, vol. 4 (1327-1357), at 425-425 679-684 (Belin-Le-Prieur, w/d [1821-1833]). Source: <gallica.BnF.fr>., 11–13

§ **1.05.** Oin-Lacroix, Histoire des Anciennes Corporations et Métiers et des Confréries Religieuses de la Capitale de la Normandie, at 555 (Lecointe, 1850); Isambert et alii, Recueil Général des Anciennes Lois Françaises, Depuis l'An 420, Jusqu'à la Révolution de 1789, vol. 11 (1483-1514), at 663 (Belin-Leprieur, 1827). Source: <gallica.BnF.fr>., 13–15

§ **1.06.** E. Gosselin, *Les Potiers, Briquetiers, Tuiliers et les Émailleurs en Terre, de Rouen*, part 1, in Revue de la Normandie, 8th year, vol. 1, at 612, 622 (E. Cagniard, 1869). Source: <gallica.BnF.fr>., 15–17

§ **1.07.** Jean de Renou, Les Oeuvres Pharmaceutiques, 2nd Part, Boutique Pharmaceutique ou Antidotaire, at 472, 482, 483 (1638) (Louis de Serre, translator from Latin). Source: <www.bhv.univ-tous.fr>., 17–19

§ 1.08. Statuts, Ordonnances, Arrests et Reglemens des Marchands Apoticaires-Epiciers & des Marchands Epiciers-Ciriers-Droguistes et Confiseurs de la Ville, Fauxbourgs & Banlieue de Rouen, at 105-106 (Jacques-Joseph Le Boullenger, 1742). Source: < gallica.BnF.fr >., 20

§ 1.09. Antoine Mornac, In Senatu Parisiensi Patroni Observationes, Liber Decimous-Octavus, De periculo et commodo rei venditae, vol. 1, at 1073 (Montalant, 1721). Source: Google Books., 20–21

§ 1.10. Jacob Larwood and John Camden Hotten, The History of Signboards, from the Earliest Times to the Present Day, at 158-159, 341 (6th edition, John Camden Hotten, 1866). Source: < archive.org >., 21–24

§ 1.11. Statuts et Ordonnances pour les Marchands Apoticaires-Épiciers et les Marchands Épiciers-Grossiers-Droguistes de la Ville, Fauxbourgs et Banlieu de Paris, at 22, 23 (Prault, 1764). Source: < gallica.BnF.fr >., 24–25

§ 1.12. Elie Seignette, Traité du Faux Polychreste, pour Faire Connaître combien il difère de celui qu'ont inventé Jean Seignette, Docteur en Médecine, & Elie Seignette son Frère (Perez, 1675); Histoire de l'Académie Royale des Sciences, Année M.DCCXXXI, at 34, 35 (Panckoucke, 1764). Mercure de France dédié au Roi, 1751, vol. 1, at 208. Source: < gallica.BnF.fr >., 25–30

§ 1.13. Pomet fils (edit.), Pommet [Marchand Epicier et Droguiste], Histoire Générale des Drogues Simples et Composées, vol. 2, at 183-184 (new edit., Etienne Ganeau, 1735); Claude Blondeau and Gabriel Gueret, Journal du Palais ou Recueil des Principales Decisions de Tous Les Parlemens et Cours Souveraines de France, vol. 1, at 901-904 (Denys Thierry & Jean Guignard, 1701); Le Paulmier, L'Orviétan, Histoire d'une Famille de Charlatans du Pont-Neuf, au XVIe et XVIIe siècles, at 141-142 (Librairie Illustrée, 1893); Hyacinte Boniface, Arrests Notables de la Cour du Parlement de Provence, Cour des Comptes, Aydes et Finances du Même Païs, vol. 3, at 401 (Veuce d'Horace Molin, 1708). Source: < gallica.BnF.fr >., 30–44

§ 1.14. Statuts et Règlements en Faveur des Marchands Merciers, Ciriers, Graissiers, Epiciers et Droguistes de la Ville de Saint-Quentin (P. Boscher, 1730). Source: < gallica.BnF.fr >., 45

§ 1.15. Bulletin de la Société Française de l'Histoire de la Médecine, vol. 3, at 346 *et seq.* (Alphonse Picard et Fils, 1904). Source: < archive.org >., 46–47

§ 1.16. Mercure de France Dédié au Roi, Janvier 1752, vol. 1, at 210-211 (Pissot, Nully, Barrois, and Duchesne, 1752); Suite de la Clef, ou Journal Historique sur les Matières du Tems, Janvier 1753, vol. 53, at 224 (Ganeau, 1753). Source: < gallica.BnF.fr >., 47–50

§ 1.17. Nicolas Toussaint des Essarts, Causes célèbres, curieuses et intéressantes de toutes les cours souveraines du royaume, avec les jugemens qui les ont décidées, vol. 11, at 225-242 (1874). Source: < gallica.BnF.fr >., 50–52

§ 1.18. William Bacon, An Essay on the Virtues, Uses, and Effects of Some Valuable Genuine Patent and Public Medicines, Invented and Prepared by Men of Science, at 8 (1792); William Bacon, An Essay on the Virtues, Uses, and Effects of Some Valuable Genuine Patent and Public Medicines, Invented and Prepared by Men of Science, at 32-33 (1792). Source: < archive.org >., 52–55

§ 1.19. Collecção de decretos, avisos, e outras ordens regias a favor da verdadeira, e unica agoa de Inglaterra da composição do Doutor Jacob de Castro Sarmento, Preparada por José Joaquim de Castro, na sua Real Fábrica de Lisboa, at 13-15, 30, 32-34, 67-68 (Impressão Régia, 1814). Source: < wellcomecollection.org > ; André Lopes de Castro, Aviso ao Público a Respeito da Agoa de Inglaterra da Composição do Doutor Jacob de Castro Sarmento Fabricada nesta Corte com Publica, e Innegavel Aceitação (Simão Thaddeo Ferreira, 1799). Source: < archive.org > ; Diário da Regência, No. 121, Wednesday, May 23, 1821, Supplement. Source: Google Books., 55–62

§ 1.20. Francis Vesey and John Beames, Reports of Cases Argued and Determined in the High Court of Cancery, in the Time of Lord Cancellor Eldon, with Notes, and Reference to American Cases, by Edward D. Ingraham, vol. 2 (1813-1814), at 219 (H.C. Carey and I. Lea, 1823). Source: < archive.org > ., 63

§ 1.21. L. Créteur, Lois et Réglements sur la Pharmacie en Belgique, depuis les Temps les Plus Reculés jusqu'à Nos Jours, at 183 *et seq.* (G. Mayolez and Germer Baillière, 1870): Jules Sauveur, Histoire de la Législation Médicale Belge, at 226 and 326 (Aug. Decq, 1862). Source: < gallica.BnF.fr > ., 63–65

§ 1.22. Reports of Cases in Chancery, Argued and Determined in the Rolls Court during the Time of Lord Langdale, Master of the Rolls, vol. XIII, 1850, 1851, at 210 *et seq.* (Stevens and Norton, 1853). Source: < archive.org > ; Le Tintamarre, critique de la réclame, satire des puffistes, February 24, 1861. Source: < gallica.BnF.fr > ; The Chemist and Druggist, February 14, 1863, at 45-47; April 22, 1893, at 544-545. Source: < wellcomelibrary.org > ; Le Droit d'Auteur, the official journal of the Bureau of the International Union for the Protection of Litterary and Artistic Works, July 15, 1893, at 86 *et seq.*; John Cutler and Grank G. Underhay (eds.), Reports of Patent, Design, Trade-Mark, and Other Cases, vol. 20, at 525 (Darling & Son, Ltd., 1903). Source: < archive.org > ., 65–74

§ 1.23. Dr. Commet, L'Abbeille Médicale – Revue des Journaux et des Ouvrages de Médecine, de Chirurgie, de Pharmacie, vol. 6, 6th year, 1849, at 82-83 (1849). Source: < gallica.BnF.fr > ; Observations sus l'Histoire et les Effets du Rob Anti-Syphillitique de M. Boyveau-Laffecteur, at 155-156 (self-publication, 1810). Source: < archive.org > ; Bulletin des Arrêts de la Cour de Cassation rendus en Matière Civile, vol. 47, year 1860, at 31-32 (Imprimerie Impériale, 1861). Source: < gallica.BnF.fr > ., 75–81

§ 1.24. Decisions of the Commissioner of Patents and of United States Courts in Patent and Trade-Marks Cases – 1898, at 687-688 (Government Printing Office, 1899). Source: < archive.org > ., 81–84

§ 1.25. Source: < uspto.gov > ; John Cutler (edit.), Reports of Patent, Design, Trade Mark, and Other Cases, vol. 18, at 191 *et seq.* (Darling & Son, 1901); Rowland Cox, A Manual of Trade-Mark Cases, at 158 (Houghton, Mifflin and Co., 1881). Source: < archive.org > ; Source: < www.nexis.com > ; La Propriété Industrielle, Organe Officiel du Bureau International de l'Union pour la Protection de la Propriété Industrielle, 8th year, no. 4, April 1st, 1892, at 45, 46. Source: < gallica.BnF.fr > ; The Chemist and druggist, April 16, 1910, at 37. Source: < www. wellcomelibrary.org > ., 85–93

§ **1.26.** John Cutler and Frank G. Underhay, Reports of Patent, Design, Trade Mark and Other Cases, vol. 23, at 725 *et seq.* (Darling & Son, 1906). Source: <archive.org>., 93–97

§ **1.27.** 153 Fed. Reporter 735 (1907). Source: Google Books., 97–100

§ **1.28.** Eugène Pouillet, Traité des Marques de Fabrique et de la Concurrence Déloyale en Tous Genres, at 115-120, 610-611, 659-660, 957, 1142 (6th ed., Marchal & Godde, Succ., 1912). Source: <gallica.BnF.fr>., 100–104

§ **1.29.** House of Commons, Report of the Select Committee on Patent Medicines, at xii-xiii (1914). Source: <archive.org>., 104–105

§ **1.30.** Source: <casetext.com>; Source: <uspto.gov>; John Cutler and Frank G. Underhay, Reports of Patent, Design, Trade Mark and Other Cases, vol. 22, at 501 *et seq.* (Darling & Son, 1905). Source: <archive.org>; La Propriété Industrielle, Organe Officiel du Bureau International de l'Union pour la Protection de la Propriété Industrielle, 23th year, no. 7, July 31, 1907, at 99. Source: <gallica.BnF.fr>; The Coleman Journal, Alberta, Canada, March 19, 1936 and December 16, 1937. Source: <archive.org>., 105–117

§ **1.31.** Source: <casetext.com>., 117–121

§ **1.32.** Source: <www.who.int/nutrition/publications/code_english.pdf>; Source: <extranet.who.int>, 121–126

§ **1.33.** Source: <www.planalto.gov.br>., 126–128

§ **1.34.** *Marks and International Nonproprietary Names for Pharmaceutical Substances (INNs) – Document prepared by the Secretariat*, SCT/16/3, of 1 September 2006. Source: <www.wipo.int>., 128–129

§ **1.35.** Boletín Oficial del Estado, August 20, 2011., 130–131

§ **1.36.** <www.wto.org>; <www.health.gov.au>., 131–135

§ **2.01.** Scribonii Largi, Medici Vetustissimi, de compositione medicamentorum liber, at 69-70 (Andream Catandrum, 1529). Source: <archive.org>., 138–139

§ **2.02.** W.H.S. Jones (transl. and ed.), Pliny, Natural History, with an English Translation in 10 Volumes, vol. 7, Libri XXIV-XXVII, at 5 and 137-138 (Harvard Univ. Press, 1966). Source: <gallica.BnF.fr>., 140–141

§ **2.03.** C.J.S. Thompson, The Mystery and Art of the Apothecary, at 103-104 (John Lane The Bodley Head Ltd., 1929). Source: <archive.org>., 141–142

§ **2.04.** Francesco Scipione, *Notizie sopra Jacopo e Giovanni Dondi dall'Orologio*, in Saggi Cientifici e Letterari dell'Academia di Padova, vol. II, at 469, 473-474 (1789). Source: <archive.org>., 142–143

§ **2.05.** J. Aubrey Rees, The Worshipful Company of Grocers – An Historical Retrospect, 1345-1923, at 79-80 (Chapman and Dodd, 1923). Source: <archive.org>., 143–144

§ **2.06.** Alfred Franklin, Dictionnaire Historique des Arts, Métiers et Professions exercés dans Paris depuis le Treizième Siècle, at 439 (H. Welter, 1906). Source: <gallica.BnF.fr>., 144–145

§ **2.07.** Alessio Piemontese, Foreword to the first edition of De Secreti, 1555. Source: <archive.org>, <gallica.BnF.fr> and Google Books., 145–152

§ **2.08.** Bulletin de la Société Française d'Histoire de la Médecine, vol. 12, at 372 *et seq.* (1913). Source: <archive.org>., 152–153

§ 2.09. Printed by George Edward Eyre and William Spottiswoode, 1857. Source: < archive.org > ., 153–155

§ 2.10. Paul Dorveaux, LES APOTHICAIRES DE METZ, LEURS SATUTS (Honoré Champion, 1909). Source: < gallica.BnF.fr > ., 155

§ 2.11. CERTAIN NECESSARY DIRECTIONS, AS WELL FOR THE CURE OF THE PLAGUE, AS FOR PREVENTING THE INFECTION; WITH MANY EASY MEDICINES OF SMALLCHARGE,VERY PROFITABLE TO HIS MAJESTIES SUBJECTS. SET DOWNE BY THE COLLEDGE OF PHYSICIANS BY THE KINGS MAJESTIES SPECIALL COMMAND. WITH SUNDRY ORDERS THOUGHT MEET BY HIS MAJESTIE, AND HIS PRIVIE COUNCELL, TO BE CAREFULLY EXECUTED FOR PREVENTION OF THE PLAGUE. ALSO CERTAINE SELECT STATUTES COMMANDED BY HIS MAJESTIE TO BE PUT IN EXECUTION BY ALL JUSTICES, AND OTHER OFFICERS OF THE PEACE THROUGHOUT THE REALM. (Robert Barker, 1636). Source: < archive.org > ., 156–157

§ 2.12. A. Baudot, ETUDES HISTORIQUES SUR LA PHARMACIE EN BOURGOGNE AVANT 1803, at 279-280 (A. Maloine, 1905). Source: < gallica.BnF.fr > ., 157–158

§ 2.13. Mary Anne Everett Green (edit.), CALENDAR OF STATE PAPERS, DOMESTIC SERIES, OF THE REIGN OF CHARLES II, 1664-1665, at 303 (Kraus Reprint, 1968); Mary Anne Everett Green (edit.), CALENDAR OF STATE PAPERS, DOMESTIC SERIES, OF THE REIGN OF CHARLES II, 1667, at 360, 431, 439, 508 (Logmans, Green, Reader, and Dyer, 1866); Mary Anne Everett Green (edit.), CALENDAR OF STATE PAPERS, DOMESTIC SERIES, OF THE REIGN OF CHARLES II, NOVEMBER 1667 TO SEPTEMBER 1668, at 239 (Eyre and Spottiswoode, 1893); Mary Anne Everett Green (edit.), CALENDAR OF STATE PAPERS, DOMESTIC SERIES, OF THE REIGN OF CHARLES II, NOVEMBER 1667 TO SEPTEMBER 1668, at 466 (Eyre and Spottiswoode, 1902). Source: < babel.hathitrust.org > ., 158–159

§ 2.14. Mary Anne Everett Green (edit.), CALENDAR OF STATE PAPERS, DOMESTIC SERIES, OF THE REIGN OF CHARLES II, NOVEMBER 1667 TO SEPTEMBER 1668, at 224 (Eyre and Spottiswoode, 1893); Mary Anne Everett Green (edit.), CALENDAR OF STATE PAPERS, DOMESTIC SERIES, OF THE REIGN OF CHARLES II, OCTOBER OF 1668 TO DECEMBER OF 1669, at 239 (Eyre and Spottiswoode, 1894). Source: < babel.hathitrust.org > ., 159–160

§ 2.15. C.J.S. Thompson, THE MYSTERY AND ART OF THE APOTHECARY, at 182-183 (John Lane The Bodley Head Ltd., 1929). Source: < archive.org > ., 160–161

§ 2.16. Jonathan Goddard, A DISCOURSE SETTING FORTH THE UNHAPPY CONDITION OF THE PRACTICE OF PHYSICK IN LONDON, AND OFFERING SOME MEANS TO PUT IT INTO A BETTER; FOR THE INTEREST OF PATIENTS, NO LESS, OR RATHER MUCH MORE, THAN OF PHYSICIANS. London, 1669. Source: < quod.lib.umich.edu; BIOGRAPHIA BRITANNICA OR THE LIVES OF THE MOST EMINENT PERSONS WHO HAVE FLOURISHED IN GREAT BRITAIN AND IRELAND, vol. 4, at 2217 (1757); Martin Lister, A JOURNEY TO PARIS IN THE YEAR OF 1698, at 243-245 (Jacob Tonson, 1699); Christopher Merrett, A SHORT VIEW OF THE FRAUDS, AND ABUSES COMMITTED BY APOTHECARIES; AS WELL IN RELATION TO PATIENTS: AND OF THE ONLY REMEDY THEREOF BY PHYSICIANS MAKING THEIR OWN MEDICINES, at 57-58 (2nd ed., James Allestry, 1670); Lex Talionis, SIVE VINDICIAE PHARMACOPORUM: OR A SHORT REPLY TO DR. MERRETT'S BOOK; AND OTHERS WRITTEN AGAINST THE APOTHECARIES: WHEREIN MAY BE DISCOVERED THE FRAUDS AND ABUSES COMMITTED BY DOCTORS PROFESSING AND PRACTICING PHARMACY, at 5 (1670). Source: < archive.org > ., 161–167

§ 2.17. J.H. Aveling, The Chamberlens and the Midwifery Forceps—Memorials of the Family and an Essay on the Invention of the Instrument, at 132-136 (excerpts) (J. & A. Churchill, 1882). Source: <archive.org>., 167–168

§ 2.18. Bulletin de la Société Française de l'Histoire de la Médecine, vol. 21, at 282 *et seq.* (1927); Johan Jacob Waldschmidt, Opera Medico Practica, vol. 1, at 462 (Bernardini Gerssarj, 1727); Royal Society, Philosophical Transactions, Giving Some Accompt of the Present Undertakings, Studies and Labours of the Ingenious in Many Considerable Parts of the World, No. 96, July 21, 1673, at 6078, 6079 (John Martyn, 1673). Source: <archive.org>., 168–170

§ 2.19. C.J.S. Thompson, The Mystery and Art of the Apothecary, at 233-235 (John Lane, 1929). Source: <archive.org>; Nicolas de Blégny, Le Remède Anglois pour la Guérison des Fièvres, Publié par l'Ordre du Roi, Avec les Observations de Monsieur le Premier Médecin de sa Majesté, sur la Composition, les Vertus, et l'Usage de ce Remède, at 5-12 (Estienne Michallet, 1683). Source: <gallica.BnF.fr>., 2.19–173

§ 2.20. De Vigneul-Marville, Mélanges d'Histoire et de Littérature, vol. 1, at 48-53 (new ed., Claude Prudhomme, 1713); Maurice Bouvet, *Les laboratoires autorisés au XVII siècle (suite et fin)*, *in* Bulletin de la Société d'Histoire de la Pharmacie, 13th year, no. 46, at 56-57 (1925). Source: <www.persee.fr>; Nicolas Nupied, Journal des Principales Audiences du Parlement, depuis l'année 1685, jusqu'en 1700, vol. 4, at 278-279 (Comp. des Libraires Associés, 1757); Helvetius, Méthode pour Guérir toute Sorte de Fièvres sans Rien Faire Prendre par la Bouche, Preamble (Widow Nicolas Oudot, 1694). Source: <gallica.BnF.fr>., 173–180

§ 2.21. Printed by Eyre and Spottswoode, Printers to the Queen's Most Excellent Majesty, 1857. Source: <archive.org>., 180–183

§ 2.22. Brisseau, Pierre (1626-1717). Lettre d'un médecin à un de ses amis, touchant les remèdes secrets. 1708. Source: <gallica.BnF.fr>., 183–186

§ 2.23. Printed by George Edward Eyre and William Spottiswoode, Printers to the Queen's most Excellent Majesty. 1857. Source: <gallica.BnF.fr>; Source: <wellcomelibrary.org>., 186–188

§ 2.24. M. Gallon, Machines et Inventions approuvées par l'Académie Royale des Sciences depuis son Etablissement, avec leur Description, [vol. 2], at 121, 191, 379, and 467 (Antoine Boudet, 1778). Source: <archive.org>., 188–192

§ 2.25. Lettre de M. de G. à M. de M. à Aix-La-Chapelle Sur l'Elixir d'Or et Blanc de M. le Général de la Motte, Nouvelle Edition Corrigée et Augmentée (Veuve Quillau, 1757); *Annonces, Affiches et Avis Divers*, Dix-Neuvième Feuille Périodique, du Mercredi, Février 27, 1754, at 35-36. Source: <gallica.Bnf.fr>., 192–196

§ 2.26. Extracted from Jacques de Drouas, *Un Remède au XVIIIème Siècle — Le Sachet Antiaplopéctique d'Arnoult*, *in* Bulletin de la Société de l'Histoire de Paris et de l'Île de France, 113e et 114e années, 1986-1987, at 413-414 (Libr. d'Argence, 1988); Arrêt du Conseil du Roi (Imprimerie Delaguette, 1748); Mercure de France Dédié au Roi, Juillet 1751, at 137 *et seq.* (Cailleau, Pissot, Nully, Barrois, 1751); Brochure (P. G. Simon, 1772). Source: <gallica.BnF.fr>; Journal de Paris, 3

Frimaire, IXme Année de la République [November 24, 1802], at 380; Leaflet, w/d. Source: <gallica.BnF.fr>., 196–204

§ 2.27. J. de Castro Sarmento, *Da Quina Quina, e em especial, das Minhas Agoas de Inglaterra, in* Materia Medica Physico-Historico-Mechanica, at 402 *et seq.* (Guilherme Strahan, 1758). Source: <archive.org>., 204–206

§ 2.28. Methode de M. Keyser (sel-publication, 1762). Source: <gallica.BnF.fr>., 206–208

§ 2.29. Alfred Franklin, Les Médicaments, at 212-215 (E. Plon, Nourrit et Cie., 1891). Source: <gallica.BnF.fr>., 208–209

§ 2.30. Source: <gallica.BnF.fr>., 210–212

§ 2.31. Jourdan, Isambert, and Decrusy, Recueil des Anciennes Lois Françaises depuis l'An 420 jusqu'à la Révolution de 1789, Du 10 mai 1777 au 31 Decembre 1778, at 395 et seq. (Belin-Leprieur, 1820); L. Créteur, Lois et Réglements sur la Pharmacie en Belgique, depuis les Temps les Plus Reculés jusqu'à Nos Jours, at 127-129 (G. Mayolez and Germer Baillière, 1870); Avis au Public sur l'Examen des Remèdes pour lesquels on Demande des Permissions ou Brevets, Royal Society of Medicine, Paris, November 21, 1778 (ed. Ph. D. Pierres, 1778); Histoire de La Société Royale de Médecine, Année MDCCLXXIX, at 1-2 (Imprimerie de Monsieur, 1782). Source: <gallica.BnF.fr>; Nouveau Plan de Constitution pour la Médecine en France, présenté à l'Assemblée Nationale par la Société Royale de Médecine, 1790, at 126-128. Source: <archive.org>;, 212–220

§ 2.32. William Woty, The Patent, A Poem (printed for the author by G. Kearsley, 1776). Source: Google Books., 220–221

§ 2.33. Editor of Health News, *Exposures of Quackery: Being a Series of Articles Upon, and Analyses of, Various Patent Medicines*, vol. 1, at 13 *et seq.* and 33 *et seq.* (Savoy House, w/d). Source: <archive.org>., 221–224

§ 2.34. J.B. Duvergier, Collection Complète des Lois, Décrets, Ordonnances, Règlements, et Avis-du-Conseil d'Etat de 1788 à 1824, vol. 2, at 281 and 369 (A. Guyot et Scribe, 1824). Source: Google Books., 224–225

§ 2.35. Brevets d'invention, 1791-1844. 3. Brum-Desmarest. Edit. by INPI. Source: <gallica.BnF.fr>., 225–228

§ 2.36. Printed by George Edward Eyre and William Spottiswoode, Printers to the Queen's most Excellent Majesty. 1856. Source: <archive.org>., 228–230

§ 2.37. L. André-Pontier, Histoire de la Pharmacie, Origine, Moyen Âge, Temps Modernes, at 254-255 (Octave Doin 1900). Source: <gallica.BnF.fr>., 231

§ 2.38. Bulletin des Lois de l'Empire Français, 4th series, vol. 13, at 152-155 (Imprimerie Impériale, 1811). Source: <gallica.BnF.fr>; Dewandre and Delebecque, Pasicrisie ou Recueil Général de la Jurisprudence des Cours de France et de Belgique, 3ème Série, Partie de Belgique,1854, 2ème partie, at 309-310 and 351-352 (Meline, Cans et Cie., 1854). Source: Google Books;, 232–238

§ 2.39. The Repertory of Arts, Manufactures, and Agriculture, vol. 29, second series, at 14-16 (Repertory Office, 1816); William Carpmael, Law Reports of Patent Cases, vol. 1, at 431-432 (A. Macintosh, 1843). Source: <archive.org>., 238–240

§ 2.40. Lewis Merlin, The Treasure of Health, Or a Wonderful Collection of the Most Valuable Secrets in Medicine (Printed for the Society, 1819). Source: < archive.org >., 241–244

§ 2.41. Collecção das Leis do Brazil de 1820, at 28 (Imprensa Nacional, 1889). Source: < www2.camara.leg.br >., 245

§ 2.42. Extrait des Procès-Verbaux des Expériences Publiques Faites à Paris, avec la Quintessence antipsorique, dite Eau de Mettemberg, renouvelées dans les Hospices de Lille, et confirmées dans les Hôpitaux de Lyon, par ordre du Gouvernement (Courcier, w/d). Source: < gallica.BnF.fr >; Découverte Importante pour la Santé Publique, ou Méthode Particulière Pour guérir les Métastases de la Gale, par Mettemberg (de Sainte-Marie-aux-Mines). (Self-publication, w/d); Affiches, Annonces, et Avis Divers, ou Journal Général de France du Dimanche 13 Brumaire (4 Novembre 1804); Diário de Madrid of Tuesday, 1st January 1811, at 206; Preamble and closure to the Specification of Mettemberg's invention, as submitted to the British High Court of Chancery, in compliance with the terms of the patent of invention granted to him on February 26, of the same year (1825). (Eyre and Spottiswood, 1857). Source: < archive.org >., 245–251

§ 2.43. P.B. Wilcox (edit.), Condensed Reports of Decisions in the Supreme Court of Ohio, at 800-802 (IsaacN. Whiting, 1832). Source: < archive.org >., 251–254

§ 2.44. Michel Pelletier, Brevets d'Invention, Marques de Fabrique, Modèles et Dessins, Nom Commercial, Concurrence Déloyale, at 345 et seq (Baudry et Cie., 1893). Source: < gallica.BnF.fr >., 254–255

§ 2.45. Source: < archive.org >., 255–257

§ 2.46. Joseph W. England (edit.), The First Century of the Philadelphia College of Pharmacy, 1821-1921, at 128 (Phil. Coll. of Pharm., 1922). Source: < archive.org >., 258

§ 2.47. The Congressional Globe, 30th Congress, 2nd session, at 464 and 697. Source: The Library of Congress, < memory.loc.gov >., 259–260

§ 2.48. Edmund H. Bennett and Chouncey Smith (eds.), English Reports in Law and Equity: Containing Reports of Cases in the House of Lords, Privy Council, vol. 6 (1851), at 14-36 (Charles C. Little and James Brown, 1852). Source: < babel-.hathitrust.org >., 260–265

§ 2.49. Dewandre and Delebecque, Pasicrisie ou Recueil Général de la Jurisprudence des Cours de France et de Belgique, 3ème Série, Partie de Belgique, 1857, 2ème partie, at 309-310 (Administr. Centrale de la Pasicrisie, 1857). Source: Google Books., 266–267

§ 2.50. José Máximo de Castro Neto Leite e Vasconcellos, Collecção Official de Legislação Portugueza, Anno de 1863, at 105 (Imprensa Nacional, 1864); Collecção Official de Legislação Portugueza, Anno de 1899, at 1898-1899 (Imprensa Nacional, 1900). Source: < net.fd.ul.pt/legis >., 268–270

§ 2.51. S. Limousin, Notes sur l'Inhalation d'Oxigène, at 7, 8 (self-publication, 1866). Source: < gallica.BnF.fr >; Description des Machines et Procédés Pour Lesquels des Brevets d'Invention Ont Été Pris Sous le Régime de la Loi du 5 Juillet 1844, year 1872, vol. 3, Arts Chimiques, 8. Substances Organiques et Leur Conservation, at 14, 15 (Imprimerie Nationale, 1874). Source: Google Books;Source:

< uspto.gov > ; Bulletin des Arrêts de la Cour de Cassation, Matière Criminelle, no. 12, at 420, 421 (1879). Source: < gallica.BnF.fr > ; Exposition Universelle de 1878 - Palais du Trocadéro - Congrès International de la Propriété Industrielle, Tenu à Paris en 1878, Compte-Rendu nos. 1, at 1, 6, 7, and 3, at 4, 5 (Libr. des Public. Legislatives, 1878). Source: < gallica.BnF.fr > ., 270–278

§ 2.52. Collecção Official da Legislação Portugueza, anno de 1869, at 322-323 (Imprensa Official, 1870). Source: < net.fd.ul.pt > ., 278–282

§ 2.53. John S. Billings, American Inventions and Discoveries in Medicine, Surgery, and Practical Sanitation, at 1-9 (Damrell & Upham, 1891). Source: < archive.org > ., 283–285

§ 2.54. House of Commons, Report of the Select Committee on Patent Medicines, at xii-xiii (1914). Source: < archive.org > ., 285–286

§ 2.55. AMA, The Propaganda for Reform in Proprietary Medicines, vol. 2, at 542-543, and 493-494 (Press of AMA, 1922). Source: < archive.org > ., 286–289

§ 2.56. Source: < www.planalto.gov.br > ., 289–291

§ 2.57. Source: < law.justia.com > ; Source: < www.govinfo.gov > ., 291–299

§ 2.58. Source: < uspto.gov > ; Source: < www.govinfo.gov > ., 300–305

§ 2.59. Source: < www.planalto.gov.br > ; Source: < portal.anvisa.gov.br > ., 305–307

§ 2.60. Source: < www wto.org > ., 307–309

§ 2.61. Source: < bvsms.saude.gov.br > ., 309–311

§ 2.62. Source: < www.wto.org > ., 312–314

§ 2.63. Source: < www.legifrance.gouv.fr. > ; Source: < www.parl.ca > ; Source: < un docs.org/A/74/L.56 > ; Source: < www.unaids.org > ; Source: < www.who.i nt > ; Source: < geneva.usmission.gov > . Source: < www.wto.org > ., 314–326

Illustrations

Figs. 1, 2, 5-7, 9a, 10, 19, 23, 25, 26. Source: < gallica.BnF.fr > ., 4, 9, 24, 29, 36, 71, 81, 151, 248, 273, 276

Figure 3. Source: < collections.vam.ac.uk > ., 17

Figure 4. Source: < gallica.BnF.fr > ., 19

Figs. 8, 9b, 11, 18-24. Source: < archive.org > ., 59, 74, 84, 148, 151, 192, 230, 244, 248, 257

Figure 12. Source: < wellcomelibrary.org > ., 93

Figure 13. Source: < www.wipo.int > ., 126

Figs. 14, 15. Source: Google Images., 126, 128

Figure 16. Source: < ultrafarma.com.br > ., 134

Figure 17. Source: < www.health.gov.au > .135

Figure 27. Source: < memoria.bn.br > ., 281

Figure 28. Source: < www.csarmento.uminho.pt > , 282

Figure 29. Source: < uspto.gov > ., 304

Index